Thomas Barlow, Catholic Church, Regnans in Excelsis

Brutum Fulmen

The Bull of Pope Pius V Concerning the Damnation of Q. Elizabeth. Second Edition

Thomas Barlow, Catholic Church, Regnans in Excelsis

Brutum Fulmen
The Bull of Pope Pius V Concerning the Damnation of Q. Elizabeth. Second Edition

ISBN/EAN: 9783337260477

Printed in Europe, USA, Canada, Australia, Japan

Cover: Foto ©Lupo / pixelio.de

More available books at **www.hansebooks.com**

BRUTUM FULMEN:
OR THE
BULL
OF
Pope Pius V.

Concerning the
Damnation, Excommunication, and Deposition
OF
Q. ELIZABETH,

As also the
Absolution of her Subjects of their *Oath of Allegiance*, with a Peremptory Injunction, upon Pain of an *Anathema*, never to Obey any of her Laws or Commands.

With some *Observations* and *Animadversions* upon it,

By *THOMAS* Lord Bishop of *Lincoln*.

Whereunto is Annex'd the Bull of Pope *Paul* the Third, Containing the Damnation, Excommunication, &c. of King *Henry* the Eighth.

The Second Edition.

Come out of her my People, that ye partake not of her Sins and Plagues,
Rev. XVIII. 4.

THE EPISTLE TO THE READER.

Reader,

WHoever thou art (Protestant or Papist, Courteous or Censorious) having made these Papers publick, thou hast a liberty to read, and a right to judge; and that thou maist do it impartially, (not out of hate or kindness to me, but upon a serious and just Consideration of the Cause) I shall neither importune thy Favour, nor deprecate (when

The Epistle to the Reader.

'tis just) *thy severest Censure.* **For,** 1. *'Tis truth, I have impartially desired, and not indiligently sought; and if (by the blessing of God) I have found it,* Magna est veritas & prævalebit, *it will prevail, in despight of all Enemies and Opposition;* φίλο⸱ ὡς ἀσδείς⸱, nat super, non immersalibis undis. *Truth we know (especially Divine Truth, which concerns our Souls and their Salvation) ever had, and, so long as* there are *Devils and wicked Men, will have in this* World *many Enemies; who will indeavour (what they cannot do) to suppress it;* premi potest veritas, opprimi non potest. *They may dipp, and (for some time) keep it under water, but they cannot drown it. If these Papers contain truth, (as I hope they do) then I am sure that every Intelligent Reader, and pious lover of Truth, will be its Patron; and (though in this Epistle I do not sollicite him) ready to vindicate it from the Objections of its Adversaries. But (on the other side) if my Reader relate to* Rome, *and be possess'd with strong delusion to believe (against Reason and Divine Revelation) his Catholick Cause, the Papal Monarchy and Infallibility, it will be in vain for me, in this Epistle, to desire (what I believe I (a) cannot have) his Favour. However, he shall have my Pity and Prayers,* That God Almighty would be graciously pleased to open his Eyes, and bless him with the Knowledge and Love of the Truth.

(a) The reason why I cannot expect the favour or assent of my Adversaries, (especially of the Jesuits) is, because *Maldonate* tells us, That *Luther* and *Calvin* (Arch-Hereticks) are not to be followed though they speak things consonant to Scripture ——— *Cum sacris literis consentanea docent, Non Sequendi.* Nay Calvinists and Lutherans, Even When They Speak Truth, are no more to be hearken'd to, Then To The Devil. *Lutherani & Calvinistæ à Deo, & Ecclesia tanquam perniciosissimi Hæretici declarati, non magis, Etiam Cum Vera Dicunt, audiendi sunt, Quam Diabolus.* Maldonat Comment. in Matth. 16. vers. 6. p. 336. C. Nor is this *Maldonat's* peculiar Opinion; for the *Censor Librorum*, who approves his Commentaries on Matth. tells us, That *Omnia in illis juxta Orthodoxam Apostolicæ ac Romanæ Ecclesiæ Doct. inam Summa Cum Eruditione exponi.* Ita Joh. Clavius De illo Libr. Censor.

2. We

The Epistle to the Reader.

2. *We know 'tis true, what the great Roman Orator long since said*——Humanum est errare, labi, decipi, &c. *The wisest men have their mistakes*; Bernardus non videt Omnia, & quandóque bonus dormitat Homerus. *Since Adam fell, the best men have their Infirmities, and sometimes err, even when they desire and seek Truth. Since the Prophets, our blessed Saviour and his Apostles, left the World, I know no man Infallible; nor any, save the Pope, who (against evident Reason, and the sense of Christendom) pretends to it. For my own part, I do humbly acknowledge my many and great Infirmities; and for these Papers*——Hominem pagina nostra sapit, *there may be mistakes and errors in them; yet it is my hope and (not ungrounded) belief, that there are none such as may prove pernicious, or (in the main) dangerous* ----Non hic Centauros, non Gorgonas, Harpiasve invenies. *No such prodigious and pernicious errors, as our Popish Adversaries maintain, and (so far as they are able) vindicate: such I mean as their stupid Doctrine of Transubstantiation (contradictory to Natural Reason, Divine Revelation, and all our Senses) their Idolatrous Adoration of a piece of Bread, with* Divine (b) *worship due to God only*) *their Sacrilegious robbing the Laity of half the Sacrament in the Eucharist, contrary to our blessed Saviour's express (c* Command, *and the practice of the Christian* (d) *World (even of the Church of* Rome *her self) for above a thousand years (as their own great and learned Writers confess) &c. I say, such errors as these, I do (and have reason to) believe, the Reader will not find in these Papers. Though it be certain and confess'd, that every one, even the best and most learned Writers are fallible; yet so long as they*

(b) *Nullus dubitandi Locus, quin cultus Latriæ qui Vero Deo debetur, sic huic Sacramento exhibendus.* Concil. Trid. Sess. 13. De Eucharistiâ cap 5.

(c) Matth. 26. 27. And they obey'd, and did all drink. And Marc. 14. 23.

(d) Cardinal Bona, De Rebus Liturgicis, l. 2. c. 18. p. 491, 492. Parif. 1672. Lindanus Panopliæ, l. 4. c. 56. p. 342. Colon. 1575.

they rationally build their Conclusions upon the clear Principles of Nature, Scripture, or Universal Tradition, They may be sure enough, (and so may their Reader too) that they are not actually false, nor what they so write erroneous. However if the Reader find any errors of what nature soever, and can make it appear, that they are indeed errors, I shall not (as I said before) deprecate his severest Censure, but concur with him, and Censure them my self, as much as he; and do hereby promise publickly to retract them, and heartily thank him for the discovery. For in this Case my Reader and I shall both be Gainers, and (in a several way) Conquerors----(e) Vicimus utérque nostrum, palmam Tu refers mei, Ego erroris; *my Reader has overcome me, by manifesting my mistakes, and I (by his help) have overcome those errors;* otherwise, in Cyprian's *Opinion and language*, (f) Non vincimur cum offeruntur nobis meliora, sed instruimur. *He, who by his Adversaries help and concluding Arguments, gains the knowledg of Truth, is (in that good Father's Opinion) not conquered, but instructed. But if the Intelligent Reader discover any error in these Papers, and can, and will really make it appear to be so, let him call it what he will, Victory or Instruction, I shall thankfully submit, and both love that truth, and him for the discovery of it.*

3. *I know that this Tract of mine (as every one of the like nature) is already prohibited and damned at* Rome; *for the Rules* (g) *prefix'd to the* Index Librorum Prohibitorum, *contrived by the Authority of the* Trent Council, *declare all* Books of (h) Controversies *between* Catholicks *and* Hereticks (Protestants *and* Papists) *in any Vulgar Tongue, prohibited*

(e) Vid. Hieronym. adversus Luciferianos, in fine. Tom Operum. 1. p. 230. Col. 2. G.

(f) Cyprian Epist. 71 ad Quintum fratrem, p. 140. in Editione Rigaltij, Paris. 1648.

(g) Extant dictæ Regulæ Indici Tridentino præfixæ, in Calce Concilij Tridentini. Antv. 1633.

(h) *Libri Vulgari Idiomate de Controversiis inter Catholicos & Hereticos nostri temporis differentes, non passim permittantur, sed de iis, idem servetur quod de Bibliis Vulgari Linguâ scriptis Statutum est.* Ibidem Reg. 6.

The Epistle to the Reader.

hibited and damned; neither to be (i) had nor read by any Papist, under pain of Excommunication, and many other Penalties contained in their Canons, Papal Constitutions, and their Expurgatory Indices. So that although our blessed Saviour, by his holy (k) Spirit, in the Gospel, command all (even the Common people, for to those he writes) to Examin and try all things, to use that understanding and discretion God has given us, to distinguish truth from error (for that is evidently the meaning of those words, πάντα δοκιμάζετε, prove all things, as (l) sober and learned Papists confess) & when we have done so, then we must hold fast that which is good. I say, in this Case, in the choice of our Religion, wherein the eternal weal or woe of our Souls is concerned; though Christian prudence require it, and our blessed Saviour, (by his Apostle) command, that we should not believe every Spirit, but try before we trust, and diligently examin Things till we be assured of truth; yet his pretended Vicar, with an Antichristian Pride and Impiety, contradicts this, and commands the contrary. He forbids all Examination; Those under his Tyranny (at least the unlearned and common people) must believe as the Church believes; that is, all that he proposeth, though it be Transubstantiation, or any thing evidently repugnant to their Reason and Senses too: They must (m) renounce their own Reason, and if he say that is white, which they see black, they (n) are to believe what he says, and not their own Senses. All means for the People to examin, whether it be truth or error, which the Pope and his Church proposes, is prohibited, and deny'd them; nor is it only the Books of Protestants which write of Religion, but the Bible and Sacred Scripture too; even

(i) *Legentes, aut habentes, pœnas in Sacris Canonibus, Constitutionibus Apostolicis, & Indicibus Librorum prohibitorum contentas, incurrere volumus.* Ita Bulla Greg. 15. data Rom. 30. Decemb. 1622.

(k) 1 Thess. 5. 21. & Joh. 4. 1.

(l) *Omnia probate*, i.e. *Per Discretionem dijudicate.* Dr. Hen. Holden in Locum.

(m) *Sublato Omni Proprio Judicio, paratus semper sit animus, ad Obediendum Ecclesiæ.* Vide Exercitia spiritualia Ign. Loyolæ. Tolosæ, 1593. p. 172. Reg. 1.

(n) *Si quod Oculis nostris apparet Album, Ecclesia Nigrum definierit, debemus quod nigrum sit pronunciare.* Ibid. Reg. 13. p. 176.

The Epistle to the Reader.

and promote the Papal Greatness and Interest, (on which their own depends) will give licence to none to read such Protestant Writings, save to those, who (for fidelity to their Catholick Cause and Learning) they judge able and willing to Answer and Confute them: That is, None shall have Licence to read such (to them) dangerous and damned Books, save such as have (a) solemnly Promised, Vow'd, and Sworn firmly to believe and constantly to hold and profess to their last breath (and, to the utmost of their Power, indeavour that others, under them do so too) their new *Trent-Creed,* and so the whole Mass of their Popish Errors and Idolatries contained and commanded in it. *The Case being evidently this; that (if their Papal Constitutions be obligatory and obey'd) none are to read or have these Papers, save such as have promised, vow'd, and sworn never to believe them; as I have little reason to desire or hope for their favour, so (be it known unto them) I do as little fear their Confutation, or (what I am like enough to have) their Calumnies.*

4. *Although I well know (to say nothing of others) that all our English Papists (both in their Words and Writings) do constantly call themselves* Catholicks, *and* Roman Catholicks; *yet they must pardon me, if in these Papers, I neither do, nor justly can call them so:* Papists *I do call them, and (I hope) they will not be offended, or take it ill, that I do so.* For (b) Baronius *(their great Cardinal and Annalist) having said,* That the Hereticks (we know whom he means) call'd them Papists; *he adds,* That we could not honour them with a more glorious Title than that of Papists, and therefore he desires that they may have the honour of that Title while they live,

---

(a) *Hanc Catholicam fidem, extra quam nemo salvus esse potest, quam in præsenti Profiteor, & veraciter* Teneo, *eandemque Integram, usque ad extremum vitæ spiritum, constantissime retinere, & confiteri, & a meis subditis, vel illis quorum cura ad me spectat, Teneri, & Prædicari, quantum in me erit, curaturum. Ego idem N. Spondeo, Voveo, ac Juro.* Ita in Bulla Pij Papæ 4. super forma Juramenti Professionis fidei, in Concil. Tridenc. Sess. 24. De Refor. c. 12. p. 452. Editionis Anverp. 1633.

(b) *Recentio es Heretici Catholicos homines Papistas vocant; & certo nullo sublimiore Gloriæ Titulo Exornari potuissent. Sint ideo nobis viventibus, hæc semper Præconia Laudum, & post mortem, Tituli Sepulchrales, ut sit Semper Dicamur Papistæ.* Baronius Notat. ad Martyrologium Rom Oct 16. B. p. 707. Col. Agripp. 1610.

The Epistle to the Reader.

live, and that (after death) it may be writ upon their Tombs and Sepulchral Monuments. *For my part, so long as they believe and profess their new* Trent-Creed, *and the Popes* Monarchical Supremacy, *I shall (according to the Cardinal's desire) call them Papists, and if it be so honourable a Title (as he says it is) let them have it, I shall not envy them that honour, but pity their error, who glory in that which is indeed their sin and shame: For the other Title of* Catholick, *which our Adversaries, (without and against reason) appropriate to themselves; we grant, and know, that anciently it was, and (when rightly used) is a word of a good sound and signification, when it was applied to persons,* (as a Catholick Bishop, or Catholick Doctor, &c.) *it signified such persons as were*, 1. In respect of their Faith, Orthodox; *who intirely believed and profess'd the true Christian Faith, rejecting all pernicious and dangerous errors, and so were* no Hereticks. 2. In respect of their Charity, *such as were in Communion with the Church of Christ, without any uncharitable Separation from it, and so no* Schismaticks. *Now that our Adversaries of* Rome *are (as they pretend) such Catholicks, is absolutely deny'd; not only by Protestants, but (except themselves) by all Christians in the World, and that upon evident and great reason; Considering,* 1. *Their many and monstrous* (c) Errors *(contradictory to Sacred Scripture, and the sense and belief of the Christian World for a thousand years after Christ our blessed Saviour) which they approve and publickly receive as Articles of their Faith, in their new Creed, the* Trent-Council, *and* Roman Cate-

(c) Concerning the Errors, Superstition and Idolatry of the Church of *Rome*, (with which I charge them) I do not here name the Particulars, much less the proofs of them. It is not the business of this Epistle. But many of our learned Writers have long since effectually done it. Such I mean, as Bishop *Jewel*, Bishop *Morton*, *Davenant*, *John White*, *Chillingworth* and Dr. *Crakanthorp*, and (to omit many more) lately, my learned Friend Dr. *Stillingfleet* Dean of *Pauls*. The Reader (if he please) may consult these and find satisfaction. Something also is said to that purpose, in the following Papers. But if my Popish Adversaries (who are not easily, if at all to be satisfy'd) require me particularly to make good my Charge, I shall undertake it; & hope (by the blessing of God, and the help of the Writings of

those learned persons I have named) to say that which might (though may be it will not) satisfie my Adversaries.

chism;

The Epistle to the Reader.

chism; Considering also their many Superstitions and stupid Idolatry, professed and practised by them in their sacred Offices (their Missal, Breviary, Horæ B. Virginis, their Ritual and Pontifical, &c.) I say, these things impartially considered, they may be (and really are) Idolatrous Hereticks; but 'tis impossible they should be, (what they against greatest evidence pretend to) true Catholicks. 2. Considering the unchristian (indeed Antichristian) Pride and Tyranny of the Pope and his Party, Excommunicating, Cursing and Damning all Christians, save themselves, (without and against that Charity which the Gospel requires) and so Schismatically cutting off from the Body of Christ whole Kingdoms at a Clap (as Pius the Fifth does, (d) in the following Bull) which are things inconsistent with the Christian Temper and Charity of a true Catholick; I say these things considered, and that the Pope and his Party are really guilty of such uncharitable Actions, dividing and violating the Union of the Church; it evidently follows, that they are so far from being true Catholicks that they are great and formal Schismaticks; And therefore they must pardon me, if in these Papers, I do not call them (what really they are not) Catholicks; and for the same reason, I do not call them Roman Catholicks. For, as it is neither reason nor sense to call him an English Gentleman, who is no Gentleman at all; or him a Sorbon Doctor, who never saw Paris, or ever had or desired that Degree; so it is alike irrational to call him a Roman Catholick, who really is an Erring Schismatick, and no Catholick at all.

5. I know some (otherwise learned and pious) Writers, who say that those words Roman Catholick

(d) *Declaramus prædictam Elizabetham Hæreticam, tique Adhærentes Anathematis Sententiam incurrisse, esseque à Christi Corporis unitate præcisos.* In dicta Pij 5. Bulla §. 3.

The Epistle to the Reader.

lick *are inconsistent, and imply a Contradiction, as signifying a* particular Universal. *But this (I confess) is a manifest mistake. For not only* particular Persons, *(of which before) but* particular Churches, *in this or that City (be it great or little) have anciently and usually been call'd* Catholick Churches, *without any Contradiction or Impropriety. In an Epistle of a* (e) *great Council at* Antioch, *we find the* (f) *Bishop of that City call'd a* Catholick, *and that particular Church a* (g) Catholick Church. *So in the Subscriptions to* Nazianzen's *last Will and Testament,* Optimus Bp. of Antioch, *subscribes thus;* Optimus Bp. of the Catholick (h) Church at Antioch; *and the rest of the Bps: who subscribe that Testament, (and they are six or seven) use the same Form. So* Nazianzen *subscribes himself* Bp. of the Catholick Church in Constantinople; Amphilochius B.shop of the Catholick Church in Iconium; *and so all the rest. In the Appendix to the* Theodosian Code, *Pope* Vigilius *begins his Encyclical Epistle thus* —— Vigilius (i) Episcopus Ecclesiæ Catholicæ Urbis Romæ: Bp. of the Catholick Church of the City of Rome. *So Pope* (k) Leo *the great (and* (l) *many more Bishops of* Rome) *uses the very same form. The Popes stiled themselves* Catholicæ Ecclesiæ (non Orbis, sed) Urbis Romæ Episcopos. *The Antichristian stile of* Universal Bp. (*as Pope* (m) Gregory *the Great calls it*) *was not yet usurped at* Rome. *The Bishops of* Rome *then, and their Church, were* Catholick, *and so was every Orthodox Bp. and his Church, as well and as much as they.* Constantinople, Iconium, Antioch, &c. *and their*

(e) Synodus innumerabilium fere Episcoporum (as Valesius renders it) apud Euseb.Hist.l.7. c.29.p.278.D.

(f) Φρόνημα καθολικὸν ἔχοῦσα, homo professionis Catholicæ. Even Paulus Samosatenus, till he was discovered to be an Heretick, was call'd a Catholick. Ibid. c. 30. p. 282.B.

(g) Καθολικῆς Ἐκκλησίας Ἐπίσκοπος, speaking of the Church of Antioch. Euseb.Ibid. p 282.6.

(h) Ὄπτιμος Ἐπίσκοπος τῆς κατὰ Ἀντιόχειαν Καθολικῆς Ἐκκλησίας: Testam. Nazian cum Invert. contra Julian Græcè Ætonæ 1610. p. 126. & apud Leunclavium, Juris Græco-Rom. Tom. 2. p. 203 vide Epiphan. Edit. D. Petav. Parif. 1622. Tom. 2.p.2.

(i) Vid. App. Cod. Theod. per Sirmondum p.218.

(k) Leo Papa Ecclesiæ Catholicæ Urbis Romæ.

Conc. Chalcedon. part. 1. num. 10.12. & Act. 8. (l) The Reader may have a very large Catalogue of such Subscriptions, by *John Launoy*. Epist. part. 1. In Epist. ad Francis. Bonum. (m) Pope *Gregory* damns that proud Title, twelve several times, the places are particularly cited by *Joh. Launoy* (and he no Lutheran) in the Epistle *ad Bonum* before-named.

Bishops,

The Epistle to the Reader.

Bishops, were as truly Catholick *as* St. Peter's *Successor, or* Rome *it self: The truth is evidently this; the Pope and his Party are in this,* nec Christi, nec Petri, sed Donati Successores; *they do not follow Peter or our blessed Saviour, (as they vainly bragg) but that impious Heretick* Donatus, *whose damnable Schism and Heresie they have espoused.* St. Augustin *(who well knew it) tells us, in* (n) *several places,* That the Donatists assumed to themselves the Name of Catholick, said that their Sect was the only true Church, and so damn'd all other Christians; and upon this Heretical Opinion, they Schismatically separated from the whole Catholick Church. *The Pope and his Party (with as little reason and charity) do the very same thing; they (as the* Donatists *anciently) Heretically affirm,* That they, and they only, are truly Catholicks, and the only Members of the true Christian and Catholick Church: and then Schismatically Separate from, Excommunicate and damn all other Christians.

(n) Vide Augustinum Breviculi Collat. cum Donatistis, Collat 3. Diei Tom. 7. p. 568. Edit. Basil. 1569. & Epist. 67. ad Alipium. Tom. 2. p. 323.

6. *And further (that I may freely speak what I really believe) I am so far from believing* the Pope and his Party *to be (what they vainly pretend) the only true Christian and Catholick Church; that I do believe them (and so did thousands before* Luther, *and many whole Kingdoms and Provinces since) to be* Ecclesia Malignantium *an Antichristian Sect and* Synagogue (in fide) *highly erroneous, and* (in facto) *as highly impious. And the Pope so far from being* Peter's *Successor, and our B. Saviour's Vicar-General, that he is* (o) *that man of Sin,* ὁ Ἀντικείμενος, *That Adversary of our B. Saviour, and the great Antichrist, the Apostle speaks of,* who exalts himself (ὑπὲρ πάντα λεγόμενον Θεὸν ἢ σέβασμα) above all Kings and Emperors.

(o) 2 Thess. 2. 3, 4. See Bp. *Jewel* on this Chapter, and this Fourth Verse. Sir *Christoph. Sibtharp's* Advertisement to the Catholicks in *Ireland.* Dublin 1622. part. 3. c. 2. p. 280, 281, 282. &c. Andr. Rivet. contra Silvestrum Petrasanctam c. 28. p. 537, 538. &c. vid. Georg. Dounanium, Diatr. de Antichristo, l. 3. & 4. Lond. 1620.

The Epistle to the Reader.

Emperors. This (I hope) will in part appear by what is said in the following Papers. At present, I shall desire the Impartial Reader (who possibly may read this short Epistle, and trouble himself no further, to read what follows) to consider, That the Pope really and professedly does exalt himself above all Kings and Emperors, and so has this Mark of the Beast, and Indelible Character of Antichrist. That he does so Exalt himself, will evidently appear, thus,

1. Pope Innocent the Third tells the (p) Emperor of Constantinople (and with prodigious Error and Impudence, indeavors to prove it out of (q) Scripture) That the (r) Pope is as much greater Than the Emperor, as The Sun is greater Than the Moon. So Innocent the third; and (that we may be sure his Successors liked it well) Gregory the Ninth approves, and refers it into the Body of Canon-Law: And (s) Greg. the Thirteenth approves it too; and (with the other Decretals) confirms it for Law; and 'tis continued in all Editions of that Law, ever since. It is then certain and confess'd, That the Pope Exalts himself above all that is call'd God, above all Kings and Emperors; and that he is far greater than they. And if you inquire of the Proportion, how much he is greater? I say, 2. That their approved and received Glosses on their Law, (with some difference of Opinion) calculate how many times the Sun is greater than the Moon, and then infer the Pope's Greatness above the Emperor. And here

1. The Author of the Gloss, (Bernardus de Botono was the man) a good Lawyer, but (sure I am) no good Astronomer, tells us, (ignorantly and ridiculously) ----- That the Sun is greater than the Moon, (and consequently the Pope greater than the Emperor

(p) Vide Cap. Solitæ.6. Extra de Major.& Obedientia, and the Lemma to that Chap. which is this ---- Imperium Sacerdotio subest, & ei Obedire Tenitur.

(q) 1 Pet. 2. 13. (which place evidently proves the contrary) Jer.1.10. Gen.1.16. Joh.21. 16. Matth.16.19.

(r) Quanta est inter Solem & Lunam, tanta inter Pontifices & Reges differentia cognoscitur. Dicto Cap Solitæ 6.

(s) Bulla Romæ data 1580. Juri Can. præfixa.

The Epistle to the Reader.

(t) *Cum igitur terra sit septies major Luna, Sol autem octies major terra: restat ergo, ut Pontificalis Dignitas Quadragesies septies sit Major Regali.* Glossa verbo. Inter Solem & Lunam. Cap. Solitæ 6. Extra de Major. & Obedientia. I quote the Edition of the Canon Law at Paris, 1612.

(u) *Alias quinquagies septies. Ita Nota in Margine, ad dictum Cap. Solitæ verbo, inter Solem & Lunam.* Ibid.

(x) *Manifestum est, quod magnitudo Solis continet magnitudinem terræ Centies quadragies septies & duas medietates.* Vid. Additionem ad Glossam verbo. Inter Solem & Lunam. Cap. Solitæ. 6.

(y) *Palam est, quod magnitudo Solis continet magnitudinem Lunæ septies millies septingenties & quadragies quater, & insuper ejus medietatem.* Ibidem id dicta additione ad dictam Glossam.

(z) *Aurum non tam pretiosius est plumbo, quam Regia Dignitate sit Altior Dignitas Sacerdotalis.* Gratian Can. duo sunt 15. Distinct. 96.

peror) (t) Forty seven times. *This is pretty weil, but much short of that Magnitude the Pope meant, (if he knew what he said) when he affirm'd,* That he was as much greater than the Emperor, as the Sun was greater than the Moon.

2. *And therefore another* (u) *Canonist*, would have the Sun greater than the Moon (and so the Pope greater than the Emperor) Fifty seven times.

3. *But this (as too little) does not please the Pope's Party and Parasites; and therefore* Laurentius *(another Canonist) says,* That it is (x) manifest that the Sun is greater than the Moon (so the Pope than the Emperor) an hundred forty seven times. *I omit the fractions; for if the Pope be* 147. *times greater than the Emperor, methinks it might satisfie his Ambition, so that he needed not stand upon the fraction, or little overplus.*

4. *But this also comes far short of that Magnitude, which they ascribe to the Sun above the Moon, (& so to the Pope above the Emperor) for they tell us* (y) That the Sun is greater than the Moon (7744½) seven thousand seven hundred, forty four times, and one half more. *To such a prodigious greatness, does the Bishop of* Rome *exalt himself. So that if St. Paul say true, (That he is Antichrist, who exalts himself above all Kings and Emperors) then it will evidently follow, that the Pope is Antichrist; for never man did, or (without Antichristian Pride and Impiety) can so exalt himself. They sometimes tell us in their Law,* ---- (z) That the Papal Dignity is to be preferr'd to the Imperial, more than Gold is to Lead; *and (if* Gratian

The Epistle to the Reader.

say true) it was the Pope who said so. And the Gloss gives the reason of this Papal (a) Greatness above all Kings; Because Kings and Princes are to submit their Necks to the Popes Knees; (he might have said, and their (b) Mouths to the Popes Feet, which the Emperor is bound to kiss). That this is Impious and Antichristian Doctrine, I think evident; and I have some reason to believe that intelligent and impartial Judges will think so too, and yet it has heretofore, and still is approved and (as Catholick) received at Rome. *For,* 1. *That Decretal of Pope* Innocent *the Third, was by* Gregory *the Ninth made a Law, and (amongst other Decretals) by him commanded to be received as Law, in all* (c) *Universities and Papal Consistories, about* 450. *years ago, and so continues to this day.* 2. *For the Glosses before-mentioned, they are not only in the* (d) *old Editions of their Law, but were approved and confirmed afterwards by* (e) Gregory *the Thirteenth (and so stand approved and confirmed to this day) who expresly tells us,* That the Law being by his (f) command receiv'd, corrected and purged; no man (for the future) should dare to add, detract, or change any thing in it.

(a) *Quia Colla Regum & Principum submittuntur Genibus Sacerdotum.* (By *Sacerdotes* here the Popes are principally meant, as is evident both by the Text and the Gloss) Glossa ad dictum Can. verbo. Duo sunt.

(b) *Papa excipit Imperatorem ad osculum pedis —— ut primum videt Papam, detecto Capite, illum, genu terram tangens, veneratur—— & Pontificis pedes Devotè osculatur.* Lib. Sacrarum Ceremoniarum, Rom. 1560. l. 1. Tit. 5 p. 22. Col. 2, 3.

(c) *Volentes ut hac tantum Compilatione utantur universi in Judiciis & in Scholis, &c.* Greg. 9. in Literis Acad. Bononiensi, dat. 1230. Juri Canonico Præfixis. Edit. Lugd. 1661.

(d) Edit. Parif. 1520. cum Glossis. (e) Vide Bullam Greg. 13. datam Romæ, Anno 1580. Corpori Juris Canonici præfixam. (f) *Nulli liceat Libris Canonici Juris, de mandato nostro Correctis, Recognitis, & Expurgatis quicquam addere, det. abere, vel immutare, &c.* Ibid. dicta Greg. 13. Bulla.

In short, whether the Champions of the Church of Rome *and Catholick Cause, (as they call it) will think what is said in these Papers, worthy of any Answer, or no, I know not. But in case they do, I shall make them (if I mistake not) a very fair offer, which (if accepted) will much lessen their pains and labour,*

C

The Epistle to the Reader.

bour, yet so, as (if they perform the Condition annexed) they may (as to my self) effectually do their business, and make me their Proselyte: The thing I mean is this; If they can from Scripture, (by any one Cogent and Concluding Argument) prove any one of these following Propositions (and unless they be all proved, their Papal Monarchy cannot stand) I will grant the rest, and give them the Cause. I say then, if they can make it appear,

1. That our blessed Saviour before his Ascension, did constitute *Peter* his Vicar, and gave him such a Monarchical Supremacy and Jurisdiction (as is (g) now contended for) over the Apostles and the whole Church. *For if Peter had no such Power he could not transfer it to his Successors; it being impossible, that they should have that Power (Jure Successionis) which their Predecessors never had.*

2. If they can prove that St. *Peter*, while he lived, did exercise such Power and Supream Jurisdiction, even over the Apostles, &c. *By their own* (h) *Computation* St. *Peter lived* 34. *or* 35. *years after the Ascension of our B. Saviour, and was (as they say) Bishop of* Antioch 7. *and of* Rome 25. *years. Now if it neither do, nor can appear, that in all that time he exercised any such Monarchical Power or Jurisdiction; we may safely conclude, either that he had no such Power (which is most true) or betray'd his trust in not making use of it, for his Masters Glory, and his Churches good; which (I suppose) our Adversaries will not say. In this Case,* Idem est non esse & non apparere;

(g) They tell us, that it was our B. Saviour himself, who Constituted *Peter* and his Successors Supream Monarchs of the Catholick Church. *Christus Catholicam Ecclesiam, uni Soli in Terris Petro, Petrique Successori Rom. Pontifici, in Potestatis Plenitudine, tradidit Gubernandam.* So Pius the Fifth in his Bull of Excommunication of *Eliz. In Principio.* And *Bellarmine* says——*Successio ex Christi Instituto, & Jure Divino est, quia Ipse Christus Instituit in Petro Pontificatum; ideo quicunque Petro succedit, à Christo accipit Pontificatum.* De Rom. Pont. l. 2. c. 12. §. *ut autem. Cum Papa in Petri Cathedra Sedeat, summum in to Dignitatis gradum, nonnullis Humanis Constitutionibus, sed Divinitus datum agnoscit.* Catechis. Trident. Part. 2. c. 7. De Ordinis Sacramento. § 28. vide Can. Sacrosancta. 2. Dist. 22. & Glossam & Turrecrematam. Idem. (h) *Baronius* says, that *Peter* suffered Martyrdom *Anno Christi* 69. and therefore 34. or 35. years after our blessed Saviours Passion. Annal. Tom. 1. ad Ann. 69. §. 1.

and

The Epistle to the Reader.

and therefore our Adversaries must pardon us, if we do not believe (what they cannot prove) *St.* Peters *Monarchy*.

3. *But let it be supposed* (*which neither has been, nor can be proved*) *that* Peter *had, and executed such Power*; let them make it appear that it was not Personal and Temporary, to cease with his Person, (as the Apostleship did) but to be transferred to some (*i*) Successor. *For if it was temporary, and ceas'd with* St. Peter's *Person, then whoever* (*after* Peter's *death*) *pretends to that Power, is not bonæ fidei possessor, but an Impious and Antichristian* Usurper.

4. *But let all those Particulars be supposed,* (*which being untrue, cannot possibly be proved*) *that* Peter *had and executed such Power, and that it was to be transmitted to his Successor;* Let them make it appear that the Bishop of *Rome* was that (*k*) Successor, that *Peter* was (as they say) 25. years Bp. of *Rome,* or 25. days, or that he ever was at *Rome:* For, *if it be so far from truth that* Peter *was* 25. years Bp. of Rome, *that it cannot appear from Scripture, that he was ever Bishop there at all, or that he ever was at* Rome. *It will evidently follow, that the Pope is not* St. Peter's *Successor, and so can have no Title* (Jure Successionis) *to that Supremacy, they say,* Peter *had: It being impossible that the Pope should succeed* Peter, *if he never preceeded him in the Bishoprick of* Rome.

5. *Let them make it appear*, that our blessed Saviour, while on Earth, either exercis'd or had such a Temporal Monarchy, as the (*l*) Pope now chal-

(i) *Bellarmine* says, that 'tis evident in Scripture, that *Peter's* Supremacy was to descend to a Successor —— *Aliquem Petro Succedere, deducitur Evidenter ex Scripturis.* De Rom. Pon. l. 2. c. 12. §. Observandum Tertio.

(k) *Bellarmine* tells us, That it is not expresly in Scripture, that the Pope is *Peter's* Successor, but that must be proved by Apostolical Tradition. *Rom. Pontifice. succedere Petro, non habetur expresse in Scripturis, sed habetur ex traditione Apostolica.* Bellarm. dicto loco.

(l) They constantly tell us, the Pope has two Swords; and of the Temporal Sword they say —— *Figurat Pontificalis hic gladius potestatem summamTemporalem, à Christo ejus Vicario collatam; juxta illud, data est mihi omnis Potestas in Cælo & in Terrâ, & alibi, dominabitur à Mari usque ad Mare, & à Flumine, usque ad Terminos*

Orbis Terrarum. Liber Sacrarum Cerimoniarum Ecclesiæ Rom. Romæ. 1560. Lib. 1. Tit. 7. De Ense benedicendo, p. 36. Col. 1.

The Epistle to the Reader.

lenges as his Vicar. *For unless this appear, all their pretences to such Power, (as Vicars of our B. Saviour) will be vain and irrational; it being impossible that the Pope or Peter should derive from him that Power which he himself neither had, nor ever here on Earth exercis'd.*

These are the Foundations upon which the Papal Monarchy (Spiritual and Temporal) is built; and if these fail, the whole Fabrick will and must fall; and therefore they are concern'd, by some real and rational proof, to make them good. Now if our Adversaries can and will make it appear, from Sacred Scripture, that Peter *ever had or exercised such a Power, as is pretended; that it was not personal in him, but to be transmitted to his Successor; that he was* 25. *years Bp. of* Rome, *and actually transferred that Power to his Successor there; or that our B. Saviour ever had or exercis'd such a terrene & temporal Power, as they pretend the Pope (as his Vicar) has from him: I say, let them make all, or any one of these Particulars appear from Scripture, and I will confess, and retract my error. Nor is the Condition unjust or unequal, when I require Scripture proof. For they themselves constantly affirm that the Pope has right to his Monarchical Supremacy* Jure Divino; *by the Constitution of our B. Saviour, and Divine Right; and this their Popes, Canonists and Divines (with great noise and confidence, but no reason) indeavour to prove from Scripture, miserably mistaken and misapply'd. I know, that their late* (m) *Jesuitical Methodists (so much* (n) *magnify'd by their Party) require of Protestants to confute their Popish Doctrines (Transubstantiation, the Sacrifice of the Mass, Purgatory, &c.) by express words*

(m) Vide Methodum Veronianam, seu modum, quo quilibet Catholicus potest Solis Bibliis, Religionis prætensæ Ministrum evidentèr mutum reddere, &c. Authore Francisco Verono Parisiensi, Soc etatis Jesu Theolog. Colon. Agrip 1610. Vide Jac. Masenij meditatam Concordiam Protestantium cum Catholicis, ex verbo Dei. Edit. Colon. 1661.

(n) Francisc. Veroni Scientiam, è doctissimâ Societate Jesu prodeuntem, veneramur, sententiam libenter sequimur, & labores, optimo successu à Deo donatos, honoramus. Adrian. & Petrus Wakenburch in Exam. Princip. fidei, &c. Exam. 3. §. 1. num. 4. p. 111.

The Epistle to the Reader.

words of Scripture) *not admitting of Consequences, however deduced from plain Texts as Premisses. This method of theirs (being irrational and (o) demonstrated so to be) I shall not tye them too: But if they can prove any of the aforesaid Positions by the express words of Scripture, or by good Consequences deduced from it, or (what they pretend to) Universal and Apostolical Tradition; I shall admit the proof. Nay, I shall make our Popish Adversaries two further, and (if that be possible) fairer Offers.*

1. *Let them prove by any just and concluding reason whatsoever, that any Christian Church in the World acknowledg'd, or the Church of* Rome *her self assumed and publickly pleaded for such a Papal Supremacy, as* (p) *now they pretend to, for* 1000. *years after our B. Saviour; and (for my own part) I will confess and retract my Error.*

2. *Let them prove, by any such concluding reason, that any Church in the World (Eastern or Western, Greek or Latin) did acknowledge (what now the Pope and his Party so earnestly and vainly contend for) the* Popes Infallibility, *and his Supremacy over all General Councils, for* 1500 *years after our blessed Saviour; and for my part,* Cedat Julus Agris, manus dabimus captivas, *I will retract what here I have affirmed, and be (what I hope I never shall be) their Proselyte.*

To Conclude, I have no more to say, (my Adversaries will think I have said too much) save only to desire the Readers, who sincerely and impartially desire truth and satisfaction, to read and consider the Margent as well as the Text. In this, they

(o) Vide Disput. de fidei ex scripturis demonstratione, contra novam nonnullorum Methodum, Per Joh. Dallæum. 8°. Genevæ, 1610.

(p) They do now pretend to *potestatem Summam Temporalem*; as the Book of their Sacred Ceremonies (a little before cited) tells us, That our blessed Saviour gave *Peter* (and in him the Pope) *Cælestis & Terreni Imperij Jura.* Can. Omnes, 1. Dist. 22. Power to depose Kings and Emperors, absolve their Subjects from Oaths of Allegiance, and dispose of their Dominions. Plat. in vita Greg. 7. Conc. Lateran. sub Innocent. 3. Can. de Hæret. 3. Hence it was, that *Bonif.* 8. (that Prodigy of Antichristian Pride and Impiety) in the Solemn Jubilee shewed himself to the People the first day in his Pontificalibus, and the next day, *Imperiali habitu, Istula Cæsa-*

rea Insignis, gladium ante se nudatum jussit deferri & sedens alta voce testatur; Ecce duo gladij. Vide Paralip. ad Chron. Urspergen. ad An. 1294. p. 344.

have

The Epistle to the Reader.

have my *Positions*, and the *proofs* of them, in plain *English*: In the *Margent*, the *Authorities* and *Authors* I rely upon, in their own words, and the *Language* in which they writ: and I have (for the Readers ease, not my own) cited not only the *Authors* and their *Books*, but the *Chapter*, *Paragraph*, *Page*, and mostly the *Editions* of them: That so the Reader may with more ease, find the places quoted, and judge whether I have cited and translated them aright. It is notoriously known, that our *Popish Adversaries* have published many forged *Canons* and *Councils*, many spurious (a) *Decretals*, and suppositious *Tracts*, under the names of *Primitive Fathers*, and *Ancient Bishops*; that they have shamefully corrupted the *Canons* of *Legitimate* (b) *Councils*, and thousands of other *Authors*; making them (by adding and substracting words or Sentences) say what they never meant, or not to say what indeed they did both mean and say: and this they themselves have (without shame or honesty) publickly own'd, in their *Expurgatory Indices*; and after all this fraud and falsification of Records, these *Apocryphal Books* and suppositious *Authors* are continually produced by them (for proofs of

(a) It is notoriously known how many Decretal Epistles have been forged, and fathered upon the Ancient Bishops. I shall only instance in the fifth Epistle of that pious Pope and Martyr, *Clemens* the first; in which he pleads for a *community* of all things in the world, even of *wives. Communis usus Omnium, quæ sunt in hoc mundo, Omnibus esse Debuit. In Omnibus Sunt Sine Dubio, & Conjuges. Joh. Sichardus* and *James Merlin* have that Epistle, and those very words; and *Gratian* has referr'd them into the Canon Law. Can. dilectissimis. 2. Caus. 12. Quæst. 1. and there they are still in all the Editions of that Law, even that corrected and approved by Pope *Gregory* the Thirteenth. (b) I shall instance only in one, the 28. Canon of the Council of *Chalcedon*, as it is shamefully corrupted in Gratian. Can. Renovant. 6. Dist. 22. where, 1. It is in the Original, δεί ομεν, definimus, statuimus; for which *Gratian* has, *Petimus*. 2. In the Original Canon, it is πρεσβυτέρῳ Ῥώμῃ, Senior Roma; but *Gratian* has *Superior Roma*. 3. In the Original, it is, Ἴσα πρεσβεῖα, Æqualia Privilegia; But *Gratian* has *Similia privilegia*: as being unwilling that *Constantinople* should have equal priviledges with *Rome*. 4. In the Original Canon, it is ——— ϰ ἐν τοῖς Ἐκκλησιαστικοῖς, &c. That *Constantinople* should be equal to *Rome*, in Ecclesiastical Matters, *etiam in Ecclesiasticis*. But *Gratian* (in contradiction to the Canon) says, *Non tamen in Ecclesiasticis, &c.* So it was in *Gratian*, in the old Editions; only in the later Editions of *Gratian* (An. 1612, 1618, 1661, &c.) this last corruption is acknowledg'd, and (which is not usual) mended. But other corruptions remain still, in their last and best Editions of *Gratian*.

their

their Errors) against Protestants who well know, and (as many sober men of their own Communion) justly condemn such impious Roman Arts ——— Nec tali auxilio, nec defensoribus istis Christus eget. *Truth needs no such forg'd and false Medium's to maintain it ; nor will any honest man use them. Sure I am, I have not, in this Discourse, built the truth of my Positions upon the Testimonies of our own Protestant Authors, (knowing that our Adversaries would with scorn reject their Testimony) nor of any supposititious or spurious ones. The Testimonies and Proofs I have quoted, and rely upon, are drawn from* Scripture, *the* genuine Works of the ancient Fathers and Councils, *or (which* ad hominem, *must be valid) from* their own Councils, *the* Popes Bull, *their* Canon Law, *their* Casuists, School-men, Summists, *the* Trent Catechism, *the* Book of the Sacred Ceremonies of the Roman Church, *their approved and* received Publick Offices, *(such as their* Missal, Breviary, Ritual, Pontifical, &c.) *which Authorities (if I do not misquote, or mistake their meaning) are, and (to them) must be just proofs of those Positions for which I have produced them. But let the Evidence of the Testimonies, and the Authority of the Authors quoted, be what it will ;* I have little hope, that they will gain any assent from our Adversaries ; *so long as they believe the* Infallibility of their Pope and Church, *and their Learned Men are* solemnly sworn, firmly to believe their new Trent Creed (*the whole Body of Popish Errors*) to their last breath, *and to* Anathematize and damn what Doctrine soever contradicts it. *For while they are*

possess'd

The Epistle to the Reader.

possess'd **with** *these Principles, it may be truly said of* **them***, what was said of the* Luciferian Hereticks *in St.* Hierome —— Facilius eos Vinci posse, quam persuaderi, *you may sooner baffle, than perswade them: They will (in despite of Premisses) hold the Conclusion; nor shall the clearest demonstration overcome their blind Zeal and Affection to their Catholick Cause. However that God Almighty would be graciously pleased to bless us and them, with a clear knowledge of Sacred Truth, with a firm belief, and (in dangerous times) upon undaunted and pious profession of it, is and shall be the Prayer of*

Thy Friend and Servant

Oct. 3.
1689.

in Christ

T. L.

The

The Damnation and Excommunication of *Elizabeth* Queen of *England*, and her Adherents, with an Addition of other punishments.

Damnatio & Excommunicatio Elisabethæ *Reginæ* Angliæ, *eique Adhærentium, cum aliarum pœnarum Adjectione.*

Pius Bishop, Servant to God's Servants, for a perpetual memorial of the matter.

Pius Episcopus, Servus Servorum Dei, ad perpetuam Rei memoriam.

HE that reigneth on high, to whom is given all Power in Heaven & in Earth, committed one Holy, Catholick and Apostolick Church (out of which there is no Salvation) to one alone upon Earth, namely, to *Peter* the Prince of the Apostles, and to *Peter*'s Successor the Bishop of *Rome*, to be governed in fulness of Power. Him alone he made Prince over all People, and all Kingdoms, to pluck up, destroy, scatter, consume, plant and build, that he may contain the faithful that are knit together with the band

Regnans in Excelsis, cui data est Omnis in Cœlo & in Terra Potestas, unam Sanctam, Catholicam & Apostolicam Ecclesiam (extra quam nulla est salus) soli in terris, videlicet, Apostolorum Principi Petro, *Petrique Successori Romano Pontifici, in Potestatis plenitudine tradidit Gubernandam. Hunc unum super omnes Gentes, & omnia Regna Principem constituit, qui evellat, destruat, dissipet, disperdat, plantet, & ædificet, ut fidelem populum, mutuæ Charitatis nexu constrictum, in unitate Spiritus contineat, salvumque & in-*

of Charity, in the Unity of the Spirit, and present them spotless, and unblameable to their Saviour.

columem suo exhibeat salvatori.

§. 1. In discharge of which Function, we which are by God's goodness called to the Government of the aforesaid Church, do spare no pains, labouring with all earnestness, that Unity, and the Catholick Religion (which the Author thereof hath for the trial of his Children's Faith, and for our amendment, suffered to be punished with so great Afflictions) might be preserved uncorrupt: But the number of the ungodly hath gotten such power, there is now no place left in the whole World, which they have not assayed to corrupt with their most wicked Doctrines: Amongst others, *Elizabeth*, the pretended Queen of *England*, a Slave of Wickedness, lending thereunto her helping hand, with whom, as in a Sanctuary, the most pernicious of all men have found a Refuge. This very Woman having seized on the Kingdom, and monstrously usurping the place of Supream Head of the Church in all *England*, and the chief Authority and Jurisdiction thereof, hath again brought back the said Kingdom into miserable destruction, which was then newly reduced to the Catholick Faith and good Fruits.

§. 1. *Quo quidem in munere obeundo, Nos ad prædicta Ecclesiæ gubernacula Dei Benignitate vocati, nullum laborem intermittimus, omni operâ contendentes, ut ipsa Unitas, & Catholica Religio (quam illius Auctor ad probandam suorum fidem, & correctionem nostram, tantis procellis conflictari permisit) integra conservetur. Sed Impiorum numerus tantum potentia invaluit, ut nullus jam in Orbe locus sit relictus, quem illi pessimis doctrinis corrumpere non temârint, adnitente inter cæteros flagitiorum servâ Elizabeth, pratensâ Angliæ Reginâ; ad quam, veluti ad asylum, omnium infestissimi profugium invenerunt. Hæc eadem, Regno occupato, supremi Ecclesiæ capitis locum, in omni Angliâ, ejusque præcipuam Authoritatem atque Jurisdictionem monstruose sibi usurpans, regnum ipsum jam tum ad fidem Catholicam & bonam frugem reductum, rursus in exitium miserum revocavit.*

§. 2.

§.2. For having by strong hand inhibited the exercise of the true Religion, which *Mary* lawful Queen of famous memory, had by the help of this See restored, after it had been formerly overthrown by *Henry* the Eighth, a Revolter therefrom; and following and embracing the Errors of Hereticks, she hath removed the Royal Council consisting of the English Nobility, and filled it with obscure men, being Hereticks, oppressed the Embracers of the Catholick Faith, placed impious Preachers, Ministers of Iniquity, abolished the Sacrifice of the Mass, Prayers, Fastings, Choice of Meats, Unmarried Life, and the Catholick Rites and Ceremonies. Commanded Books to be read in the whole Realm containing manifest Heresie; and impious Mysteries and Institutions, by her self entertained, and observed according to the Prescript of *Calvin*, to be likewise observed by her Subjects; presumed to throw Bishops, Parsons of Churches, and other Catholick Priests, out of their Churches and Benefices; and to bestow them and other

§. 2. *Usu namque veræ Religionis, quam ab illius desertore* Henrico VIII. *olim eversam, Claræ M m.* Maria *Regina legitima, hujus Sedis Præsidio reparaverat, potenti manu inhibito, secutisque & amplexis Hæreticorum erroribus, Regium Consilium ex* Anglicâ *Nobilitate confectum diremit, illudque obscuris hominibus Hæreticis complevit, Catholicæ Fidei cultores oppressit, improbos Concionatores, atque Impietatum Administros reposuit, Missæ Sacrificium, Preces, Jejunia, Ciborum dilectum, Ritusque Catholicos abolevit. Libros manifestam Hæresim continentes, toto Regno proponi, impia Mysteria, & instituta ad* Calvini *Præscriptum à se suscepta, & observata, etiam à subditis observari mandavit. Episcopos, Ecclesiarum Rectores, & alios Sacerdotes Catholicos, suis Ecclesiis, & Beneficiis ejicere, ac de illis & aliis Ecclesiasticis rebus, in hæreticos homines disponere, deq; Ecclesiæ causis decernere ausa, Prælatis, Clero, & Populo, ne Romanam Ecclesiam agnoscerent, neve ejus Præceptis, Sanctionibusque Canonicis obtemperarent, Interdixit; plerosque in nefarias leges suas venire, &* Romani Pontificis *Auctorita-*

D 2 Church

Church Livings upon Hereticks, and to determine of Church Causes, prohibited the Prelates, Clergy, and People to acknowledge the Church of *Rome*, or obey the Precepts and Canonical Sanctions thereof, compelled most of them to condescend to her wicked Laws, and to abjure the Authority and Obedience of the Bishop of *Rome*, and to acknowledge her to be sole Lady in Temporal and Spiritual matters, and this by Oath; imposed Penalties and Punishments upon those which obeyed not, and exacted them of those which persevered in the unity of the Faith and their Obedience aforesaid, cast the Catholick Prelates and Rectors of Churches in Prison, where many of them, being spent with long languishing and sorrow, miserably ended their lives. All which things, seeing they are manifest and notorious to all Nations, and by the gravest Testimony of very many so substantially proved, that there is no place at all left for Excuse, Defence, or Evasion.

§. 3. We seing that impieties and wicked actions are multiplied one upon another; and moreover, that the persecution of the faithful, and affliction for Religion, groweth every day heavier and heavier, through the

tem atque obedientiam abjurare; seque solam, in Temporalibus & Spiritualibus Dominam agnoscere jurijurando coegit; pœnas & supplicia in eos qui dicto non essent Audientes, Imposuit; easdemque ab iis, qui in unitate fidei, & prædicta Obedientia perseverarunt, Exegit. Catholicos Antistites, & Ecclesiarum Rectores in vincula conjecit, ubi multi diuturno Languore & Tristitia Confecti, Extremum vitæ diem misere finiverunt. Quæ omnia cum apud Omnes Nationes perspicua & notoria sunt, & gravissimo quamplurimorum Testimonio, ita comprobata, ut nullus omnino locus Excusationis, Defensionis, aut Tergiversationis relinquatur.

§. 3. *Nos multiplicantibus aliis atque aliis super alias Impietatibus, & facinoribus, & præterea fidelium persecutione, Religionisque afflictione, impulsu & Operâ d. Elizabeth quotidie magis Ingravescente, quoniam illius animum ita obfirma-*
In-

Instigation and Means of the said *Elizabeth*; because we understand her mind to be so hardned and indurate, that she hath not only contemned the godly Requests and Admonitions of Catholick Princes, concerning her healing and conversion, but also hath not so much as permitted the Nuncios of this See, to cross the Seas into *England*; are strained of necessity to betake our selves to the Weapons of Justice against her, not being able to mitigate our sorrow, that we are drawn to take punishment upon one, to whose Ancestors the whole State of Christendom hath been so much bounden. Being therefore supported with his Authority, whose pleasure it was to place Us (though unable for so great a burthen) in this Supream Throne of Justice, we do out of the fulness of our Apostolick Power, declare the aforesaid *Elizabeth*, being an Heretick, and a favourer of Hereticks, and her Adherents in the matters aforesaid, to have incurred the sentence of Anathema, and to be cut off from the Unity of the Body of Christ.

§. 4. And moreover, we do declare Her to be deprived of her pretended Title to the Kingdom aforesaid, and of all Dominion, Dignity, and Priviledge whatsoever.

tum atque induratum Intelligimus, ut non modo pias Catholicorum Principum de sanitate & conversione, preces, monitionesque contempserit, sed ne hujus quidem sedis ad ipsam hac de causâ Nuncios in **Angliam** *trajicere permiserit; ad Arma Justitiæ contra eam de necessitate conversi, dolorem lenire non possumus, quod Adducamur in unam animadvertere, Cujus majores de Republicâ Christianâ tantopere meruêre. Illius itaque Auctoritate suffulti, Qui Nos in hoc Supremo Justitiæ Throno, licèt tanto Oneri Impares, voluit Collocare, de Apostolicæ potestatis plenitudine declaramus prædictam* Elizabeth *Hæreticam, hæreticorumque fautricem, eique adhærentes in prædictis, Anathematis sententiam incurrisse, esseque à Christi Corporis unitate præcisos.*

§. 4. *Quin etiam ipsam prætenso Regni prædicti jure, necnon omni & quocunque Dominio, Dignitate, Privilegioque privatam.*

§. 5.

§.5. And also the Nobility, Subjects, and People of the said Kingdom, and all others, which have in any sort sworn unto her, to be for ever absolved from any such Oath, and all manner of Duty, of Dominion, Allegiance, and Obedience; As we also do by Authority of these Presents absolve them, and do deprive the same *Elizabeth* of her pretended Title to the Kingdom, & all other things abovesaid. And we do Command and Interdict all and every the Noblemen, Subjects, People, and others aforesaid, that they presume not to obey her, or her Monitions, Mandates, and Laws: And those which shall do the contrary, We do innodate with the like Sentence of Anathema.

§.6. And because it were a matter of too much difficulty, to convey these Presents to all places wheresoever it shall be needful; our will is, that the Copies thereof, under a publick Notaries hand, and sealed with the Seal of an Ecclesiastical Prelate, or of his Court, shall carry altogether the same Credit with all People, Judicial and Extrajudicial, as these Presents should do, if they were exhibited or shewed. Given at *Rome*, at St. *Peters*, in the Year of the Incarnation of our Lord, 1570. the Fifth of the Calends of *May*, and of our Popedom the Fifth year.

§.5. *Et etiam Proceres, subditos, & populos dicti Regni, ac cæteros omnes qui illi quomodocunque juraverunt. A Juramento hujusmodi, ac omni prorsus Dominii, Fidelitatis, & obsequii debito, perpetuo absolutos, prout Nos illos Præsentium Auctoritate absolvimus, & privamus eandem* Elizabeth *prætenso Jure Regni, aliisque Omnibus supradictis. Præcipimusque & Interdicimus Universis & singulis proceribus, subditis, populis, & aliis prædictis, ne illi ejusve monitis, Mandatis, & Legibus audeant obedire. Qui secus egerint, eos simili Anathematis Sententia innodamus.*

§.6. *Quia vero difficile nimis esset, Præsentes quocunque illis Opus erit perferre, volumus, ut eorum exempla, Notarij publici manu, & Prælati Ecclesiastici, ejusve Curiæ Sigillo Obsignata eandem illam prorsus fidem in Judicio, & extra illud, ubique Gentium faciant, quam ipsæ Præsentes facerent, si essent exhibitæ vel ostensæ. Dat'* Romæ, *apud Sanctum* Petrum, *Anno Incarnationis Dominicæ* 1570. 5.*Cal. Maij Pontificat' nostri Anno* 5.

SOME ANIMADVERSIONS AND OBSERVATIONS

Upon the Impious

Damnation and Excommunication

OF

Q. Elizabeth

BY

PIUS V. *Anno* 1570.

Extat hæc Bulla in Bullario Romano. Romæ 1638. Tom. 2. pag. 229.

Before I come to a particular and distinct Examination of the several Parts and Paragraphs of this Impious Popish Bull, I shall in general observe, 1. That *Pius* V. was not the first or only Pope, who usurped this Extravagant and Antichristian Power over Kings and Emperors; to damn, depose,

Observ. 1.

pose, and deprive them of all their Royal Rights and Imperial Jurisdiction; for both his Predecessors and Successors approved, and with prodigious pride and impiety, exercis'd such Power. That this may appear, I shall give the Reader some instances, extant upon Record, in their own Popish Annals and Histories.

1. Pope (*a*) *Constantine* in a Council of *Italian* Bishops (it was about the Year 714.) Anathematise's all who deny'd the worshipping of Images, and (*b*) *particularly, and by name damns the Emperor* Philippicus *to the Torments of Hell.* So *Carolus Sigonius* tells us, and *Martinus Polonus*, and the *Fasciculus Temporum* concur with him.

2. After Pope *Constantine*, *Gregory* the second, and *Gregory* the third, succeed (*c*); and both of them Excommunicate the Emperor *Leo Isaurus*, for this only Crime, because he was against worshipping of Images; and though the *Italians* had sworn Allegiance to him, yet they null that Oath: And the Historian commends these Actions of those two Popes, as excellent Examples for Posterity. And *Platina* says, that *Gregory* the third (*d*) *Excommunicated the Emperor* Leo, *and deprived him of his Empire*.

3. To *Gregory* the third, succeeded Pope *Zachary*, and (if *Gratian* say true) he (*e*) deposed *Childericus* King of *France*, and absolves his Subjects from their Oaths of Allegiance, and gives his Kingdom to *Pipin*: And this he did, not for the *great Crimes of* Childeric, *but because he was unprofitable, and unfit for the Government*; not that he was *Insufficient* (says the (*f*) *Glosse*) but because *he was Effeminate, and dissolute with Women*. And from this Canon, *Joh. Semeca* (the Glossator) infers, *That the Pope may depose the Emperor*, and proves it by citing other Canons; And by the Authority of Pope (*g*) *Gelasius*, who tells *Anastasius* the Emperor, that he had power to Depose him, and proves it from the Example of this Pope *Zachary*. I know, that what *Gratian*, and

the

(*a*) Carolus Sigonius de Regno Italiæ, lib. 3. pag. 58.
(*b*) *Omnium Consensu, omnes qui Imaginibus venerationem negarent, damnati; & Philippicus ipse Nominatim, Diro in eum composito Carmine,* Pœnis Inferorum devotos. ibid.
(*c*) Car. Sigonius de Regno Italiæ. lib. 9. p. 219. *Extabant præclara Gregorij* 2. & 3. *exempla, qui Leoni Isauro Imperatori, Sacris Interdicere, & Jurata* Italiæ *obedientiâ spoliare non dubitarant, uno eo Crimine, quod Imaginibus se Inimicum præbuisset.*
(*d*) *Gregorius* 3. Leonem *Imperio & Communione fidelium privat.* Plat. in vita Gregorij 3.
(*e*) Zacharias Papa *Regem* Francorum, *non tam pro ejus Iniquitatibus, quamquod erat inutilis deposuit: & Franciginas à juramento fidelitatis absolvit.* Gratian. Can. alius. Caus. 15. Quæst. 6.
(*f*) *Non quod insufficiens sed quod dissolutus erat cum mulieribus, & effaminatus.* Gloss. ibid. verbo *Inutilis*. (*g*) Gloss. ibid. verbo *Alius*.

the Canonist, say, of Pope *Zachary*'s Deposing *Childeric*, is evidently untrue, (and by many (*h*) demonstrated so to be) yet it stands uncensur'd in their last and best (*i*) Edition of the Canon Law, which Pope *Gregory*. XIII. (*k*) approved and publish'd, as most correct. And they further tell us, That *Clement*. VIII. published an (*l*) Exact Correction of all the Glosses and Additions to the Canon Law, and yet this of Pope *Zachary*'s deposing *Childeric* (and, what the Gloss says of it) is neither left out, nor any way censur'd. Whence it is evident, that they approve the Doctrine of deposing Kings, and (having no just reason for it) forge Instances to prove it.

4. Pope *Hildebrand*, or (*m*) *Gregory*. VII. deposeth the Emperor *Henry* IV. *by the Authority given* (*n*) *by God,* (as he says) *of binding and loosing both in Heaven and Earth:* And then he (*o*) *absolves his Subjects from their Oath of Fidelity, and then prohibits them to obey him.* This Bull is dated at *Rome, Anno Domini* 1075. and five years after he Excommunicates, and Deposes him again 1080. And *implores the Assistance of* Peter *and* Paul, *in this his Excommunication and Deposition of the Emperor; that the World may* (p) *know, that as they have power to bind and loose in Heaven; so they have power on Earth to give and take away Empires, Kingdoms, Principalities, Dukedoms, Earldoms, and (according as they shall deserve, and he is* (q) *Judge of that) the possessions of all men.* This power he says, Peter had; and so he, and the Bishops of Rome *have it too, and that from God, as Vicars of Christ, and* Peter's *Successors.* And so by this most Erroneous and Impious Doctrine, the Popes have a Power (which neither *Peter*, nor any, nor all the Apostles ever had) to dispose of all mens Temporal Estates in the World, whether they be Supream or Subjects.

(*h*) Vid. Joh. Launoium Epist. Tom. 7. p. 117, 118, &c. & p. 245, 246, &c. Hottomanni Franco-Galliam, c. 13. p. 96. 97, 98.
(*i*) Vid. Edit. Paris 1612 & 1618.
(*k*) Vid Bullam Gregorij. 13. dat. Romæ. 1. Die Julij. 1580.
(*l*) Vide Indicem Librorum Prohibitorum Lusitanicum Olysipone, 1624. p. 350 in Carolo Molinæo.

(*m*) Vide Bullarium Romanum Romæ. Anno 1638. Tom. 1. p. 49.
(*n*) Potestate à Deo data Ligandi & Solvendi in Cœlo, & in Terra. Ibid.
(*o*) Omnes Christianos à vinculo Juramenti, quod sibi faciunt, aut facient, absolvo, & ut nullus ei serviat, sicut Regi, interdico. Ibid. §. 1.
(*p*) *ut Mundus intelligat, quia si potestis in Cœlo ligare & solvere, potestis in Terra Imperia, Regna, Principatus, Marchias, Ducatus,* Comitatus, & Omnium Hominum possessiones, pro meritis tollere, unicuique & Concedere. In dicto Bullario Roman. Bullæ Excommunicationis. Hen. 4. §. 10. p. 51. Col. 1. (q) Sive Roman. Pontificem Supremum in Ecclesiâ Dei Judicem. Ita Gregorius. 13. in Bulla data Romæ. 8. Apr. 1575. In Ecloge Bullarum Lugduni. 1582. p. 359. Col. 2.

5. After

Observations on the Pope's Bull

(r) Vide Bullam. 13. Gregorii. 9. datum Romæ. Anno 1239. In Bullario Romano, Tom. 1 p. 89. 90.

5. After this, Pope *Gregory*. IX. (r) Excommunicates the Emperor *Friderick*. II. Absolves his Subjects from their Oaths of Allegiance, lays an Interdiction all his Cities, Castles, and Villages, Excommunicates all that favour him, or any way assist or obey him, commands the *German* Bishops (upon pain of Excommunication) solemnly to publish this Excommunication with all their Impious Solemnities, ringing of Bells, lighting and then extinguishing Candles, &c.

(s) Vid. Constitutionem Ejus 3: dat. Lugduni 1245. In Bullario Romano, Tom. 1. p. 94, 95.

(t) Damnatio & Excommunicatio Friderici. 2. Ibidem.

(u) Cum Fratribus & Sacro Concilio, deliberatione diligenti habitâ. Ib. dictæ Constitutionis. §. 6. Bullarij dicti. p. 95. Col. 1. lin. ultimâ.

(x) Non sine Omnium audientium & Circumstantium stupore & horrore. Matth. Paris in Hen. 3. ad Annum 1245. p. 668. lin. 33.

6. After this, Pope (s) *Innocent* IV. (in the like form) Excommunicates and Deposes the said *Frederick*. The *Lemma* or Title prefix'd to the Bull is thus (t) *The Damnation and Excommunication* of Frederick. II. &c. And lest this might be thought a rash and inconsiderate Act of the Pope, he himself tells us, That (u) *he did diligently deliberate about it, with his Brethren* (the Cardinals he means) *and the Sacred Council*, the General Council of Lions.) I know, that *Matthew Paris* says, that he publish'd that *Excommunication in that Council, not without the* (x) *Horror and Amazement of all who heard it*. But *Platina* tells us, That *it was done by the* (y) *general and concurrent consent of the Council*. And *Innocent* himself expresly says, That it was done (*Frederick* Excommunicate) by the (z) *Council it self*; (and therefore the Major part must concur.) and if it was not so, that Pope was not only fallible, but actually false: And it is a considerable Observation which *Matthew Paris* has, (and therefore I shall not omit it) when he tells us———*That some did positively affirm*, (and he believed it) *that* (a) *Innocent*. IV. *did above all things earnestly desire to ruin the*

(y) *Fredericum Omnium Consensu Imperio & Regnis privavit*. Platina. in vita Innocentij. 4. p. 209. Col. 1. Edit. Col. Agripp 1626. (z) *Quem* (*Fridericum*) *Concilium generale Lugdunense Cassaverat & condemnaverat*. Matthew Paris in Hen. 3. ad An. 1250. p. 773. lin. ultimâ. (a) *A nonnullis affirmative dicebatur, quod Dominus Papa sitienter & super Omnia desiderabat, Fridericum* (*quem magnum Draconem vocabat*) *pessundare, ut ipso suppeditato & conculcato, Reges Francorum & Angliæ, aliosque Christianitatis Reges,* (*quos omnes Regulos & Serpentulos esse dicebat*) *facilius, Exemplo dicti Friderici perterritos, Conculcaret, & Bonis suis, ac Prælatos eorum, ad Libitum spoliaret*. Matth. Paris. in Hen. 3. ad dictum Annum 1250. p. 774. lin. 2. &c.

Emperor

Emperor Frederick, (*whom he called the great Dragon*) *that, he being trampled upon, the King of* France, England, *and other Christian Kings,* (*whom he call'd diminutive Kings, and little Serpents*) *affrighted with the sad Fate of* Frederick, *might more easily be kept under, and they and their Prelates spoiled of their Goods, and by him plundered.* So that although he, and other Popes did pretend, (as appears by their Bulls) that they deposed Kings for the Extirpation of Heresie, the Preservation of the Catholick Faith, and Christian Religion; yet 'tis evident to any intelligent and impartial Judge of their Actions, that it was their prodigious ambition and covetousness, their inordinate and erroneous desire of Dominion, of Rule and Riches, which made them usurp and exercise a power to depose Kings and Emperors, which St. *Peter* (from whom they pretend to have it) never had, nor pretended to.

7. Pope *Paul.* III. (*b*) Excommunicates, Curses, Deposes and Damns *Henry.* VIII. of *England*, and all who adhere to him, favour or obey him; absolves his Subjects from all Oaths of Allegiance; commands them all, under pain of Excommunication, not to obey him, or *any* (*c*) *Magistrate or Officer under him; nor to acknowledge the King or any of his Judges or Officers to be their Superiors.* And further (with a strange Impiety and Impudence) he declares King *Henry* and his Complices and Favourers and their Children and Descendents to be Infamous, incapable to be Witnesses, make Wills, or be Heirs to any; Incapable to do any legal Act, and *that in any Cause* (*d*) *of Debt, or any other Cause Civil or Criminal, none should be bound to answer them, and yet they bound to answer every body.* And to omit the rest, (for I shall at the end of these Observations, set down the whole Bull) he commands the (*e*) Ecclesiasticks (Secular and Regular) *to quit the Kingdom, and not to return, till the Persons Excommunicate, de-*

(*b*) Vide Bullam. 7. Pauli. 3 dat. Romæ. 3. Cal. Sept. Anno. 1535. In Bullario Romano. Tom. 1. p. 514. Editionis Romæ. 1638.

(*c*) *Mandantes, ut ab Henrici Regis, suorúmque Officialium, Judicum & Magistratuum quorumcunque Obedientiâ penitùs & omninò recedant, nec illas in superiores recognoscant, néque eorum Mandatis Obtemperent.* Dictæ Bullæ. §. 10.

(*d*) *Et Nulli ipsis, sed ipsi aliis su-per* (*qocunque debito, & negotio, tam Civili, quam Criminali, de jure respondere teneantur.* Ibid. §. 11. (*e*) *Prælatis quóque & Cæteris personis Ecclesiasticis mandat sub pœnis in Bulla Contentis, quatenùs de Regno Angliæ discedant, nec revertantur, donec dicti Excommunicati, privati, maledicti, & damnati meruerint absolutionis Beneficium.* Ibid. §. 13. p. 516.

prived, cursed and damn'd (the King and all his Loyal Subjects he means) *be absolved from their Censures.* This Bull, though fram'd and ready to be publish'd, yet the Execution of it was suspended for three years, and then actually published in the Year 1538. which was the fifth year of Pope *Paul.* III. as appears by the Date of it, in the aforesaid Bullary. And when it was published, as it was in it self highly Impious, so (to *Hen.* VIII, and his Loyal Subjects) it was ridiculous; and all the Effect it had was, that it increased their hate and contempt of the Antichristian pride and folly of its Author. It appeared (what indeed it was) *Brutum fulmen,* and that King had too great a courage and understanding, to be frighted with an *Ignis fatuus,* Papal Squibs, and Wild-fire, which could neither warm or burn him.

8. Lastly; as the Popes proceeding *Pius.* V. so those who followed, approved and (so far as they were able) put in practice that execrable Doctrine of Deposing Kings. Pope *Gregory.* XIII. did immediately succeed *Pius* V. and renues and confirms his Bull for deposing Queen *Elizabeth,* and absolving her Subjects from their Oaths of Allegiance (as is testified not only by (*f*) *Cambden,* but by the Romish Priests themselves, (the (*g*) Seculars, who seem'd most moderate) and in prosecution of that damnatory Sentence, the said Pope *Gregory* did constitute *Fitz-Gerald* (an *Irish* Rebel against the Queen) General of all the *Irish* Rebels; that so he and they by Fire and Sword might Execute the Sentence of those two Popes, deposing that Queen This is expresly testify'd by *Fitz-Gerald* (*h*) himself, in an Edict publish'd by him, after he was General, declaring the Ju-

(*f*) Cambdens *Elizabeth.* lib. 3. p. 360, 361. ad Annum 1588.

(*g*) See a Book with this Title ----- *Important Considerations* &c. written by the Secular Priests here in *England*, printed *Anno* 1601. and reprinted with other Tracts, with this Title ------ *A Collection of several Treatises concerning the Reasons and Occasion of Penal Laws, &c.* London 1675. In which Collection, pag. 76. the Secular Priests tell us, that Pope *Gregory.* 13. did excommunicate Queen *Elizabeth.* (h) *Gregorius.* 13. *in Ducem ac Generalem hujus belli Capitaneam, Nos Elegit, ut ex ipsius Diplomate constat: Quod tanto magis fecit, quia ejus Prædecessor Pius.* 5. *Elizabetham hæresium Patronam Omni Regia Potestate privaverat.* Vid. Edictum Illustriss. D. Jac. Geraldini, de Justitia ejus belli, quod in Hibernia pro fide gerit. 'Tis Extant in the History of the Irish Rebellion. *Lond.* 1680. in the Appendix, p. 8.

stice

stice of that *Irish* War, which (he says) was undertaken for the Catholick Faith, and restoring it in *Ireland*. To *Gregory*. XIII. *Sixtus Quintus* immediately succeeds, *and confirms the damnatory Sentences of his two Predecessors, and* (as he who well knew, tells us) *Excommunicates and* (i) *deposes the Queen, Absolves her Subjects from their Oaths of Fidelity, and published a Croisado, as against Turks and Infidels* (indeed as afterwards evidently appear'd against *England* and Queen *Elizabeth*) *and gave* (what he never had to give) *plenary Indulgence to all who should assist in that War*. Nor is this all; Cardinal Allen (k) *writ a Traiterous and Seditious Book, to Exhort all the* English *and* Irish *Papists, to joyn with the* Spanish *Forces* (*against their Queen and Country*) *under the Prince of* Parma: *and Pope* Sixtus V. *sends* Allen (*with that Book, and his own Bull*) *into the* Low-Countries, *and there a great number of those Books and Bulls were Printed at* Antverpe, *to be sent into* England. Were it necessary, many things now might be said, pertinent to this purpose; but (I suppose) the Instances already given, will be sufficient to convince Intelligent and Impartial Persons, That Pope *Pius*. V. was neither the first nor last, who usurped this Extravagant Power to Depose Princes; seeing several of his Predecessors and Successors, for above. 600. years, have owned, approved, and (as they had opportunity) put that Power in practise: This in General premis'd, I come now to consider the Bull of *Pius*. V. wherein he damns and deposeth Queen *Elizabeth*; wherein two things occur very considerable;

(i) Cambdens *Elizabeth*. lib. 3. p. 360, 361.

(k) Cambden ibid. lib. 3. p. 364.

1. The 'Ἐπιγραφὴ, or Title prefix'd to the Bull.
2. The Particulars contain'd in it.

For the first; the Title prefix'd to the Bull is thus:——— ———*The Damnation of* Elizabeth, *&c.* where, though *Damnation* may seem a very hard word (as indeed it is, in the sense they use it, as shall by and by appear) yet it is not unusual; but occurs in other Bulls of the like nature: So we find it in

Observation.

in the Bull of Pope *Innocent.* IV. wherein he Excommunicates the Emperor *Frederick.* II. For the *Lemma* or *Title* of that Bull is thus---(*l*) *The Damnation & Deposition of* Frederick. II. So in the Bull of Pope *Paul.* III. Excommunicating *Henry.* VIII. the Title prefix'd to it is---(*m*) *The Damnation of* Henry. VIII. *and his Favourers*, &c. So that *Pius.* V. Damning Queen *Elizabeth*, was not singular (though Impious) he had some of his Predecessors Forms to follow. I say, his Predecessors; for I do not find that any Bishops in the World (save those of *Rome*) ever used such Unchristian, and indeed Anti-christian Forms of Excommunicating and Damning Kings and Emperors. And it is observable, and well known to those who diligently read and consider the Papal Bulls now extant, (of which there is a vast (*n*) number) that the Popes of later Ages, when they go about to justifie some extravagant Act of their usurped Power; they usually cite (*o*) the Bulls and Constitutions of their Predecessors, who had done the like; not for matter *of fact barely*; but to *prove a Right*; that because their Predecessors had done so formerly, therefore they (who succeeded in the same Power) might do it too. Now, although to argue thus, *à Facto ad Jus*, be evidently inconsequent and irrational: (no better than this———*Peter* (*de facto*) deny'd and forswore his Master: *Ergo*, His Successors (*de jure*) may do so to.) Yet, if their Principles were true, (as I suppose they may think them) such Arguing would be more concluding. For, Pope *Leo.* X. expresly (*p*) affirms, and publickly declares, in one of their General Councils, that it is more clear than light it self; *That none of his Predecessors, Popes of* Rome, *Did ever Err, in any of their Canons or Constitutions.* Now if this were true, (as

(*l*) *Damnatio & Depositio Friderici.* 2. Vid. Bullarium Romanum, Romæ, 1638. Tom.1. p.94. Col. 7. Edita erat Bulla ista An.1245.

(*m*) *Damnatio Hen.* 8. *ejusque Fautorum, &c.* In Bullario Romano. ibid. p.514. Col.2. Edita dicta bulla, Anno 1535. & postea 1538.

(*n*) Vid. *Bullarium Romanum* Lugduni. 1655. In 4. Tomis in Folio, & Eclogen Bullarum & motu propriorum P i.4. &c. Lugduni. 1582. 8°. & *NovamCollectionem*, &c. Eman. Roder. Turnoni. 1609. fol. where in that one Volume you have above. 500. Bulls, with the Names of 46. Popes, who published them.

(*o*) Vide Constitut. 22. Julij Papæ. 2. In Bullario Romano Tom.1. p. 378. Et Constitut. 81. Gregorij.13. In dicto Bullario Tom. 2. p. 348. vide Extravag. Communes,l. 5. Tit.9. cap. Unigenitus. 2. (*p*) *Docuissimus cum* (*Lutherum*) *Luce clarius, Sanctos Rom. Pontifices Prædecessores nostros, in suis Canonibus seu Constitutionibus Nunquam Errasse.* Vide Bullam Apostolicam Leonis. 10. contra Errores Lutheri, & sequacium. Dat. Romæ. 17. Cal. Julij, An. 1520. & Pontificatus sui, Octavo. Apud Fer. Crab Conc. Tom. 3. p. 715. &c. And his Predecessor, *Julius.* 2. says as much for the Church of *Rome*,——*S. Sancta Ecclesia Romana, Magistra fidei, omnium Errorum Expers, unica, immaculata*, &c. Constitutio. 27. Julij 2. data Anno. 1512. In Bullario Romano. Tom. 1. p. 384.

it is evidently false, and his Asserting it an Argument not only of his Fallibility, but of his great Error and Folly) *That none of his Predecessors ever Err'd*, then they might with more Security follow them; for certainly, it can be no great fault or danger to follow an unerring Guide. Especially if it be true which they tell us.

For 1. In their Laws and Canons, approved by their Supream Authority, and retained in publick use in their Church, we are told, (q) *That all their Papal Sanctions are so to be received, as if the Divine Voice of* Peter *himself had Confirmed them*: This (as *Gratian* there tells us) *was Pope* Agatho's *Sentence, and is Received into the Body of their Canon Law, Revised, Corrected, and Purged from all things Contrary to Catholick Verity*: So (r) *Gregory*. XIII. says, and confirms it. Whence it evidently follows; that (in Pope *Gregory's* Judgment) This Sentence of *Agatho* is not repugnant to *Catholick Verity*: And in the same place it is farther declared for Law, (Pope *Stephen*. I. is cited as Author of that Sentence) *That*, (s) *Whatever the Church of* Rome *does Ordain or Constitute, it is (without all Contradiction) perpetually to be Observed*.

2. Though this be (beyond all truth and reason) highly erroneous; yet the Jesuits (of late) have gone much higher, and in their Claromont Colledge at *Paris*, publickly (t) maintain'd these two Positions. 1. *That our Blessed Saviour left* Peter *and his Successors, the same Infallibility, he himself had, so oft as they spoke* è Cathedra. 2. *That (even out of a General Council) he is the Infallible Judge in Controversies of Faith, both in Questions of Right and Fact*. This (as to the main of it, though Erroneous and Impious) is maintain'd by others as well as Jesuits. F. *Gregory de Rives*, a Capuchin Priest, tells us (and his Book is approved by the General, and several others of his Order, and by Father *D. Roquet*, a Dominican, and Doctor of Divinity,

(q) *Sic Omnes Apostolicæ Sedis Sanctiones accipiendæ sunt, tanquam Ipsius Divini Petri voce Firmatæ sint.* Can. sic Omnes 2. dist. 19. & Ibid. Can. 3, 4, &c.

(r) Vide Bullam Greg. 13. datam Romæ. 1. Jul. 1580. Jur. Can. præfixam.

(s) *Quicquid Statuit, Quicquid Ordinat Romana Ecclesia, Ab Omnibus perpetuo & irrefragabiliter est Observandum.* Ibid. Can. Enim vero. 4. Dist. 19.

(t) *Christum ita Caput Ecclesiæ Agnoscimus, ut illius regimen, dum in Cœlos abiit, primum Petro, dein successoribus commiserit, & eandem quam habebat Ipse Infallibilitatem, concesserit, quoties ex Cathedrâ loqueretur. Datur, ergo, in Eccles. Rom. Controversiarum fidei Judex Infallibilis, etiam Extra Concilium Generale, tum in Quæstionibus Juris & Facti.* Vid. Exposit. Theseos. in Col. Claromontano propositæ. 12. Dec. 1661.

&c.

&c.) (u) That as the Authority of Christ (our blessed Saviour) if he were now on Earth, were greater than all Councils, so by the same Reason, the Authority of the Pope (who is Christs Vicar) is greater than all Councils too. That the Priviledge of Infallibility was given to the Pope, not to Councils; and then Concludes, That the (x) Church of Rome (he means the Pope) is Judge of Controversies, and all her Definitions and Determinations are De Fide. Thus De Rives. And three or four years before him, Lud. Bail (a Parisian Doctor and Propenitentiary) expresly affirms, That the (y) Word of God is threefold. 1. His written Word in Scripture. 2. His unwritten Word, in the Traditions of the Church. 3. The Word Declared or Explain'd; when doubtful passages in Scripture or Tradition are explain'd, and their meaning determin'd by the Pope, whether in, or out of Councils; and this (he says) is the most approved way, in which men acquiesce, and think they need look no further. And hence he Infers, That seeing this is so; we (z) ought not to be afraid to follow the Pope's Guidance in Doctrines of Faith and Manners, but acquiesce in his Judgment, and submit all our writings to be Corrected by him. I neither will nor need Cite any more Authorities, to prove the aforesaid Particulars; That Their Popes may damn and Depose Kings and Emperors (especially if they be Hereticks) and think they have (as Christs Vicars) a just Prerogative and Power to do it. Sure I am, that these Positions (though Erroneous and Impious) are generally maintain'd by the Jesuits, Canonists, (a) Schoolmen, and their Followers (which are very many) receiv'd into the Body of their Canon Law of their best, and (as they themselves say) their most Correct Editions, and approved, and (when they had opportunity) practis'd by (their Supream Powers) their

---

(u) Si Christi Authoritas non penderet à Concilio, & adhuc in terris viveret, sed Omni Concilio Major esset. Eâdem Ratione, & Pontificis Authoritas, quæ ipsius Christi Vicaria est, Concilio superior est.——Privilegium Infallibilis veritatis, non Concilio, sed Pontifici à Christo Collatum est. Luc. 22.32. Gr. de Rives Epitome Concil. in Principio prælud. 5.

(x) Ecclesia Romana est Judex Controversiarum in Rebus Fidei, & Ipsius Determinationes Sunt De Fide. Ibid. Prælud. 9. Edit. Lugd. Anno. 1663.

(y) Verbum Dei, vel est Scriptum in Scripturis: vel non scriptum, Traditionibus: vel Explicatum, cum dubia in verbo Scripto aut Tradito Explicantur. Quod fit Præsertim per Papam, sive Extra Concilia, seu in Conciliis. Isque modus ultimus Magis probatus est, & Majori suavitate ei Plures acquiescunt, ut nihil ulterius Contendendum existiment. Lud. Bail in Prin. Apparatus ad summam Conc. De triplici verbo Dei.

(z) Quæ cum ita sint, nec Nos debemus vereri ejus ductum sequi, In Doctrinâ Fidei & Morum, ejus Judicio Nos sistere, & scripta Omnia corrigenda submittere. Idem in Calce præfationis ad Lectorem, Tom. I. præfixam. (a) Vide Aquinatem. 2.2. Quæst. 11. Art. 3. utrum Hæretici sint tollerandi? negat. & ibid. Quæst. 12. Art. 2. utrum Princeps propter Apostasiam à fide, amittat Dominium in Subditos, ita quod ei obedire non tenentur? He affirms it, and says——Ejus Subditi à Dominio ejus & Juramento Fidelitatis (si sit Excommunicatus) Ipso facto liberantur.

against Queen Elizabeth.

Popes and General Councils. I would not be mistaken; I do not say that all who now do, or for this Six hundred years last past, have liv'd in the Communion of the Church of *Rome*, either do, or did approve such Papal Positions or Practices. I know the *Sorbon* and *University of Paris*, and many in other Countries, have publickly Declared their disbelief and dislike of them; Especially in (*b*) *Germany*, in the time of *Hen.* III. *Hen.* IV. *Frederick* II. *&c.* not only private Persons, but some Synods declared the Papal Excommunications and Depositions of their Emperors, not only Unjust and Impious, but Antichristian. I grant also, That *Father Caron* in his *Remonstrantiâ Hibernorum* (if some have rightly told the Number) has cited Two hundred and fifty Popish Authors, who deny the Popes Power to depose Kings: And though I know that many of his Citations are Impertinent; yet I shall neither deny nor doubt, but that there are many thousand honest Papists in the outward Communion of the Church of *Rome*, who dislike this Doctrine. But this will neither Justifie or Excuse the Church of *Rome*, so long as her Governing and Ruling part publickly approves and maintains it. For, 1. Father (*c*) *Caron* himself tells us, that (notwithstanding his Book, and all his Authorities for Loyalty to Kings) The Divines of *Lovane*, The *Pope*'s *Nuncio*, the Cardinals, four or five Popes, (*Paulus.* V. *Pius.* V. *Alexander.* VII. *Innocentius* X. (he might easily have reckon'd many more) did condemn his Doctrine, *The Inquisitors damn'd his Book*, and *his Superiors Excommunicate him.* 2. It is confessed, That the Supream Infallible Power of their Church, resides either in the Pope, or Council, or both together; And 'tis also certain, That their Popes, in their approved, and (in (*d*) publick use) received Canon Law, in their Authentick Bulls, (publish'd by themselves) in their General Councils (and (*e*) with their Consent) have approved, and (for these Six hundred years last past) many times

(*b*) Vid. Johan. Aventinum Annal: Bojorum. Lib. 5,6, 7. Carol. Sigonium de Regno Italiæ. Matth. Parif.&c. Ad An.1078 p.10,11. & p. 13. lin. 1. & p. 668. lin. 30. & 773. lin. 49. & p. 774. lin. 1. 2. & p. 875. where *R. Groshead* (for his Tyrannical Usurpations) calls the Pope Antichrist.

(*c*) Remonstranr: Hibernorum, part. 1. Cap. 3. &c.

(*d*) *Volentes (verba sunt Gregorij. Papæ. 9.) ut hac Tantum Compilatione universi utantur, & in Judiciis & Scholis,&c.* Bulla Greg. 9. Decretal. præfixa.

(*e*) Innocent. 4. Excommunicates *Friderick.* 2. in the General Council at Lions, *Omnium Consensu, &c.* Platina in vita Innocent. 4. And Pope *Innocent* himself said constantly that the Council of *Lions* Excommunicated

and Deposed that Emperor. Matth. Paris in Hen. 3. Ad Ann.1250. p. 773. lin. 58. 59. And Pope *Paseh.* 2. tells us, that he Excommunicated the Emperor *Hen.* 4. *Judicio Totius Ecclesiæ*. Carol. Sigonius de Regno Italiæ,!. 9. p. 237. lin. 18.

F practis'd

practis'd this Doctrine of Deposing Kings; nor has the Church of *Rome* (I mean the Governing and Ruling part of it) by any publick Act or Declaration disown'd or censur'd it, as doubtless she would, had she indeed disliked it. *Quæ non prohibet, cum possit, jubet.* If any man think otherwise, and can really shew me, that their Popes & General Councils have not formerly approved, or since have disown'd and disapprov'd this Doctrine: I shall willingly acknowledge my mistake, and be thankful to him for a Civility, which (at present) I really believe I shall never receive. However, *Grata supervenient quæ non sperantur.*

Observ. 3.

3. Seeing it is Evident that Pope *Pius* V. (and his Predecessors in the like Cases) calls the Anathema and Curse contain'd in this Bull, *The Damnation of Q. Elizabeth*; The next Query will be, What that hard word signifies, and what they mean by it, in their Bulls? For the Solution of which doubt, and Satisfaction to the Query: 1. I take it to be certain and confess'd; that the word *Damnum* (from whence *Damnation* comes) signifies a (*f*) *diminution*, or (*g*) *loss of some good things*, had and enjoyed before, or of a right to future good things, and then *Damnation* (as to our present Case) will be a judicial sentence, which (by way of punishment) imposes such loss and diminution. 2. As the *Damnum* or loss may be either of Temporal things here (as loss of Honours, Liberty, Lands or Life) or of Spiritual and Eternal things, (as Heaven and Salvation) hereafter; so the *Damnation* also (according to the Nature of the sentence, and the mischief intended by it) may be Temporal or Eternal, or both; if it penally inflict the loss both of Goods Temporal and Eternal. 3. I say then (and I hope to make it evident) that the mischief intended by this Papal Bull, and Excommunication (so far as the malice and injustice of an Usurped Power could) endeavoured to be brought upon that good Queen, was not only *Temporal*, but also *Spiritual and Eternal*. This the word *Damnation*, in the Ἐπιγραφή, or Title of the Bull, (in their Popish Construction) intends and signifies. For the Temporal mischiefs intended to be brought upon that good Queen,

(*f*) *Damnum à demendo, quia damnum est Rei diminutio unde Damna Lunæ, apud Gellium.* Noct. Atticarum lib. 20. Cap. 8. And *Varro; Damnum à demptione* lib. 4. de Regibus. So *Isidore* lib. 5 Orig cap. 22.

(*g*) *Damnum est amissio eorum quæ habueras* Quinctilianus Declamat 120. And a good Lawyer tells me, that ——— *Damnare; est rem sine remedio sublevandi tormentis seu Ignominiæ sententialiter deputare.* Panormitan. in cap. Damnamus. in. 2. Norab. de summâ Trinit. & fide Catholicâ.

against Queen Elizabeth.

Queen, there is no question; they are all particularly named in the Bull it self, as we shall see anon. For the Spiritual, that is, a seclusion out of Heaven and Happiness, and Eternal Damnation of Body and Soul; that these also were the intended and designed Effects of this Impious Bull and Excommunication, is now to be proved. And here it is to be Considered,

1. That they constantly say, and (having strong Delusion) possibly may believe it; That Hereticks (and such the Queen is declared to be in the Bull) dying Excommunicate, (as that Queen did, and all true Protestants do) are *Eternally Damn'd*. For, 1. A very great (h) *Canonist* of our own Nation, (while Popish Superstition unhappily prevail'd here) tells us, *That every Excommunicate Person is a Member of the Devil*. And for farther proof of this, he Cites (i) *Gratian* and their Canon Law, (and he might have Cited other as pertinent places in *Gratian*) who tells us, in another Canon (k), *That Excommunication is a Damnation to Eternal Death*. And *John Semeca* the Glossator gives us their meaning of it; *That it is certainly true, when the* (l) *Person Excommunicate is incorrigible, and contemns the Excommunication*, (as for my part I really do contemn all their Excommunications, as *Bruta fulmina*, which neither do, nor can hurt any honest Protestant) so that by their Injust Law, and most uncharitable Divinity, not only Queen *Elizabeth*, but all Protestants (who are every Year Excommunicated by the Pope, in their *Bulla* (m) *Cœnæ Domini*) are *Eternally damned*, and that *è Cathedra*. A Sentence Erroneous and Impious; and (though it be the Popes, whom they miscall *Infallible*) inconsistent with Truth, or Christian Charity.

2. But we have (both for Learning and Authority) a far greater Author than *Lindwood* or *Gratian*, and (in our days) long after them; I mean Cardinal *Baronius*; who tells us ——— (n) *That Pope* Gregory. VII. *did not only depose the Emperor* Hen. IV. *but Excommunicate, and Decree him*

(h) *Excommunicatus est membrum Diaboli*. Lindwood ad Cap. *Sæculi Principes*. verbo Reconciliatoris. De Immunit. Ecclesiæ.

(i) Gratian. Can. Omnis Christianus. 32. Caus. 11. Quæst. 3.

(k) *Excommunicatio est Æternæ Mortis Damnatio*. Idem Gratian. Can. Nemo 41. Caus. 11. Quæst. 3.

(l) *Est Perpetua Damnatio cum ab Excommunicato contemnitur*. Gloss. ad dictum Can. verbo mortis.

(m) This *Bulla Cœnæ* often (with some alterations) occurs in *Bullario Romano*. vid. Constit. 25 Julii. 2. Tom 1. pag. 382. Edit. Romæ. 1638. & Constit. 63. Pauli. 5. Tom. 3. p. 83. ubi reliqua, hujus Bullæ Exemplaria dicto Bullario comprehensa, indicantur.

(n) *Non modo deponi, sed etiam Excommunicari, & in Æterno Examine Damnari Decrevit*. Baronius Annal. Tom 8. ad An. Christi 593. num. 86.

Observations on the Pope's Bull

to be *Eternally Damn'd*. And for this he (*o*) Cites Pope *Gregory's* own Epistles, who surely best knew his own mind, and the meaning of his own Decree.

3. But we have greater Authors and Authority for this, than *Baronius*; for Pope *Paschal*. II. tells us, (*p*) *That he had Excommunicated the Emperor* Hen. IV. *in a Council*; and adds, *That by the Judgment of the whole Church, he lay bound under an Eternal Anathema*. And after this Pope *Paul*. III. (*q*) *Damns* (that's the word) *and Excommunicates our King* Hen. VIII. *and all his Favourers and Adherents; And we smite them* (saith he) *with the Sword of an Anathema, Malediction, and Eternal Damnation*. In the Year 1459. *Pius* II. (with the Unanimous Consent of his Council, at Mantua, *Excommunicates and Damns all those* (*even* (*r*) *Kings and Emperors*) *who shall Appeal from the Pope to a General Council, and that they shall be punish'd as* (*s*) *Traytors and Hereticks*. Pope *Julius*. II. afterwards confirms this Constitution of his Predecessor, as to all the Punishments contain'd in it; Excommunicates and Curses all Persons, Ecclesiastical and Secular, of what Dignity soever (though Kings) who shall offend against that Constitution; and *Decrees that they shall have* (*t*) *their Portion & Damnation with* Dathan *and* Abiron. The Damnation then intended and threatned in this Impious Bull of *Pius*. V. (as in other Papal Bulls of the like nature) is not only some *Temporal loss and damage* (though that also be included and expressed) but the *Eternal Damnation of Body and Soul*. Which further appears by that Famous (or indeed Infamous, Erroneous and Ridiculous) Constitution of *Boniface*. VIII. wherein having said, *That there is but one Catholick Church, out of which, there is no Salvation, and that our Blessed Saviour made* Peter *and his Successors his Vicarii, Vice-Gerents, and Heads of that Church*; he adds, *That* (*u*) *whoever are not of that Church, and in Subjection*

(*o*) Gregor. 7. lib.4. Epist.2. & 23. & lib. 8. Epist. 21.

(*p*) *Henricus.* 4. *primum à Gregorio Papâ, dein ab Urbano, Postremo à Nobis, Judicio Totius Ecclesiæ, Perpetuo Anathemate Obligatus est.* Car. Sigonius de Regno Italiæ. lib. 9. pag 237.

(*q*) *Henricum, Ejusq; fautores, Adhærentes &c. Excommunicatos Decernimus, eosque* Anathematis, Maledictionis, & *Æternæ Damnationis mucrone percutimus*. In Bulla Damnationis Hen. 8. Dat. Romæ. Cal. Sept. An. 1535.

(*r*) *Si Imperiali, Regali, aut Pontificali Dignitate præfulgeant* §. 3. dictæ Bullæ.

(*s*) *Pœnis quæ Læsæ Majestatis & Hæreticâ pravitatis reis Imponuntur*. Ibidem.

(*t*) *Decernentes eos pro Schismaticis, & de Catholicâ fide male sentientibus, cum* Dathan *& Abiron partem & Damnationem habere*: Constit. 22. Pii. 2. § 6. vid. P. Crab. Concil. Tom. 3. p. 650. Col. 2. & ibi formam ——— sub pœnâ Maledictionis Æternæ. (*u*) *Porro subesse Rom. Pontifici Omni humanæ Creaturæ declaramus, dicimus, definimus, & pronunciamus Omnino esse de Necessitate Salutis*. Constit. Bonifacii. 8. dat. Romæ. Ann. 1301. Pont. Ann. 8. Cap. unam sanctam. 1. De Major. & Obed Extrav. Communes.

and

against Queen Elizabeth.

and Obedient to the Pope, can have no Salvation. And *Pius V.* in this very Bull, expresly says the same. For, 1. He says, *That out of the Apostolick* (x) *Church* (he means evidently his own Roman Church) *there is no Salvation.* 2. He declares Queen Elizabeth *an* (y) *Heretick, that she and all her Adherents had Incurr'd an Anathema and Malediction, were Excommunicate, and cut off from the Body of Christ.* So that Queen *Elizabeth*, and all her Loyal Protestant Subjects, who never were, nor could be, (as without great Error and Impiety they could not) subject to the Pope, nor Members of his Apostolical Church, are (by this Bull) *Eternally Damn'd.*

4. But this is not all; for we have greater Evidence, that by the word *Damnation* in their Bulls, wherein all Hereticks, (Protestants you may be sure, who without Truth or Charity, they call so) are Curs'd and Excommunicated, they do and must mean *Eternal Damnation.* For, 1. Pope *Leo* X. in the *Lateran* (z) Council, (which with them is General and Oecumenial) innovates and establisheth (with the Approbation and Consent of that Council) the aforesaid Doctrine and Constitution of Pope *Boniface,* VIII. 2. The *Trent* Council doth so too, and absolutely Anathematizes and Damns all those who do not believe their whole new Creed; (in which there is not one true Article, but all Erroneous, many Superstitions and Impious) and tells us, *It is the Catholick* (a) *Faith, without the belief of which, no man can be saved, and swear firmly to believe it to their last breath, and Anathematize all who do not.* And, (which is further very considerable and pertinent to confirm what is abovesaid) they do in that Oath promise, vow, and swear to receive and imbrace (b) *All things delivered, defined, and declared in their General Councils, and All* (c) *the Constitutions of their Church ;* For these Particulars are parts of

(x) *Ecclesia Apostolica, extra quam nulla est Salus.* In Prin. Bullæ. Pii. 5.

(y) *Declaramus Elizabetham Hæreticam eique Adhærentes Anathematis sententiam incurrisse, esseque a Christi Corporis unitate præcisos.* Ibid. §. 3.

(z) *Cum de necessitate Salutis sit, Omnes Christi fideles Romano Pontifici subesse, prout Divinæ Scripturæ & Sanctorum Patrum Testimonio edocemur, & Constitutione Bonifacii Papæ 8. quæ incipit unam Sanctam, declaratur. ------ Constitutionem ipsam Sacro præsenti Concilio Approbante Innovamus, & Approbamus.* Conc. Lateran. sub Leone. 10. Sess. 10. apud P. Crab. Conc. Tom. 3. p. 697. Col. 1.

(a) *Contraria Omnia & Hæreses, ab Ecclesia Damnatas & Anathematizatas Ego pariter Anathematizo. Hanc veram Catholicam fidem, Extra quam*

Nemo Salvus esse Potest, quam veraciter teneo, & ad Extremum vitæ Spiritum, Constantissime retinere, spondeo, voveo, juro. Conc. Trident. Sess. 24. De Reformat. in Calce Cap. 12. p. 452. Edit. Antverp. 1633. (b) *Omnia à Conciliis Oecumenicis tradita, definita, & Declarata, Indubitanter recipio, & profiteor.* Ibid. p. 452. (c) *Apostolicas Traditiones, reliquasque Ejusdem Ecclesiæ Constitutiones firmissimè admitto & amplector.* Ibid. p. 451.

that

(d) Conc. Trident. Sess. 24. De Reformat. cap. 12. *Provisi de Beneficiis*, &c. *Tentantur fidei publicam facere professionem in Rom. Ecclesiæ Obedientiâ se permansuros spondeant ac Jurent.* p. 432. dictæ Editionis. And that we may know that the Faith they are to profess and swear to, is the Creed of *Pius*. V. in the afore-named Edition of the Council of *Trent*, at *Antverp.* 1633. *Pius* 5. his Creed, and the *Forma Juramenti Professionis Fidei*, is placed immediately after that 12. cap. Sess. 24. De Reformat. pag. 450.

Observ. 4.

(e) Jer. 1. 10.
(f) *Petro & Successoribus, Ecclesiam, in plenitudine Potestatis gubernandam tradidit. Hanc unum super Omnes Gentes, & Omnia Regna Principem constituit, qui Evellat, Destruat, Dissipet, Disperdat, plantet & ædificet; ut fideles Salvos exhibeat Salvatori.*

that new Creed, to the Belief and Profession of which they are sworn. And the *Trent* Council it self (as well as the Pope in that Creed) *(d)* requires that they make such a Profession. Whence it evidently follows, that all their Bishops, all Regulars of what Order soever, who are provided of Monasteries, Religious Houses, &c. All *Canons* and *Dignitaries* in their Church, all who have any *Cure of Souls*, and all *who profess and teach* any of the Liberal *Arts*, &c. (for all these are required to take that Oath) are sworn to *receive*, *believe*, and *profess* all the *Definitions* of the *Lateran Council* under *Leo*. X. and the *Constitution* of Pope *Boniface*. VIII. which denounces Damnation to all those who submit not to the Pope, and embrace not their Popish Religion; and hence it further, and as evidently follows, that not only Queen *Elizabeth*, but all good Protestants then, and ever since, (who neither did, nor without great Error and Impiety, could so submit to their Popes, or believe their New Creed) are, by their Papal and uncharitable Divinity, *Eternally Damn'd*. So that it is not only some Temporal mischief or loss, but the *Eternal Damnation of Body and Soul*, which is threatned, and Declared to be the Effect and Inevitable Consequence of this against Queen *Elizabeth*, and such other Excommunications of those whom they call Hereticks.

4. In the beginning of this Impious Bull, we are told by the Pope, *That our Blessed Saviour committed the Government of his Church (with all plenitude and fulness of Power) to Peter and his Successors.* And that we might know, how great the Power was over all Kings and Kingdoms, he miserably misapplies a Text in *(e) Jeremy*; and says —— *(f) That our blessed Saviour did Constitute* Peter *alone a Prince*, *over All Nations, and all Kingdoms, to Pull up, and Throw down, to Dissipate and Destroy, to Plant and Build* (in Ordine ad Spiritualia) *in Order to the Salvation of his Faithful People*; so that (if we may believe this Infallible Expositor) the same Power which God gave *Jeremy* over all *Nations and Kingdoms*, *to pull up and destroy them*; the very same did our blessed Saviour give to *Peter* and his Successors. Nor is

Pius.

Pius. V. the only Pope who makes use of that Text to prove their extravagant Papal Power over Kings: Pope *Alexander.* III. having told some of his Brethren, how the (g) *Emperor held his Stirrup when he mounted his Palfrey;* In his next Constitution, (having said, That the Diligence of the Bishops and Pastors was necessary to pull up, and cut off Hereticks, and wicked-men in the Church) he Cites the place of *Jeremy* to prove it; and says, *That the Power over Nations and Kingdoms, to pull up, cast down, and destroy, was given to* Jeremy (h), *and In Him, to the Evangelical Priest, to* Peter *and his Successors,* as he there expresly explains it. And Pope *Paul.* III. tells us; ——— (i) *That he was Vicar of Christ, our blessed Saviour, and plac'd in the Throne of Justice Above All Kings in the whole World, According to the Prophecy of* Jeremy; And then Cites the words of *Jeremy* before mention'd. And (to omit others) Pope *Boniface.* VIII. Cites the same Text (though to as little purpose) to the same end; to prove *the* (k) *Popes power above Kings,* so as to punish and depose them. And before him *Innocent.* III. in his wild and irrational Epistle to the Emperor of *Constantinople* (l), Cites the same Text of *Jeremy,* and another (*Gen.* 1. 16.) more impertinent (if that be possible) to prove the vast Power of Popes above all (m) Kings and Emperors. By all which, Papal Bulls and Constitutions (as by many others of the like nature) it may evidently appear, that they challenge a Power to depose Kings, and that they bring the Text of *Jeremy* as a ground and proof of it.

But although their Popes brag, *That they have* (n) *all Laws in the Archives of their own breasts,* and that they are Supream and Infallible Judges in all Controversies of Faith; yet their whole Discourse and Deductions from the Text of the Prophet *Jeremy,* is inconsequent, and indeed ridicu-

(g) *Cum Ascenderemus Palfredum nostrum, Fridericus Imp. Stapham tenuit. &c.* Constit. 8 Alexand. 3. In Bullario Rom. Tom. 1. p. 65. Col. 2.

(h) *Deus Jeremiam, & in illo Evangelicum Sacerdotem instruxit dicens; Ecce Constitui Te super Gentes & Regna, ut Evellas, destruas, dispirdas, &c. quæ Potestas imminet in Romano Antistite, qui à Christo, ut sit Caput Ecclesiæ, accepit.* Ibid Constit. 9. p. 65 Col. 2.

(i) *Ejus Vicis gerentes in terris, & in Sede Justitiæ Constituti, Juxta Jeremiæ Vaticinium, &c. super Omnes Reges universæ Terræ.* In Bullâ Damnationis Hen. 8. data Rom. 1535. & 1538.

(k) *Spiritualis Potestas terrenam judicare debet, si bona non fuerit: sic Verificatur Vaticinium Jeremiæ, Constitui Te super Gentes, &c.* Cap. unam Sanctam. 1. de major. & Obed. Extrav. Communes. (l) Cap. Solicit. 6. Extra. De Major. & Obedientia. (m) *Deus Papam Totius Orbis præcipuum obtinere voluit Magistratum.* Bonif. 8. in Bulla. 6. Decretalium præfixa. (n) Dictum Bonif. 8. Cap. *Licet Romanus.* De Constitut. in. 6. *Romanus Pontifex jura Omnia in Scrinio pectoris sui censetur habere.*

lous,

lous, and no ways concerns either *Peter*, or any of his pretended Successors. For,

1. This Power which God gave to *Jeremy*, was Personal, to himself only, not hereditary or after his death to be continued to any Successor; much less to *Peter*, who came above Six hundred years after. That the Popes of this or former Ages, were Successors to *Peter*, both the Popes themselves, and Popish Authors universally affirm; but (as yet) I have found none (except the Pope and some few of his Party) who say that either *Peter*, or any Pope, was Successor to *Jeremy*. It's true, Pope *Alexander*. III. (in the Place quoted a little before) says; *That that Power over Nations and Kingdoms, to pull up, dissipate, and destroy*, &c. *was (by God) given to* Jeremy, *and in Him to* Peter. So that (by this wild Supposition) *Peter* succeeded into that Power, which before him, *Jeremy* had. But (notwithstanding his Infallibility) this is *gratis dictum* without any shadow or pretence of Reason: For he who succeeds into a Right which another possess'd before him, must do it either, 1. *Per generationem & Jure Sanguinis*; as a Son succeeds his Father, or the next Heir, *In jus defuncti*: and that *Peter*, or any Pope did this way succeed *Jeremy*, as none (with any reason) can, I suppose none will say. 2. *Per Consecrationem & Jure Ordinis*; so one Bishop succeeds another in the same Bishoprick. Neither could *Peter* succeed *Jeremy* this way; for *Jeremy* was never Bishop of *Rome*, or any other place, and then 'tis impossible that they should succeed him in a Place he never had, and be Successor to one who never was their Predecessor. 3. A man may be said to succeed another, who has a new Commission given him, to Execute an Office, which (though intermitted) some had long before him. So suppose the King should give one a Commission to be High Constable of *England*, after the Place had been long void; he who had such Commission, may be said to succeed him, who had that Office last, though One or Two hundred years before. Now if the Pope (or any for him) can shew, that our blessed

Saviour

Saviour gave *Peter* the same Commission, which God gave *Jeremy*, and set him over Nations and Kingdoms, to pull up, dissipate, and destroy, &c. (as Pope *Pius* V. expresly says (o) he did, in this His Impious Bull against Q. *Elizabeth*) then I will Confess, that in this Sense *Peter* may be called *Jeremy*'s Successor. But that our blessed Saviour gave *Peter* any such Commission (though the Pope say it) is absolutely untrue; not only without any foundation or ground of Reason for it in Scripture, (and nothing else can prove it) but point blank against it. *As our Saviour's Kingdom was not of this World*, no Temporal Power or Dominion; so he neither exercis'd any such Power himself, nor gave *Peter* or his Apostles, (who, all of them had Equal Power with *Peter*) any such (p) *Temporal Power over Nations and Kingdoms, to pull up, destroy, and dissipate, &c.* All the Power they had was *Spiritual*; they could punish no man (unless miraculously, which the Pope pretends not to) *in his person*, by loss of *Life*, or *Liberty* (by Imprisonment) nor *in his purse*, by imposing and exacting Pecuniary Mulcts; as has been, and might be further demonstrated, were it now my business: only (by the way) I crave leave to observe, That Pope *Pius* in this Bull, makes that Commission, which he says, our blessed Saviour gave *Peter*, far larger than that which God gave *Jeremy*. For he tells us, 1. *That our blessed Saviour did* (q) *Constitute* Peter *a Prince, to pull up, and destroy, &c.* but there is no such thing in *Jeremy*'s Commission. 2. That *Peter* was Constituted a Prince *over* (r) *All Nations, and All Kingdoms*; but *Jeremy* had not such Universal Power, as is evident from the (s) Text. But to make this further appear, it is to be Consider'd,

2. That *Jeremy* was a Priest, and a Prophet; so that if *Peporal Sword, Quoad Executionem* only: the Power of the Temporal Sword belongs to the Emperor, but the Pope makes him Emperor, and gives him that Power: and this he proves out of a Decree of Pope *Innocent.* 3. Cap. Venerabil. 34. Extra. De Elect. & Electi Potestate. (q) *Hunc unum* (Petrum scilicet) *Principem Constituit, &c.* Ibid. in dicta Bulla. (r) *Super Omnes Gentes, & Omnia Regna.* Ibid. (s) Jer. 1. 10.

(o) *Regnans in Excelsis* (i. e. *Christos*) *Ecclesiam soli Petro & Successoribus tradidit Gubernandam* And then it immediately follows —— *Hunc unum* (Petrum scilicet) *super Omnes Gentis, & Omnia Regna Principem Constituit, qui evellat, destruat, dissipat, disperdat, plantet, &c.* Bulla dicta in Principio.

(p) Pope *Nicol.* 1. (and he as Infallible as any of his Successors) tells us, That *Ecclesia non habet Gladium nisi spiritualem, qui non occidit, sed vivificat.* In Iprandus in vita, Nicol. 1. Cap. 107. But he lived above 800 years since, and though Gratian records it for Law (Can. inter hæc. 6. Cauf. 33. Quæst. 2.) yet the Case is alter'd since and the Gloss upon that Canon (verbo Gladium) tells us, that the meaning is, that the Pope has not the Tem-

ter and his Successors succeeded him, it must be in one of those two Capacities. But, 1. 'Tis certain, that neither *Peter*, nor any Christian Bishop did, or could succeed him, as a Priest; he being a Priest of *Aaron's* Order, which absolutely ceased at our Saviour's death. 2. Nor did he succeed *Jeremy* as to his Prophetical Office. 1. Because that was, Extraordinary, Temporary, and Expired with his Person. The Prophetical Office was not Hereditary or Successive. 'Tis true, some Prophets preceded in time, and some afterwards followed: So (*t*) *Jeremy* was after *Isaiah* about One hundred sixty five years; *Ezekiel* after him Four and thirty years; *Daniel* after him Twenty years. But each Prophet had a new Call and Commission, and that for particular and different purposes, as is evident by the Prophesies themselves. 2. *Jeremy* and those Prophets were Θιοπνευσοι, Divinely Inspired, and that to an Infallibility, and their Prophecies (as Divine, and the Word of God) referr'd into the Sacred Canon of Scripture; now although *Peter*, (not by Succession from *Jeremy*, but by a new Call and Commission from our blessed Saviour) was Θιοπνευσος, and had such an Assistance of the Holy Spirit, as made him Infallible, and his Doctrine Divine Truth; yet such assistance being personal in him, (as it was in all Prophets before him) his Successors cannot, without Impudence and Impiety pretend to it; though *some of the* (u) *Canonists, the Jesuits, and Papal Parasites,* would have us believe (what the (*x*) World knows to be false) that they are Infallible.

3. But that I may (in short) come to the main scope and hinge of the Question; the truth is Evident, That all these Popes in the Exposition and Application of this Text in *Jeremy*, (notwithstanding their pretended Supremacy and Infallibility) are miserably mistaken, and put a sense upon it, which, before them, never any Father or Ancient Author did; no nor their own Learned Writers of later times, even when Popery most prevail'd; a sense (if I may call it so) inconsistent with the true

and

(*t*) Vide Corn. A Lapide in Prin. Argument. Comment. sui in Jeremiam.

(*u*) For proof of this, see the Quotations before Observ. 2.

(*x*) Pope *Honorius*, & Pope *Vigilius* anciently condemned for Hereticks in General Councils; and of later times, the General Councils of *Pisa, Constance*, and *Basil* condemned others.

and certain meaning of *Jeremy*. For when 'tis in that Text, *I have set thee over the Nations and Kingdoms, to pull down, dissipate, destroy, plant, and build*; That which (y) *Alexander*. III. (and other Popes after him) Cite this Text for, is, to infer a Power in *Jeremy*, (and from him, in them) so far, to pull down, dissipate, and destroy, as to *Depose Kings and Emperors, and Absolve their Subjects from all Oaths of Allegiance*: Though the Text mean nothing less; nor can any such Impious Conclusion, by any (save possibly Popish) Logick, be deduced from it. For when the (z) Text says, *I have set thee over the Nations, to pull down, and destroy, &c.* 1. The meaning is not, that *Jeremy* (by this Commission) had Power and Jurisdiction, (*per modum Imperantis*) as a Prince and Superior, *to pull down and destroy any man, much less Kings and Emperors*; nay so far was he from that, that he quietly and patiently submitted to the Authority and Commands of Injust and Impious Superiors, (as is evident in his Prophecy) and was several times (a) Imprison'd and cast into Dungeons, with great danger of his Life, at *Jerusalem*; and when carried Captive into *Egypt*, by some Rebellious Jews, who would not obey the Word of God by him, he was more miserably used, and at last, by them (b) murder'd and martyr'd. So far was *Jeremy* (after God had given him that (c) Commission) from pulling down, or destroying any man, that (on the contrary) he patiently submitted to his Superiors, and was by them (though most unjustly) punished, pull'd down, and at last destroy'd. 2. But the meaning of that Text evidently is, *I have set thee over Nations and Kingdoms, to pull down, destroy, and dissipate*, &c. *Per modum Prophetantis, & Quid Judicio Justo facturus esset Deus, prædicentis*; As a Prophet, to foretell what God would do; that (unless they repented) he would pull down, destroy, and dissipate those Nations and Kingdoms, against which (by God's express Command) he Prophesied. *Jeremy* had no Commission, no Power or Authority to pull down, or destroy any one single Person, much less Kings

(y) Vide Constitut. 9. Alexand. 3. In Bullario Rom. Tom. 1. p. 65. Col. 2.

(z) Jer. 1. 10.
(a) He is beaten by *Pashur*. Jer. 20, 1. Apprehended & Arraigned. Jer. 26. 8. Imprison'd by *Zedekiah*. Chap. 32. 3. and beaten and imprison'd by the Princes. Jer. 37. 15. by them put into a Dungeon. Jer. 38. 6

(b) *A suis Concivibus in Taphnis Ægypti, Lapidibus Obrutus, Martyr occubuit*. Ita Hieronymus, Tertul. Doroth. Epiphan. Isiodor. &c. Corn. A. Lapide Comment. in Jerem. in Argumento.

(c) The Commission was given him, when he was a Child. Jer. 1. 6. 7. when he was 14. or 15. years old. So Corn. A Lapide in Prin. Argumenti Commentariis suis in Jeremiam præfixi.

and Emperors; nor did he ever do, or attempt any such thing; he only Prophecied, and premonish'd them from God, that Destruction would come upon them for their sins, but it was God only who could and did execute that Sentence, and when they repented not, destroyed them. So in Scripture, the Prophet is said to do that, which he foretells will be done. *Joseph* in Prison, tells *Pharaoh*'s Butler and Baker, That *within three days the one should be restored to his Place, and the other hanged*. This coming to pass (not by any Power of *Joseph*, for he was a Prisoner) yet the (*d*) Text says, That *He restored the one, and that He hang'd the other*. And this, those Popes, who so often urge this Text of *Jeremy*, might have easily and certainly known, had they studied Scripture and Divinity as much as Human Policy (as too (*e*) many of them do not) For what I have said is expresly said in the very Text of *Jeremy*'s Prophecie; as he who compares and considers (*f*) two or three Chapters in it, may evidently see. Sure I am, (to say nothing of the Fathers and Ancient Writers of the Church) what I have said of the true meaning of this place in *Jeremy*, is acknowledg'd even by the Jesuits and Canonists (the greatest Flatterers of the Pope, and Sticklers for his pretended Supremacy) who Expound the Text as I have done done. I shall instance in One or Two.

1. *Corn: A. Lapide* (a Noted and Learned Jesuit) Expounding this Place of *Jeremy*, says thus —— (*g*) *I have set thee over the Nations, that thou should pull up: That is*, (saith he) *that thou shouldst Threaten my Enemies, that unless they repent, I will pull them out of the Countries, where I have placed them*. And then he tells us truly, that this is the Opinion of *Hierome, Theodoret, Rabanus, Vatablus, Lyranus, Dion-Carthusianus*, and others. And then he adds —— (*h*) *That it is God* (not *Jeremy*) *who Pulls up, and Plants the Nations*. So that when 'tis said —— *I have set thee To pull up, and plant the Nations*: it is all

(*d*) Gen. 41. 13.
(*e*) It is a memorable Story we are told to this purpose; not by any *Lutheran*, but a Learned *Sorbon* Doctor, an ear-witness of it, who says, That when Pope *Innocent* X. was pressed to Determine the Controversie between the Jesuits and *Jansenists*, He (who was bred a Lawyer) told them that he was *No Divine*, that Divinity was not *His Profession, nor had he studied Divinity*. Monsieur de St. Amour in his Journal Part. 3. Cap. 12. & p. 320.

(*f*) Vide Jer. 18. 7 8. &c. Jer. 25. 15. 16. 17. &c. & Cap. 42. 10. & 45. 4.

(*g*) *Constitui Te ut Evellas*, i. e. *ut Intermineris Hostibus meis, (quos Regionibus suis Plantavi) ni inde per Bulla, &c. evulsurum, nisi respuerint*. A Lapide. in Jer. 1. 70.

(*h*) *Ita Deus: lantat & Evellit Gentes: nam Jeremias reipsa nec plantavit nec Evulsit Gentes. Ergo, ut Evellas & Plantes; Idem est quod, ut has Gentes evellendas, illas plantandas A Deo mineris ac Prædices. dem Ibidem*.

one

one as if he had said——*I have set thee to Threaten and Preach that God would* **Pull** *up and Plant those Nations.* This is that we say and prove to be the meaning of that Text in *Jeremy*, and the Jesuit fully Consents, and Acknowledges it to be true.

2. Pope *Innocent.* III. in his (*i*) Epistle to the Emperor of *Constantinople*, (amongst several other places of Scripture) brings this Text of *Jeremy*, *to prove the Priest* (especially *Peter*'s Successor the Pope) *to be* (k) *Superior to all Kings*: and yet *Bernardus de Botono* (the (*l*) Author of the Gloss there) when he comes to Explain that Text ——*I have set thee over the Nations, to pull up, and plant*; he has nothing *of Deposing and setting up Kings*: but Conceives the meaning to be ——That *Jeremy* was set over (*m*) Nations, *To pull up Vices, and plant Virtues*. He truly Conceives that *Jeremy* was not Constituted *a Prince*, with Dominion and Jurisdiction over Kings and Emperors; to set them up, or pull them down, at his pleasure; (to which purpose many of the Popes produce it) but *a Prophet*, to foretell them, what God would do. That is, *He would plant them*, if they were Penitent; if not, pull down and destroy them. So the Author of the Gloss; and they tell us, that he (*n*) *writ most Learned Glosses* upon the Decretals of *Gregory*. IX. which (*o*) afterwards had the Approbation of Pope *Gregory*. XIII. Be it concluded then, that *Pius*. V. and those other Popes before mention'd (notwithstanding their Infallibility) have miserably mistaken the true meaning of this place of *Jeremy*. And indeed he who reads and seriously Considers the several Places of Scripture, which the Popes of the last 600 years have explained in their Bulls and Decretals, and produc'd as proofs of their extravagant and usurp'd Supremacy; I say, he will have just reason to believe, that Popes are not the best Expositors of Scripture. For Instance; (to omit others) I shall refer the Reader to those (*p*) 8. or 9. Places, which Pope *Innocent*. III. and *Boniface*. VIII. have Cited, and Explain'd, in two of their Constitutions, both Extant in their

(*i*) Cap. Solitæ. 6. Extra de Major. & Obedientia.

(*k*) Ostendit Sacerdotium præeminere Regibus, dicto *Jeremiæ* Glossa ad dictum Cap. verbo. Solitæ Benignitatis.

(*l*) Vide Corpus Juris Can. cum Glossis; Paris. 1612 In Nota, Titulum. Tom. 2. Immediate (seu pagina proxima) sequente.

(*m*) Constitui Te, ut Evellas] *Vitia scilicet. & plantes*] *Virtutes*. Glossa ad dictum Cap. Solitæ. verbo, Constitui Te, &c.

(*n*) Glossas Eruditissimas Edidit. Vid.dictam Notam in Prin. Tom. 2. Juris Can. Paris. 1612.

(*o*) Vid. Bullam Greg. 13 Corp. Juris Can. præfixam.

(*p*) 1. Peter. 2. 13. 14. Jer. 1. 10. Gen. 1. 16. 17. &c. Joh. 21. 16. Matth. 15. 18. 19. Luc. 22. 38. Rom. 13. 1. 2. Gen. 1. 1. 1. Cor. 2. 15.

Observations on the Pope's Bull

their (q) Canon Law, in the places before Cited, where the Expositions and Applications of those places, by those Popes, are not only evidently Erroneous, but (being repugnant to all good Sense and Reason) exceedingly rediculous: such as may give their Adversaries reason to believe that the Authors of such wild Interpretations, are rather Fools than Infallible.

5. Pope *Pius.* V. Here in the beginning of this his Bull, calls (r) *Peter* (as other Popes and their Parasites usually do) *Prince of the Apostles; and tells us, that our blessed Saviour did set and constitute him a Prince over all Nations and Kingdoms.* From whence, they (Illogically and without any shadow of Just Consequence) would Conclude, *Peter's* Supremacy, his Dominion and Authority even over all the Apostles. For although *Peter* in the Gospel (when the Names of the Twelve Apostles are numbred) is called (s) πρῶτος, *Primus*; and amongst Latin Authors anciently (*Princeps Apostolorum*) *The Prince of the Apostles*; yet that (t) Papal Supremacy, which the Popes and their Party generally attribute to him, that they (as his Successors) might have it themselves, cannot thence be concluded. So (u) *Erasmus* tells us, (out of St. *Hierome*) *That the Apostles in the other Evangelists, are not reckon'd in the Order they are in* Matthew; *lest any man should think, that* Peter *were first of all the Apostles, because he is reckon'd in the first Place.* Matthew *reckons* Thomas *before himself; but* Mark *after him:* Matthew *reckons* Andrew *before* James *and* John, *but* Mark *after them. So St.* Paul *reckons* James *before* Peter *and* John, *though* Matthew *puts* Peter *first.* And *Erasmus* there says further, that *Hierome* intimates, *That the Apostles were all (as to their Apostolick Office) Equal.* That which makes me believe, that what *Erasmus* Observes out of *Hierome*, is true, is this; The Spanish Inquisitors have damn'd it, and (in their *Index* (x) *Expurgatorius*) commanded it to be

blotted

(q) That of *Innocent.* 3. Cap. Solitæ. 6. Extra de Majorit. & Obed. And that of *Boniface.* 8. Cap. Unam Sanctam. 1. Eodem Tit. Extrav. Commun.

Observ. 5.
(r) *Christus Ecclesiam Apostolorum Principi tradidit gubernandam; & hunc unum Super Omnes Gentes & Omnia Regna Principem Constituit.* Dictæ Bul'æ principio.
(s) Matth. 10. 2.
(t) *Petrus Apostolorum Primus & Primas, poterat Apostolis præcipere, & si in fide aut moribus errarent, Corrigere, &c.* Corn. A Lapide in Matth. 10. 2.
(u) *Cæteri Evangelistæ Matthæum præponunt Thomæ, Matthæus Thomam Præfert. Paulus ad Galat.* 2. 9. *Jacobum primo loco recensit, ante Petrum & Johannem. Existimat. Hieronymus* (so *Erasmus* says) *Ejus esse, Ordinem Apostolorum distribuere, Qui illos Elegit: innuens, Authoritatem Apostolis Omnibus Parem fuisse, quod ad Apostolici muneris functionem attinet.* Erasmus in Locum. 1667. p. 289. Col. 1.
(x) Index Librorum Prohib. & Expurg. Madriti.

blotted out. But *Erasmus* adds further, —— (y) *That it cannot Logically and firmly be concluded, from the order wherein the Apostles are number'd, which of them is to be preferr'd before the rest, because where many are number'd, there is a necessity we begin with some one, and 'tis not material which we begin with.* And This the Inquisitors let pass, without a *Deleatur*; they do not condemn it to be blotted out, and so seem to approve it, otherwise it had not pass'd; so that (even by our Adversaries consent) all that can be rationally Inferr'd, from that Text, where in numbering the Apostles, *Peter* is called πρῶτος, *first*, is only (z) a *Primacy* of Order, (which we willingly grant) but no Primacy (much less a Supremacy) of Authority, Dominion, and Jurisdiction over the rest of the Apostles; which the Pope and his Party desire, and we justly deny. 2. And as πρῶτος or *Primus*; so *Princeps*, or *Prince* (amongst the best Latin Authors) usually signifies *Order Only*, or some *Excellent Quality* in those who are call'd *Principes*, without any (a) *Authority or Jurisdiction* over those in relation to whom they are so call'd. And that the Rest of the Apostles were call'd *Principes* as well as *Peter*, I have Authentick warrant even the *Roman Breviary*, restored according to the Decree of the Council of *Trent*, publish'd by *Pius*. V. (The very Pope who publish'd this Impious Bull against Queen *Elizabeth*) and then Revised by the Authority of *Clement*. VIII. and *Urban*. VIII. and Printed at *Antverp*. 1660. In this *Breviary*, we have this (b) Hymn, in the Office for the Feast of St. *Peter* and *Paul*;

> *Ecclesiarum Principes,*
> *Belli Triumphales Duces,*
> *Cœlestis Aulæ Milites,*
> *Et vera Mundi Lumina,* &c.

Now in this Hymn *Peter* and *Paul* too, are call'd *Ecclesiarum Principes*, Princes of the Churches; For being a Hymn for the Feast of those two Apostles; *Ecclesiarum Principes* cannot relate to less than two; nor Properly to any but them

(y) *Certe ex Ordine recensionis, non Efficaciter Colligitur Quis Cui sit præferendus; siquidem ubi multi numerantur, aliquis primus sit oportet.* Erasmus ibidem, in Matth. 10. 2.

(z) So the word πρῶτος usually signifies; *Eusebius* calls *Simon Magus*, πρῶτος πάσης αἱρέσεως Ἀρχηγός. *primus Dux Hæretsos, scilicet Primus Ordine Temporis, non Jurisdictionis.* Euseb. Hist. Lib. 2. Cap. 13. p 51. Edit. Valesii.

(a) So *Homer* & *Virgil* are call'd *Poetarum Principes*. So in *Tully, Patroni Principes*, Eminent Advocates. So *Plato* & *Aristotle, Philosophorum Principes*, and yet no Dominion or Jurisdiction meant in these Expressions.

(b) Dicti Breviarij Part. æstivâ, ad Diem. 29. Junij, in Festo SS. Apostolorum Petri & Pauli. p. 476. & in Festo S. Andreæ. Nov. 30. Ibidem pag. 780.

them two in that Place. Though elsewhere it (*c*) relates to all the Apostles; as in the Place cited in the Margent; when after the Invitatory, (as they call it) (*d*) *Come let us adore the Lord, King of the Apostles*; it follows thus;

> Æterna Christi munera,
> Apostolorum Gloria,
> Palmos & Hymnos debitos,
> Lætis canamus mentibus.
> Ecclesiarum (*e*) **Principes**,
> Belli Triumphales Duces,
> Cœlestis Aulæ Milites,
> Et vera Mundi Lumina, &c.

So that if we may believe their own Authentick Breviary, Publish'd and Carefully Revised by these Popes, according to the Decree of the *Trent* Council; All the other Apostles (under our blessed Saviour, and by his Authority) were *Princes* of the Christian Church as well as (*f*) *Peter*. Now I desire to know, how these things will Consist? (*g*) *Pius*. V. in this Bull against Queen *Elizabeth*, says, That *our blessed Saviour Committed the Government of his Church to One Only*, to Peter, *and Constituted him Only a Prince over all Nations and Kingdoms*, (so he in his Bull) and yet the same Pope, in this *Roman Breviary*, (for it was Approved and Published by him) and the Hymn here cited, says, That all the Apostles were *Ecclesiarum Principes*; and if so, then *Peter* was not the *Only Prince* to whom the Government of the Church was Committed; no, the Commission of every Apostle (given by our blessed Saviour) was as unlimited and as large as *Peters*. This will appear in all the Particulars of it, equally given to all, as they are expresly set down in Scripture, from whence alone, we can surely know, what their Authority and Commission was. Our blessed Saviour tells them, and us,——(*h*) 1. *As my Fa-*

(*c*) Vide Commune Sanctorum in Calce Partis Æstivæ, dicti Breviarij, & in Communi Apostolorum & Evangelistarum. pag. 4.

(*d*) Ad matutinum, Invitatorium. *Regem Apostolorum Dominum, Venite adoremus.*

(*e*) Vide Card. Cusan Opera. p. 836. & Gratian. Cauf. 2. Quæst. 7. Can. Beati. 37. & Theodoret in Gal. 2.p.270.where *Peter* and *Paul* are call'd μεγάλοι κỳ πρῶτοι Ἀπόστολοι. & in 2. Cor. 11.6. p.251. *Principes Apostolorum alij præter Petrum.* Vid. Bellarmin. de Rom. Pontif. l. 1 c.12 p. 861. *Potestas clavium transivit ad alios Apostolos, & ad Omnes Ecclesiæ Principes,*&c. These are the words of Pope *Leo* (and he Infallible) cited there by *Bellarmine*.

(*f*) *Hoc erant utique & Cæteri Apostoli Quod fuit Petrus, Pari Consortio præditi & Honoris & Potestatis.* Cyprian de Unitate Ecclesiæ. p. 208. Edit. Rigaltij. (*g*) *Ecclesiam suam uni Soli, Petro Commisit gubernandam; & hunc unum Super Omnes Gentes & Regna Principem Constituit.* Bulla dicta in Principio. (*h*)Joh. 20.21.

ther

ther sent me, so send I you. There we have the Author and Authority of their Commission. The same blessed Saviour of the World sends them all. 2. Then he breath'd upon them, and said, (*i*) *Receive ye the Holy Ghost.* There we have the Principle inabling them to discharge that great Office and Trust reposed in them; It was that Holy Spirit, which gave them, 1. *Infallibility in their Doctrine.* 2. *Power to work Miracles for* (*k*) *Confirmation of it.* 3. **Then he** adds, (*l*) *whose sins ye retain, they are retained, &c.* **Here** we have the great Spiritual Power given them for the calling and governing the Church, which is elsewhere called, (*m*) *The Power of the Keys;* which consists in *binding and loosing, retaining and remitting sins.* For so 'tis Explain'd by our blessed Saviour in the Place last cited, and is (by our Adversaries) (*n*) confess'd. So that 'tis evident that the Power of the Keys, the Power of binding and loosing, of retaining and remitting sins, is equally given to all the Apostles, to every one as well as *Peter.* 4. He Assigns them their Place and Province, where, and the way how they were to Exercise their Apostolical Power ——(*o*) *Go and Teach All Nations, baptizing them, and teaching them to observe all things, whatsoever I have Commanded you.* Their Diocese was the World ——(*p*) *Go ye into All the World, and preach the Gospel to every Creature* (every man.). And the administring the Sacraments, and teaching men to believe and observe the whole Gospel, was the business they were to do in that their Diocese. 5. And *to incourage* them to this great and difficult Work, he graciously promises his Presence and Divine Assistance; *Lo, I am* (*q*) *with you Always, even to the End of the World.*

These are the Powers and Promises given to the Apostles, and (which to me seems Evident) without difference or distinction, Equally to all; to *Simon* the *Cannite,* (for (*r*) so it should be writ) as well, and as much as to *Simon Peter.* If any think otherwise, if he can, and will (by any Cogent Reason) make it appear either, 1. That the foregoing Powers and Promises were not Equally given to all the Apostles. 2. Or that some other Power or Promise was

(*i*) Ibidem. vers. 22.

(*k*) Mark. 16. 20.
(*l*) Ibid. vers. 23.

(*m*) Matth. 16. 19.

(*n*) *Ministri Ecclesiæ ad Remissionem peccati, Per Virtutem Clavium Ministerialitèr operantur.* Lyran. in Joh. 20. 23. Vid. Tirinum, Menochium, &c. in Matth. 16. 19.
(*o*) Matth. 28. 19. 20.
(*p*) Mark. 16. 15.
(*q*) Matth. 28. 20.
(*r*) *Simon,* who Matth. 10. 4. is call'd *Simon* the *Canaite,* in the Syriack Version there, and Luk. 6. 15. is call'd *Simon* ζηλωτης, which is the Greek word for *Cannita,* or *cinnæus.* For the Syriack ܟܢܢܐ *canna* signifies ζηλωτης. Vid. Ang. Caminium, in Explicat. locorum. N. Test. p. 51.

was (in Scripture) given peculiarly to *Peter*, whereby he had an Authority and Dominion over the other Apostles and the whole Church, to make *him Only a Prince over all Nations and Kingdoms,* (as Pope *Pius.* V. in this his wild Bull confidently affirms) I say, he who can and will make both or either of these appear, shall have my hearty thanks for the Discovery, and I shall (for the future) have a better Opinion of *Peter's* Supremacy, which (at present) I take to be a groundless Error, without any proof or probability.

Objectio.
(s) Vide Constitut. Bonif. 8. Cap. unam Sanctam. 1. De Majorit. & Obed. Extrav. Communes. & Innocent. 3. Cap. Solicitæ. 6. Extra. de Major. & Obedientiâ.

(t) Matth. 16. 18. 19.

(u) *Promittit hic Christus Petro, quod ipse & Successor Ejus Omnis, sit Ecclesiæ Supremum Caput, Princeps & Monarcha.* Jac. Tirinus in Matth. 16. 18. 19.

(x) *Quamvis mortalis homo sit Petrus Ejusque Successor, tamen Cœlesti præditus Potestate, & quod illi è Cathedrâ decreverit, habendum est tanquam ab Ipso Deo Decretum.*

I know that the Popes in their (s) Constitutions, and their Party usually urge that place in (t) *Matthew* to prove *Peter's* (and thence their own) vast and Monarchical Supremacy over the whole Church, (even the Apostles themselves not excepted) the words These———*Thou art Peter, and upon This Rock, I will build my Church.*———*And I give unto thee, The Keys of the Kingdom of Heaven.* From this Place, (most irrationally, and without any Sense or Consequence) they infer, *That* (u) *Peter, and every Successor of his, was Constituted Supream Head, Prince and Monarch of the Universal Church.* So that what Peter or his (x) *Successor shall* (è Cathedrâ) *Determine and Decree, is to be received, as if God himself had decreed it.* So *Tirinus,* and their Canon Law, in their most Correct Editions. Though this be Erroneous, and evidently Impious, yet *Tirinus, Gratian,* and their Canonists are not singular in this point, another Learned Jesuit (in his Commentary on this Place) tells us, That when our blessed Saviour says, *On this Rock will I build my Church*; he speaks of (y) *Peter, as the Fundamental Rock, on which the Church is built.* And he adds— (z) *That though our blessed Saviour was chiefly that Fundamental Rock, yet* Peter *and the Popes of* Rome *succeeded him, as his Vicars, with Supream Power, &c.* This place, they con-

Idem Ibidem, ad vers. 19. Gratian. Can. 2. *Sic Omnes.* dist. 19. (y) *De Petro ut Fundamentali Petra loquitur Christus.* Joh. Stephan. Menochius in Matth. 16. 18. (z) *Christus est Fundamentalis Petra Præcipuè, sed ei Successerunt Petrus & reliqui summi Pontifices, ut Ejus Vicarii cum Summâ Potestate.* Menochius Ibid. p. 41. Col. 2. vid. Gratian. Can. In nono. Dist. 21.

ceive,

ceive, concerns no Apostle but *Peter*, and proves his, and his Successors Supremacy.

To this, I say, 1. That all they say, in this particular, is *gratis dictum*; for they only say it, without any pretence of proof. If we will take their bare word, we may, otherwise we may chuse; for they bring no proof to prove their Exposition of this Text, such as might command and necessitate our Assent. And then a bare denial, is Answer enough to a bare Assertion. For (as St. *Hierome* says in the like case) an unproved Position, *eâdem facilitate rejicitur, quâ Affirmatur*. 2. When they say, *our blessed Saviour was the chief Fundamental Rock on which the Church was built, and that St.* Peter *and the Popes succeeded him, with Supream Power.* They consequently must say Two things; 1. That our blessed Saviour left his Place and Office of being the Fundamental Rock, to *Peter*, when he left this World. For if he kept it, and still do keep it, neither the Pope nor *Peter* could be his Successors. No man can be Successor and succeed into a Place till his Predecessor leave it. *Linus* neither did, nor could succeed *Peter* in the Bishoprick of *Rome*, whilst *Peter* liv'd, and possess'd it himself; so that by this Erroneous and Impious Doctrine, they have displac'd our blessed Saviour from being the Fundamental Rock, on which the Church is built, and instead of him, have plac'd *Peter* first, and then particular Popes successively. And then let the World judge, in what a miserable Condition the Church of Christ must be. 1. When the Fundamental Rock on which it was built, was an (*a*) *Idolater*, as *Marcellinus* was. 2. Or an *Heretick*, as (*b*) *Liberius*, (*c*) *Honorius*, (*d*) *Vigilius*, &c. were. 3. Or an *Impudent whorish Woman*, as *Johannes Anglicus*, or Pope (*e*) *Joan* certainly was. 4. Or when many Popes together, no less than Fifty (by the Confession of their own Learned men) were (*f*) *Apostatici potius quam Apostolici*.

Responsio. 1.

(a) *Marcellinus Pontifex ad Sacrificia Gentium ductus, Deos alienos Adoravit.* lat.in vit.Marcel.

(b) *Cum Arianis sentiebat, &c.* Plat. in vit. Liber.

(c) *Honorius* Synod. 6. damnatur. Act. 18. vid. Theoph.Chronagraph. p. 299. 301. Anastas. Biblioth.in vitis Pontif. p. 54. Francis. Combesis in Auctario Biblioth.Græc. Patrum. Tom.2.p.66.Synodus Nicena.2.apud Joverium. Part. 1. p.106.Col 2.

(d) Vid. Synod. 5. & Rich. Crakanthorp. in Vigilio Dormitante. Ed. Richerium in Hist. Annibalis Fabroti,

Concil Generalium p. 302. (*e*) Vid. Plat. in vitâ Johan. 8. & Notas Car. ad vitas Pont. Anast. p. 290. (*f*) Vid. Genebrardi Chronol. circa initium seculi. 10. l. 4. p. 807. ad Annum. 901.

5. Or when the Popes were such (*g*) Monstrous Villains, as *were put into, and out of St.* Peter's *Chair by Impudent Whores, made Popes by Violence and Simony,* such (as even in Baronius *his Judgment*) *none should, or dared call true Popes, whose names were recorded only to fill up the Catalogues of the Roman Bishops.* 6. Or in the Vacancies, when for (*h*) two or three years, and (if some (*i*) Writers say true) sometime for Eight years, there was no Pope at all, and so (by this Doctrine) the Church had no *Fundamental Rock at all, for several years together.* 7. Lastly, Or when they had for near (*k*) Fifty years together, *two or three Popes* at the same time; when it was Impossible they should be all Legitimate, and true Successors of St. *Peter,* and (what they pretend to) Vicars of Christ our blessed Saviour; and which, or whether any of them, were such indeed, none did, or could know: Nay, 'tis certain, (and must by our Adversaries be confess'd, unless they will deny their own received Principles) that sometimes, all of the Pretenders were Impious Usurpers of the Papal Chair, without any Just Right or Title to it. Then the first Council of (*l*) *Pisa* met (and it was a General One, consisting of above. 600. (*m*) Fathers) there were Two Popes in being (such as they were) *Gregory*. XII. and *Benedict*. XIII. who were both (*n*) Damn'd and Deposed, as *Perjur'd Persons, Schismaticks, and Hereticks, &c.* and that *by an unanimous Consent and Decree of that Great Council.* At the Council at *Constance* (four or five (*o*) years after) there were three Popes; the two beforenamed, *Gregory* and *Benedict*, (who would not sit down, though damn'd at *Pisa,* and *John*. XXIII. For the two former, what Villains they were, the Council of *Pisa* has told us. For *John.* XXIII. the Council of *Con-*

(*k*) *Tunc fœdissima Rom. Ecclesiæ jacie*, cum Romæ Dominarentur sordidissimæ Meretrices, quarum arbitrio, Intruderentur in Sedem Petri earum Amasij Pseudopontifices, qui non nisi ad signanda tempora, in Catalogo Rom. Pontif. scripti: Quis enim à scortis intensos sine lege, legitimos dicere possit Romanos fuisse Pontifices?* Baronius Annal. Tom. 10. ad An. 912. §. 14. p. 663. vid. eundem ad An. 897. §. 8. p. 624. & ad An. 925. §. 10. p. 688. Edit. Annal. *Antverp.* 1618. vid. loca & hic adde.

(*h*) Post Clem. 4. vacat Sedes. Ann. 3. m. 2. dies. 10. Post Nicolaum 3. vacat. Sedes. Ann. 3. Post Clement. 5 vacat Sedes. Ann. 2. m. 3. d. 17. Platina in Ejus vita.

(*i*) Sunt qui scribunt, post mortem Nicolai. 1. Sedem vacasse Ann. 8. mens. 7. d. 9. Platina in Calce vitæ Nicolai. 1. (*k*) In that great Schism, commonly reckon'd for the 27. Schism in their Church; which begun about the year 1378. *Urbanus*. 6. being Pope at *Rome,* and *Clem*. 7. at *Avignion.* (*l*) Anno Dom. 1409. or as others. 1410. (*m*) Longus A Coriolano. Summa Con. p. 857. Col. 2. (*n*) *In maximâ Prælatorum Frequentiâ, utérque Pontifex ab iis damnatus, utróque tanquam Perjuro, Schismatico, Hæretico è Pontificatu dejecto.* Idem Ibidem Col. 1. (*o*) Concil. Constantiense Anno. 1414.

stance gives him this Character———(*p*) *That he was a Person (all the time he was Pope) notoriously Scandalous to the Church, that his Life was damnable, and he in his Conversation guilty of Impieties not to be nam'd:* And the Council adds, (in their Definitive Sentence of his Deposition) (*q*) *That he had broke his Vow, his Oath, and Promise made to God, and his Church, that he was Notoriously Simoniacal, and by his dishonest and detestable Life and Manners notoriously Scandalous, &c.* Now if these (and such other) Popes be the *Fundamental Rock* upon which the Church is built, (and this they say, and would have us believe it) She must of necessity be in a miserable Condition, and the Gates of Hell must prevail against her; when they evidently prevail against the Rock, upon which (they say) she is built; for if the Rock and Foundation fail, that which is built upon it, must evidently fall and come to Ruin. This is the first Consequence of their Doctrine, manifestly Erroneous; but this is not all; For there is a second Consequence of it, both Erroneous, and indeed Blasphemous. For, 2. when *they say*, that our *blessed Saviour was the Fundamental Rock on which the Church was built*, and that *Peter* and the Popes after, did succeed him in that Place and Office, *cum Potestatis plenitudine*, (says *Pius.* V. here) *Cum Summâ Potestate* (as others Generally) Hence it follows, That the present Pope has (and every one of his Predecessors had) the same Power required to the being of a Fundamental Rock, which our blessed Saviour had. For if they succeed him in the *same Place*, and with *a Supream Power*, then they have the *same Place* and Power our blessed Saviour had. His Power neither was, nor could be greater than *Potestas summa*; (*summo non datur Superius*, there can be nothing higher than the highest, nor superior to the Supream) and if *Peter* had, and every pitiful Pope has *potestatem Summam*, then they have a Power as great, and equal to that our blessed Saviour had before he Resigned it to his Successors: But I might have saved the Labour of proving this; for 'tis Acknowledg'd and expresly Affirm'd in their *Roman Catechism* (*ex Decreto Concilij Tridentini, jussu* Pii. V. *Edito*) in which they say that

Peter

(*p*) *Nobis Legitimè Constat. Johan. Papam.* 23. *à tempore quo fuit assumptus, usque nunc, Papatum in Scandalum Ecclesiæ notorium rexisse; vitâque sua Damnabili ejúsque Nephandis moribus, populis exemplum vita Male præbuisse.* Concil. Constant. Sess. 10.

(*q*) *Johan.* 23. *Schismatis nutritivum, à voto, promisso, & Juramento per Ipsum Deo, Ecclesiæ & huic Concilio præstitis derimativum, Simoniacum notorivm, suis Inhonestis & Detestabilibus vita & moribus Ecclesiam Dei & Populum Christianum notorie scandalizantem.* Idem Concil. Sess. 12. in sententia contra Johan. 23. definitivâ.

Peter was (r) *Caput & Princeps Omnium Apostolorum*. And then it there follows, *Christus* (s) *Petrum Universi Fidelium Generis Caput, ut Qui ei successit Eandem Plane Totius Ecclesia Potestatem habere voluerit.* It was our blessed Saviour's will, That *Peter* should have *The same Power our blessed Saviour had. Sed Apage nugas Impias & Blasphemas.* The bare recitation of such wild Positions, should and will be Confutation enough to all sober Christians, who are solicitous to maintain our blessed Saviours Honor, and will never give that Place or Power to the Pope or *Peter*, which is solely and eternally due to their Redeemer.

3. But further, when our Adversaries, upon that Place of *Matthew* [*Thou* (t) *art* Peter, *and upon this Rock I will build my Church*] would have us believe, *That* Peter *was that Rock, while he liv'd, and his Successors after him*; And thence infer their Supremacy. They must pardon our Infidelity, if we believe it not. For, 1. They do or might know, that not only Protestants, but the Fathers, and (u) Ancient Ecclesiastical Writers generally, by *Rock* in that Text, understand *not* Peter's *Person*, but *either the Profession of his Faith* he there made, or our blessed Saviour. But our Adversaries like not this Doctrine; And therefore when *Hilary* had truly said —— *Unum hoc est immobile fundamentum, Una hac est felix fidei Petra, Petri Ore Confessa* ; and *Erasmus* had put this Note in the Margent, *Petram Interpretatur Ipsam Fidei Professionem*; and when the same *Erasmus* on *Matth.* XVI. 18. had cited *Augustin* for the same sense of the place, which *Hilary* gives ; And had put in the Margent —— *Ecclesia non est fundata super Petrum.* The (x) *Spanish* Inquisitors command it to be blotted out of *Erasmus* his Text and Margent ; Although *Hilary* and *Augustin*, and many others (as they well knew) said the same thing. 2. And this truth is so Evident, that not only the Fathers, and Ancient Authors, but Sober and Learned men in the Church of *Rome*, even in darkest times when Popery unhappily prevailed, were of the same Judgment ; And by the *Rock* in this Place of *Matthew*, [*upon this Rock I will build my Church*] understand not *Peter*, but that *Confession of his Faith*

(r) Catechismus Romanus. Part. I. cap. 10. §§. 11. 12.
(s) Ibid §. 13. p. 117. Edit. Parif. 1635.

(t) Matth. 16. 19.

(u) Vid. Chrysost. in Matth. 26. Hom 82. pag. 702. Edit. 1607. Isiod. Pelusiota. l. 1. Epist. 235. Aug. Retract. l. 1. c. 20. & De verbis Dom. Serm. 13. Tom. 18. Col. 58. ita Cyrillus & Anonymus in Catetena Nicetæ Serrarum Episcopi ad Matth. 16. 18. vide Catenam Græcam in Matth. per possinum Jesuitam Cap. 16. 18. Hilarius Pictaniens. De Trinitate. l. 2. p. 25. Edit. Erasmi. Theophylact. in Matth. 16. 18.

(x) Index Librorum Prohibit. & Expurg. Madriti. 1667. in Desid. Erasmo. p 289. Col. 1.

against Queen Elizabeth

Faith there made, to be meant. So (*y*) *John Semeca*, Author of the Gloss upon *Gratian*, and (*z*) *Nic. Lyranus*, and *Ansel. Laudunensis*, Author of the (*a*) *Interlineary Gloss*, upon his Text of *Matthew*; by the *Rock* on which the Church was built, understand *Christ* (our blessed Saviour) *and not Peter* (*b*). And a late Learned *Sorbon* Doctor (though he would seem to say, that *Peter* was that Rock) yet acknowledgeth, that by that Rock, the (*c*) Faith *of Peter might be meant*, and not his Person. Nay, which is more considerable (and may seem strange to the Reader) the Fathers of the *Trent* Council expresly say, *That the* (*d*) *Creed or Profession of Faith, which the Church of* Rome *useth,* (the *Constantinopolitan Creed* they mean, and there set it down) *is The Firm and Only Foundation, against which the Gates of Hell can never prevail*; and our present (*e*) Text is in the Margent Cited for it, whence it evidently appears, that those Fathers at *Trent* have Declared, That the Creed, or true Faith of Christ, is that firm Rock, and The

(*y*) *Super hanc Petram*; i. e. *super fidei Tuæ soliditatem.* Can. loquitur. 18. Caus. 24. Quæst. 1. verbo. Petram, in Glossâ.

(*z*) *Super hanc Petram, quam Confessus es*; i. e. *Christum*. Lyranus in Matth. 16. 18.

(*a*) *Super hanc Petram*, i. e. *Christum in quem credis.* Glossa Interlinearia in dictum Locum.

(*b*) So Gregorius Magnus in 7. Psalmos Pœnitential. Tom. 2. Operum Parif. 1619.

pag. 908. D. *Christus est Petra, à quâ Petrus Nomen Accipit, & Super Quam se ædificaturum Ecclesiam dixit*——*Quod Ecclesia nullis Persecutionibus sit superanda, Ipse Super Quem ædificata est, Ostendit, cum ait, Portæ Inferorum non prævalebunt contra eam.* So Strabo Fuldensis in his Ordin. Gloss. on Matth. 16. 18. circa Ann. 840. And after them *Lyranus* (in the Place cited) who though he was a Franciscan Frier, and flourished almost Four hundred years ago, and in many things (as those times were) Popish enough; yet he was not come so far, as to make *Peter*, or any but Christ, the Rock on which the Church was built: And again, on the 1 Cor. 3. 11. *Solus Christus est Fundamentum Ecclesiæ, quod ex se firmitatem & stabilitatem habet.* And the Gloss on their own Canon Law, says, That Christ was the Rock; for *Boniface.* 8. in that famous Extravagant. Cap. Unam Sanctam. 1. Indeavouring to prove the Papal Supremacy from several places in Scripture; he adds, That the Authority given to *Peter* and his Successors by our blessed Saviour, was not Human but Divine. *Hæc Authoritas licet homini data, non humana, sed potius Divina, ore divino Petro data & Successoribus, &c.* The Gloss on these words, *Est autem hæc Authoritas.* p. 191. says thus——*Hæc Authoritas est Divina; quia firmata est in Petra firma, in Christo, qui erat verus Deus: & quod sit Divina, quia fundata in eo; patet ex Evangelio; quia Christus loquebatur cum dixit, super hanc Petram; id est, super meipsum (qui sum Petra, & qui significor per Petram) ædificabo Ecclesiam meam.* Ita Gloss. verbo, *Est autem hæc Authoritas.* Ad. Cap. Unam Sanctam. 1. Extrav. Commun. (*c*) *Super hanc Petram*, i. e. *Super Ipsum Petrum, seu Petram seu Cepham, vel Super Fidem Petri quæ est Catholica.* Dr. Hen. Holden in Annotat. in Nov. Testam. Parif. 1660. ad Matth. 16. 18. & ad 7. Matth. verf. 25.

(*d*) *Synodus Statuit, præmittendam esse Confessionem Fidei*——*Symbolum fidei; quo Romana Ecclesia utitur, tanquam Principium*——*ac Fundamentum firmum ac unicum, contra quod portæ Inferi nunquam prævalebunt.* Conc. Trident. Sess. 3. Feb. 4. Ann. 1546.

(*e*) Matth. 16. 18.

Only

Only *Foundation* on which the Church is built, and against which the Gates of Hell cannot prevail; and if *that Faith* be the *only Foundation* of such firmness, then the Pope is not. For if there be another, then that is not (what the *Trent* Fathers say it is) the *Only Foundation*. And lastly, it is very considerable, what (*f*) *Stapleton* (their Learned Professor at *Doway*, and great Champion of their Church) confesseth (and without great Impudence, he could not deny it) that not only *Chrysostome*, *Cyril*, and *Hilary*; but four Popes, *Leo*, *Agatho*, *Nicholas*, and *Adrian* (each of them the first of that name) have, in their *Decretal Epistles*, declared, That the Rock on which the Church was built, was not *Peter's Person*, but *his Faith or Confession of it*. This was the Opinion of those ancient Popes, and they as infallible sure as any of their Successors. By the way, (that we may observe the Contradiction amongst our Adversaries, notwithstanding the pretended Infallibility of their Church) The *Trent Catechism* says —— (*g*) *That* Peter *Only was the Rock on which our blessed Saviour built his Church*. And this the Author (or Authors) of the Catechism pretends to prove out of *Cyprian*, and some others there named. So that if the *Trent Council* say True: the *Creed*, or the *Confession of the Catholick Faith*, is the *Only Foundation* on which the Church is built, but if the *Trent Catechism* be in the Right, *Peter Only is that Rock and Foundation*. Now seeing it is impossible, that both these Positions should be true, it Evidently follows, that there is an Error in the *Council* or *Catechism*, or (which I rather believe) in both. That this may further appear, I say,

4. That 'tis certain, and generally Confess'd, That *a Lively Faith, and a firm belief of the Gospel, is a Rock and Foundation against which the Gates of Hell cannot prevail*. Our blessed Saviour tells us, That *he* (h) *who hears his sayings, and doth them*; (he who really and practically believes the Gospel) *builds upon a Rock*. And St. *John* tells us, That *such Faith is* (i) *victorious, nay victory, and cannot be overcome*. Hence it is, that in the Liturgy of St. *James*, in the

---

(*f*) Per Petram, Confessionem Fidei intelligunt Chrysostomus, Cyrillus, Hilarius, & Rom. Pontifices, Leo magnus, Agatho, Nicolaus, & Adrianus primus in suis Decretalibus. Stapleton, Princep. Fidei Doct. Demonstr. Contrav. 2. l. 6. c. 2. p. 207. 208.

(*g*) *Loquitur Dominus ad Petrum; Ego dico Tibi, quia Tu es* Petrus, *& Super hanc Petram adificabo Ecclesiam meam Super Illum unum adificat Ecclesiam.* Catechis. Trid. ex Decreto Conc. Trid. à Pio 5. Editur. Part. 1. Cap. 10. de 9. Symbol. Art. §. 12. p. 115. Edit. Paris. 1635.

(h) Matth. 7. 24. 25.

(i) 1 Joh. 5. 4. 5.

the Administration of the Eucharist, they pray——*That God would bless the Sacred Elements, that they might be effectual, to the* (k) *Establishment of the Holy Catholick Church, which he had Founded and Built upon the Rock of Faith.* But though Faith and a firm belief of the Gospel, be a Rock, yet 'tis not (as the *Trent* Fathers say) *the Only Rock,* on which the *Church is built. Peter* was a *Rock* too; this our Adversaries Confess, and earnestly Contend for. But neither was he the *Only Rock* (though the *Trent Catechism* and Popish Writers commonly say so) nor such *a Rock,* as they (without any Reason or Just Ground) would have him. That this may appear, it is to be Considered,

(k) *Orat Sirvdos, ut Sacra Symbola Omnibus cedant,* εἰς ϝηεϰγμον της αγιας, κ, Καθολικης Ἐκκλησιας ἣν ἐθεμελιωσας ὁτι την Πέτραν της πίστεως, In Lit. ac. Græc. Parif. 1550. p. 20. vid. Fabr. Stapulensem in Matth. 15. 18. So

Pope Nicol. 2. *Ecclesia super Petram fidei fundata.* Gratian. Can. Omnes. 1. Dist. 22. And the Apostle in his Canonical Epistle (Jude 20.) adviseth all, *to build up themselves on their most holy Faith.*

(1.) That (by Evident Scripture) our *blessed Saviour is the Prime and Chief Fundamental Rock on which the whole Church is built.* (1) *Behold* (says God by *Isay*) *I lay in* Sion, *for a Foundation a Stone, a precious Corner Stone,* a *Sure Foundation, &c.* I know that in the Vulgar Latin of (m) *Sixtus.* V. and (n) *Clemens.* 8. it is untruly render'd——*Lapidem pretiosum in Fundamento Fundatum.* Whence (o) *Bellarmine* will have it meant of *Peter,* and so of the Pope; who (in his Opinion) is *Lapis pretiosus in Fundamento fundatus.* But had the Cardinal consulted the *Hebrew Text,* or the Version of the *Septuagint,* or (p) *Hierom's* Version of both, and his Notes upon them; he might have seen his Error : But though *Bellarmine* Expound this place of *Isay,* to be meant of *Peter*; yet (q) *Peter himself* (who understood that Text as well as the Cardinal) refers it to our blessed Saviour, so does (r) *Paul* too; and if this be not sufficient to Convince the Cardinal, and such other Papal Parasites; our blessed Saviour expounds it not of *Peter,* but himself, and that

(l) Isa. 28. 16.

(m) Edit. Rom. 1590.
(n) Edit. Rom. 1592.
(o) Bellarmine, in Præfat. ad Libr. de Pontif. Rom. vid. R. Crakanth. Contra Spalatens. Cap. 81. §. 3. p. 612.
(p) Vid. Hieronym. in Issiæ 28. vers. 16. Isiodor. Clarius in. 1. Cor. 3. 10. *Fundatissimum Fundamentum Christus.*

(q) 1 Pet. 2. 6. 7. 8. and Act. 4. 11. (r) Rom. 9. 33. & 10 11. 1 Cor 3. 11. & 1 Cor. 10. 4.

after

after he had (f) said to *Peter*——*Thou art* Peter, *and upon this Rock I will build my Church.*

(2.) This being granted (as of necessity it must) that our blessed Saviour is *the first Immoveable Rock, and most sure Foundation on which the Church is built*; It is also granted, and must be so, (Scripture expresly saying it) That *Peter is a Foundation too, on which the Church is built.* But in a way far different from that our Adversaries dream of; (for they do but dream, nor will any Considering and Intelligent Person think them well awake when they writ such things) For, 1. When we say, *That Peter is a Foundation on which the Church is built*; our meaning is not, that he has by this, any Prerogative or Superiority, much less (what our Adversaries pretend) any Monarchical Supremacy over the rest of the Apostles, and the whole Church; for every one of the Apostles is, as well and as much a Foundation of the Christian Church, as *Peter.* The (t) Apostle tells us, That the *Church is a spiritual House, which is built upon* (u) *The Foundation of the Apostles and Prophets, Jesus Christ being the Chief Corner-stone.* And St. *John* to the same purpose speaking of the Church, the New Jerusalem, says——(x) *The City had Twelve Foundations, and in them the names of the Twelve Apostles of the Lamb.* In these Texts all the Apostles (*James* and *Paul*, as well as *Peter*) are foundations of the Church equally, and without any distinction or difference; no Prerogative given to *Peter* above the rest; much less that vast Monarchical Supremacy which is pretended to. Both the Greek and Latin Fathers say, That the *Gospel*, the *Christian Faith*, or *the Creed* (which contains the Sum of it) or *Peter's Confession of our blessed Saviour to be Christ the Son of the Living God*, (which is the Chief Fundamental Article of our Faith, I say, That (in those Father's Judgment) *this Faith is the Foundation on which the Church is built*; St. *Augustin*, Explaining the Creed to the *Catechumens*, has these words——
(y) *Know you* (saith he) *that this Creed is the Foundation quod ædificium Ecclesiæ surrexit.* Aug. lib. 3. de Symbolo ad Catechum:n. Tom 9.

(f) Matth. 21. 24. But though *Paul* and *Peter*, and our blessed Saviour himself do expound the word *Rock* on which the Church is built, not to be meant of *Peter*, but *Christ the Messiah*, (as appears by the foregoing Texts) yet *Maldonate* the Jesuit (whose words I shall cite anon) says ——*That 'tis very far from sense so to expound it.* Maldonate in Matth. 16. 17. p. 339. Col. 1. E. And yet Card. *Cusanus* says, *That Christ was that Rock.* Operum p. 826. And so *Cyrill* in the Aurea Catenâ Græc. Patrum in Psalmos David. 50. per Dan. Barbaram Patriarcham Aquilejensem; Venet. 1569. ad vers. 2. Psal. 39. (aliâ. 40. p. 400. 401. So Gregorius Magnus in 7. Psal. Pœnitent. Tom 2. p. 980. D. So Chrysostom, &c

(t) 1. Pet. 2. 5.
(u) Eph. 2. 20.
(x) Rev. 21. 14.

(y) *Noveritis Symbolum hoc esse Fundamentum super*

against Queen Elizabeth.

on which the *Edifice* or *Building of the Church is raised*. To the same purpose *Theophylact* tells us——(z.) *That the Faith which Peter confess'd, was to be the Foundation of the faithful, that is of the Church.* This is a Truth so evident, that a Learned Jesuite, having cited and approved (a) *Alcazar*, (a zealous Roman Catholick) for this very same Opinion, does not only receive and approve, but largely and undeniably prove it, out of *Clemens Romanus, Augustine, Hierome, Ruffin,* the (b) *Trent Council*, and (c) *St. Paul:* And then adds——(d) *That other Councils and Fathers say the same.* Another (e) Learned Jesuite confesses, That it was the Opinion of many Ancient Fathers (yet he endeavours to confute it) that those words ——(*upon this Rock I will build my Church*);] are thus to be understood——Upon this *Faith*, or *Confession of Faith which thou hast made, That I am Christ the Son of the Living God*) will *I build my Church* ; And then he cites many Fathers to prove it; and immediately quotes St. *Augustine*, and (with little respect or modesty) says ——*That* (f) *Augustine's Opinion was further from sense, then those he there cited; because he made Christ the Rock on which the Church was built.*

(z.) Ἡ ὁμολογία ἣν ὡμολόγησας. Θεμέλιον μέλλει εἶναι τῶν πιστευόντων. Theophylact. in Matth. 16. 17, 18.

(a) *Alcazar*'s words are these——*Censeo Apostolos ideo fundatores Ecclesiæ dici; quia fidei summam ediderunt, & effusi Cruoris Testimonio, necnon prædicatione & miraculis in hominum animis insueverunt.* Corn. A Lapide in Apocal. 21. 14. p. 112. Col. 2. C.

(b) Conc. Trid. Sess. 3: *Apostolicum Symbolum vocat firmum atque unicum Fundamentum, contra quod portæ Inferi non prævalebunt.* Idem, ibid. Col. 2. E. 1 Cor. 3. 10. *ut Sapiens Architectus Fundamentum posui.* Idem, ibidem.

(d) *Idem dicunt alia Concilia & Patres.* Ibid. (e) *Sunt inter veteres Authores, qui Interpretantur super hanc Petram; i. e. super hanc Fidem; aut super hanc Fidei Confessionem quâ me Filium esse Dei vivi dixisti: ut Hilarius, Greg. Nyssenus, Chrysostomus, Cyrillus Alexandrinus, Ambrosius in Epistolas Pauli, &c.* Maldonat. in Matth. 16. 17. p. 339. Col. 1. E. (f) *Longius etiam à sensu recedens Augustinus interpretatur, super hanc Petram, i. e. super meipsum, quia Petra erat Christus.* Maldonat. ibid.

(3.) I take it then for certain, and confess'd, (and so does a very (g) Learned Jesuite too, that the *twelve Foundations,* in that Place in the *Revelation* before cited, (*Cap.* 21. 14.) signifies the Twelve Apostles on whom the Wall of the *New Jerusalem*, or the Church of Christ was built;

(g) *Certum est apud omnes hæc* 12. *Fundamenta* (Rev. 21. 14.) *significare* 12. *Apostolos; ipsorum enim humeris quasi innixus Ecclesiæ murus recumbit. Ideo enim eorum nomina fundamentis Inscripta sunt, ut significetur ipsis esse fundamenta & fundatores (hæc enim duo eodem recidunt) Ecclesiæ.* Corn. A Lapide in Apoc. 21. 14. p. 312. Col. 1. D.

and therefore their Names (as St. *John* says) were written on those Foundations, to signifie, that the Apostles (*Paul* as well as *Peter*) were Founders or Foundations of the Christian Church. And that this may more distinctly appear, and from Scripture it self, that every Apostle, (as well as *Peter*) is a Foundation of the Christian Church; we are to consider. First, That in Scripture the Church is commonly call'd (*b*) *a House*, the *House of God*; and every good Christian is a (*i*) *lively Stone* which goes to the *building of that spiritual House*. 2. Our blessed Saviour *call'd and sent ad his Apostles*, (as well as *Peter*) to (k) build this House. He gave some *Apostles — — for the edifying* (εἰς οἰκοδομὴν) or *building the body of Christ*, That is, the (*l*) Church. 3. The *Apostles all of them*, *Paul* (*m*) as well as *Peter*) were *Master-Builders* of this House. Evident it is (in the Text cited) that St. *Paul* was a *Master-Builder*, and St. *Peter* was no more; nor is he any where in Scripture, expresly said to be so much; though I believe, and grant he was. 4. The Means by which these *Master-Builders* edify'd and built the Church, were these: Their diligent *preaching of the Gospel*, (first, and more infallibly Communicated to them, then to any others) Their pious and exemplary Conversation, which made their Preaching more effectual, and gave Reputation to it, and themselves; Their confirming with Miracles, and sealing the Truth of it, with their Blood and Martyrdom. 5. Hence, the *Gospel it self* and our Christian Faith, is call'd the *Foundation of the Church*; as may appear by what is said before, and by St. *Paul*, who expresly (*n*) calls it so. For that *Foundation*, which he there says he *had laid* at *Corinth* (as may appear from the Context) was the (*o*) *Gospel* he had preach'd among them. So that (by the Authorities above cited) I think it may appear, that Divines (Ancient and Modern, Protestant and Papist) seem to agree in this; That there is a double Foundation of the Church, *Doctrinal* and *Personal*: The first is the *Gospel*, or those holy Precepts, and gracious Promises contain'd in it; On the belief and practise

(*b*) 1 Tim. 3.15. 1 Cor. 3.9.16.
(*i*) 1 Pet. 2.5.
(*k*) Eph. 4. 11. 12.
(*l*) Eph. 1. 22. 23. *The Church which is his Body*.
(*m*) 1 Cor. 3. 9, 10. *And I* (says *Paul*) *as a Master-Builder*.
(*n*) *We are God's building, and as a skilful Master-builder, I have laid the Foundation.* 1 Cor. 3. 11, 12. where σοφὸς, *peritum, significat*. σοφὸς, ὁ τῶν Θείων ἔμπειρ@. Hesychius.
(*o*) *Fundamentum posui; i.e. prima initia fidei Annunciavi.* Lyranus. *Annunciavi vitæ æternæ fundamentum*, id est, Christum. Fab. Stabulensis. Τὸ τῆς Εὐσεβείας Θεμέλιον. Theodor. vid. Cor. A Lapide in Apocal. 21.14. p. 312. Col. 2. &. vid. Gr. t. in 1 Cor. 3. 10. Rom. 15.20. Hebr. 6.1 Ita etiam Lyranus & Glossa Interlineata.

practife whereof, the Church folely relies for Grace here, and Glory hereafter; And therefore, they are commonly and juftly call'd the Foundation on which the Church is built. Whence it is very ufual in Scripture, to fay, that by Preaching the Gofpel, the (p) *Church is edify'd or built*. And becaufe our bleffed Saviour immediately call'd all his Apoftles, gave them Authority, and the Infallible Affiftance of his Spirit, and fent them to preach the Gofpel, and they (with great fuccefs) did it, converting Nations, building or founding Churches) therefore they were call'd *Mafter-Builders, Founders,* and *Foundations* of the Chriftian Church; as our (q) Adverfaries confefs. Now (as to this Particular) as the Apoftles were *Founders* or *Foundations* of the Chriftian Church; *Peter* had no Preheminence or Prerogative above the other Apoftles; He was no more *Petra*, a Founder or Foundation of the Church, then the other Apoftles. Nay in this (if any) certainly St. *Paul* might challenge a Preference and Preheminence above *Peter* himfelf, or any of the reft. For he (with truth and modefty enough, (r tells us ——— *That in preaching the Gofpel he laboured more then they All*: (And (ſ) *Irenæus* gives the reafon of it) His Sufferings were (t) more, He planted more Churches, He writ more Epiftles, then they all; (his being Fourteen, and all the reft but Seven, and they (in refpect of his, fhort ones too; which then were, and ever fince have been, and (while the World ftands) will be Doctrinal Foundations of the Chriftian Church. But that which makes more againft *Peter*'s Supremacy, and for St. *Paul*'s Preference before him, (at leaft his Independence upon *Peter* (as the Supream Monarch of the Church) is; That he tells the *Corinthians*, *That the care of* (u) *All the Churches lay upon him*. Nor that only, but that he *made Orders and* (x) *Conftitutions for all thofe Churches*, which they were bound to obferve ——— *So I Ordain*

(p) Act. 9. 37. 1 Cor. 14. 3. 5. So St. *Paul*'s Authority was given him for Edification, or building the Church. 2 Cor. 10. 8.

(q) *Ideo enim Apoftolorum nomina Fundamentis Ecclefiæ infcripta funt.* Rev. 21. 14. *ut fignificetur ipfos effe Fundamenta & Fundatores (hæc enim duo eodem recidunt) Ecclefiæ.* Corn. A Lapide ubi fupra, in Apoc. 21. 14. p. 312. Col. 1. D.

(r) 1 Cor. 15. 10. *I laboured more abundantly then they All.* And 2 Cor. 11. 23.

(ſ) *Plus reliquis, quia illi, ut plurimum, Judæis prædicabant, quorum facilis Catechizatio, cum Legem & Prophetas admiferunt.) Paulus Gentibus, qui utráſque negabant.* Irenæus adverf. Hærefes l. 4. c. 41. p. 379. C. Edit. Feu-Ardentij.

(t) 2 Cor. 11. 23.

Vid. Originem contra Celfum, Græco-Lat. p. 49. (u) 2 Cor. 11. 28. Πασῶν Ἐκκλησιῶν μέριμνα. (x) 1 Cor. 7. 17. ὕτως ἐν ταῖς Ἐκκλησίαις πάσαις Διατάσσομαι.

(faith

(saith he) *in All the Churches.* So our English truly renders it. I know the Vulgar Latin (which the *Trent* (y) Fathers ridiculously declare Authentick) renders it otherwise —— *So I teach in all Churches :* but the *(z) word* there, signifies not to teach, but *properly* to *(a) Ordain* and *Legally Constitute, Define,* and *Command.* So that thereupon Obedience becomes due from those who are concern'd in such Constitution or Ordinance. And this *Theodoret* took to be the true meaning of that Text; and therefore he says, That *Paul's Ordaining in all Churches,* was giving *them a* (b) *Law,* which they were to obey. So that here are two things expresly said of *Paul* in Scripture, and that by himself, who best knew, and was *Testis idoneus, & ἀξιόπιστος,* a Witness beyond all Exception. 1. That the care of all the Churches lay upon him. 2. That he made Ecclesiastical *Laws and Constitutions for them All :* whereas (in Scripture) no such thing is said of *Peter,* or any other Apostle. Upon consideration of the Premises, some of the Ancients have call'd St. *Paul, A Preacher to the whole World;* So (c) *Photius* and *Nicolaus Methonensis Episcopus,* speaking of several Apostles Officiating at several places; as of *James* at *Jerusalem, John* in *Asia, Peter* and *Paul* at *Antioch, &c.* He adds; concerning (d) *Paul* —— *That he did particularly Officiate to the whole World.* And to the same purpose *Theodoret,* Expounding the words of the Apostle —— *That the care of All the Churches lay upon him;* He says, That the (e) *sollicitude and care of the whole World lay upon* Paul. More than this cannot be said of *Peter,* nor is there half so much said of him, as of St. *Paul* in Scripture. Had *Peter* told us —— *That the Care of All the Churches lay upon him;* and that he made *Orders and Constitutions, to be observed in All Churches,* (both which are expresly said of St. *Paul*) the Canonists and Popish Party, would have had some pretence (who now have

(y) **Conc.** Trid. Sess. 4. in Decreto de Edit. Sacrorum Librorum.

(z) Διατάσσομαι; Inde διάταγμα, Edictum, διάταξις, Constitutio. Glossæ veteres In Calce Cyrilli, &c.
(a) Διατάττομαι, τὸ προςτάσσομαι, καὶ πρυτάτ[ω· οἷον ὁ Βασιλεὺς διατάττηται τοῖς ὑφ᾽ ἑαυτῷ ὑπηκόοις — ἐξ ἀνάγκης καὶ διατάττομαι, ἢ τῷ Βασιλέως προσαγῇ. Phavorinus. verbo διατάττομαι.
(b) Τοῖς ἄπω κληθεῖσιν ἐκεῖνα νενομοθέτηκεν —— πᾶσι νομοθετῶν τὰ κατάλληλα. Theod. in 1 Cor. 7. 17. *Oecumenius* and *Theophylact* say to the same purpose, on the same place. Confer 1 Cor. 16. 1.
(c) Τῆς οἰκυμένῳ κῆρυξ. Photius Epist. 117. p. 158. & ibid. p. 109.
(d) Παῦλος δὲ ἰδίως, καὶ πάσῃ τῇ οἰκυμένῃ. Paulus autem peculiariter Orbi universo. Nicol. Methon. de Corp. & Sang. Christi in Magna Bibl. Patrum: Tom 12. p. 519. (e) Πάσης τῆς οἰκουμένης μέριμναν τὴν μέριμναν. Universi Orbis Terrarum sollicitudinem mecum gero. Theod. in 2 Cor. 11. 28.

none)

against Queen Elizabeth   47

none) for *Peter*'s Supremacy. I urge not this, to ascribe to *Paul*, that Supremacy we deny to *Peter*; (For neither had they, nor any other Apostle, any such thing) but only to shew, That St. *Paul* (his Labours, Sufferings, the many Churches founded by him, and his Canonical Writings consider'd) may be thought (not without reason) a more eminent Founder of the Christian Church, then St. *Peter*. 2. But as it is, and must be confess'd by Divines, Ancient and Modern, Protestants and Papists, That the Gospel is the Doctrinal Foundation, and that *Petra*, on which the Church is built; So there is also a Personal Foundation, evidently mention'd in Scripture. I mean Persons, on whom the Christian Church is built: And they are

    1. Our blessed Saviour.
    2. His Apostles.

1. That our blessed Saviour is a Rock, and that κατ' Ἐξ-οχὴν, the most firm and immoveable Rock on which the Church is built, is evident from the (*f*) *Scriptures* before cited. Such a Rock, as *Peter* neither was, nor could be, much less any of those they call his Successors. For, 1. Our blessed Saviour was, and still is a Rock on (*g*) which (as *Irenaus* tells us) the *Universal Church*, both before and since his coming into the World, was built. He was (*h*) *promised by God* presently after the fall of *Adam*, and then successively by (*i*) *all the Prophets*; His Death and Passion was a Propitiation, as well for the Sins of those who (*k*) *lived before*, as ours who live after it; and those Promises of the Messiah were such, as all the Patriarchs, Prophets, and

1. Our blessed Saviour.
(*f*) Vide Matth. 21.42. Rom. 9.33. & Rom. 10.11. & 1 Cor. 3.11.& 1 Cor. 10.4.& Act.4.11. & 1 Pet.2. 6, 7, 8. & Isai. 28.16. The Septuagint translate it thus ——— ἰδοὺ ἐγὼ ἐμβάλλω εἰς τὰ θεμέλια Σιὼν λίθον πολυτελῆ, ἐκλεκτὸν, ἀκρογωνιαῖον, ἔντιμον, εἰς τὰ θεμέλια

αὐτῆς. Vide Hieronymum in locum; & 1 Pet. 2. 6, 7. ubi Isaiam citat, & eadem pene verba habet, quæ apud 70. Interpretes hodie Extant. Vide Procopium in Isai. 44. p. 504. & Fabr. Stapulensem in Matth. 16.18.   (*g*) *Christus lapis summus Angularis Omnia sustinens, & in unam fidem Abrahæ Colligens eos, qui in utróque Tistamento apti sunt in ædificationem Dei.* Irenæus lib: 4. cap. 42. pag. 380. Edit. Feuardentij.   (*h*) Gen. 3. 15.   (*i*) Act. 13. 18. 24. Luc. 1. 70. & Luc. 24. 27.   (*k*) Heb. 9. 15.

Pious

Pious men before Christ did (*l*) *know and believe*. Nay, (if we believe *Eusebius*) the Promises of the Messias, were (*m*) *clearly and distinctly revealed to the Ancient Patriarchs and Prophets* (though in a less degree and measure of clearness) and their Belief and suitable Obedience such, that (though they had not the *name*, yet they might truly be (*n*) call'd *Christians before Christ*. The Apostle tells us, That *the* (*o*) *Gospel was preached to Abraham*, and so it was to all the *Ancient Church*, by the (*p*) *Prophets*; who foretold them of the Incarnation, Passion, and Resurrection of Christ. It was the Gospel St. *Paul* every where preach'd, and yet he says, that *He preached No* (*q*) *other Things, then those which the Prophets and Moses did say should come*. And this is a Truth so manifest, that (to say no more of the Ancient Christian Writers) (*r*) *Peter Lombard*, and the Popish Schoolmen, writing *de Fide Antiquorum*, of the Faith by which the Saints, before our blessed Saviour, were saved; *they all say*, that they then (as we now) were saved by Faith *in Christ their Redeemer*. The difference was, 1. They believed *in Christo Exhibendo*, we *in Christo Actu Exhibito*. 2. *Their Faith* before our blessed Saviour's coming, was more imperfect and implicite; *Ours* (since he is come, and the Gospel clearly publish'd) much more Perfect and Explicite. This I say, to prove that our blessed Saviour was the Rock, on which the Church under the *Old Testament* was built, and (in this Particular) such a Rock and Foundation of the Church as *Peter* never was, nor could be; it being impossible he should be a Foundation of that Church which was founded almost Four thousand years before he was born. 2. Our blessed Saviour is a Rock and Foundation, on which the whole *Christian Church* is built, even the Apostles themselves, as well as others: who (all of them, (*s*) *Peter* as well as *Paul*)

(*l*) Hebr. 11. 13. Vid. Euseb. Hist. l. 1. c. 2. p. 6. B. Edit. Valesij. Τότον κὶ, οἱ ἀπὸ τῆς πρώτης ἀνθρωπογονίας μάντες, &c. *Omnes ab origine Generis humani qui justitiæ laude floruerunt, ut Abraham, Moses, & Quicunque postea justi, Omnes Christum agnoverunt, eique tanquam Dei Filio, debitum cultum Exhibuerunt*. Et Demonstrat. Evang. l. 1. Capp. 5. 6.

(m) Σαφῶς τοῖς Χριςὸν ἥδεσαν. *Christum distincte cognitum habuerunt.* Euseb. Hist. l. 1. c. 4. p. 16. B.

(n) Ἔργῳ Χριςιανὸς εἰ χὶ μὴ ὀνόματι. *Si non nomine, reipsa tamen Christianos.* Idem plane habet Augustinus, Retract. l. 1. c. 13.

(o) Galat. 3. 8.
(p) Luc. 24. 25. 26. 27. 44.
(q) Act. 26. 22, 23. and Act 28. 23.
(r) Lombard. Sent. l. 3. Dist. 25. vide Johan. Martinez de Ripalda ad dictam Distinctionem.

(s) *Augustinus in Evang. secundum Matth. Serm.* 13. Tom. 10. p. 58. O. Basil. 1569. *Super hanc Petram quam confessus es, dicens, Tu es Christus Filius Dei vivi, ædificabo Ecclesiam meam. Id est, Super meipsum ædificabo Ecclesiam meam. Super Me ædificabo Te, non Me super Te ——— Non in Pauli, nec in Petri Nomine baptizati sumus, sed Christi; ut Petrus ædificetur super Petram, non Petra super Petram.* Ibid. p. 59. A.

against Queen Elizabeth.

in respect of Christ (who is the great immoveable Rock, which sustains the (*t*) whole Building) are *Superstructions*; though otherwise, in respect of the Christian World converted by their Preaching, they *are call'd Foundations*; yet only Secundary Foundations, all of which are built upon the Principal and prime Foundation Jesus Christ (*u*). So in the like Instance, all the Apostles (*Peter* as well as the rest) were both *Sheep* and *Shepherds*. 1. Sheep, in respect of Christ, who is the (*x*) *great* and (*y*) *chief* Shepherd. *My* (*z*) *Sheep hear my voice,* (says our blessed Saviour:) The Apostles did so; when he call'd them, they heard and obey'd him. Again, *I lay* (*a*) *down my life for my Sheep*; so he did for his Apostles, else they could not have been saved; And therefore they also are his Sheep. 2. Yet they were Shepherds too (sent by, and subordinate to the great and chief **Shepherd** *Jesus Christ*) in respect of the Church and Christians, over which the (*b*) Holy Ghost had set them. 3. Our blessed Saviour is such a *foundation and founder of his Church,* as does not find, but make these *Lively Stones,* which are the Materials with which he builds it. He gives his Spirit, and by it Grace and a Lively Faith, which things alone make men Lively Stones, and fit for that Building. This no Apostle, (not *Peter*, much less any succeeding Pope) ever did, or could do; nor (without great folly and impiety) can pretend to. 4. Our blessed Saviour is such a Rock, such a Foundation and Founder of the Church, as was and is Proprietary and the sole true Owner of it; 'tis *his House, purchased with his precious Blood*;

(*t*) Ἀπάντων γὰρ θεμέλιος ὁ Χριστός, &c. *Omnium siquidem fundamentum est Christus, qui sibi ad mota, fixa firmáque sustineat.* Procopius in Cap. 44. Isaiæ p. 504. And a little after———— Τεθεμελίωκε, &c. *Ecclesiæ idem fundamentum fecit, qui Ipst Fundamentum est, super quod & nos, tanquam Lapides pretiosi, superstruimur.* Procopius ib. pag. 519. *Omnis Ecclesiæ Compages innititur & incumbit, ut nunquam cadat, summo Angulari Lapide Christo Jesu.* Augustin. Enarrat. in Psal. 86. Tom 8. pag. 955. Operum Basil. 1569.

(*u*) *Fundamentum est solus Christus vel fides Ipsius.* Object. Apoc. 21. 14. *Apostoli sunt Fundamenta.* Sol. 1. *Fundamentum proprie,*

est illud quod habet firmitatem & stabilitatem in se; sic Solus Christus est Fundamentum. 2. *Improprie, illud quod adhæret primo Fundamento; sicut sunt Lapides primarij Fundamento inh*[...]*, sic Apostoli dicuntur fundamenta qui primitus Adhæserunt Christo.* Lyranus in 1 Cor. 3. vid. Pet. Lombard. in locum. pag. 73. C. D. *Christus primus Lapis & Angularis; super Christum Apostoli & Prophetæ, super illos, Nos ædificati sumus.* Maldonatus in Matth. 16. pag. 342. And again———— *Multi in eodem Fundamento Lapides sunt; summus & primus solus est Christus, & præter illud, Fundamentum Aliud nemo potest ponere; super illud autem, et*[...] *alia sunt, quæ eo nituntur, Fundamenta: nam & Apostoli & Prophetæ Fundamentum Appellantur, sed ipso summo Angulari Lapide Christo Jesu.* Eph. 2. 20. Maldonat. in Matth. 7. 24. p. 178.

(*x*) Τὸν ποιμένα τῶν προβάτων τὸν μέγαν. Hebr. 13. 20. (*y*) Ἀρχιποίμην. 1 Pet. 5. 4. (*z*) John 10. 27. (*a*) John 10. 15. (*b*) Act. 20. 28.

and he ever had, and still hath a Magisterial and Imperial power over it, to rule and govern it; He is *(c) King of Saints.* 'Tis true, the Prophets and Apostles are called Foundations and Founders of the Church; Those of the *Judaical Church,* before our blessed Saviour's Incarnation; these of the *Christian Church,* after it. But the Power, and the Authority, the Prophets or Apostles had, (even the greatest of them (*Moses,* or *Peter*) was only *Ministerial,* the Authority of *Servants,* deriv'd from our blessed Saviour, and exercised under him. So the Apostle tells us —— *(d)* That Moses *was faithful in all his House* , (i. e. in the Judaical Church) *As a Servant ;* but Christ *as a Son,* over his *Own House* , whose House *Are We, &c.* So in the Christian Church , the Apostles (all of them) were Prime and *Principal Ministers,* from and under Christ, to call and build the Church. They were Servants of Christ, and (for his *(e)* sake *)* of the Church: they had *Ministerium,* but not *Imperium.* Neither *Peter,* nor any other, had that vast Monarchical Supremacy over the whole Church, which is (not without great Error and Impiety) pretended to ; when they blasphemously say —— *That* Peter *(f) was our blessed Saviour's Successor, and (by him) Constituted the Head of the Universal Church, with the very same Power our blessed Saviour had.* But this they say only, without any Proof or Probability; and so *transeat cum cæteris erroribus.*

2. But although we say, (and have evident Reason and Authority for it) That our blessed Saviour was the one and *only prime and chief foundation and founder of the Church,* and all the Apostles (*Peter* as well as the Rest *) Superstructions* in respect of him ; yet we know and acknowledge, that (both in Scripture and Antiquity) they are called *Foundations and Founders* of the Christian Church in respect of the Churches, call'd, *Converted,* and Constituted by them ; but all Equally so ; *Peter* was no more a foundation than *Paul,* or *James,* or *John.* For, 1. They were all *immediately call'd* by our *(g)* blessed Saviour, without any dependence *(h)* upon *Peter,* or any body else, (as is Evident in the Text it self)

(c) Rev. 15.3.

(d) Hebr. 3.5.6. Μωσῆς ἐν οἴκῳ, ut famulus: Christus ἐπὶ τὸν οἴκον, super domum, ut Filius & Dominus.
(e) 2 Cor. 4.5.
(f) Christus Petrum universi fidelium Generis caput Constituit—ut qui Ei Successit, Eandem Plane Totius Ecclesiæ Potestatem habere voluerit. Catechismus Tridentinus Part. 1. c. 10. §§. 11. 12. & præcipuè. §. 13. p. 317. Edit. Paris. 1635.
2. The Apostles.
(g) Matth. 10.1. 2.3. &c. Mark. 3. 14. Luk. 9.1. &c.
(h) Paulus Apostolus non ab hominibus nec per hominem, Gal. 1.1. ὁ δεσπότης ἐρχόμενῳ, &c. *Dominus eum vocavit cælitus, homine non usus administro.* Theodoret in loc. *Non Petro.* Estius in locum.

self) And this is generally confess'd by the Popish Commentators, even the Jesuits, such as *Tirinus*, *Menochius*, &c. I say, all the Apostles had this *immediate calling* to their Apostleship, from our blessed Saviour, except *Matthias*; and he was not chosen by *Peter* (who neither knew nor had any such Supremacy, as without all reason, is now ascribed to him) but the (i) *Colledge of the Apostles*, and consent of the faithful there present. And though a learned Jesuit, (zealous for *Peter*, and the Popes Supremacy) *would have* Peter *to be the* (k) *Director in that business* (the **Election of Matthias**) yet he cannot deny, but it was done by the *common* (l) *consent of the Apostles and Brethren*. 2. As the Apostles all of them, (*Matthias* excepted) had their *call* Immediately and Equally from our blessed Saviour, without any dependance upon St. *Peter*; so they had their *Commission immediately* from him, and in it, the very same Power, equally given to all. The same power given to any one, (even St. *Peter*) was given to every one. This is Evident, 1. From those plain Texts where their (m) Commission and Apostolical Power is given them by our blessed Saviour, before the Resurrection; when they were sent to *the* (n) *Jews* only; and the very same Power equally given to all. 2. And from those other (as clear and plain) Texts, wherein (after the Resurrection) they had commission and Authority given them by our blessed Saviour, to *preach to* (o) *all Nations*; where it is——— *As my Father sent me, so I send you*, and *Go ye, &c.* All equally sent, no difference or distinction of the Persons, as to any Priviledge or Precedence, no Degrees of Power more or greater in one, than every one. Their Commission and Authority given in it, was the very same, and equally given to all the Apostles. These Truths are so evident in the Text, that some sober Popish Writers do both profess and industriously prove them. *Franc: A Victoria*, (prime Professor of Divinity at *Salamanca* in *Spain*, and (as they esteemed and called him) an (p) *Excellent and Incomparable Divine*) proposes and proves these two Conclusions. 1. *All the* (q) *Power the Apostles had, was* (by them) *received immediately from Christ.*

(i) *Matthias à Collegio Apostolorum factus est Apostolus, Ita Estius in Gal.* 1. 1.

(k) *Hæc omnia facta sunt dirigente Petro, qui totius Operis fuit Choragus.* A Lapide in Cap. 1. Act. Apost. p 57. Col. 1. C.

(l) *Apostoli cæterique fideles communi consensu Nominarunt duos,* &c. A Lapide, Ibidem.

(m) Matth. 10. 1. 2. 3. &c. Mark. 3. 13. 14. 15. Luk. 9. 1.

(n) Matth. 10. 5. 6.

(o) Matth. 28. 18. 19. Mark. 16. 15. 16. John. 20. 22. 23.

(p) *Francis. A Victoria. SS. Theol. Salamanticensis Academiæ, in primaria Cathedra Professore Eximio & Incomparabili.* Ita habet Libri sui Epigraphe seu Titulus.

(q) *Omnem Potestatem, quam Apostoli habuerunt, receperunt Immediatè à Christo.* Victoria Prelect. 2. De Potest. Ecclef. Conc. 3. p. 84.

2. *All*

2. All the (r) *Apostles had Equal Power with* Peter: And then he Explains his meaning thus―――(s) *That every Apostle had Ecclesiastical Power in the whole World, and to do every Act, which* Peter *had power to do.* But then (to please the Pope and his Party) he *Excepts those Acts which were proper and belong'd* (t) *peculiarly to the Pope*; *as Calling of a General Council.* But this is *gratis dictum*, without any pretence of proof, or probability from Scripture, and evidently contradictory to the known practice of the Christian World, after the Emperors became Christians, who alone (and not the Pope) call'd all the Ancient Councils; as is fully proved by a late and Learned (u) *Sorbon* Doctor.

(r) *Apostoli Omnes habuerunt æqualem Potestatem cum Petro.* Ibid. Conc. 4. p. 85.
(s) *Quod sic Intelligo; quod quilibet Apostolus habuit Potestatem Ecclesiasticam in toto Orbe, & ad Omnes Actus ad quos Petrus habuit* Ibid.
(t) *Non loquor de illis Actibus, qui spectant ad solum summam Pontificem, ut Congregatio Generalis Concilij.* Ibidem.
(u) Vid. Hist. Conc. Generalium, per Ed. Richerium Doct. & Socium Sorbonicum. Colon. 1680. where he clearly proves, the first Eight General Councils were call'd by the Emperors.

5. But to proceed; That place in (x) *Matthew* is urged in the foregoing Objection, to prove the Monarchical Supremacy of *Peter*――― *I give unto thee, the Keys of the Kingdom of Heaven, and whatsoever thou shalt bind on Earth, shall be bound en Heaven, &c.* Now that I may give a short and distinct Answer to this place: I consider,

1. That this Text is generally urg'd (though most Impertinently) to prove *Peter's* and the Popes Power over Kings and Emperors. So (y) *Innocent*. III. Cites it to prove, that the *Emperor is subject to the Pope*. To the same purpose Pope *Boniface*. VIII. produceth it, in his Impious and (as to the Nonsence and Inconsequence of it) ridiculons (z) Extravagant; which (a) *Bellarmine* approves, and *Leo*. X. and his (b) *Lateran Council* (which they call a General one) Innovates and Confirms; and yet a late (c) Jesuit, expresly tells us, (and you may be sure, with the (d) Approbation of his Superiors) *That the Keys were given Only to* Peter. These, and many more, quote this place to the same purpose.

(x) Math. 16. 19.
(y) Cap. Solicit. 6. Extra De Major. & Obedientiâ. vid. Baron. Tom. 11. ad ann. 1076. §. 25. 26.
(z) Cap. unam Sanct. 1. De Major. & Obedientia. Extravag. Com
(a) Bellarm. de Pont. Rom. l 5 c. 7. §. Item; & §. sic enim.
(b) Conc. Lateran. sub Leo. 10. Sess. 11. apud Binium. Tom. 9. p. 153. A. B.
(c) Honoratus Faber Societatis Jesu, libro cui Titulus―――*Una Fides, Unius Ecclesiæ* Rom. Delingæ. 1657. Cap. 19. *Cujus Lemma est; Claves Regni Cœlorum Dantaxat Petro Datæ fuerunt.* (d) *Prodiit dictus Liber, cum facultate Superiorum, & Privilegio Cæsareo.*

2. It

2. It is certain (and (*e*) confess'd) that our blessed Saviour in this place of *Matthew*, does not *Actually give* St. *Peter* the Power of the Keys (be what it will) but (*pro futuro*) promise that he will give it. For it is in that Text, δώσω, *dabo*, *I will give*, not *I have given*, or *do give*; and therefore they must shew some other place in Scripture, where that Power is actually given to *Peter*, and that to him alone; else, (if it be given to the other Apostles as well as to him) it will be impossible to prove his Prerogative and Supremacy over the other Apostles, from that Power, which they have as well as he.

(*e*) Dabo ait, non do; promittit, non dat. Luc. Brugensis in Matth. 16. 19. Ita etiam Faber Stapulensis in dictum locum, ut & alij. Vide Catenam Græcorum Patrum in Matthæum à Nicetà Serrarum Episcopo Collectam, & à Balth. Corderio Jesuita Editā.

Tholos. 1647. & ibi Cyril. p. 548. ubi ait, *Christum Claves Petro promisisse*. Matth. 16. 19. *Sed non dedisse*. Joh. 20. 22, 23. —— Ὅ τῷ δώρῳ καιρὸς ἦν ἤ τῆς Ἀναςάσεως ὥρα, ὅτε εἶπε, λάβετε πνεῦμα ἅγιον, ἄν τινων ἀφῆτε τὰς ἁμαρτίας, ἀφίενται αὐτοῖς, &c.

3. But it is certain, that the *Power of the Keys* (be what it will) was (by our blessed Saviour) afterwards given to all the Apostles, as well, and as much, as to *Peter*. So it evidently appears by St. (*f*) *Matthew*, in the place cited. Where our blessed Saviour speaking to all his Disciples, as well as *Peter*, hath these words —— *Verily I say unto You*, ('tis all (*g*) of them he speaks to) *whatsoever you shall bind on Earth, shall be bound in Heaven; and whatsoever you shall loose on Earth, shall be loosed in Heaven*. Here his Promise made before to *Peter*, Chap. 16. 19. is made Good to him, and the Power of the Keys given him; but 'tis manifest, that it is (in the same time and place) equally given to all the Apostles, as well as to *Peter*. Their own Authentick Offices, now and heretofore in Publick use in the Church of *Rome*, do attest this truth. In one of which, they are taught to Invocate the Apostles in this Form —— (*h*) *Orate pro eo Omnes Sancti Apostoli, Quibus à Domino data est Potestas Ligandi & Solvendi*. The Power of Binding and Loosing, (and so the Power of the Keys) was given to all the Apostles, as well as to *Peter*. This the (*i*) *Manual of the Church of* Salisbury *acknowledges*, that the Power of binding and loosing, was given to Paul as well as Peter; and further

(*f*) Matth. 18. 18.

(*g*) τὰς κλεῖς Πέτρῳ παρέχει, &c Petro dedit Claves cum Ligandi Potestate; eam vero Potestatem tradidit & Discipulis Omnibus. Procop. in Isaiæ Cap. 61 & p. 715, 716. Potestatem tribuit Apostolis. Hieronym. in Matth. 18. 18. so even the Popish Commentators upon that place; Menochius. Luc. Brugensis, &c.

(*h*) Processionale juxta Ritum Ecclesiæ Romanæ restitut. Paris. 1663. p. 205. In Commendatione Animæ.

(*i*) Manuale dictum. Lond. 1554. p. 72.

further adds —— (k) *That every Priest is Vicar of Peter and Paul, and (Vice Petri & Pauli Ligat & solvit) binds and looseth in their stead and place.* The (l) *Ancient MS. Missal belonging to the Abbots of* Evesham, says the very same thing; So does (m) their *St. Anselme*: and the Old (n) *Ordo Romanus* expresly says; *That the Power of the Keys, or the Power of binding and loosing, was* (by our blessed Saviour) *given to all the Apostles*, and (in them) *to all their Successors*. Vide Bandinum, Lombardum, &c. Sent. Lib. 4. Dist. 18. 19. and the rest there. Their *Trent Catechism* (published by Pope *Pius*. V. according to the Decree of the *Trent Council*) assures us, *That every* (o) *Bishop and Priest has the Power of the Keys given him by our blessed Saviour*. Hence it is, that in their *Roman* (p) *Pontifical*, in their Ordination of a Priest, this *Power of the Keys, of remitting and retaining sins, is given to every one Ordain'd to that Office*, and (which may seem strange) *in the very* (q) *same words* our blessed Saviour used, when he gave that Power to *Peter* and the other Apostles. Nor is this all; Their Oecumenical Council of *Trent* approves and (by a Synodical Definition and Decree) confirms all this; and says further, *That our* (r) *blessed Saviour, before his Ascention, left All Priests His Vicars, as Presidents and Judges, who By the Power of the Keys, should Pronounce Sentence of the Remission and retaining of Sins*. And this they there prove out of this very *Place* (s) *of Matthew*, from which they would (and generally endeavour to) prove the *Popes* (t) *Absolute Monarchical Supremacy, And Power to depose Kings and Emperors*. To omit all other Instances (which are too many) sure I am, that Pope *Innocent*. IV. built his Power to Depose the Emperor *Friderick* upon this

---

(k) *Quilibet Sacerdos est Vicarius Petri & Pauli, &c.* Ibid. p. 73.

(l) Missale dictum MS. In Formulâ Absolutionis. p. 111, 112.

(m) Apud Eadmerum Hist. Novorum, per Seldenum lib. 1. pag. 27.

(n) Apud G. Ferrarium De Cath. Eccl. Divinis Officiis Romæ. 1591. p. 39. in absolut. plurali & p. 40. in Absolut. singulari. Col. 1. A. B.

(o) Catechis. Roman. Paris. 1635. Part. 2. c. 11. De 10. Symboli Artic. §. 4. 6. *Dominus Episcopis tantum & Sacerdotibus hanc Potestatem dedit*. Et Idem habemus §. 9. Ibidem.

(p) Pontificale Romanum. Romæ. 1611. p. 52. De Ordinat. Presbyteri.

(q) Joh. 20. 22. 23. *Accipe Spiritum Sanctum, quorum remiseritis peccata, remittantur eis; & quorum retinueritis, retenta sunt.*

(r) *Christus Ascensurus in Cœlos, Sacerdotes sui Ipsius Vicarios reliquit, tanquam Præsides ac Judices, ad quos omnia mortalia crimina deferantur; quo, Pro Potestate Clavium, remissionis & retentionis Sententiam pronuncient.* Concll. trid. Sess. 14: De Poenitentia. c. 5. (s) Matth. 16. 19. Conc. Trident. Ibid. c. 6. (t) *Summam Absolutámque Potestatem, Supremum Caput, summumque Pastorem.* Luc. Brugensis in locum Matth. 16. 19.

one

one Text — (n) *We* (saith that Pope) *being Christ's Vicar, and it being said to us, in the Person of* Peter, *whatsoever thou shalt bind on Earth, shall be bound in Heaven, &c. do Depose that Emperor, and Absolve all his Subjects from their Oaths of Allegiance, &c.* From the Premisses, and Authorities above-cited, I think 'tis Evident, 1. That in that Text, *Matth.* 16. 19. *The Power of the Keys*, was only promised, but not actually given to *Peter.* 2. When it was really and (*de facto*) given him, *Matth.* 18. 18. it was as well, and as much given to all the other Apostles as to him: as (besides what is aforesaid) is attested, and expresly affirmed by Pope (*x*) *Gregory* the Great, in his Book of the Sacraments, published by *Hugo Menardus*, a Learned *Benedictine Monck*; where Pope *Gregory* (and he as Wise and Learned, and as Infallible as those who follow him) teaches them to pray thus; *O God, who hast Committed the Power of Binding and Loosing To the Apostles, &c.* He knew not (it seems) any Supremacy given to *Peter* by our blessed Saviour, when he gave him *Potestatem Clavium*, The Power of the Keys; seeing the same Power was given to other Apostles, who never claim'd any such Supremacy. 3. Lastly, I desire then to know, by what Logick they can prove St. *Peter*'s Supremacy over all the Apostles, for having a Power (the Power of the Keys) which every Apostle had has well as He.

(u) *Nos Christi Vices tenentes, in terris, Nobisque in Petri Prijoná, dictum sit, Quodcunq; Ligaveris, &c. Imperatorem Privamus, & Subditos à Juramento fidelitatis absolvimus.* Apud Eimum. Conc. Tom. 7. Part. 2. p. 854.

(x) Vide Sacramentarium Gregorij Magni, per Hugonem Menardum Parisi. 1642. p. 113. In Vigilia SS. Petri & Pauli. Where they pray thus—— *Deus, qui Ligandi Solvendique Licentiam Tuis Apostolis Commissisti, &c.* Barlaam de Primatu Papæ. lib. 2. confesseth that the Keys were given to Peter —— ἀ μὴν αὐτός μόν@, &c. *Sed non illi soli, sed Pari cum ipso Dignitate, unicuique è duodecim.* And then he proves it from Matth. 18. 18. and Joh: 20. 22. 23. The Learned *Dan: Huetius* cites this, In Notis ad Originem. Part. 2. p. 46. Col. 1. but neither gives, nor pretends to give any Just Answer to it. Only he says—————— Barlaamum corrupit ἐλληνικὴ ζύμη. This was easily said, and *Barlaam* might as easily have answered, Doctillimum Huetium corrupit ὀφρὺς Δυτικὴ.

4. There is *one* place (y) *more* (and but one) wherein the Power of the Keys is actually given to *Peter*; The words are these —————— *As my Father sent me, so send I you; And he breathed on them, and said; Receive the Holy Ghost; whose soever sins ye remit, they are remitted, and whose sins ye retain, they are retained.* Where, 1. It is certain and con-

(y) Joh. 20. 21. 22. 23.

confess'd, That though the *Power of the Keys*, be not here expresly nam'd, yet to *retain and remit* here in *John* signifies the very same thing, That to *bind* and *loose* in *Matthew*, where only the Power of the Keys is named. This the *Trent Catechism*, and the *Trent Fathers* themselves must, and do acknowledge, (as will manifestly appear by the Places cited in the (z) Margent) and the most Learned Commentators on this Place in *John*, allow it, and tell us truly, (a) That *remittere* here in *John*, is the very same with *solvere*, to loose, in *Matthew*, and so *retinere* here, the same with *ligare* in *Matthew*. 2. And 'tis as certain, (from the express words of the Text) and the undoubted meaning of them) that the Power of the Keys is here given equally to all the Apostles, as well as *Peter*; For so the words of their Commission, *I send you* (mine Apostles) *and he breathed on Them*; (his Apostles) *whose Sins ye* (my Apostles) *retain, &c.* The Authority and Power here mentioned, is (without distinction or difference of Degree) equally given to all; to *James*, and *John*, and *Jude*, as well as *Peter*. 3. Nay more; it is (b) Confess'd, and positively and truly affirm'd, by a very Learned Popish Author, That all the Apostles (as well as *Peter*) are by this Commission *Vicars* and *Successors* of Christ, and have the Power of the Keys (to *bind* and *loose*, *retain* and *remit* sins) equally given to them All. Now, if this be true, then it will inevitably follow, That all the Arguments they usually bring to prove the Pope's Monarchical Supremacy (even over Kings and Emperors) because he was Christ's Vicar, and had the Power of the Keys given him; I say, All such Arguments, from such Topicks, will not only be inconsequent, but indeed altogether impertinent and ridiculous. For if this Argument be good and concluding, *The Keys were given to* Peter, *and he is the Vicar of Christ:* Ergo, *He is the sole Supream Monarch of the whole Church*, Then this will be as good and concluding —— *Every Apostle* (as well as Peter) *was the Vicar of Christ, and had the Keys given him:* Ergo, *Every Apostle*

was

(z) Vid. Catechis. Trid. part. 1. c. 11. §. 4. et. loca in Margine notata, in Edit. Paris. 1635. p. 129. & Ibid. §. 9 p. 132. & part. 2. c 5. De Poenit. §. 12. p. 309. 310. & Ibid. §. 55. p. 339. 340 & Conc. Trid. Sess 14. De Poenit. c. 5. & 6.

(a) *Remittuntur eis, verè & reipsâ Judicio meo Patrisque Coelestis, Soluta sunt in Coelo; quomodo loquitur* Mat. 16. 19. Luc. Brugensis in Joh. 20. 23. Comment. Tom 4. p. 134. Vid. Catenam Græc. Patrum in Johan. per Corderium, ad Joh. 20. 23. p. 459. and *Ammonius* there.

(b) *Ego, filius Dei, perfunctus Vicibus meis, mitto Æquali Authoritate in Mundum universum, vos. quos creavi Apostolos meos,* —— *Ordino vos Successores meos*—— —*Apostoli tanquam Legati ac Vicarij Christi, sustinentes Personam ipsius absentis.* Luc. Brug. in Joh. 20. 21. Comment. in 4. Evang. Tom. 4. p. 172.

was *sole Supream Monarch of the whole Church.* And then (by this wild Logick) we shall have Twelve or Thirteen Persons, *and every one of them sole Supream Monarch of the whole Church.* That the Power of the Keys, was by our blessed Saviour, given to All the Apostles as well as *Peter,* seems to me evident by the Premisses, and that all of them (as much and as **well as He**) were *Christi Vicarij,* Christ's Vicars, may be as evident, and must be confess'd, even by our Adversaries; unless they will deny the plain Truth of Scripture, and their own received Principles. For, 1. Our blessed Saviour tells us —— *As my* (c) *Father sent me, so send I you.* Christ was our great (d) Apostle sent immediately by his Father, so that he was *Legatus & Vicarius Patris,* his Father's *Vicar* and *Ambassador* (as St. (e) *Ambrose* says) And our blessed Saviour sends his Apostles, as his *Vicars and Ambassadors.* So the same Father tells us, in *the* (f) *same place*; and St. *Paul* says as much of (g) *himself* and the other Apostles —— *He hath committed to us the Word of Reconciliation; now then We are Ambassadors, for Christ, as though God did beseech you by us; we pray you in Christ's stead.* All the Apostles were (by our blessed Saviour) Commission'd and sent as his Ambassadors, what they did was in *Christ's stead* and *place.* They were his *Vicars,* and what they did was as his Deputies, *Vice-Christi,* supplying his place. Thus (h) *Lyranus,* and the *Interlinatory* (i) *Glossator,* (and they no *Lutherans*) Explain that place; so the Famous Bishop of *Paris,* and Father of the School-men, *Peter* (k) *Lombard*; so Pope (l) *Gregory* the Great; nay the Jesuites (*Instituta Societat. Jesu. Tom.* 3. pag. 262. 263. acknowledge their Superiors (though they be neither Popes nor Apostles) to be *Vicarios Christi,* Christ's Vicars. And that I may neither trouble the Reader, nor my self with more Testimonies; Their own Authentick Offices, which have been, or are approved, and publickly used in their Church, expresly say the very same thing; That the Apostles (All of them as well as *Peter*) were *Christ's Vicars*; particular-

(c) Joh. 20. 21.
(d) Hebr. 3. 1.
(e) *Deus erat in Christo, quasi in Vicario & Legato.* Ambros. in 2 Cor. 5. 19. Explicat. Ambr f cap. 16.
(f) *Deus pro Christo Vicarios dedit Apostolos, ut pro ipso prædicarent reconciliationem.* Idem Ib.
(g) 2 Cor. 5. 19. 20.
(h) *Obsecramus pro Christo; i.e. Loco Christi, cujus sumus Ministri.* Lyranus in loc. 2 Cor. 5. 20.
(i) *Ministerium reconciliationis dedit nobis; i.e. Vicariis Apostolis.* And again, *Legatione fungimur pro Christo; i. e. Vice-Christi.*
(k) *Dedit quosdam Apostolos,* i. e. *Vicarios Prædicationis* i. e. Lombard. in Eph. 4 p. 171. & rursus in 2 Cor. 5. 19. 20. *De i' Ministerium reconciliationis nobis Apostolis, Vicariis Christi.* p. 125. Col. E.
(l) Vide Johan. Lanoium Ep. Tom. 6. p. 192.

ly, the present *Roman* (m) *Missal*, as does manifestly appear by the place quoted in the Margent. This then being certain, and (by our Adversaries) confess'd, That every Apostle (as well as *Peter*) was *Christ's Vicar*, and had *the Power of the Keys given him* by our blessed Saviour, at the same time, and in the *very same* (n) *words* when and wherein they were given to *Peter*: I say, this being granted (as it is, and must) it will be absolutely impossible for them to prove any Superiority in *Peter* (much less a Monarchical Supremacy) over the other Apostles, from his Title of *Christ's Vicar*, or *the Power of the Keys*, both which every Apostle had as well and as much as He, unless you will say, That very Power which only makes *Peter* Equal to the rest, makes him their Monarch and Superior. Sure I am, if this Argument be good (and they have no better) *Peter is Christ's Vicar, and has the Power of the Keys*: Ergo, he is Superior to John. Then this will be good too —— *John is Christ's Vicar, and has the Power of the Keys*: Ergo, He is Superior to Peter. But enough (if not too much) of this. For the Arguments they bring for the Popes Supremacy (drawn from his being *Christ's Vicar*, and having *the Power of the Keys*), are such as rather deserve pity, or scorn, then any serious Answer, were it not that their greatest men (for Place and Learning, even (o) *their Infallible Popes* in their Authentick Bulls) per-

(m) Vid. Missal. Roman. ex Decret. Conc. Trid. restitutum, Pij 5. jussu Edit. Clement. 8. Authoritate recognitum, Antv. 1619. Inter Præfationes Missæ fine notis, p. 219. ubi in Præfat. De Apostolis, Sic Orant —— *Æquum est Te Domine suppliciter exorare, ut gregem tuum, Pastor æterne, non deseras; sed per Apostolos tuos, continuâ protectione Custodias; ut iisdem Rectoribus gubernatur; quos operis Tui Vicarios eidem contulisti præesse Pastores.* Hanc Orationem iisdem **plane** verbis conceptam, habes in Missali secundum usum York, inter Præfationes Missales, in Calce Tom. 1. & in Missali secundum usum Ecclesiæ Salisburiensis. Inter Præfationes Missales: And *Guil. Estius* the Learned Professor and Chancellor of the University of *Doway*, expresly approves, and confirms this, in his Comment on 2 Cor. 5. 20. *Postquam Sublatus est Christus in Cælum, Nos (Apostoli) Ullius Vices Germanus in terrâ. Deus igitur primus Author, Christus Minister principalis, Nos (Apostoli) Ministri secundarij, atque Vicarij, A Deo & Christo Missi.* (n) Matth. 18. 18. Joh. 20. 22. 23. (o) So Pope *Bonif.* 8. urges that Place. Matth. 16. 19. *Quodcunque Ligaveris, &c.* Cap. unam Sanctam. 1. De Major. & Obed. Extrav. Commun. And *Innocent.* 4. justifies his Deposing the Emperor, (as is aforesaid) from those words —— *Quodcunque Ligaveris*, and the Power given to *Peter* and the Pope by them. Binius Conc. Tom. 7. part. 2. p. 854. Edit. Parisi. 1636. And *Greg.* 7. cites the same Place, to the same purpose. Lib 8. Epist. 21. And the same *Gregory* grounds his Excommunication of the Emperor *Henry* the Fourth upon the power of the Keys. *Mihi est Potestas data Ligandi in Cælo & Terrâ. Hac ideo Fiduciâ Fretus, Henrico totius Regni Teutonicorum & Italiæ gubernacula contradico, & Omnes Christianos à vinculo Juramenti, quod sibi fecere, aut facient, absolvo.* Baronius Annal. Tom. 11. ad Ann. 1076. §§ 25. 26.

petually

against Queen Elizabeth. 59

petually urge them, to prove *the Pope Superior to Kings and Emperors,* and to have (what Pope *Pius* the Fifth in This Impious Bull against Queen *Elizabeth* pretends to) Power to Depose them, and Absolve Subjects from all Oaths of Allegiance and Fidelity. The Premisses considered, I think it is evident, and (I doubt not but) Impartial and Intelligent men think so too:

1. That every Apostle, as well as *Peter*, was *Christ's Vicar*, and had the *Power of the Keys Committed to him*, by our blessed Saviour, and that *Immediately* without *Any dependence on Peter*, or any other; Sure I am, that Cardinal *Cusanus* (though a zealous Assertor of the Pope's Supremacy) was convinc'd of this Truth (as to St. *Paul*, and so he might for the Rest) and does *in Terminis* acknowledge it. He says, *That both* Peter *and* Paul were (p) *Ecclesiæ Principes, Princes of the Catholick Church*; *That they* (both of them) *had the* (q) *Power of the Keys, power to bind and loose*; and both of them had it (r) *Immediately* from our blessed Saviour; That as *Peter* was (s) *Primate*, as to the *Jews*; so *Paul* was *Primate* as to the *Gentiles*; and so, that (in this Primacy) *Peter* was not subject to *Paul*, nor (t) *Paul to Peter*, but each of them had that *Primacy Immediately from Christ*, without any dependence on each other. And this *Cusanus* there proves out of *Ambrose, Augustine* and *Hierome*.

(p) *Petrus & Paulus ambo Principes.* Card. Cusanus Epist. 2. De usu Communionis ad Bohemos. Operum, p. 836. Edit. Basil. 1565.

(q) *Nec Mysterio caret, Romanum Pontificem. Authoritate Petri & Pauli Ligare & Solvere.* Idem ibid. (r) *De utriusque tam Petri inter Judæos, quam Pauli inter* Gentes Primatu, *Immediate à Christo utrique collato.* And this he proves, out of *Ambrose* on *Galat.* 2. 7. who says the same thing. Idem. ibidem. (s) *Potuit utérque ubique* **Ecclesias** *fundare, tam in circumcisione, quam præputio; Licet Principalis commissio cum Primatu, Petri fuerit in Circumcisione, & Pauli in Præputio.* Idem ibidem. (t) *Nec in hoc Alter Alteri Suberat, sed Ambo sub Christo immediate.* Idem ibidem.

2. And as every Apostle, as well as *Peter*, was *Vicar of Christ*, and had *the Power of the Keys*; so it appears by the Premisses, and is *confess'd by our Adversaries* (in the Places before cited) that all of them transferred that Title and Power to their Successors; so *that every Bishop*,

L 2 and

Observations on the Pope's Bull

(u) *Cyprian* says, That the Bishop is ——— *Judex Vice Christi*, and that the Bishops, *Apostolis Vicariâ Ordinatione succedant.* This *Rigaltius* observes; And adds, *Ecce Episcopos, ævo jam Cypriani, Vicarios Christi,* Rigalt. Observat. in Epist. Cypr. p. 73. And a little after, ——— *Episcopus est Dei Sacerdos, & Vicarius Christi.*

(x) *Synodus declarat Episcopos, qui in Apostolorum locum successerunt.* Conc. Trid. Sess. 23. De Sacrament. Ordin. c. 4.

(y) *Christus Ascensurus, Sacerdotes sal ipsius Vicarios reliquit, &c.* Conc. Trid. Sess. 14. de Pœnit. c. 5. de Confessione.

and every Priest, after the Apostles, is *Christ's* (u) *Vicar*, and has the Power of the Keys. Whence it evidently follows, that the Bishops of *Rome* (notwithstanding their great noise, and groundless pretence to the contrary) are no more our blessed Saviour's Vicars, nor have any more Power of the Keys, then any, (I say again, then any) other Bishop in the World; the Pope and Bishop of *Rome* no more then the Bishops of *Roan* and *Rochester.* For their own Oecumenial and (with them) Infallible Council of *Trent*, assures us of two things. 1. That all Bishops are (x) *Apostolorum Successores,* Successors of the Apostles. 2. That our blessed Saviour, when he was about to Ascend into Heaven, (y) left *Sacerdotes* (that (z) is Bishops and other Priests) his *Vicars*, and gave them the *Power of the Keys, to bind and loose, to remit and retain sins.* To conclude this Point; If the Pope and his Party, have no better ground in Scripture, (then the Places above-mentioned) to prove and support that vast Papal Supremacy, they most vainly and irrationally pretend to; the whole Fabrick must of necessity fall. It being impossible that so vast a Superstruction as their Popish Monarchy should be so sustain'd, by such Reasons which are so far from being Cogent, that they are altogether Impertinent.

(z) Vid. ibid. c. 6. de Minist. Sacramenti Pœnitent. where it is evident, that by *Sacerdotes,* c. 5. all Bishops and Priests are meant; And that it should be sure that they are meant, in the Index of that Council these words are expresly set down, ——— *Sacerdotes sunt Vicarij Christi.* And refer to the 14. Sess. c. 5. before cited. In Edit. Conc. Trid. Antv. 1633.

Object.

Well; but if these will not prove (what they are produc'd for) the Pope's Supremacy; other Texts they bring, with as much noise and confidence as they did the former, and (if that be impossible) with less Reason or Consequence. For Instance, they cite (to prove the Pope's Supremacy over the whole Church, even over all the other Apostles) *Joh.* 21. 15, 16, 17. *Pasce Oves meas, Feed my Sheep.*

And

And tell us, — (a) *That our blessed Saviour leaving the World, did Create* Peter *his Vicar, and highest Priest, and Prince of the Universal Church, which he had promised before,* Matth. 16. 18. *and now perform'd that promise.* And again (they say) ——(b) *It appears from this place, That* Peter *(and his Successors Popes of* Rome*) is Head and Prince of the Church, and that all the Faithful, even the Apostles are made Subjects to him, to be fed and ruled by him.* This place is urged by Pope *Innocent* the Third to the like (though God knows little) purpose: who would have us understand by those words, *Feed my Sheep*; that our *blessed Saviour* (c) *meant all his Sheep, all good Christians. That he might shew,* (says that Pope) *that they were none of our blessed Saviours Sheep, who would not acknowledge* Peter *and the Popes of* Rome *to be their Masters and Pastors.* And (to name no more) Pope *Boniface* the Eight indeavours to prove, that our blessed Saviour by those words, *Feed my Sheep, meant universally all his Sheep* (d) —— *because he does not say singularly these or those, but generally Feed my Sheep: And from this Place so Expounded, they would prove* Peter's, *and so the* Pope's *Monarchical Supremacy over all Christians, even the Apostles, Kings, and Emperors.*

(a) *Christus in Cœlum abiturus, hic suum Creatum Vicarium designat ac summum Pontificem creat Petrum; Promiserat Christus id ipsum Petro.* Match. 16. 18. *Sed hoc loco præstat ; eumque Principem & Pastorem totius Ecclesiæ constituit.* Corn. A Lapide in Joh. 21. 15. p. 546.

(b) *Ex hoc loco patet S. Petrum (& ejus Successores Romæ Pontifice.) esse Caput & Principem Ecclesiæ, Omnesque fideles, & jam Apostolos ipsi Subjici, & ab eo pasci & regi debere.* Idem ibid. p. 547. Col. 2.

(c) *Ait Christus* Petro & Successoribus: *Pasce Oves meas*; *non distinguens inter has oves & alias: & alienum à suo ovili demonstraret, qui Petrum & Successores Ipsius, Magistros non recognosceret & Pastore.* Cap. Solicit. 6. Extrav. de Majorit. & Obedientiâ. (d) *Pasce Oves, inquit, & generaliter non singulariter has vel illas: per quod commississe sibi Intelligitur universas.* Cap. unam Sanctam. 1. De Major. & Obedientiâ. Extrav. Commun. Ita Tirinus Reliquique passim, in Joh. 21. 15.

1. Were it not certain, that there is no possibility that any man should bring a true and concluding Reason to prove an erroneous and false Position; it would hardly be credible that otherwise Learned men, furnished with great Parts of Art and Nature, should bring such miserable Stuff, such misapply'd and misunderstood Scripture, to prove that great (e) *Article* of their Popes Supremacy; which being a manifest Errour, without any Foundation in Scripture or

Answer.
(e) The Pope's Supremacy consists in this, that he is, *Petri Successor, & Christi verus & legitimus in terris Vicarius.* Catechis. Trid. Part. 2. c. 7. §. 28. p. 391. Edit. Paris. 1635. And this an Article of their Creed. (I mean their new Creed) to which they swear (all who have any Dignities, Cure of Souls, &c. Vide Bullam Pij Papæ 4. Super forma professionis fidei in Concil. Trident. Sess. 24. De Reformat. post. cap. 12. Edit. Antverp. 1633.

Pri-

Primitive Antiquity, I cannot blame them, for not bringing (what they neither have, nor can have) better Arguments; but that they bring any at all, to establish that, which they ought, and with evident and cogent Reasons, might confute.

2. As Antiquity did, so we do grant (all that with any Reason or Just ground they can desire) that *Peter* had a Primacy of Order (but not of Power or Jurisdiction) amongst the Apostles. For the Evangelist naming the Apostles, (*f*) says——*The First was Peter.* First in Order, or (if you will) first *respectu vocationis*; as first call'd by our blessed Saviour; not to be one of his Disciples; for so *Andrew* was call'd before him (as is evident in the (*g*) Text) but in respect of his Call to be an Apostle. For when, out of his Disciples he chose Twelve to be his Apostles, *Matthew* (in the Place cited) saith; *The first was Peter.* So we grant to the Bishop of *Rome* (what anciently was given him) a *Primacy of Order*, and Precedency, before all the Bishops in the *Roman Empire*; but not *Jure Divino*, by Divine Right (which without all Reason, (*h*) they pretend to) but by the Consent of the Ancient Fathers and Councils. And for this, we have the Synodical Definition and Declaration of Six Hundred and Thirty Fathers in an Ancient and received General Council; who said——(*i*) *That because Old* Rome *was the Imperial City, therefore the Fathers had rightly given Priviledges to the Episcopal Seat of that City.* Where it is evident, that in the Judgment of that great and good Council, (and of the General Council of (*k*) *Constantinople* too, which they there Cite.) 1. That the Priviledge and Precedency the Bishop of *Rome* had, was not Convey'd to him *by any Divine Right* (as they now pretend) *non à Christo vel Petro, sed à Patribus*; it was the Fathers who gave them. 2. And the Reason

(*f*) Matth.10.2.

(*g*) Joh. 1, 40, 41, 42.

(*h*) Catechis. Trid. in the place and Section last cited, says—— *Romanus Pontifex est Episcoporum Maximus; Idque Jure Divino.* That's the Lemma to that Section. And then 'tis added, That the Supream Jurisdiction of the Pope, *Nullis Synodicis, aut Humanis Constitutionibus, sed Divinitus data est.*

(i) Καὶ γὰρ τῷ θρόνῳ, &c. *Etenim Antiquæ Romæ Throno, quod urbs illa Imperaret, Jure Patres Privilegia dederunt.* Conc. Chalcedon. Can. 28. Apud Bin. Tom. 3. p. 446. (*k*) Conc. Const. 1. Can. 5. apud Bin. Conc. Tom. 1. pag. 661. *Episcopus Constantinopolitanus habere debet Primatus Honorem Post Romanum Episcopum, quia Civitas illa est nova Roma.*

why

why they gave him such Priviledge, and Precedency, was not because he was *Christ's Vicar* and *St. Peter's Successor*, but because *Rome* was *Urbs Imperialis*, the great Metropolis of the *Roman Empire*. I know the Popes Legats in that Council, did what they could to hinder the passing that Canon, and Pope *Leo* out of it, (when the Canon was passed) did oppose it, as much as he was able, but in vain. For the Canon was *Synodically passed*, by the Concurrent Consent of the whole (*l*) Council, (the Popes Legats excepted, which was acknowledg'd by the (*m*) Judges, and then (*n*) Confirm'd by the Emperor, and Received into the *Codex Canonum Ecclesiæ Universæ*. That which troubled the Pope, was, that *Constantinople* should have *Equal Priviledges* with *Rome* (Precedency only excepted) even in all *Ecclesiastical business*; and that (by the Canon of that great Council, and Confirmation of the Emperor) the Patriarch of *Constantinople* should have so vast a Territory under his Jurisdiction, to wit, Three whole Dioceses, (*Thracica, Asiana, Pontica,*) more than (by any Law of God or Man) the Pope ever had under him. And 'tis here observeable, that although this Canon (giving Equal Priviledges to the Bishop of *Constantinople*, as to him of *Old Rome* (Precedency only excepted) absolutely deny'd that Monarchical Supremacy and Jurisdiction over all Patriarchs, (which the Popes were then nibling at, and have since openly own'd) yet *Leo* in his Epistles to the (*o*) Emperor, (*p*) *Anatolius*, (*q*) *Pulchoria Augusta*, &c. wherein he writes fiercely against this Canon, never pretended (as afterwards, and now they do) That *the Bishops of* Rome *had by Divine* (*r*) *Right*, as (Vicars of our blessed Saviour) *a Supream Jurisdiction over all Bishops and Patriarchs in the whole World*: but complains of *Anatolius* (*s*) *his pride*, (*Catalina Cethegum*)

(*l*) Vid. Binium Conc. Tom. 3. Edit. Paris 1636. p. 461. & p. 464. Ἐπίσκοποι ἐδόκουν, αὐτα δίκαια ἦθος, ταῦτα πάντες λέγομεν, ταῦτα πάντα οἴην ἀρέσκει, &c.

(*m*) Οἱ ἐνδοξότατοι Ἄρχοντες εἶπον ὅσα διαλελαλήμαμεν πᾶσα ἡ Σύνοδος ἐπίνευσεν. Binius ibidem. p. 463. E. F. & 464. D.

(*n*) Vide Edictum Valentiniani & Marciani. ibid. p 476, 477. "Ἅπαντες Τοίνυν, &c. Universi ideo quæ à Synodo Chalcedonensi Constituta sunt, Custodire debent. Et vide ibid. p. 477, 478. Edictum Marciani, de Confirmatione Synodi Chalcedonensis.

(*o*) Binius ibid. Conc. Tom. 3. p. 480.

(*p*) Ibid. pag. 479. (*q*) Ibid. pag. 481. (*r*) So Pope *Nicol.* 1. tells us, That *Primatus Sedis Romanæ non à Patribus, aut Imperiali Civitate, sed à Cbristo & Beato Petro.* Vid. Binium Conc. Tom. 6. p. 508. Col. 2. F. Edit. Paris. 1636. & pag. 513. Col. 2. C. So the Trent Catechis. part. 2 cap. 7. §. 28. *Papa Rom. Supremum habet —— Non ullis Synodicis, aut humanis constitutionibus, sed Divinitus,* &c. See the Authorities they there urge for it. p. 391. Edit. Paris. 1635. (*s*) Apud Binium ubi supra. pag. 479. E.

the

the Violation of the *Nicene Canons*, and the wrong done to the Patriarchs of *Alexandria* and *Antioch*. To talk of such a Monarchical Supremacy then, as the Popes have since pretended to; Pope *Leo* neither did, nor durst, it was a Doctrine unheard of in those purer times; and had he challenged it then, as due to him by *Divine Right*, as he was *Christ's Vicar*, he would have made himself Odious, and (having no ground for such a Challenge) ridiculous to the Christian World. But when (notwithstanding all his Legates could do in the Council, or he out of it) **the Canon pass'd, by the Unanimous Consent of the Council, and was Confirm'd by the Imperial and Supream Power of the Emperor**; (for the Pope does Petition and (*t*) Supplicate to him as his Superior) though the Pope in a private Epistle to *Pulcheria Augusta* (with great Insolence, **and without any ground**) pretends to (*u*) Cassate and null that Canon by the Authority of St. *Peter*, (who never had any such Authority to Null any Just Imperial or Synodical Constitutions) yet that Canon was approved, received, and (as *de Jure* it ought) Obey'd by the *Eastern Churches*, both then, and ever (*x*) after. When these Pretensions of the Pope and his Legates prevailed not, nor were regarded by the Council, or Emperor, or the Eastern Church; other Arts were used at *Rome*, to conceal that Canon (which they could not Cassate) from the knowledge of the *Western Church*. And to this end, 1. They Corrupt the *Codex Canonum Ecclesiæ Universalis* (the most Authentick Book, next to the Bible, the Christian Church has, or ever had) (*y*) *Dionysius Exiguus* a Roman Abbot, begins that Impious Work; and in his *Latin Translation* of that *Code* (amongst other things) leaves out that Eight and twentieth Canon of the Council of *Chalcedon*, and (*z*)

(*t*) *Clementiam vestram Precor, & Sedulâ Suggestione Obsecro,&c.* Ita Leo Papa in Epist Marciano Imperatori, apud Binium.Conc Tom.3.p.481.Col. I. B.

(*u*) *Consensiones Episcoporum* (even those in the General Council at *Chalcedon* he means) *in irritum mittimus, & per Authoritatem Beati Petri, Generali Definitione Cassamus*. Leo Papa in Epist.ad Pulcheriam,apud Binium. Tom. 3. p. 482. B.

(*x*) It was *in terminis* Confirm'd in the sixth General Council at *Constantinople*. Can. 36. And the second General Council at *Constantinople*. Can. 5. gives the same Precedence to the Bishop of *Byzantium*, which the Council of *Chalcedon* does.

(*y*) Dionysius Exiguus Abbas-Romanus sub Justiniano, Circa An. 540. as Trithemius, or 520 as others. (*z*) So Isiodor. Jac. Merlinus. Paris. 3535. Codex Canonum vetus Eccl. Romanæ, Edir. 2. Mogont. 1525. dein Paris. 1619. Editio Latina prisca Canonum, Apud Justell. Biblioth. Tom.1.p.300.So Pet.Crabb.Joverius.Joh.Sichardus.Post Opera D. Clement.Paris.1568. &c.

others

others of the Popish Party, follow him. 2. They *Corrupt the* (a) *Canon it self*; and by putting in other words in their false Translation, they make it contradict the *Greek Canon*, and the certain Sense of the Council that made it. So in *Gratian*, the Corruptions of this Canon, are thus———

(a) **Can.** Renovantes. 6. Lift. 22. *Petimus, ut Constantinopolitana Sedes Similia Privilegiis, quæ Superior Romæ habet, accipiat; Non tamen in Ecclesi-*

asticis rebus magnificetur ut illa, &c. So Gratian in the Old **Editions**, as is Confess'd. Vid. Corpus Jur. **Can.** Cum Glossis. Parif. 1612. & sine Glossis. Parif. 1618. & ibi Notas ad hunc Canonem.

1. For ἴσα πρεσβεῖα (*æqualia Privilegia*) in the Original Greek; *Gratian* has *Similia Privilegia*; *like*, but not *equal* Priviledges.

2. For Πρεσβυτέρα Ῥώμη, (*Senior Roma*) *Gratian* has *Superior Roma*——*Old Rome* must be Superior to *New Rome*, or *Constantinople*, if Forgery and Falsification of Records can do it: for better Grounds they have none.

3. For, ϗ ἐν τοῖς Ἐκκλησιαστικοῖς, *etiam in Ecclesiasticis magnificetur ut illa*. *Gratian* impudently reads, *non tamen in Ecclesiasticis*, &c.

But notwithstanding all that Pope *Leo* or his Legates could do, and all their other Indirect Arts afterwards, this Eight and twentieth Canon of the Council of *Chalcedon* was received in the Christian World, and long after Confirm'd by General Councils, not only by the *Synodus 6. Generalis*, which was held *Anno* 681. (of which a little before) But the Eighth General Council under Pope *Adrian* II. about the Year 870. gives that (b) Precedency to the Patriarch of *Constantinople*, which the Canon of *Chalcedon* before gave him; And this acknowledged and referred into the Body of their (c) Canon Law, in the best Editions of of it, Revised and Corrected by Pope (d) *Gregory* XIII.

(b) *Definimus neminem Mundi Potentum, quenquam qui Patriarchalibus præsunt Sedibus, in honorare præcipué sanctissimum Papam Senioris Romæ; deinceps autem Constantinopoleos Patriarcham, deinde Alexandriæ, &c.* Ita Synodus. 8. habita sub Adriano Papa. Can. 21. And

this an approved Council at *Rome*. (c) Gratian. Can. Definimus. 7. Dist. 22. Vid. Glossam Ibid. (d) Vid. Bullam Greg. 13. dat. Romæ. 1. Julij 1580. Juri Canonico præfixam. Edit. Parif. 1612. & 1618.

And 'tis to be observed, that this *Synodus* 8. was Subscribed by the Pope or his Legates there, and was then, and still is approved and received at *Rome*: Nor need we wonder at it, For what it did, was carried chiefly by the Popes Authority, who was by that Council basely and servilly flatter'd; they calling him *Most* (e) *Holy and Oecumenical Pope, and Equal to the Angels*, &c. This Title *Oecumenical*, the Pope took kindly then, though his Predecessor (f) *Gregory* the Great abhorr'd it, as *Antichristian*. But to return to the **Objection**.

(e) Τῷ κυρίῳ ἰ-
οσιωτάτῳ, ἁγιωτά-
τῳ, μεγίστῳ Ἀρ-
χιερεῖ ἢ Οἰκουμε-
νικῷ Πάπα Ἀδρι-
ανῷ. In Epist. Synod. 8. ad Adrianum. Apud Binium Conc. Tom. 7. Part. 1. p. 984. (f) Vid. Greg. Maj. Regist. l. 4. Epist. 32. & 34. 36. 38. & l. 6. Epist. 30. & l. 7. Epist. 30. pag. 220.

3. And here before I give a Particular and Distinct Answer to this Place of *John*, (*Feed my Sheep*) on which they commonly (and vainly) build the Popes Supremacy; I shall crave leave, a little to explain, the nature and measure of that Power which they give the Pope under the name of his Supremacy. And here they say, *That our blessed Saviour gave his own Power to* Peter, *made him his Vicar, Head and Pastor of all the Faithful in the World; and that in* most *ample Words, when he bad him, Feed his Sheep,* **and** *that it was our blessed Saviours Will, that all* Peter's *Successors should have the very same Power, which* Peter *had*; (so the *Trent* (g) *Catechism* tells us) And this is that Plenitude of Power by which they Erroneously and Impiously Depose Kings and Emperors, and (as *Pius* V. does, in this Bull, we are now speaking of, against Queen *Elizabeth*) absolve their Subjects from their Oaths of Allegiance, and sworn or natural Fidelity. This premised, I shall proceed to a direct (and I hope a full and satisfying) Answer to that **place** in *John*, *Feed my Sheep*, &c. And here I consider,

(g) *Salvator Noster Petrum suæ Potestatis Vicarium præfecit; & universi Fidelium generis Caput & Pastorem Constituit, cum illi Oves suas pascendas, Verbis Ampissimis Commendavit; ut qui ei successit, Eandem plane Totius Ecclesiæ Regendæ Potestatem habere voluerit.* Catechis. Trid. ex Decreto Conc. Trid. à Pio 5. Editus. Part. 1. c. 10. §. 13. p. 117. Edit. Paris. 1634. Vid. N. Rigaltij Observat. Galeatam, Notis suis in Cyprianum præfixam.

1. That

against Queen Elizabeth. 67

1. That if the Supremacy was first given to *Peter*, in those words———(*h*) *Pasce Oves, Feed my Sheep*, (as is confess'd, and by our Adversaries positively affirm'd in the Objection) which was after our blessed Saviours Resurrection: then it is evident he had it not before: It being impossible he should have it before it was given him. And then it will as Evidently follow, that all those places in the Gospel, spoken of, or to *Peter*, before our blessed Saviour's Passion, are Impertinently urged to prove *Peter's* Supremacy, which he had not till after the Resurrection. And yet *Innocent* III. *Boniface* VIII. and other Popes in their Bulls and Papal Constitutions, the Canonists, School-men, and Commentators usually Cite *many places* in the Gospel (besides this, *Pasce Oves*) to prove that *Peter* had the Supremacy before our blessed Saviour's Passion; which here they Confess was not given him till after the Resurrection. That they do urge many such Places is known to all Learned men, vers'd in these Controversies; but if any man doubt of it, and desire Satisfaction, I shall refer him to what a Learned Popish Writer (and *Capucine*) has said in the (*i*) Margent, where he tells us, how many places are Cited for the Supremacy.

(*h*) John 21.15, 16.

(*i*) Vide Epitomen Canon. &c. per Greg. De Rives Capucinum. Lugd. 1603. Tract. de Primatu, p. 3, 4. where for *Peter's* Supremacy, he cites Matth. 16. 17, 18.

19. *Super hanc Petram: & dabo tibi claves:* Matth. 10. 2. *Primus Petrus.* Matth. 17. 27. *Christ paid tribute only for himself and Peter.* John 1. 43. *Thou shalt be called Cephas.* John 21. 7, 8. *Peter alone cast himself into the Sea.* Matth. 14. 28. *He calls Peter only to come to him; Et ita unicum se Christi Vicarium designavit.* Matth. 18. 21. Matth. 19. 27. Mark. 14. 37. *He said only to Peter, Simon sleepest thou.* Others Cite for *Peter's* Supremacy, Luke 22 38. *Here are two Swords.* So Pope *Bonif.* 8. *Cap. Unam Sanctam.* 1. Extrav. Commun. vide Glossam verbo, Cœlestis. Can. Omnes. 1. Dist 22. Though their proofs from all those Places, (and they have no better) are not only Inconsequent, and Erroneous, but indeed Ridiculous. Vid. Tho. Campegium, Episc. Feltrensem, De Potestate Romani Pontificis. Venet. 1555. Cap. 4. 5. Opus Paulo. 4. Papæ dedicat. ubi loca hæc & plura, ad probandum Papæ Suprematum, vanè adducit, & ridicule explicat. **vid. etiam** Bellarmin. De Romano Pontif. lib. 1. cap. 10, 11, 12. & inde ad cap. 24. Inclusivè.

2. When our blessed Saviour says, *Pasce Oves, Feed my Sheep*, and *Feed my Lambs*; he useth two words ——— ποίμαινε and βόσκε. Both which words the vulgar Latin

M 2 renders,

renders, *Pasce, feed* my Sheep and Lambs: Now their Commentators on this place, (to very little purpose) make a great stir and pudder to shew (what (*k*) none denys) that ποιμαίνω signifies to *rule* and *govern*. But let the word signifie what it will, in the Civil State, yet in the Ecclesiastical and Scripture Sense of the Word, where our blessed Saviours Lambs and Sheep (that is the Faithful) are to be fed, every Bishop and Presbyter (as well as *Peter*) are ποιμένες, *Pastores,* and may and ought ποιμαίνειν, to feed the Flock of Christ. So, 1. St. *Paul* tells us, (*l*) who from *Miletum*, sends for the *Presbyters* of *Ephesus*, (I say Presbyters, for *Timothy*, who was their first Bishop, was with *Paul* at (*m*) *Miletum*, and so was none of those he sent for) and when they came, he exhorts *them to take heed unto themselves, and the Flock*, (*n*) *To feed the Church of God, &c.* where St. Paul (when he bids the *Presbyters feed the Church*) useth the very same word our blessed Saviour doth, when he bids *Peter feed his Sheep*. 2. So (*o*) *Peter* himself (who little dream'd of any Supremacy given him by those words, *Feed my Sheep*) writing to the *Asiatick* Dispersion of the *Jews*, and Exhorting the Jewish Elders, (or Presbyters) to a diligent Care, *in feeding the Flock*; he useth the very same word to them, our blessed Saviour did to him, ποιμάνατε (says he) *Feed the Flock*; he thinks it their duty, as well as his, to feed our blessed Saviour's Sheep. And that which further, and (*ad hominem*) more strongly confirms what I have said (in this Particular) is; That our Adversaries grant (though in Contradiction to the Sense many of them give of those words, *Feed my Sheep*, when they would build the Popes Supremacy upon them) that the word ποιμαίνω, both as it signifies to *rule* and *feed*, **and** so the *duty* of *ruling* and *feeding* our blessed Saviours Sheep, is so far from being Peculiar to *Peter*, or proving his Supremacy, that it is the Duty, not only of *Peter*, but of every Bishop in the Christian World, both to *rule* and *feed* our blessed Saviour's *Sheep*. This the (*p*) *Trent Catechism* expresly affirms, *That all Bishops*

(*k*) 'Tis certain, and confess'd, that ποιμαίνω signifies to rule. Kings are call'd ποιμένες λαῶν, populi pastores. So *Menelaus* & *Agamemnon* usually in *Homer*, and in *Hesychius* ποιμὴν Βασιλεὺς. And ποιμαίνω λαῶν, κ̇ ὁ τῶν πρεσβυτῶν. And the Gloss. veteres in Calce Cyrilli, ποιμαίνω, pecora pasco; and ποιμαίνω ἐπ' ἀνθρώπων, Rego.
(*l*) Act. 20. 17. Τοὺς πρεσβυτέρους τῆς ἐκκλησίας. *The Presbyters of that Church.*
(*m*) Act 20. 4. 6.
(*n*) Vers 28. cap 20 ποιμαίνειν τὴν Ἐκκλησίαν, &c.
(*o*) 1 Pet. 5. 2. ποιμάνατε τὸ ἐν ὑμῖν ποιμνίον.
(*p*) *Episcopi* (says that Catechism) *singulis Episcopatibus præpositi sunt, ut Cæteros Ecclesiæ Ministros, & fidelium populum Regant, & eorum saluti summâ curâ Prospiciant; unde in Sacris Litteris Pastores Ovium Spe Appellantur.* Catechis. Trid. part. 2. cap. 7. § 26. p. 389, 390. Editionis p-TH. 1635.

(as

against Queen Elizabeth.

(as well as *Peter*) are Paſtores, *Paſtors to Rule as well as Feed the Flock and Sheep of our bleſſed Saviour*; and to prove this, they Cite the Two very (*q*) places which I (a little before) produced to the ſame purpoſe, whence it manifeſtly appears, That even in our Adverſaries Judgment, (when the Popes Supremacy is a little out of their Head) *the feeding our bleſſed Saviour's Sheep, is not Peter's Supream Prerogative, but a Duty required of every Biſhop in the World.*

3. But this (though enough) is not all; we have greater (and with them Infallible, and therefore undeniable) Authority to confirm what I have ſaid, and Confute our Adverſaries, as to their proof of *Peter's*, or the Pope's Supremacy, from thoſe words, *Feed my Sheep*. For their *Trent Council* (which if the Pope ſay true, was (*r*) Divinely Inſpired, and therefore Infallible; and if he do not ſay true, he himſelf was not only fallible but actually falſe) expreſly tells us, *That not only every Biſhop, but every one* (ſ) *who had Cure of Souls, was bound by the Law of Chriſt in the Goſpel, to rule and feed his Sheep, by offering Sacrifices for them, by preaching the Word, Adminiſtring the Sacraments, by good Example, by a Paternal Care of the Poor, and all other Paſtoral Offices*. And this is there proved by Texts, quoted in the Margent; which (with ſome others) are the very ſame with thoſe I have (a little before) cited out of the (*t*) Acts of the Apoſtles, and (*u*) St. *Peters* Epiſtle: Nor thoſe only, but this very place of (*x*) St. *John* (on which they would build *Peter's* Supremacy) is cited in the Margent, as containing a *Precept* obliging (not *Peter* only, but) *All, who had Cure of Souls, to feed Chriſt's Sheep*. Now if thoſe words, *Feed my Sheep*, contain *Præceptum*, a Precept, Obliging all Paſtors to a Paſtoral Duty; then they do not contain (what they pretend) *Donum*, a Donation of Supremacy.

(*q*) Act. 20. 28.
1 Pet. 5. 2, 3.

(*r*) *Dominus Patres Tridentinos Divinitûs Inſpirare dignatus eſt.* Pius Papa 4. in Bullâ ſuper formâ Juramenti profeſſionis Fidei.

(ſ) *Præcepto Divino Mandatum eſt Omnibus, quibus Animarum Cura Commiſſa eſt, Oves Agnoſcere, pro iis Sacrificium offerre, verbi prædicatione, Sacramentorum Adminiſtratione, ac bonorum operum Exemplo paſcere, pauperum curam paternam gerere, & in Cætera Munia Paſtoralia incumbere —— ideo Synodus eos admonet, ut præceptorum divinorum Memores, in Judicio & veritate Paſcant & Regant.* Concil. Trid Seſſ. 21. De Reformat. cap. 1. Edit. Antverp. 1633. pag. 284. (*t*) Act. 20. 28. (*u*) 1 Pet. 5. 2.

(*x*) John 21. 15, 16.

4. But

4. But Pope *Boniface* the Eighth, and Pope *Innocent* the Third, in their before-mention'd (y) Constitutions, tell us; that by *Oves meas*, our blessed Saviour means, *All his Sheep*, All Christians in the World; Because he does not speak *singulariter* of *these* or *those*; but *generaliter* of his *Sheep*. Whence they, (and many after them) conclude, That our blessed Saviour Committed all his Sheep Universally to *Peter's* Care, so that even the Apostles, (being his Sheep) were committed to *Peter's* Care, and by Consequence, he became their Pastor and Superior. Certainly they who reason at this rate, and so irrationally, may possibly be fit Pastors to feed Sheep and Oxen, and such other brutish Cattle, but surely not to feed Men and Christians. For, 1. *Feed my Sheep*, (as all know, unless they be such as those two Popes were) is *an indefinite Proposition*: and then any Novice or young Sophister in the University, could have truly told them, That *Propositio indefinita in materiâ Contingenti*, (as this evidently is) *aquivalet particulari*. When we say men are young, or wise, or learned; we mean, not all, but some are such. So he who says, *Christ's Sheep are to be fed by* Peter; must mean some of them are to be fed by him, *pro loco & tempore*, as he had place and time to meet with them. It being impossible he should feed them (z) all. There were many thousands of our blessed Saviour's Sheep, whom *Peter* never did, nor could see, nor they hear him: And certainly his gracious Lord and Master would not tye him to Impossibilities. 2. When they say, (which is evidently untrue) that by those words—*Feed my Sheep*, all the Faithful are meant, and are committed to Pe-

---

(y) That of *Bonif.* 8. Cap. Unam Sanctam. 1. De Major. & Obed. Extrav. Commun. And that of *Innocent.* 3. Cap. Solicitæ, 6. extra eodem Titulo.

(z) *Maldonat.* speaking of *Matth.* 28.19. where our blessed Saviour gives Commission to all his Apostles —— *Go ye therefore into All the World, &c.* He says thus——*Non fieri poterat ut singuli omnes terræ partes peragrarent, Gentésque omnes docerent; neque erat necessarium. Quid enim erat Opus, ut Omnes à singulis, modo Omnes ab hominibus, aliæ ab aliis docerentur.* Maldonat. in Joh. 21. 15. 16. &c. §. 65. p. 1889. E. This he says, and truly. But then he should have consider'd, that if it was impossible for every one of the Apostles to teach all the World; then it will be impossible for any one. Impossible for *Peter* to feed all Christ's Sheep in the whole World: and yet this he indeavours to prove ——— *Quicunque intra Ecclesiam erant, Petro pascendos tradit. Dicit enim pasce Oves, non hâs, aut illas, sed pasce Oves meas. Omnium ego suarum Ovium curam illi dedit.* Ibid. §. 62.

ter's care and charge; and therefore the (a) Apostles themselves (being our Saviour's Sheep as well as others) are part of his Charge; and under his Jurisdiction. This they say indeed usually, but (miserably mistaken) only say it. For they neither have, nor can have any just Ground or Reason for it. For it is certain, 1. That our blessed Saviour, is (to his whole Church) the only (b) High Priest, the (c) Prince *of all the Pastors*, and the Grand (d) *Shepherd of the Sheep*; and as King, has Imperial Power to Rule and Govern them. 2. It is certain, the Apostles (from and under him) are *Pastores* and Shepherds, as well as *Peter*, to feed the Flock. But their Power is *Ministerial*, not *Imperial*. Even the Apostleship it self is (e) Διακονία, a Ministery, and they Ministers of *Christ*, and his (f) *Church*. Now though in respect of Christ the great Shepherd, they are Sheep, even *Peter* himself: yet (on Earth) they are Shepherds only, not Sheep, neither in respect of the Church, over which our blessed Saviour has set them to be Shepherds; nor in relation one to another. *Paul*, or *James*, or *John*, are no more Sheep in respect of *Peter*, to be *fed* and *ruled* by him, then he to be *fed* and *ruled* by them: And therefore to say (as our Adversaries vainly do) that in those words, *Feed my Sheep*; *Peter* is Commanded to feed and rule the rest of the Apostles, as his Charge, (who were Shepherds only, and Sheep to no Superior Pastor, except our blessed Saviour; And by their Apostolical Commission (g) Equal to himself) is irrational; without any ground in Scripture, or purer Antiquity. There is another Metaphor concerning the Apostles, and their feeding and building the Church, which may illustrate this business, All the Apostles (as well and as much as *Peter*) are in Scripture call'd *Foundations of the Church*, converted, fed, and confirm'd by them. In respect of Christ, our blessed Saviour, (who is the only prime and principal firm Rock on which the Church is built) they are (*all of them*) *Superstructions*; but in respect of the Christian Church, Foundations; and that with-

(a) *Ex hoc loco* (Joh. 21.15.) *patet Sanctum Petrum (& Ejus Successores Romanos Pontifices) esse Caput & Principem Ecclesiæ, Omnesque fideles, etiam Apostolos Ipsi Subjici & ab eo Pasci & Regi debere.* Corn. A Lapide, in Joh. 21. 15. p. 547. Col. 2.
(b) Heb. 4. 14. Τὸν Ἀρχιερέα.
(c) 1 Pet. 5. 4. Ἀρχιποίμην.
(d) Heb. 13. 20. Τὸν ποιμένα τῶν προβάτων τὸν μέγαν.
(e) Act. 1. 17 25.
(f) 2 Cor. 4. 5.
(g) *Hoc erant Cæteri Apostoli, quod fuit Petrus; Pari consortio præditi & Honoris, & Potestatis.* Cyprian. de Unit. Eccles. p. 208. Edit. Rigaltij *Pastores sunt Omnes Apostoli, sed Grex unus, qui ab Omnibus unanimi Consensione Pascatur. Pasce Ovis meas*, belong'd equally to all the Apostles, as well as to *Peter*, in Cyprian's Opinion, as shall appear anon.

without any dependence upon *Peter*; he is not the Foundation on which they are built, but both he and they immediately upon the prime Rock and Foundation, *Jesus Christ*: So that as the Apostles are *Superstructures* in the House of God (the Church) in respect of Christ, the prime firm Foundation; and none of them *Superstructures* in respect of *Peter*: being neither built upon him, nor made Superstructions by him, by his Feeding or Ruling them: So they (and *Peter* too) are *Sheep* in respect of our blessed Saviour, the great Shepherd of the Sheep; but not in respect of *Peter*; they are Shepherds as well as he, and never committed to his Care or Cure, that (as his Sheep) he should feed and govern them: And as all the other Apostles (in respect of *Peter*) were Foundations and Shepherds of the Church, co-ordinate with, and equal to him: So all other Bishops, the Apostles Successors, were equal to *Peter's* pretended Successor (the Bishop of *Rome*) and no way bound to give any Reason of their Administration to him, as to their Superior; much less as to a Supream Prince & Monarch of the Christian World, as the Canonists, Jesuites, and the Popish Party, do now erroneously and impiously miscall him. This was *Cyprian's* Opinion, in the Place but now cited; And *Rigaltius* (a Learned *Roman Catholick*) though he (b) seem to say much for *Peter's* and the Popes Supremacy; yet he confesseth, (as upon a serious Consideration of several Passages in (i) *Cyprian*, and the *African Councils*, well he might) That *Cyprian's* (k) *Opinion was, That all Bishops were equal, and were bound to give an Account of their Administration to our blessed Saviour only, and not to any Superior Bishop, no not to* Peter's *Successor, the Pope*. Nor is it any way probable, that a Person so excellent and knowing as *Cyprian*, should think otherwise; seeing in his time (as is notorious and well known to all who know Antiquity) there was no Patriarch or Archbishop Superior (by any Law of God or Man) to the Ordinary Bishops, (as may, and when there is an Opportunity, shall be made good.) It is true, *Cyprian*

(b) Nic. Rigaltius in Observatione Galeata, Notis suis ad Cypriani Opera præfixa.

(i) Vid. Cypr. Epist. 67. p. 128. 129. Edit. Rigaltij. & Epist. 72. Ibid. p. 142. in Calce dictæ Epistolæ, &c. & Epist. 55. p. 95.

(k) *Singulis Pastoribus Episcopis portionum gregis esse adscriptam, quam regat unusquisque; Actus sui, sive administrationis suæ rationem redditurus; Non Romæ, sed in Cœlis; Non Cornelio, sed Christo ——— Negat* (Cyprianus) *Ecclesiæ Romanæ ullas esse Partes in causâ Novatiani, peractâ jam in Africâ cognitione damnati*. (There lay no Appeal to the Pope, as Superior to the Bishops of *Africa*). Rigaltius in Notis ad Cypriani Epist. 55. p 95. & Notarum p. 77. 78.

(if

(if it be he, and not the Interpolator of that Tract) says, *That the Primacy* (l) *was given to* Peter; *and that the Church of* Rome *was the* (m) *Principal Church*. Now this *Primacy* and *Principality Cyprian* speaks of, is, by me before, and now freely granted. *A Primacy of Order and Precedency*, not of *Jurisdiction*, or that *Monarchical Authority*, which (anciently was not pretended to by themselves) they now contend for. And this Primacy, which anciently was allowed to the Bishop of *Rome*, was not from *our blessed Saviour's gift*, but the greatness of *that Imperial City*; *Non à* (n) *Petro, sed à Patribus*, (as the Canon of *Chalcedon* tells us.) And that which makes it more probable, that I have given the true sense of *Cyprian*, is, That *Rigaltius* (a Learned *Roman Catholick*) in his Dissertations and Notes on *Cyprian*, Explains *Cyprian's* meaning just as I have done, reducing the *Primacy* and *Principality* of the *Roman Church*, not from any Prerogative given to that Bishop or Church by our blessed Saviour, *but from the greatness of that* (o) *Imperial City*: And then cites the Canon of the General Council of *Chalcedon*, which *in Terminis*, and (when Translated) in plain *English*, says the very same thing I have done. And indeed that Canon, made by Six hundred and thirty Fathers Synodically met, in a legitimate General Council, confirm'd by (p) *Imperial Edicts*, and received into the *Codex Canonum Ecclesiæ Universæ*, does Authentickly and utterly overthrow that vast Monarchical Supremacy, which the Pope and his Party for some Ages last past (without any just ground) contend for. If any of our Adversaries think otherwise, (as possibly they may) I shall make them this fair offer; Let them bring me any Canon, of any General Council (of equal Authority and Antiquity with this of *Chalcedon*) by which they can prove the Popes pretended Supremacy, (or any one Article of their own new *Trent Creed*.) And for the future, I shall acquiesce, and they shall have my Thanks and Subscription.

(l) Cyprian de Unitate Ecclesiæ, p.208. apud Rigaltium. Hoc erant cæteri Apostoli, quod fuit Petras, Pari consortio præditi honoris & potestatis; sed Primatus Petro datur.

(m) Cypr. Epist. 55. ad Cornelium, p. 95. Ad Petri Cathedram, & ad Ecclesiam principalem, unde unitas ἐξορτᾶ est.

(n) Διὰ τὸ Βασιλεύειν τὴν πόλιν, &c. Quia urbs illa Imperaret, Patres dederunt Privilegia. Conc. Chalced. n. Can. 28.

(o) Ad Ecclesiam principalem] Id est, in urbi principali constitutam. Rigaltius ad Epist. Cypr. 55.p 78. Notarum.

(p) Justin. Const. Novel. 115. c.3 §. 14. Græco-Lat. Ludg. 1571. p.745. & Novel. Const. 131. c. 1. ibid. p. 1056. where the Emperor says— τῶν γὰρ προειρημένων &c. dictarum quatuor Synodorum dogmata, sicut Sanctas Scripturas accipimus, & Canones sicut Leges Observamus.

6. *Pius*

Observ. 6.
(q) *Christus Catholicam Ecclesiam uni soli in terris, Apostolorum principi Petro, Petrique Successori Rom. Pontifici, in potestatis plenitudine tradidit gubernandam.* Ita Bulla dicta in principio.

(r) *Christus Petrum universi fidelium generis Caput & Pastorem constituit, cum illi Oves suas pascendas commendavit, ut qui ei Successisset, Eandem plane totius Ecclesiæ regendæ potestatem habere voluerit.* Catechis. Trid. part. 1. De 9. Symboli Art. §. 13. p. 117. Parif. 1635.

(s) *Cum in Petri Cathedrâ sedeat, ut Petri Successor, Christique Vicarius in terris, universali Ecclesiæ præsidet.* Ibid. part. 2. c. 7. §. 28. p. 391.

6. *Pius* the Fifth in his Bull says further ——— (q) *That our blessed Saviour committed the Care and Charge of the Universal Church, with a plenitude of Power to govern it, to one only, that is to* Peter *the Prince of the Apostles, and His Successors.* Here I consider,

1. That although it be certain, (from Scripture, and evident Testimonies of pure and primitive Antiquity) that *Peter* never had, nor Executed any such Monarchical Supremacy over the other Apostles, and the whole Christian Church, as is now vainly pretended to; yet 'tis as certain, that the Pope (and his Party) cry up, and magnifie St. *Peter's* Power, that he (as his Heir and Successor) may possess the same Power. For this they say, (and without any just proof, say it only) *That it was our blessed Saviour's will, that* Peter's *Successor should have* (r) *the very same Power* Peter *had*; and this because he was (s) *Christ's Vicar,* (though every Bishop in the World, (as shall, God willing, appear anon) be Christ's Vicar as well, and as much as he) *and sate in* Peter's *Chair, as his lawful Successor.*

2. But admit, (*dato non Concesso*) which is absolutely untrue, That *Peter* had such a Supremacy and Monarchical Power (as they erroneously pretend to) yet it might be *Personal*, to himself, and for his Life only, (as his Apostolical Power was; as to that part of it, which was properly Apostolical) and not Hereditary, to be transferred to any Successor. So that the Hinge of the Controversie will be here, and our Adversaries concern'd to prove two Things. 1. That *Peter's* Power (be what it will) was not Personal, but Hereditary, and to be Transmitted to his Successor. 2. And that the Pope and Bishop of *Rome* was his Legal Successor. For if they do not, upon just Grounds, make both these good, good night to their pretended Supremacy.

For the first; That the greatest Power St. *Peter* and the Apostles had, was Extraordinary and Personal, not to be Transmitted to any Successor (what Power they did transmit,

mit, I shall anon shew) will be Evident, in these Particulars.

1. *Peter* and the Apostles, had *Vocationem à Christo Immediatam*. Our blessed (t) Saviour cal.'d them all (except *Matthias*) immediately; as is evident from the Text. And, sure I am, that the Pope cannot pretend to such an immediate Call.

2. The Apostles (every one as well as *Peter*) had a Power given them to do Miracles, *to Cast out* (u) *Devils, and heal all manner of Diseases and Sicknesses*. Nor can *Peter*'s Successor (whoever he be) pretend to this.

3. The Jurisdiction, which was by our blessed Saviour given to every Apostle, (to *James* and *John*, and *Paul* as well as *Peter*) was Universal; the whole World was their Diocese. Not that every one could possibly be in every place, but where ever any of them came, they had Authority to Preach, Administer the Sacraments, Constitute and Govern Churches. So *Paul* did at (x) *Antioch* and *Rome*, as much, and (y) *more than Peter*; though they pretend that *Peter* alone (and not *Paul*) was first Bishop of both those Places. That every Apostle (as well as *Peter*) had Universal Jurisdiction and Authority over the whole World, is in Scripture evident by the Commission our blessed Saviour gave them———(z) *Go and teach all Nations, baptizing them in the Name of the Father, Son, and Holy Ghost: Teaching them to observe whatsoever I have commanded you*. And again,——(a) *Go ye into all the World, and Preach the Gospel to every Creature*. Here I observe, 1. That the Apostles in their first Mission, were sent to the (b) *Jews, and them only*. But now their Commission is inlarged; and they are equally sent (every one as much as any one) *to all Nations* (says *Matthew*) To all the World, (κόσμον ἅπαντα, πάσῃ οἰκουμένῃ, as (c) *Eusebius* explains it) says St. *Mark*; *Idem Jurisdictionis Apostolicæ & Orbis Termini*; The whole World was their Diocese; every ones Jurisdiction extended so far, and *Peter*'s could not extend no further. 2. For the Persons they were to preach to, they were *Every Man in the*

(t) Matth. 10.1. Mark 3. 14. Luk. 9. 1.
(u) Ibid. Matth. 10.1.
(x) It does not appear in Scripture that *Peter* ever was at *Antioch*, save once, Gal 2.11. But *Paul* was many times, and long there, and constituted that Church. See Act. 11. 25. Act.14.21.28. Act. 15.35. Act. 18. 22. 23.
(y) *Paul* was there two whole years, Act. 28. 30. writ them a long and excellent Epistle; but 'tis certain *Peter* never writ to them, nor can it appear from Scripture that he was ever 2 weeks, much less 2 years, at *Rome*. Where St. *Paul* is by *Origen*, said to be (next Christ) *primus Ecclesiarum Fundator*. Orig. contra Celsum, l. 1. p. 49. Græco-Lat.
(z) Mat. 28.19.20.
(a) Mark 16.15.
(b) Mat.10.5.6.
(c) Euseb.l.3. Demonstrat. Evang. p. 125.and he has our B. Saviour's word for it, Mat. 24. 10. ἐν ὅλῃ τῇ οἰκουμένῃ.

the World. It is πάση κτίσει, to every Creature, (every Rational Creature, who (if Infancy and Infirmity hinder'd not) was capable. They were to *Convert Pagans*, and make them our blessed Saviour's *Disciples and Sheep*, and then *feed them*, with the Word and Sacraments: Μαθητύσατε, (says *Matthew*) *Convert*, and make them *Disciples*, and then *Baptize* and *Teach them to observe whatever I have Commanded you*. Those words, *Feed my Sheep* (on which without any Just Reason, they would build *Peter*'s Supremacy) contain only an *Indefinite Proposition*, which (as every one who understands Logick, must confess) is only *equivalent to a Particular*; But here the Commission, given by our blessed Saviour, (to every Apostle as well as *Peter*) is *expresly Universal*; *Preach to every Creature*: that is, *Feed All my Sheep*. This is a Truth so evident, that a Learned (d) *Roman Catholick confesseth* and fully proves it. Only (to save the Popes and his own Credit) he says, *That to call General Councils belong'd only to Peter and the Pope, by their Supremacy, and not to any other*. But this is, *gratis dictum*, and an evident untruth. For the Pope (by no Law of God or Man) has, or ever had Power, to call any General Council: And for many Ages never pretended to it; which I only say now, and (when there is a convenient time) can and will make it (e) Good. In the mean time, I think 'tis certain, either 1. That by those words, *Feed my Sheep*, (on which they build the Popes and *Peter*'s Supremacy) our blessed Saviour gave *Peter* no Supream Power to call General Coun-

(d) Franc. Victoria. Relect. Theol. Lugd. 1587. Relect. 2. de Potestate Ecclesiæ Concl. 4. p. 85. where he tells us, *Apostoli Omnes habuerunt Æqualem potestatem cum Petro. Quod sic Intelligo; quod Quilibet Apostolorum habuit potestatem Ecclesiasticam in Toto Orbe, & ad Omnes Actus ad quos Petrus habuit. Non tamen loquor de illis Actibus, qui spectant ad solum summum Pontificem, ut est Congregatio Generalis Concilij*. And this he there proves; as to their Power over the whole world, and to Acts; only (and he dared do no otherwise) he excepts some few, to which no Pope, for many Ages, pretended. In the present *Roman Breviary* the Universal Jurisdiction of *Paul* (as well as *Peter*) is acknowledg'd; *Paul* an Apostle, *Prædicator veritatis per universum Mundum*. In Festo Cathedræ Petri Antiochiæ. Febr. 22. (e) A Learned Papist, Doctor of the *Sorbon* (newly come to my hand) has saved me the labour, and *ex professo*, and *data opera* proved, that all the Eight first General Councils were call'd solely by the Emperors: The Popes did indeed (as he evidently proves) sometimes Petition the Emperors, to call a Council at such a time or place; but they were always both call'd and confirm'd by the Emperors. Vid. Edm. Richer. D. Sorbon. in Hist. de Conc. General. Colon. 1680.

cils,

cils, that by them he might feed his Sheep: Or, 2. That the Apostles and Primitive Christians in their times, knew no such thing. For, 1. When a *Controversie* arose at *Antioch*, about Circumcision, they send not to *Peter*, as Supream Head of the Church, desiring him to call a Council; but *to the* (f) *Apostles and* **Elders**. Had they known and believ'd, that *Peter* had been Invested with such Power and Supremacy, as is now pretended; it had been Civility and Duty in them, to have sent to him in the first place; But they send to the *Apostles and Elders*; without any notice taken of (what they knew not) *Peter*'s Prerogative. 2. It neither does, nor can appear, that *Peter* call'd that Council. 3. Nor did he (as Head and President of the Council) speak (g) first; but the Question was much disputed, before *Peter* spoke any thing. 4. Nor did *Peter* (after the Question was debated) give the Definitive Sentence; For 'tis evident (h) in the Text, That *James* the Less, Son of *Alphæus*, and Bishop of *Jerusalem*, gave that *Definitive Sentence*, which both *Peter* and the whole (i) Council acquiesc'd in. 5. Nor did *Peter* send his Legats to *Antioch*, to signifie what he, and the Council had done, but the (k) Apostles and the whole Church chose and sent their Messengers. 6. Nor are the Letters sent in *Peter*'s Name, or any notice taken of any Primacy or Prerogative of his, above the other Apostles; No, the Ἐπιγραφὴ is, (l) *The Apostles, Elders, and Brethren send Greeting*. 7. Nor was that *Decree* publish'd To the Churches in *Peter*'s Name, as made or (m) confirm'd by him, more than any other Apostle. 8. Nay, the Apostles send *Peter* on a (n) Message to *Samaria* (and he obeys and goes) which had been a strange piece of Presumption, had either he or they known his (now pretended) Monarchical Supremacy. 9. So far were those *Primitive Christians*, from knowing or acknowledging the now pretended Monarchical Supremacy of *Peter*, that even in the Apostles times and Presence, they *question* and (o) call him to an *Account for his Actions*. Διακρίνοντο, *Disceptabant adversus*

(f) Act. 15.2.
(g) Act. 15.7.
(h) Act. 15. 19. 20. 21.
(i) Act. 15. 22.
(k) Ibidem.
(l) Act. 15. 23. Vide dictum Edmundum Richerium D. Sorbonicum, in Hist. Conc. Generalium, lib.1.c 13. § 5. pag. 401. Edit. Colon. 1680. Ubi ex Card. Alliaceno, & Concilio hoc Apostolico Act. 15. demonstrat. Petrum Primatum (qualem Jesuitæ vellent) non habuisse, sed Primatum illum Monarchicum ab Hildebrando, seu Gregorio 7. retroductum. Ibid. §. 2. 5.

(m) Act. 16. 4.
(n) Act. 8. 14.

(o) Act. 11. 2. 3.

sus illum (says the vulgar Latin) *tanquam valde offensi expostulabant* (says *Chrysostom*.) And honest *John Ferus* (a *Roman Catholick*) tells us, (*b*) *That he was Compell'd to give a Reason of his Actions to the Church; nor was* Peter *offended at it, because he knew that he was not a Lord, but Minister of the Church.* But now (as (*c*) *Ferus* there goes on) the Case is alter'd; *for wicked Popes*, (as though they were Lords and not Ministers) *will not be Question'd for any thing, or reprov'd.* Had the Canon Law been then in force, (which his pretended Successors have approved, and by their Supream Authority publish'd) he might have told those who Question'd him, (*d*) *That he was to judge all men, and none him; nor was he to be reprov'd by any mortal man, though by his Impiety and ill Example, he carried thousands to Hell with him.* 10. Nay, St. *Paul* does not only (*e*) question St. Peter's *Actions, but to his face, before the People publickly condemn them, and that justly; for* (he says) *he was to be blamed:* which he neither would, nor indeed well could have done, had he known *Peter* to have been so far his Superior as to have (by Divine Institution) a Monarchical Jurisdiction and Power over him. 11. Lastly, St. *Paul* himself tells us, (*f*) *That he was in nothing Inferior to the Chiefest Apostles*; not to *Peter*, *James*, or *John*, whom (*g*) elsewhere he reckons the chiefest. I know they say, *That Paul was equal to* Peter *as to his Apostolical Office, but Inferior to* Peter, *as he was* (*h*) *Supream Pastor over the Apostles, and the whole Church.* But this is *gratis dictum*, and indeed a begging of the Question, and taking that for granted, which never was, nor ever will be proved. However, 'tis certain, 1. That every Apostle (as well as *Peter*) had an *Universal supream* (*i*) *Authority and Jurisdiction*, in any part of the World, and over any Christians wherever they came. 2. That this largeness of their Jurisdiction, was Apostolical, and Personal to themselves, which they neither did, nor could trans-

(*b*) *Petrus Apostolorum Primus, rationem reddere Ecclesiæ cogitur, nec indignè fert, quia non Dominum sed Ministrum Ecclesiæ se agere sciebat.* Ferus in Act. 11.2.

(*c*) *Impij autem Pontifices Nunc nec ab Ecclesiâ argui, aut in Ordinem cogi volunt, quasi sint Domini non Ministri.* Ibidem.

(*d*) *Si Papa innumerabiles populos secum ducit, primo mancipio Gehennæ &c. Hujus Culpas redarguere præsumat mortalium nullus: quia Cunctos ipse judicaturus, à nemine est Judicandus; nisi sit à fide devius.* Can. si Papa. 6. Dist. 40.

(*e*) Gal. 2. 11, 12, 13, 14.

(*f*) 2 Cor. 11. 5. & 12. vers. 11.

(*g*) Gal. 2. 9.

(*h*) *Locus hic non derogat prærogativæ Petri, qui totius Ecclesiæ Rector & Pastor Constitutus, etiam ipsis Apostolis Major & Superior fuit.* Estius in 2 Cor. 12. 11.

(*i*) *Qui Apostolus est, Summam habet in Omnem Ecclesiam Potestatem.* Bellarmin. De Rom. Pontif. lib. 2. Cap. 12. in Respons. 3. & Object. 2.

mit

mit to their Successors; whose Jurisdiction was limited to some City and Territory, and that particular Place, the Care and Charge whereof was committed unto them; as *Ephesus* was to *Timothy*, and *Creet* to *Titus*. 3. Our Adversaries confess this, (as to all the other Apostles) but for *Peter*, they say, *He* (k) *transmitted his Supremacy and Universal Jurisdiction over the whole Church to his Successor, and that by the Institution of our blessed Saviour, and Divine Right.* If they could prove this, the Controversie were at an end; we would acquiesce, and admit (what upon undeniable evidence we deny) the Popes Supremacy. But this they neither do, nor is there any possibility they ever should prove. For there is not one Syllable in (l) Scripture, of *Peter*'s Successor, or of what Power he received from him: and nothing but Scripture can prove our blessed *Saviour*'s *Institution*, and *Divine Law*, whereby *Peter*'s Supremacy is transmitted to his Successor. The truth is, that *Pius V.* in the beginning of this his Impious Bull, and other Popes many (m) *times* in their Bulls, Breves, and Decretal Constitutions, and their Writers generally, take it for granted, that our blessed Saviour gave *Peter* the Supremacy over the whole Church, and to *his Successors after him*: And when (n) some of them, sometimes go about to prove it, the Reasons they bring, are so far from Sense and Consequence, that they may deserve Pity and Contempt, rather than a serious Answer. But when Reason will not Convince, they have other Roman Arts to Cosen men into a Belief, that what was given to *Peter*, was likewise given to the Pope his Successor; and that is (amongst other ways) by corrupting the Ancient Fathers with false Translations. So when *Chrysostom* had said, *That the Power of the Keys, was not given to Peter only, but to the rest of the Apostles*: Pet. Possinus adds, *Successors*; and renders it thus —— *The Power of the Keys was not gi-*

(k) *Successio ex Christi Instituto, & Jure Divino est, quia ipse Christus Instituit in Petro Pontificatum, in finem Mundi duraturam, ac ideo quicunque Petro succedit, a Christo accepit Pontificatum.* Bellarmin. dicto lib. & c. §. ut autem.

(l) *Romanum Pontificem succedere Petro, non habetur expresse in Scripturis; (no, nor implicite neither) tamen succedere aliquem Petro, deducitur evidenter ex Scripturis, illum autem esse Romanum Pontificem, habetur ex traditione Apostolica.* Bellarmin dicto lib. & cap. §. Observandum Tertio.

(m) Vid. Cap. Solitæ. 6. Extra. de Major. & Obedientia. & Cap. Per venerabilem. 13. Extra. Qui filii sunt legit. & Cap. Ad Apostolicæ. 2. De Sent. & re judicata, in 6.

& Cap. pro Human. 1. De Homicidio, in 6. (n) Vid. Tho Campegium Episc. Feltrensem, de Potestate Rom. Pont. Capp. 13, 14. & Bellarminum de Roman. Pontifice, lib. 2. c. 12. &c.

ven only to Peter *And His* (o) *Successors, &c.* where *Chrysostome* (whom he Translates) has nothing of *Peter's Successors*: but truly and plainly says ———— *That the Power of the Keys was not given only to* Peter, *but to the rest of the Apostles, when our blessed* (p) *Saviour told them, whose sins ye remit they are remitted, and whose sins ye retain, they are retained.* So in the Epistle of Pope (q) *Leo* to the Bishops of *France*, and of his Legat *Paschasinus* about the Condemnation of *Dioscorus*, in the Council of *Chalcedon*, these Words occur in the Latin Copies ———— *The most holy and most blessed Pope* Leo, *Head of the Universal Church:* Where these words ———— *Head of the Universal Church*, are not in the Greek Copies; (as that Learned Archbishop ingenuously and truly (r) Confesseth) but (by Roman Arts) falsly and basely interserted, that so they might by fraud (what by no reason they can) maintain, the Pope's impiously usurped Supremacy. And that we may know, how unpleasing the publishing of such things (though evidently true) are to the Pope and his Party at *Rome*, (who are resolved, in despight of truth) to maintain the Popes pretended Supremacy) this Learned Work of that great Roman Catholick Archbishop (ſ) is damn'd by the Inquisitors, not to be printed, read, or had by any. He who seriously reads (and understands) the Latin Versions of the Greek Councils, Fathers, and other Greek and Latin Writers, may find an hundred such Frauds, to maintain (what they know they have no just Reason for) their Papal and Antichristian Tyranny: And their *Indices Expurgatorij* are Authentick Evidences, to Convince them of these Unchristian Practises, to conceal truth, and cosen the World into a belief of their pernicious Papal Errors. Nor is this all, (nor the worst) for so desperately are they set upon it, that if their Interest and the Papal Monarchy cannot otherwise be maintain'd (as 'tis impossible it should by any just and lawful means) they speak impiously and blasphemously of our blessed Saviour. *Thomas Campegius Episcopus Feltrensis*, in his Book of the Power of the Pope,

(o) Οὐ μόνῳ τῷ Πέτρῳ τοῦτο δεδώρηται, &c. Non id Petro uni Successoribusque suis reservatum. Pet. Possinus Jesuita, Catena Græc. Patrum in Matth. Tom. 1. p. 232.

(p) Joh. 20. 22, 23.

(q) Vid. Pet. de Marca de Concordia Sacerdotij & Imperij. Tom. 2. l. 5. c. 10. §. 2. p. 35. & Pet. Crab. Conc. Tom. 1. pag. 945. Col. 2. The words are these; *unde Sanctissimus & Beatissimus Papa, Caput universalis Ecclesiæ, &c.*

(r) Absunt à Contextu Græco, verba illa, *Caput universalis*, &c. loco dicto, in margine.

(ſ) Vide Indicem Librorum Prohibitorum Alexan. 7. Jussu Editum, Romæ, Ann. 1664. verbo, De Concordia Sacerdotij, &c. p 29. & p. 352. ubi extat Decretum Congregationis Judicis, in quo damnatur hic Petri de Marca Liber.

Pope, to *Paul* IV. says,——— (t) *That our blessed Saviour had not been a Diligent Father of the Family, to his Church, unless he had left such a Monarch over his Church, as the Pope,* of whom he is there speaking: And he cites Pope *Innocent,* and *Aquinas* to justifie it. *Albertus Pighius* is as high to the same impious purpose, and expresly says ——— (u) *That our blessed Saviour had been wanting to his Church in things necessary, if he had not Constituted and left such a Monarch and Judge of Controversies.* And a great (x) Canonist (if that be possible) more blasphemously says ——— *That our blessed Saviour, while he was on Earth, had power to pronounce the Sentence of Deposition, and Damnation against the Emperor, or any other; And by the same Reason, his Vicar now can do it.* And then he impiously adds ——— *That our blessed Saviour would not have seem'd Discreet, unless he had left such a Vicar, as could do all these things, &c.* So if it be granted (which is most evident and certainly true) that our blessed Saviour left no such Monarchical vicar, as the Pope; then they are not afraid to accuse him of *want of Diligence and Discretion.* And this impious Gloss is approved and confirm'd by Pope (y) *Gregory* XIII. as (we may be sure) what makes for his Extravagant Power and Papal Monarchy (how Erroneous and Impious soever) shall not want his Approbation. And thus much of the third Priviledge of the Apostles, their *Universal Jurisdiction*; equally in them all, in *James,* and *John,* and *Paul* as much as *Peter*; and this Jurisdiction Personal to all, and never transmitted to any of their Successors.

(t) *Non fuisset Christus Diligens Pater-familias, si non divisisset in Terrâ aliquem qui Vice suâ posset subvenire necessitatibus Ecclesiæ,* &c. De Potestat. Rom. Pontif. cap. 1. §. 3. pag 2.

(u) *Christus Ecclesiæ Defuisset nec de Necessariis prospexisset, Nisi Monarcham aliquem & Judicem Constituisset,* &c. Vide Albert. Pighium Controvers. 3. fol. 70, 71, 72.

(x) *Christus dum fuit in Mundo, de jure naturali, in Imperatorem & Quoscunque Alios Depositionis Sententias ferre potuisset, & Damnationis ——— & Eadem Ratione & Vicarius ejus potest. Nam non videtur Dominus Discretus fuisse, nisi unicum post se Talem Vicarium reliquisset. Fuit autem iste*

Vicarius Petrus: & idem dicendum est de Successoribus Petri. Ita Petrus Bertrandus in Addit. ad Glossas ad Cap. Unam Sanctam. 1. De Major. & Obed. Extrav. Commun. (y) Vide Bullam Greg. 13. dat. Rom. 1. Julij, Ann. 1580. præfixam. Corp. Juris Can. Parif. 1612. & 1618.

4. Besides the Immediate Call of the Apostles, their Power of doing Miracles, and their Universal Jurisdiction over all the World; they were (all of them) διαπνευσοι, Divinely Inspired by the Holy Ghost, so that they had Infallibility,

fallibility, so far, as whatever they preach'd or writ was Divine, and the undoubted Word of God. This Priviledge also was Personal, nor ever was Communicated to any of their Successors. I know that the (z) Canonists and (a) Jesuits, (in the last and worst of times) would make the World believe (without any shadow of rational ground) that *Peter* transferred his Infallibility to the Pope, and made him the Infallible Judge of all Controversies of Faith, and Fact too. A thing so evidently false, and without any possibility of proof, that 'tis a wonder, that any should have the Confidence to assert it, especially in *Paris*, the great Metropolis of a Church which constantly does, and has deny'd the Popes infallibility and Superiority to a General Council. 2. But that which might for ever silence this Irrational and Injust Claim of Infallibility in the Pope, is, that (for Matter of Fact) none of them, (though they were sometimes nibling at a kind of Supremacy) for above a Thousand Years after our blessed Saviour, either did or dared pretend to Infallibility; and if they had, they had made themselves ridiculous. For, 3. It was notoriously known, that several of their Popes were Hereticks. For instance, (b) *Liberius*, (c) *Honorius*, (d) *Vigilius, &c.* And for Heresie Condemn'd in General Councils, as is evident from the Acts themselves, and has been demonstrated, not only by Protestants, but by very Learned men of the Roman Communion. 4. And he who seriously reads, and impartially considers their Papal Bulls, Breves, and Decretal (e) Constitutions;

(z) *Sic Omnes Apostolicæ Sedis Sanctiones accipiuntur sunt, tanquam Ipsius divini Petri voce firmatæ sint.* Can. sic. Omnes 2. Dist. 19. And this the Gloss there indeavours to prove, from a spurious & ridiculous, as well as impious Canon. Can. Non Nos. 1. Dist. 40.

(a) The Jesuits in their Thesis proposed in the *Claromont* Col. 12. Dec. Ann. 1661. Impudently and Impiously say, *Christus ecclesiæ regimen primum Petro, deinSuccessoribus Commisit, & Eandem quam habebat Ipse, Infallibilitatem, Concessit, quoties ex Cathedrâ loqueretur.* And then Thes. 20. tells us ―― *Datur Infallibilis Controversiarum Judex, etiam Extra Concilium Generale, Tum in Quæstionibus Juris, tum facti.* (b) Hieronymus de Scriptoribus Ecclesiast in Fortunatiano. (c) Vid. Hist Hæresis Monothliarum, per Fran. de Combesis Dominicanum. Paris. 1648. p. 65. &c. 121. &c. ut i contra Pighium, Baronium, &c. probat evidentèr Honorium Synodo 6. damnatum. (d) Vid. D. Rich. Crakanthorp, in Vigilio dormitante. (e) Let any man read those two Constitutions before nam'd. 1. That of *Innocent* 3. Cap. Solicitæ 6. Extra de Major. & Obedient. &c. 2. That of *Bonif.* 8. Cap Unam Sanctam. 1. eodem Titulo Extravag. Commun and if he have eyes, and will Impartially use them, he will find what I say, true. Or he may (with the same success) read the Bulls and Damnations of the Emperor *Hen.* 4. by *Greg.* 7. in Bull. Rom. 1638. Tom. 1. p. 49, 50, 51. And of *Freder.* 2 Ibid. p. 94, 95. by *Innoc.* 4. And the Excommunications of the same Emperor, by *Greg.* 9. Ann. 1239. Ibid. in dicto Bullario, Tom. 1. p. 89, 90.

and

and in them how ridiculously they reason, and prophane (rather than expound) Scripture, will have abundant reason to believe, that those Popes were so far from Infallibility, that their own Writings Convince them guilty of Gross Ignorance and Folly

5. Lastly, All the Apostles were *Fundamenta Ecclesiæ, Domus Dei,* Foundations of the Church, or House of God, (as has before been evidently proved from Scripture) and this was in all the Apostles Extraordinary, and a Personal Apostolical Priviledge, to which, (as it was in the Apostles) none of their Successors (no not the Pope,) ever did, or (with any reason) could pretend. And as this Apostolical Priviledge, so the other four before mention'd (1. *Immediate Vocation.* 2. *Power to work Miracles.* 3. *Universality of Jurisdiction.* 4. *Infallibility in all things they preach'd or writ.*) I say, all these Priviledges, were extraordinary and Personal to the Apostles, and never were transmitted to any of their Successors. And this being granted, (as of necessity it ought and must) it will evidently follow, that *Peter* neither had, nor could have, that Monarchical Supremacy over the Apostles and Universal Church, to which the Pope and his Party vainly, and without any reason or ground pretend. For that Papal Supremacy and Monarchy they pretend *Peter* had, (according to their Hypothesis) consisted principally, in the Universality of his Jurisdiction over the whole Church, and his Infallibility, as a Judge, to determine Controversies of Faith; both which every Apostle had, (as much and as well as he) and therefore it was impossible, that (in these respects) he should have any Superiority (much less Supremacy) over the other Apostles, more than they over him; especially, seeing in Scripture, (to men who have good Eyes, and will impartially use them) there is not one Syllable looks that way. Nay, seeing our blessed Saviour hath expresly determin'd the contrary. The Apostles were disputing and reasoning amongst themselves, which of them should be *greatest*: (they had their Infirmities and ambi-

tious

tious desires). But our Saviour tells them —— (f) *Whosoever will be great among you* (though *Peter* be the man) *let him be their Minister*; *and whosoever will be* (g) *chief, let him be your Servant*. And again —— (h) *Be not ye call'd Masters, for one is your Master, even Christ* (not *Peter*) *and ye are Brethren*; *but he that will be greatest among you, shall be your Servant*. The Apostles had no Master under Heaven, but their blessed Saviour; it was of him, and him Only, that they learned the Gospel, and that Immediately; they had it not from (i) *any man*, nor one from another. Our blessed Saviour was *their only Master and Superior*, and they his *Scholars, subordinate to him*, and co-ordinate amongst *themselves*. He tells them, *that they are Brethren*; *Condiscipuli*, School-fellows. Names which (in themselves, and in their Master's meaning) import Equality; especially as to any Jurisdiction one over another. There may be amongst Scholars of the same School, and Brethren, an inequality, (and so there was amongst the Apostles)
1. In respect of *Age*; some might be elder, some younger. 2. *In respect of their coming to that School*; some might come before others; So *Andrew* was first call'd to our blessed Saviours School, (before *Peter* *). 3. *In respect of Natural Parts and Abilities*, some might have greater Capacities than others. 4. *In respect of their Masters Love and Kindness*, he might love one more than another, So amongst the Twelve, *John* was the *beloved Disciple*. Such inequality there was amongst them, and we willingly grant it. But to say, (as the Pope, and many of his Party most vainly do) that amongst these *Brethren*, and *School-fellows* in our B. Saviour's School, *Peter*, (or any other) had not only an *Authority and Jurisdiction*, but *a Monarchical Supremacy*, over all the rest, this is so contradictory to our blessed Saviour's plain words, and the manifest and undoubted meaning of them; that were it not, that we know men may be sway'd with worldly Interests, and sometimes have strong Delusions to believe a Lye; it were incredible that any

Learned

(f) Matth. 20. 26, 27.
(g) Πρῶτος, Primus seu Princeps, (plus est quam esse Magnum) aliis Omnibus Major (yet this the Pope would have). Luc. Burgensis. in Math. 20. 27.
(h) Matth. 23. 8, 9, 10, 11.
(i) Gal. 1. 3.

* Joh. 1. 40, 42, &c.

Learned men should (with so much Confidence, and no Reason) assert the contrary. To pass by all Testimonies of Ancient Fathers for many hundred years, and many sober Papists before *Luther*, (who neither knew, nor believed *Peter's* Monarchy over the Church and his fellow Apostles, his equals) sure I am, 1. That *Francis* (k) *Lucas Brugensis*, a Roman Catholick (in our days) eminent in their Church for Dignity and Learning, says the same thing I have done (and on the same Texts) for the Equality of the Apostles, against *Peter's* pretended Monarchy. 2. And a greater than he, (I mean (*l*) *Petrus de Marca* Archbishop of *Paris*) convinc'd with the Evidence of the former Texts, and Truth, was of Opinion, and has publish'd it to the World, That our blessed Saviour, at his Ascension, did not leave the Church establish'd in *Peter*, and a Monarchy; But in an *Aristocratie*, or the *Colledge of the Apostles*. In which Colledge *Peter* was one, not Superior (much less a Monarch) to the other Apostles; and the Apostles left the Government of the Church Establish'd in the Bishops, and *Aristocratical*; only he thinks, that both in the Colledge of the Apostles, and Councils of Bishops after them, there was (for Orders sake) to be a President, (not a Monarch, for that was Inconsistent with *Aristocratie*) And (if this will content them) we will grant it. Because we do know, that the Ancient Church allow'd the Pope the prime Place and Precedency in Councils, (for Orders sake) and that not by any *Divine Right*, (which was not in those days, so much as pretended to) but because *Rome* was the (*m*) Imperial City, and Metropolis of the *Roman Empire*; the greatness of the City usually giving greatness and Pre-

(*k*) Matth 23 8. *Omnes autem vos fratres estis.* On which words, *Luc. Brugensis* saith thus ——— *Quia fratres sumus, Neminem in alios Magisterio fungi Concedit* ——— *Fratres non Magistri Alii in Aliis Condiscipuli, nemo in alium proprie agere potest Magistratum. Nullus aliorum Magisterium mereatur, si habere vos Omnes merita debeatis Condiscipulos. Christus Solus Omnium Magister agnoscendus.* Ita L. Brugensis; Commentar. in q Evang. ad 23. Matth. 8. p. 351. vid. Hieronym in Gal. 2. 1. ubi dicit Petrum, Paulum, & reliquos Apostolos fuisse æquales.

(*l*) *Sed quia Ecclesia regenda est juxta unitatem, necessarium fuit, Institui ab Apostolis modum quendam Communionis inter Episcopos, secundum Exemplum, A Christo datum in Institutione Collegij Apostolici; quod universum Ecclesiæ Corpus repræsentabat; Ideoque præscribenda ab iis suit forma regiminis, Aristocratici nimirum, ita ut unus Præsideret.* Pet. de Marca de Concordia Sacerdotij & Imperij, lib. 6. cap. 1. § 2. pag. 58: Col. 1. (*m*) Conc. Chalcedon. Can. 28. Conc. Constant. 1. Can. 5. apud P. Crabb. Conc. Tom. 1. pag. 411.

cedency

cedency to the Bishops; such were *Constantinople*, *Alexandria*, *Antioch*, &c. I know the Inquisitors at *Rome* have damned this Book of (n) *Petrus de Marca*, but this is no Argument, that what he has said, is not true; *Grande aliquod bonum est, quod à Nerone (ab Inquisitoribus) damnatur.* To conclude this Point, if our Adversaries assent not to this manifest Truth, as (being contradictory to their worldly Interest and misconceived Infallible Pretensions) 'tis probable they will not; I shall make them this (to all unprejudiced Lovers of Truth) fair offer. Let them give me any one cogent Argument from Scripture or Universal Tradition (and nothing else can do it) whereby they can prove, the following Positions; I will thank God and them for the **discovery,** and promise hereby to be their Proselyte.

(n) But it is not only *Pet. de Marca*, but even the Popish General Councils of *Pisa*, *Constance*, and *Basil*, and the *Gallican* Church and *Sorbon*, and the Ancient Church for a thousand years after our blessed Saviour, which maintain'd the same Doctrine *Marca* did; as is evidently proved by a Learned *Sorbon* Doctor, *Edm. Rechier*. In Hist. Conc. General. l. 1. Edit. Colon. Ann. 1680. The design of the whole Book is against the **Popes** Monarchical Supremacy and Infallibility. Vide dicti lib. cap. 13. pag. 393. &c.

1. If they can (by any such Argument) prove that *Peter* (by *Divine Right*) had such a Monarchical Supremacy and Jurisdiction over the Apostles, and the whole Church, (as is vainly pretended) I will yield the Cause. But if he had no such Power, 'tis impossible he should transmit the Power (he never had) to his Successors.

2. Let it be suppos'd, (which yet is evidently untrue) that St. *Peter* had such a Monarchical Authority and Jurisdiction, even over the rest of the Apostles, let them prove by any such Argument as is before-mention'd; that it was not only Temporal, and his only for his life; that it was not to have an end and period with his Person. For if it was, then his Successor (whoever he be) can have no pretence to it. For 'tis impossible, that any Successor, can have any legal or just Claim to that Power, which vanish'd and ceas'd to be, with his Predecessor, who possess'd it only for his life.

3. Admit

3. Admit both these to be true, (which yet are equally and evidently false) that *Peter had such a Power*, and that it was *not Personal*, but to be transmitted to his Successor, seeing such transmission must either be done by our blessed Saviour immediately, or (by Power deriv'd from him) by *Peter*. Let our Adversaries make it appear, that either our blessed Saviour himself, or *Peter* (by Power deriv'd from him) did actually transmit that Power to any Successor, and I submit.

4. Lastly, Suppose all these to be (what not one of them is) true; yet unless it do appear, that the Bishop of *Rome* (and not the Bishop of *Antioch*, (where they say *Peter* was Bishop first) was that Successor of St. *Peter*, to whom such Supremacy was transmitted; he can have no pretence to it. For in this Case, *Idem est non esse & non apparere*. Let our Adversaries then make it appear, that either our blessed Saviour immediately by himself, or *Peter* (by Authority from him) did (*o*) transmit the Supremacy to the Pope, and we shall be satisfy'd; and thankful for the Discovery. And this brings me to the Second thing proposed before.

(*o*) I know that some of them (eminent for Learning and Dignity in their Church) say; That our blessed Saviour did give *Peter* power to transfer his great Authority to his Successor, and only to him, not to any of the other Apostles; But this they say only, without any pretence of proof. And I commend their prudence, not to attempt impossibilities. Johan. Franciscus Bordinus Archbishop of *Avignion*, has published his Opinion, in these words ———— *Christus universale Totius Ecclesiæ Caput Petrum constituit, qui suas Vices in Terris ageret. Quo quidem in Munere, & si dum viveret, Æquales* (mark that) *habuit cætero Coapostolos, Nulli tamen Eorum, quod à Domino accipissent, jus per Successionem in alios transferendi facultas fuit. Soli Petro id Promissum, Soli Petro id Traditum, ut Petra esset, & post Christum Ecclesiæ fundamentum.* Ita Johan. Fran. Bordinus Archiepiscopus Avenionensis, in Serie & Gestis Roman. Pontif. ad Clement. Papam 8. ad Annum Christ. 34. Tiberij 18.

2. The thing next to be enquired after is, *Whether, and how it may appear that the Bishop of* Rome *is* Peter's *Successor*. Our Adversaries say, (and vainly say it only) that *Peter* was *Supream Head* (after our blessed Saviour's Ascension) and *Monarch of the Church*; and from him, (*Jure Successionis*) the Pope derives his *Monarchical Power and Supremacy*; and that by the *Institution* and (*p*) *Command of* our

(*p*) *Petrus Romæ Sedem suam, Jubente Domino, collocavit.* Bellarm. de Rom. Pontif. l. 2. c. 1. §. 1.

our Blessed Saviour, and so not by *Humane*, but (q) *Divine Right*. This is a Position of greatest Consequence, and will require good proof. Nor is it possible to prove the Bishop of *Rome* to be *Peter's* Successor in that Bishoprick, unless it first appear that *Peter* was his Predecessor in that See. *Linus, Clemens* or *Cletus* cannot (with any Truth or Sense) be said to succeed *Peter*, unless it appear first, that he preceeded them. Our Adversaries (I confess) do constantly (with great noise and confidence) affirm, That *Peter* did preceed in the Bishoprick of *Rome*; but sure I am, that hitherto, they have not brought any, so much as probable (much less cogent and concluding) Reason to prove it: nor do I think it possible they should bring (what they neither have, nor can have) any true and concluding proof, to prove (what this is) an erroneous and false Position. And that this may not be begg'd and *gratis dictum*, I shall offer to the Impartial Reader, these Considerations.

(q) *Probatur, Roman. Pontificem Petro Succedere, in Pontificatu Ecclesiæ universæ ex Divino Jure & Ratione Successionis.* Bellarmin. ibid. lib. 2. c. 12. §. Primum ergo. *Papa in Petri Cathedrâ Sedet, summum in eo dignitatis gradum, & Jurisdictionis amplitudinem, non Humanis Constitutionibus, sed Divinitùs datum agnoscit: est Pater universalis Ecclesiæ Petri Successor, & Christi Vicarius, &c.* Catechism. Trident. Part. 2. cap. 7. §. 28. pag. 391. Edit. Paris. 1635.

1. When they (r) say, That *Peter* fix'd his Episcopal Chair at *Rome, Jubente Domino:* Let them shew that (s) Command, and there will be an end of the Controversie; we will obey our blessed Saviour's Command, and the Pope too. But this they have neither done, nor can: It being impossible, they should shew that to be, which never was, nor ever had any being.

(r) Bellarm. Locis proxime citatis, (ut & alij passim.) And Pope *Pius* the Fifth in this his Impious Bull. §. 1. *Christus Ecclesiam Catholicam uni soli Petro Petrique Successori Romano Pontifici in potestatis plenitudine Tradidit Gubernandam.* (s) *Nullum Christi, ea de re, Decretum Extat.* So A Lapide Confesses; in Apoc. 17. vers. 17. pag. 268. Col. 2. A.

2. That ever *Peter* was at *Rome*, (much less that he was Bishop there, for Five and twenty years (as is vainly pretended) cannot be made appear out of *Scripture*, or any Apostolical or Authentick Record; and therefore that he was there at all, (where he might be, as he was in many other good Cities, and no Bishop of any of them) must

must depend solely upon *human and fallible Testimonies*, (I say, Testimonies certainly fallible, if not absolutely false; which many Learned men have, and do believe). Now seeing the whole Papal Monarchy and Infallibility, depend upon *Peter's* being Bishop of *Rome*, and the grounds we have to assure us, that he ever was there, are fallible and dubious; and seeing it is irrational (if not impossible) that any considering Person, should give a firm and undoubted assent to any Conclusion, inferr'd only upon fallible and dubious premisses. Hence it evidently follows, That our Faith and belief of the Papal Monarchy and Infallibility is, and (till they find better, and more necessary premisses) must be fallible and dubious. And here I desire to be inform'd how it comes to be an Article of Faith, in their new *Roman Creed*; *That the Bishop of* Rome *is Vicar of Christ*, and (t) *Peter's Successor*; which Article (with the rest in that Creed) they promise, (u) *swear and vow, to believe and profess most Constantly, to their last breath*. With what Conscience their Church can require, or they take such an Oath, *Most constantly and firmly to believe, to their last breath*, such things, for the belief of which, they have no grounds (if any) save only fallible and very dubious, *Ipsi viderint.*

(t) *Romano Pontifici, Beati Petri Apostolorum Principis, Successori, ac Christi Vicario, veram Obedientiam spondeo ac juro.* Vid. Bullam Pij 4. super forma Juramenti Professionis fidei, in Conc. Trident. Sess. 24. p. 452. Edit. Antv. 1633.

* (u) *Hanc Catholicam fidem, extra quam nemo Salvus esse potest, quam in Præsenti profiteor, & teneo, tandem usque ad ultimum vitæ spiritum constantissime retinere, &c. Spondeo, Voveo, Juro.* Ibidem.

3. I know, that the Assertors of the Papal Monarchy (according to their Interest) are very desirous to prove out of Scripture, that *Peter* was at *Rome*; and to that end produce those words in his first *Epistle*—(*x*) *The Church which is at* Babylon *salutes you:* And by *Babylon*, they say, the Apostle meant *Rome:* And for this they cite *Papias* in (y) *Eusebius*, *That by* Babylon, Rome *is figuratively to be understood*. So that (if this be true) *Peter* writ that *Epistle* at *Babylon*, that is, at *Rome*; and

(x) 1 Pet. 5. 13. (y) *Primam Petri Epistolam Romæ Scriptam* (φασὶν) *aiunt, quam Petrus,* τροπικώτερον Βαβυλῶνα *appellat.* Eusebius Hist. l. 2. c. 15. p. 53. B. Valesio.

so must be at *Rome* when he writ it: And the proof of this depends upon the Authority of *Papias* Bishop of *Hierapolis*, and those who follow him. Now how little Credit is to be given to *Papias* in this, (or any thing else) will manifestly appear out of the same *Eusebius*; who tells us, 1. *That* Papias *was much given to* Tradition; (z) inquiring (of the Elders who had heard the Apostles) *what* Peter, *or* James, *or* John, *&c. had said: thinking he got less benefit by reading Scriptures, then by the talk of those who heard the Authors of them.* 2. *That he had by such* (a) *Tradition, strange Parables and Preachings of our blessed Saviour, and other things very Fabulous: Such as the Heresie of the Millenaries*; which he believed and propagated. *That he thus err'd, by* (b) *Misunderstanding the Apostles Doctrine:* For (as *Eusebius* goes on) *he was a man of very little understanding.* 4. *And yet* (as the same Author says) *he was the occasion that,* (c) *most of the Ecclesiastical Writers who followed him.* (Reverencing his Antiquity) *err'd with him.*

(z) *Curiose sciscitabar* (said *Papias*) *à Senioribus, quid Petrus, quid Jacobus, dicere soliti essent. Neque ex Bibliorum Lectione, tantam me utilitatem capere posse Existimabam, quantam ex hominum vivâ voce.* Euseb. l. 3 c. 39. p. 111.

(a) Ἐκ παραδόσεως ἀγράφε, *Ex Traditione non scriptâ habuit novas quasdam Struatoris parabolas & prædicationes, aliáque Fabulis propiora; inter quæ Mille Annorum spatium post resurrectionem, fore dicit.* Euseb. ibid. p. 117. (b) *Ita opinatus videtur Papias, ex male Intellectis Apostolorum narrationibus. Fuit enim Mediocri Admodum Ingenio Præditus.* Euseb. ibidem. Lit. c. (c) *Plerisque tamen post Ipsum Ecclesiasticis Scriptoribus, Ejusdem Erroris occasionem præbuit, hominis vetustate, Sententiam suam tuentibus.* Ibidem D. ita etiam Nicephorus Hist. Lib. 3. cap. 20. pag. 252. D.

Object.
(d) Colon. Allob. 1612.
(e) Parif. 1659.
(f) *Papias eadem ætate celebrus fuit; Vir imprimis disertus, & eruditus, ac Scripturarum peritus.* Euseb. Hist. l. 3. c. 36. Edit. Valesij. Sed in Edit. Christopherson. cap. 35. Græ. 30. Latinæ. Versionis.

I know, that in *Eusebius* (both in the worst Edition of him, by (d) *Christopherson*, (sometime a Popish Bishop of *Chichester*) and the best by (e) *Hen. Valesius*) we have a high Commendation of *Papias*; (f) *At the same time* (says *Eusebius*, as *Valesius* renders him) *Papias was famous; a man very Eloquent and Learned) and well skill'd in Scripture.* But *Christopherson* (his other Translator) goes higher, (as usually he does when it makes for the Catholick Cause) and in his Translation says more in Commendation of *Papias*, then is in the Text: For he tells us, *That* Papias (besides his knowledge of Scripture) *was a man* (g) *cer-*

(g) *Omnia aliarum Artium scientiâ vir plane disertissimus.* Ibidem.

tainly

tainly most learned in the Knowledge of All Other Arts. Now if this be true, then that *Character* I have given him before, is not so; and then his Antiquity (which was (*h*) great) and his great Learning, in all Arts and Sciences, as well as Scripture) consider'd; his Testimony, that *Babylon*, whence St. *Peter* writ, was *Rome*, will be more valid, and of greater Authority.

In Answer to this; I say, 1. That all this Commendation of *Papias* before mention'd, is so far from having any Authority from *Eusebius*, that 'tis a plain Forgery. *Eusebius* (as to this passage) is evidently corrupted; and this Commendation of *Papias* (by whose Ignorance or Knavery, I know not) shuffled into the Text, long after *Eusebius* his death. For, 2. *Ruffinus* (who Translated *Eusebius* his History above One thousand two hundred years ago) in the place above quoted, says only thus —— *About this time flourished* Polycarpe *Bishop of* Smyrna, *and* Papias *Bishop of* Hierapolis. So the Printed Edition of (*i*) *Ruffinus* by *B. Rhenanus*; and a very ancient and compleat MS. of *Ruffinus* (in my keeping and possession) exactly (*k*) agrees with it; and there is not one word of that Commendation of *Papias*, which is now extant in *Eusebius*: And therefore we may conclude, that anciently it was not there, but the Text of *Eusebius* (by fraud or folly) is since corrupted: For had it been in *Eusebius* when *Ruffin* Translated him, there had been no reason he should have left it out. 3. And which is yet more considerable, *Valesius* (a very Learned Roman Catholick) who last published *Eusebius*, Ingenuously confesses, that of three or four Greek MSS. of *Eusebius*, which he made use of in his Edition, not any one of them (l) *had that Commendation of* Papias; *and therefore he doubts not, but these words were* (m) *added by some ignorant Scholiast, contrary to the Judgment and Sense of* Eusebius. For (says (*n*) he) *how is it possible that* Eusebius *should call* Papias *a most Learned Man, and most skill'd in Scripture, who in the same* (o) *Book says, he was A Rude and Simple Person, of ditum, Planéque Rudem ac Simplicem.* Valesiu; ibidem.

(h) *Papias* was a friend and familiar of St. *Polycarpe*. Euseb. Hist. l. 3. c. 39 and *Polycarpe* suffered Martyrdom Ann. Christ. 167; Baron. Annot. ad Martyrolog. Rom. ad diem Jan. 26. p. 81. Col. 1.

Answ.

(i) *Quibus Temporibus floruit Polycarpus Smyrnæorum Episcopus, & Papias similiter apud Hierapolim Sacerdotium gerens.* Ruffin. l. 3. c. 35. in Excuso Rhenarci. Basil. 1528.

(k) In Cod. MS. Ruffini est. l. 3. c 32.

(l) *Totum hoc Elogium Papiæ deest in nostris Codicibus,* Valesius in Not. ad l. 3. Euseb. c. 36. p. 55.

(m) *Non dubito, quin hæc verba ab Imperito Scholiaste adjecta sunt, præter Eusebij mentem & Sententiam.* Valesius Ibidem.

(n) *Quomodo fieri potest ut Eusebius Papiam hic appellet virum doctissimum, & scripturarum peritissimum, cum in fine Libri affirmat disertè, Papiam Mediocri ingenio præ-* (o) Euseb. l. 3 c. 39.

Very Little Wit or Judgment. And his Ignorance especially appears (as in other things) in that

1. He says *that* Philip, *whose Daughters were Prophetesses, was* Philip *the*(p) *Apostle*; when the(q) Text,(had he read or remembred it) expresly says, *That it was* Philip *the Deacon.*

2. *Papias* said, (and in his Writings publiſhed his Opinion) *That hearing* (r) *Oral Traditions, was more profitable, then reading Scriptures*). That is, to hear the Stories and Tales of private and fallible Perſons (and that in Matters of Religion) was more profitable, then to read the Sacred Oracles of God, penn'd by Divinely Inſpired Infallible Perſons. St. (ſ) *John* tells us, he had writ ſo many and ſuch things, as were neceſſary and ſufficient to Salvation, yet left out thousands of things, which he thought not neceſſary. But *Papias* (with great Ignorance and Impiety) preferrs the unwritten Tradition of thoſe things concerning our B. Saviour, which the Apoſtles had omitted, as not neceſſary, nor ſo uſeful as thoſe things they had writ. And ſo in Contradiction to the Holy Spirit and St. *John* (his Infallible *Amanuenſis*) calls the Tradition of thoſe unwritten things more uſeful, which they had omitted as not uſeful at all. And this his Ignorance and want of Judgment further appears,

3. Becauſe *Eusebius* tells us, *That he had* (amongſt his Traditions) (t) *ſtrange and novel Parables and Doctrines of our bleſſed Saviour, and other things more Fabulous*; and amongſt them his *Millenary Hereſie*, of which he was Father, and (to the Infecting many others) did propagate it: And he fell to thoſe wild Opinions chiefly by his Ignorance and Miſunderſtanding of Scripture; as *Euſebius* and *Nicephorus* tell us. And yet this ſimple Perſon, and Arch-Heretick, is the principal and prime Witneſs *Rome* has, to prove that *Babylon* (in the Epiſtle of *Peter*) ſignifies *Rome*, and that *Peter* was there. For other place in Scripture, they have none, and only *Papias* (and his Followers) for that. By the Premiſſes, I think it may appear to Impartial Perſons, That ſeeing *Papias* preferr'd Tradition (or ſome mens talk before the

---

(p) Euſeb. Hiſt. l. 3. c. 39. p 112. Valeſii Edit. vide Nicephor. l. 3. c. 20.

(q) Act. 21. 8. Vid. Nicephor. Hiſt. lib. 3. pag. 252. C.

(r) Vid. Euſeb. Hiſt. l. 3 c. 39. Hieronym. de Illuſt. D. & c. 18. Nicephor. l 3. c. 20.

(ſ) Joh. 20. 30. 31. & 21. 25.

(t) Ξἐνας τινας, &c. *Novas quaſdam Servatoris parabolas ac prædicationes.*

the Scriptures) that he was a man of very weak *understanding*, and err'd by misunderstanding Scripture, that he writ Fables rather than History, and maintain'd the *Millenary Opinion*, which *Rome* now calls *Heresie*: I say, these things consider'd, his authority and credit is, (if any at all) very little; and yet 'tis all our Adversaries have (his Followers Testimonies being derived from, and depending upon his) to prove out of Scripture, that *Peter* writ that Epistle at *Rome*, or ever was there. This is a Truth so manifest, that not only (*u*) *Protestants*, but most Learned *Roman* (x) *Catholicks*, say and prove, that *Peter* writ that Epistle, not at *Rome*, but *Babylon* in *Chaldea*. And further; that he did not write it at *Rome*, will be evident from Scripture, and what their own most Learned Author confesses. For, 1. (*y*) *Baronius* tells us, *It was writ*, Anno *Christi* 45. 2. To make this probable, both he, *Petavius*, and others, generally say; *That* Peter *went to* Rome *in the second year of* Claudius; which was Anno *Christi* 44. 3. But this a very Learned *Roman Catholick* evidently (*z*) confutes from Scripture, and good Authorities; and plainly shews, that *Peter* was always in *Judea* or *Syria*, till the death of *Herod Agrippa*, which was in the fourth year of *Claudius*, and the Six and fortieth year of our blessed Saviour. And therefore it was impossible that *Peter* should write that Epistle at *Rome*, in the Five and fortieth year of our blessed Saviour, who never came thither till the year Forty six, unless they will say (and they do say things as impossible) that he writ an Epistle at *Rome* when he was not there. 4. Nay, 'tis certain from what *Luke* says in the (*a*) *Acts of the Apostles*, that *Peter* continued in *Judea* till the Council met at *Jerusalem* about the Question concerning Circumcision, and the Ceremonial Law. Sure it is, that he was present at that Council; which was *Anno Christi* 51. says (*b*)

(*u*) Scaliger in Annotat. in Joh. 18. 31. Petrus Romæ nunquam fuit: sed prædicabat τὸ διαρτω ἃ Asiæ Cujus Mitropolis erat Babylon, ex quâ scribit Epistolam suam. Vid. Johan. Rainoldum contra Hartum, &c.

(x) Tametsi Veteris Existimaverint Petrum vocabulo Babylonis significasse urbem Romam, probabilis est Scaligeri Conjecturas qui ex ipsa Babylone scriptam à Petro putat Epistolam hanc ad Judæos dispersos, &c. Petrus de Marca Archiepiscopu: Parisiensis. De Concordia Sacerd. & Imperij l 6. c. 1. § 4. p. 59. Tom. 2.

(*y*) Baronius Annal Tom. 1. ad Ann. Christ. 45. §. 16, 17.

(*z*) Hæc Sententia refelli videtur ex Actis Apostolorum, ex quibus constat Petrum, in Judæa ac Syriâ semper mansisse, usque ad ultimum Annum Agrippæ, &c. Hen. Valesius in Notis ad cap. 16. l. 2. Hist. Eccles. Euseb. p. 33, 34. (*a*) Act. 15 &c. (*b*) Baronius Annal. Tom. 1. ad Ann. 51. §. 6.

Baronius,

Baronius, Bellarmine, and others; the Learned (c) Valesius thinks (and gives his reason for it, (more probable to me, then any brought for the contrary Opinions) that the Council was held, *Anno Claudij* 7. and *Christi* 49. take which Computation you please, if St. *Peter* wrote that Epistle at *Rome*, *Anno Christi* 45. he must have writ there, several years before he came thither. 5. Nay, 'tis further Evident, (let that Council be when they will) that *Peter* was not at *Rome*, in the year 51. which *Baronius* mentions, but at *Jerusalem*. For St. (d) *Paul* tells us, that three years after his Conversion, (which was about the year 37.) he went to *Jerusalem* to see *Peter*, and found him there: And then (e) fourteen years after, (which was about the year 51.) he went to *Jerusalem* again, and then found *Peter* there. According to our Adversaries Computation, in the year 51. *Peter* had sate Bishop in *Rome* about (f) eight years; and yet St. *Paul* neither found, nor sought him at *Rome* (where he was not) but at *Jerusalem*, where he was, with the Jews, who were committed to his Charge and Cure. 6. Lastly, 'Tis evident, St. *Peter* writ that first Epistle to the *Asiatick* (g) *Dispersion of the Jews*, of which *Babylon* was the Metropolis: And sure it is, that when he says, *The Church of* Babylon *salutes you*; he intended (as all men do, who write Epistles of that Nature) that they should know where he was, and who they were who saluted them; which was impossible for them to do, if by *Babylon* he meant *Rome*. For at that time, *Rome* neither was, nor could be known to any by the name of *Babylon*; no Author (Sacred or Civil) having ever call'd it so. 'Tis true, St. *John* above (h) Fifty years after, calls *Rome*, *Babylon*. But he writing Mysterious Propheties, spoke (to use *Eusebius*'s word) Τροπικώτερον, used many Types, Figures and Metaphors, to express future things. But that *Peter*, who writ no such Mysterious Prophetical Predictions, but the plain Duties, and Promises of the Gospel, should use such Types or Figures, has neither truth nor any probability. By the

Premisses,

(c) *In Chronico Alexandrino Concilium Hierosolymitanum refertur Anno Claudij* 6. (*Christi* 48.) *melius dixissit.* 7. *Sic enim cuncta egregiè conveniunt, &c.* Hen. Valesius in Notis ad cap. 18. l. 2 Hist. Eccles. Euseb p. 37. Col. 2. A.

(d) Gal. 1. 18.

(e) Gal. 2. 1. 8. 9.

(f) They say, he sate at *Rome* 25. years, and that he was martyr'd *Neronis* 13. or *Anno Christi* 68. so that those 25. years must begin *Anno Christi* 43. And then *Anno Christi* 51. he had sate at *Rome* eight years.

(g) 1 Pet. 1. 1.

(h) The first Epistle of *Peter* was writ *Anno Christi* 45. So Baronius Annal. Tom. 1. ad Ann. 45. § 16. And the same Baronius Annal. Tom. 1. ad Annum Christi 97. § 1. tells us, that the Revelation of St. *John* was writ *Anno Christi* 97. that is, 52. years after.

Premisses, I hope it may appear, that it cannot be proved out of Scripture, that ever *Peter* was at *Rome*.

4. But let it be granted, that it could be proved out of Scripture (which is manifestly untrue) that *Peter* was at *Rome*, yet thence it will not follow that ever he was Bishop there: much less for Five and twenty years, as is vainly pretended. For, 1. That he was Bishop of *Rome* (or any place else) there is not one syllable in Scripture; and so from thence there can be no proof of his *Roman Bishoprick*. And, 2. If it be granted (which is evidently untrue) that it could (out of Scripture) be clearly proved, that he was at *Rome* a longer time, yet hence it does not follow that he was Bishop there: For he was at *Jerusalem, Samaria, Joppa, &c.* (as is evident in Scripture) and yet our Adversaries neither do, nor (with any sense or reason) can say, that he was Bishop of all those places. 3. *Irenæus* (an ancient and an approved Author) expresly says, (i) *That* Peter *and* Paul *constituted* Linus *first Bishop of* Rome; *That* Anacletus *succeeded him, and that* Clemens *(after the Apostles) was the third Bishop there.* After him, *Eusebius* says the same thing; *That after the* (k) *Martyrdom of* Paul *and* Peter, Linus *was the first Bishop of* Rome. And again, speaking of the Bishops of *Rome*, he says, *That* (l) Linus *was the first, and* Anencletus (or *Anacletus,* as he is usually call'd) *the second.* And though *Eusebius* say, *That* Linus *was* (m) *Primus post Petrum, the first Bishop of* Rome *after* Peter; yet his meaning is not, that *Peter* was Bishop of *Rome* before him, as is evident by what he says afterwards; *That* Clemens (n) *was the third Bishop of* Rome, *after the Apostles* Paul *and* Peter; and by what *Irenæus* said before him, *That* Clemens *was the third Bishop of* Rome *after the Apostles.* For if this be good consequence —— Linus *was first Bishop of* Rome *after* Peter; Ergo, *Peter was Bishop of* Rome *too.* Then this (in *Irenæus* and *Eusebius,* who both say it) will be good Consequence also; Clemens *was third Bishop of* Rome *after* Paul *and* Peter; Ergo, Paul *and* Peter *were both Bishops of* Rome. The truth

(i) *Petrus & Paulus fundantes Ecclesiam Romanam, Lino Episcopatum tradiderunt. Succedit ei Anacletus, post eum Tertio loco ab Apostolis Clemens.* Irenæus l. 3. c. 3.

(k) Τῆς δὲ Ῥωμαίων, &c. *Post Pauli Petrique Martyrium, primus Ecclesiæ Romanæ. Episcopatum suscepit Linus.* Euseb.Hist.l.3. c.2. vide Niceph. l. 3. cap. etiam 2.

(l) ΛῖνΘ δὲ ὁ Πρῶτθ, *Primus fuit* Linus, *secundus* Anencletus. Euseb. ibid. l. 3.

(m) Euseb.ibid. l. 3. c. 4. πρῶτΘ μετὰ Πέτρον.

(n) Clemens,μετὰ Παῦλον κ᾿ Πέτρον. *Tertius à* Paulo *& Petro Romæ Episcopus.* Euseb. loco dicto,c.21. vide Epiphanium adversus Hæreses.l. 1. Hæres. 27. Carpocratianorum §.5. p.107.

truth is, that neither Consequence is good. *Irenæus* and *Eusebius* did indeed believe *Paul* and *Peter* Founders of the *Roman Church*, but neither of them to be Bishops there; which a Learned *Roman Catholick* evidently saw, and publickly (o) acknowledges. By the way, let me observe; That *Eusebius* in two places here (p) cited, puts *Paul* before *Peter*: and not only *Eusebius*, (a fallible Author) but St. *Paul* himself puts *James* before (q) *Peter*. Now if *Eusebius* or St. *Paul* had known and believ'd St. *Peter* to have been (what the Pope and his Party, without any ground vainly imagine) the *Supream Monarch over the whole Church and the Apostles themselves*; it had been a great Affront and Injury to St. *Peter*, and such an Incivility as St. *Paul* would not have been guilty of. 4. And 'tis yet more considerable, what St. *Paul* says (r) in the place last cited; for there we have these things certain in the Text, 1. That *Peter* was the Apostle of the Circumcision; the Jews were committed to him, as his (s) Charge and Cure, as the *Gentiles* to *Paul*. 2. It was our blessed Saviour who (t) Commission'd both of them, and appointed them those Provinces; for none else could. He only could assign them their Provinces, who gave them the Apostolical Power to govern them. *Peter* (as our Adversaries say) was *Supream Monarch of the whole Church*, had no Superior but our blessed Saviour, and so none else to Commission him, or Appoint him his Province. 3. Both of them till that time, had diligently, and (with great Success) effectually labour'd in their (u) *several Provinces*; *Peter* amongst the *Jews*, *Paul* amongst the *Gentiles*. 4. By a mutual Agreement, they (x) consent and promise, *That* Peter (as he had (y) before, so) for (z) the future, He should go to the Jews, and make them his Charge and Cure, and Paul to the Gentiles. 5. And this Agreement was about the

(o) *Sciendum est Eusebium Apostolos In ordine Episcoporum minime Numerare.* Hen. Valesius in Annotat. ad Hist: Eccles. Euseb. l. 3. c. 21. & Notarum. p. 50. Col. 2. B.

(p) Lib. 3. Cap. 2. & Cap. 21.
(q) Gal. 2. 9.
(r) Gal. 2. 1. 7. 8. 9.

(s) Gal. 2. 7.
(t) *Unus & idem mihi Evangelium præputij, & Petro Circumcisionis credidit; me misit ad Gentes, illum posuit in Judæa.* Hieronymus in Cap. 2. ad Galatas. d.
(u) Vers. 8.
(x) Vers. 9.
(y) As is evident in the Acts of the Apostles, and by his first Epistle writ (as *Baronius* says) Ann. 45. Christi. Annal. Tom. 1. ad Ann. 45. Num. 16. vid. Euseb. Hist. l. 3. c. 1. where he says, that *Peter* preach'd the Gospel long to the *Asiatick* Dispersion of the Jews, before he came to *Rome*; and *Nicephorus* says so too. (z) And 'tis certain, that after the year 51. (of which we now speak) he took the Jews for his Charge and Cure; as is evident from his two Epistles writ to them, Ann. 68. And the Confession of *Baronius*, Annal. Tom. 1. ad Ann. 68. Num. 3.

year

year of our Lord 51. when (according to our Adversaries Computation) he was, and had been Bishop of *Rome* Eight or Nine years. 6. I desire then to know, Whether *Peter* (after this consent and agreement of the Apostles) continued Bishop of the *Gentiles* at *Rome*, (as our Adversaries pretend he did) or not? If he did, he contradicted his Commission, which our blessed Saviour had given him, to be the Apostle of the Circumcision, and neglected the *Jews*, whom he had (*a*) *Concredited* to his care, and *Committed to him*, as his proper Charge. For to take the charge of the *Gentiles* and *Jews* too, was not only against his Commission, but against that Solemn Consent and Agreement of the Apostles beforemention'd, wherein it was agreed and promised, That *Peter* should go (not to *Rome*) but to the Circumcision, and *Paul* to the *Gentiles*. Nor can it be credible that *Peter* would act in contradiction to his Commission, and his Agreement so solemnly made with the Apostles. But if at the time of that Agreement, (which was *Anno Christi* 51.) he either was not, (which is most true) Bishop of *Rome*, or then left it; then it evidently follows, That he continued not Bishop of *Rome* for Five and twenty years, as is by our Adversaries, (with great confidence and no reason) asserted. 7. And this is further manifest, from our Adversaries own Principles and Positions: *Baronius* tells us, *That* Peter *was* (*b*) *Bishop of* Antioch *seven years*; *and at* Rome *five and twenty years:* And for this he cites *Eusebius* his *Chronicon*. By the way, (concerning what *Baronius* says of *Peter's* being Bishop for so many years at *Antioch* and *Rome*) Observe, 1. That *Eusebius* says indeed, *that* Peter (*c*) *founded the Church of* Antioch; *and then*, *by our blessed Saviour's Command*, (as they say) *went to* Rome. But so far is he from saying that he was seven years Bishop there, that he expresly says, That *Euodius* was the first (*d*) Bishop of *Antioch*. 2. When he cites *Eusebius* his (*e*) *mus erat Euodius.* Idem in Chronico, ad Annum Claudij 2. Ann. 39. §. 9.

(*a*) Gal. 2. 7. πεπίστευμαι, &c. *Petro Concreditum est Evangelium præputij.*

(*b*) *Quod spectat ad Ecclesiam Antiochenam, hoc Anno* (Christi 39.) *Institutam à Petro, & septem Annis ab todem administratam, &c.* Baronius Annal. Tom. 1. ad Annum Christ. 39. §. 9.

(*c*) *Petrus Ecclesiam Antiochenam fundans, inde Romam adiit.* Euseb. in Chron. ad Ann. Claud. 1. And they say he went to *Rome*, *Our blessed Saviour commanding him so to do. Cum* 7. *Annos Antiochiæ sedisset, postea jubente Christo Romam venit.* Longus A Coriolano in summâ Conc. in Principio, in serie Pontificum.

(*d*) Τῆς Ἀντιοχείων Ἐκκλησίας, &c. *Antiochenæ Ecclesiæ Episcopus pri-*

(*e*) Baronius ibidem, ad

(f) All that *Eusebius* says is only this —— Πέτρος ὁ κορυφαῖος τῶν ἐν Ἀντιοχείᾳ πρώτην θεμελιώσας Ἐκκλησίαν εἰς Ῥώμην ἄπεισι κηρύτ]εσν εὐαγγέλιον. Ad Ann. Claudij 1.

(g) The words *Baronius* cites, as being *Eusebius* his words Ad Annum 2. Claudij, are indeed (part of them) Ad Annum 1. Claudij: but the rest (*Peter's* being five and twenty years *Bishop of* Rome) are neither at that, nor any other year of *Claudius*.

(h) Baronius Annal. Tom. 1. ad Annum Christi, 34. §. 1. & 2.

(i) Idem T. m. 1. ad Annum Christi 69 §. 9.

Chronicon to prove that *Peter* was Five and twenty years Bishop of *Rome*, and refers us, to what *Eusebius* (*f*) says) ad Ann. 2. *Claudij*. The man (who understood no Greek) is miserably mistaken; as Universally he is, when he meddles with Greek Authors, unless their Translations be true) for *Eusebius* in his Greek Text, (as all know, and may see) has no such (*g*) thing, as Five and twenty years; nay, he does not so much as say, *that he was Bishop of* Rome *at all*; much less that he was Five and twenty years Bishop there. But the Latin Copies (interpolated and corrupted, as thousands others are by Roman Arts) deceived him. But to let this pass; *Baronius* says, *That* Peter *was seven years Bishop of* Antioch, *and five and twenty of* Rome. So that (in the whole) he was Two and thirty years Bishop in *Syria* and *Italy*, and took upon him the Charge and Cure of the *Gentiles* in those Provinces. Now our blessed Saviour's Passion and Ascension was (*h*) *Anno Christi* 34. to which if 32. be added (the time wherein *Peter* was Bishop of *Antioch*, or *Rome*) the Product will be 66. So that from the Ascension of our blessed Saviour till the year 66. *Peter* had taken the Episcopacy and particular Charge of a *Gentile-Church*; and his (*i*) Martyrdom was 13. *Neronis*, that is, *Anno Christi* 68. or (as *Baronius* computes) 69. whence (by this their Account) it evidently follows, that during all the time from our blessed Saviour's Ascension to his Martyrdom (about two years only excepted) *Peter* was the Apostle and Bishop of a *Gentile-Church*. Which is, 1. manifestly untrue, and inconsistent with what is said of *Peter* in the *Acts of the Apostles*, with his Commission, in which the care of the Circumcision was concredited to him by our blessed Saviour, and with his Solemn Agreement with the Apostles to go to the *Circumcision*, as *Paul* was to the *Gentiles*. And, 2. It is without any the least ground in Scripture, by which, it neither does, nor can appear that ever *Peter* was at *Rome*, so much as for one Day, much less that he was Bishop there Five & twenty years. Nor can it appear in Scripture,

ture, that ever he was at *Antioch*, save (*k*) once; nor is there any mention of any thing he then did there; save that he diffembled, and was juftly reprehended for it, by St. *Paul*; whereas it is evident in Scripture, that St. *Paul* was at *Antioch* for a whole (*l*) year at one time, conftituted the Church there, *confirmed them* (*m*) *afterwards in the Faith*, and (*n*) ordain'd Elders to govern them, ftay'd there a (*o*) *long time*; and (*p*) *continued there preaching the Gofpel*; and yet (notwithftanding all this) if we will believe them; *Peter* was Bifhop there, and not *Paul*. The truth is; though it be evident that *Paul*, as Apoftle, did all Epifcopal Acts there; yet 'tis certain, that neither he nor *Peter*, was particularly Bifhop of that, or any other place. 3. It is utterly incredible, that *Peter* the Supream Head and Monarch of the Church (as they pretend) fhould for Two and thirty years be Bifhop, and have the particular Charge and Cure of two of the greateft Cities in the *Roman Empire*, and that while the Apoftles liv'd; and yet none of them (nor he himfelf) in any of their Writings, fhould fay one Syllable of it, nor mention fo much as one fingle Epifcopal Act done by him, in either of thofe Cities, in thofe two and thirty years; no nor St. (*p*) Luke *in the Acts of the Apoftles*, nor St. *Paul*, who liv'd long in *Antioch*, and longer in *Rome*, and had opportunity, nay (had it been true) a neceffity to mention it. He had need of a ftrong Faith, who can believe this; for my part, *Credat Judæus Apella*, &c. 4. And as for *Peter's* being Seven years Bifhop of *Antioch*, and Twenty five of *Rome*; it is further Confiderable, *That the greateft Patrons of this Popifh Pofition*, although the Acts of the Apoftles. Nay they fpeak irreverently of him, and fay, and many other things out of his Hiftory, by a Liberty or *Licence* he took to himfelf. *Hanc cum tacuit Lucas, & alia Multa Hiftoriographi Licentiâ Prætermifit. Primum Epifcopum Antiochæ Petrum fuiffe Accepimus* (fays *Hierome* there) *quod Lucas penitus Omifit*. But *Hierome* (though an excellent Perfon) had his Paffions and Errors, and in that very place, indeavours to juftifie *Peter*, as not to be blam'd, againft the exprefs words of St. Paul, Gal. 1. 11. *Luke* writ by the direction of the Holy Ghoft, and if he writ not all that *Hierome* or *Baronius* would have him, yet they fhould not Cenfure him. Vide Baronium ad Annum Chrifti, 39. §. 8.

(*k*) Gal. 2. 11, 12, 13. &c.

(*l*) Act. 11. 25.
(*m*) Act. 14. 22.
(*n*) Act. 14. 23.
(*o*) Act 14. 26. 28
(*p*) Act. 15. 35.
vid. Act. 18. 22, 23.

(*p*) I confefs *Baronius*, and *Hierom* (whom he cites, Commentariorum in Epift. ad Gal. lib. 1. cap. 2.) tells us, That *Peter* was Bifhop of *Antioch*; & are not well pleas'd that *Luke* left it out of his Hiftory in That he left that,

though

though they agree in the Conclusion, that Peter *was so long Bishop at those two places; yet they Contradict each other, and the Truth; and by their own Positions,* (*to save their Adversaries that Labour*) *utterly Overthrow and Confute that Position they endeavour to prove.* This Evidently appears in this Case, as it is stated by *Onuphrius*, *Baronius*, and *Bellarmine*.

1. (*q*) *Onuphrius* tells us, *That* Peter *remain'd constantly in* Judea, *for Nine* (*r*) *years next after our blessed Saviour's death, that is till the year of Christ* 43. *after this, he was Bishop of* Antioch *Seven years; to the year of our blessed Saviour* 50. *And then Five and twenty years he sat Bishop of* Rome; *that is,* (by his own Computation) *till the year of Christ,* 75. So that by this Account, *Peter* was Bishop of *Rome, Anno Christi* 75. And yet he there says, *That* Peter (*s*) *died, Anno Christi* 69. And then (by his Calculation) *Peter* was Bishop of *Rome* Six years after his death.

2. *Baronius* (*t*) states the Question thus. Peter *came to* Antioch *Anno Christi* 39. *and was Bishop there* (*u*) *Seven years*, that is, till the year of Christ 46. And then he says, *that from* Antioch *Peter went to* Rome, *and sat there Bishop* (*x*) *Five and twenty years*; that is, till the year 71. And so (by his own account) *Peter* must be Bishop of *Rome* two years after he was dead: For the same *Baronius* tells (*y*) us, *that* Peter *died Anno Christi,* 69. And though this Account of *Peter's* Episcopacy at *Rome*, be not only Erroneous, (but to all Intelligent Persons) Ridiculous; yet (*z.*) *Bellarmine* maintains the same Opinion, not only in Contradiction to *Onuphrius*, but to *Eusebius*, *Hierome*, *Epiphanius*, &c. (*a*) whose Opinions *Baronius* endeavours to confute. In short, as there is no ground in Scripture, that *Peter* ever was at *Rome*; so that he was Twenty five years Bishop there, neither Scripture

(*q*) Onuph. Panvin. in Annotat. ad Plat. in vitis Pont. ad vitam Petri.

(*r*) *Ex his 9. primis Annis, usq; ad Initium An. 2. Imper. Claudij, Petrum Judæa nunquam exessisse, ex quo & Paulo, apertissimè Constat.* Idem. Ibidem.

(*s*) *Petrus Cruci Affixus est, novissimo Neronis Anno, Christi verò 69.* Ibidem.

(*t*) Baronius Annal. Tom. 1. ad An. 39. §. 8, 9, &c.

(*u*) Baronius Ibidem. §. 13.

(*x*) Baronius Ibidem. §. 9. An. 39.

(*y*) Ann. Christ. 69. Capitone & Rufo Coss. Petrus & Paulus Martyrium subiere. Annal. Tom. 1. an Annum 69. §. 1. Neronis 13.

(*z*) Vide Bellar. de Script. Eccles. In Petro Apostolo; & Chronol. suæ Part. 2. ad Annum 39, & 44.   (*a*) Vide Baronium Annal. Tom. 1. ad Ann. 69. §. 2.

nor purer Antiquity affords them any proof, or probability: *Eusebius* his *Greek Chronicon*, basely (*b*) corrupted in a *Latin Version* of it, about Four hundred years after our blessed Saviour, being that they must rely upon.

(*b*) Vide Jos. Scaligeri Animadverf. in Chronologica Eusebij; Amstelod. 1658. p. 189.

5. Our Adversaries had ill luck, when they made *Peter* first Bishop of *Rome*, attributed the Supremacy to him, and (that he might have it) made the Pope his Successor. For had they chosen *Paul* in stead of *Peter*, they might have had far more (though not enough) to prove (and that out of express Scripture) both *Paul's* Supremacy, and the Popes Succession to him. For these following Particulars (every one of them) may evidently be proved out of Scripture. 1. That the *Romans* were (*c*) *Gentiles*. 2. That *Paul* (by our blessed Saviour's (*d*) Appointment) was the Apostle of the *Gentiles*, *Peter* was not, but of the (*e*) *Jews*. 3. *Paul* was two whole (*f*) years at *Rome*, Converted, and Established a Church there; but it cannot appear by Scripture, that *Peter* was ever there. 4. The Care (πασῶν Ἐκκλησιῶν) (*g*) of all *the Churches lay upon St. Paul*; no such thing in Scripture ever said of *Peter*. 5. St. *Paul* made *Orders and Constitutions* for the good Government of (*h*) *All the Churches* (without any Authority, Leave, or Commission from *Peter*) no such thing ever said of *Peter*, either in Scripture, or primitive and pure Antiquity. 6. St. *Paul* writ a Long and Excellent Epistle to the *Romans*, *Peter* did no such thing. Had the Holy Ghost in Scripture expressly told us, 1. That our *blessed Saviour had Appointed*, and Commission'd *Peter* to be *the Apostle of the Gentiles* (and such were the *Romans*), 2. *That he was two whole years residing at* Rome, *Converting and Establishing a Church there*. 3. *That the Care and Cure of All the Churches lay upon him*. 4. *That he made Orders and Constitutions for the Government of All The Churches*. 5. *That he had writ an Epistle to the* Romans, *to Confirm them in that Faith he had preach'd amongst them*: I say, had all these things been in Scripture expresly said of *Peter*, our Adversaries

(*c*) Rom. 1. 13.
(*d*) Act. 22. 21. Gal. 27. 8.
(*e*) Ibidem.
(*f*) Act. 28. 30, 31.

(*g*) 2 Cor. 11. 28. 1 Cor. 7. 17.

(*h*) Οὕτως ἐν ταῖς Ἐκκλησίαις πάσαις διατάσσομαι (hinc διάταγμα, & διάταγη, Edictum, Constitutio) So I ordain in all Churches. Versio vulg. frigidè ―― In Ecclesiis Omnibus doceo. 1 Cor. 7. 17. vide Act. 18. 2.

with great noise and confidence would (and with far more reason and probability might) have asserted *Peter*'s Supremacy, and his Roman Episcopacy, and that the Pope was, and is his Successor. But seeing not one of all these is said of *Peter*, and every one of them expresly said of *Paul*, it is Evident, that there is far more reason and probability (and that grounded upon express Scripture) that *Paul* was Bishop of *Rome* (and not *Peter*) and so the Pope might be his Successor. And yet our Adversaries (*i*) reject *Paul*, and will have *Peter* their first Bishop (though some of them impiously say, our (*k*) blessed *Saviour* was their *first Bishop*) That St. *Paul* was not Bishop of *Rome* (notwithstanding all the former things said of him, in Scripture) we believe and know, and willingly grant. But on the other side, to say, *that* Peter *was Bishop of* Rome, concerning whom no such things are said in Scripture, either in express terms, (as they are of *Paul*) or by Equivalence or any just Consequence; this we say, is very irrational. For in things Moral or Historical (and of such we are now speaking) which are Incapable of Physical or Mathematical Demonstration, the highest prudential Motives and Probabilities will, and ought to carry the Assent of all wise men: and therefore seeing it is deny'd (and justly too) that Paul *was ever Bishop of* Rome, though the Probabilities, grounded on Scripture, that he was so, be far greater than *Peter* can pretend to; for our Adversaries to say, *that* Peter *was Bishop of* Rome, must be, and is, evidently irrational. If the great probabilities we have that *Paul* was Bishop of *Rome* deserve not our Assent, certainly we cannot rationally conclude from far less probabilities that *Peter* was so.

(*i*) I confess *Bellarmine* would (out of *Irenæus* as he vainly thinks) persuade us, that both *Peter* & *Paul* were Bishops of *Rome*. *Irenæus* (says he) lib. 3. cap. 3. *fixit Catalogum Romanorum Episcoporum, & primo loco ponit Petrum & Paulum.* De Rom. Pontif. lib. 2. cap. 4. § 6. Irenæus.

(*k*) *Series & Successio Rom. Pontif. sic est: Primus Jesus Christus.* Longus à Coriol. sum. ma Concil. in Prin. in Serie Rom. Pontif. We have the very same words in the Edition of *Platina*, De viris Pont. Col. Agripp. 1626. But *Platina* (basely corrupted since his death) has no such thing in the Old Edition, 1485. But to make our blessed Saviour the first Bishop of *Rome*, is not only erroneous, but impious. 1. He never was at *Rome*. 2. *He was not sent, save to the lost Sheep of the House of Israel*, (not in Person sure, not to be a Bishop of any *Gentile* Church). 3. There was no Christian Church at *Rome* while he liv'd of which he could be Bishop. 4. Our blessed Saviour remains a Priest for ever, and cannot have any Successor: Heb. 5. 6. And therefore *Bellarm.* justly denies our blessed Saviour to have any Successor, because he is *Pontifex æternus.* Bellar. de Script. Eccles. in T. Aquin.

But

Object.

But when they would magnifie the Pope's Power and Supremacy, (having no better Arguments) they make use of several Honorary Titles given to the Bishop of *Rome*, and his See, and of some Priviledges which they take (or mistake rather) to be peculiar to the Popes, such as these. 1. The Bishop of *Rome* in many Stories and Canons, is called (*l*) *Apostolicus*. 2. His See is call'd *Sedes Apostolica*, and *Cathedra Apostolica*. 3. He is call'd *Successor Petri*. 4. *Vicar of Christ*. 5. That our blessed Saviour gave him the *Keys of the Kingdom of Heaven*, &c.

(*l*) *Apostolicus non nisi à Cardinalibus inthronizandus.* Gratian. Dist. 79. Part. 1. & Ibidem. Can. 1. *Widem* 6. Dist. 4. in Lemmate.

tèr inthronizatus non est Papa vel Apostolicus, sed Apostaticus. &, Can. si Papa mate. *Damnatur Apostolicus, suæ & fraternæ salutis negligens.*

Answer.

I confess that these, and many such (*m*) Particulars have been urged, and (as pertinent) stood upon by several Popes in their Bulls, their Decretal Constitutions and Epistles, and generally by all their Party; especially the Clergy (Secular and Regular) whose great and principal Interest it is, to maintain the Papal Supremacy : for if that fail, they irrecoverably fall with it. In some Centuries past, while gross Ignorance and Tyranny, benighted and overaw'd this Western Part of the World, such Arguments did their Business; For few could, and (the danger being very great) few, or none, durst Answer them. But after *Luther* arose, and Learning reviv'd, all knowing and impartial Persons did see and know, that all the Arguments they did (or could) bring from such Topicks, were not only Inconsequent, but indeed impertinent and ridiculous. That this may not be *gratis dictum*, I shall indeavour to make it appear by plain Instances, (and I hope effect it) that none of those Honorary Titles or Priviledges do, or can afford any just ground of that Supremacy, and Papal Monarchy, they now so earnestly contend for; And here

(*m*) *Bellarmine* gives us a Catalogue of fifteen such Papal Titles; which are these ——— *Papa, Pater Patrum, Christianorum Pontifex, summus Sacerdos, Princeps Sacerdotum, Vicarius Christi, Caput Ecclesiæ, Fundamentum Ecclesiæ, Pastor Ovilis Domini, Pater & Doctor Omnium Fidelium, Rector Domus Dei, Custos vineæ Dei, Sponsus Ecclesiæ Dei, Apostolicæ Sedis Præsul, Episcopus universalis, ex quibus Omnibus & Singulis Apertè Colligitur Ejus Primatus.* De Romano Pont. lib. 2. cap. 31.

1. It is to be observed, that the word *Apostolicus*, which (for some Ages last past) the Pope has Assumed, and
his

his Flatterers given him, as peculiar to himself, was Anciently a Title given to all Archbishops. So (*n*) *Alcuinus Flaccus* tells us, *That when a Bishop was Elected, they sent him,* ad Apostolicum, *that he might Consecrate him.* The Learned Archbishop (*o*) of *Paris*, tells me this; and also that this was the use of that word in the Sixth Century, in the time of *Gregorius Turonensis*, who was made Bishop about the year 572. but afterwards, That Title was (*p*) appropriated to the Pope. Now I desire to know of our Adversaries, how The Title, being Appropriated to the Pope, does make more for his Supremacy, than it did for the Archbishops, when it was common to them all?

(*n*) *Cum Episcopus Civitatis fuerit demortuus, Eligitur alius, & veniunt ad Apostolicum cum Electo, ut eis Consecret Episcopum.* Alcuinus de Divinis Officiis cap. 36.
(*o*) Petrus de Marca de Concordiâ Sacerdotij & Imperij. Tom. 2. lib. 6. cap. 3. §. 3. p. 67.
(*p*) *Sequens ætas abstinuit———— & deinceps Apostolici Titulus Soli Summo Pontifici attributus est ab Authoribus.* Idem Ibidem.

2. That *Rome* was *Sedes Apostolica*, and *Cathedra Apostolica*, we grant. Because we are sure St. *Paul* (though not as Bishop) *sate there*. But that *Peter* ever was there, neither we nor our Adversaries are, or can be sure. But it is, and (by our Adversaries) must be granted too; That *Jerusalem, Antioch,* and *other* (*q*) *Churches* (besides *Rome*) were *Sedes Apostolica*, and *Ecclesiæ Apostolicæ*, and *eo Nomine*, were of great esteem in the *Ancient Church*. But the Bishops of none of them then did, or could pretend to any Supremacy, much less to an Ecclesiastical Monarchy: And why *Rome* should more than they, when our Adversaries can, and will give (which as yet they never did) any Just and Cogent Reason, I shall submit. (*r*) *Tertullian* also reckons the *Apostoli-*

(*q*) The Archbishop of *Paris* next before cited, amongst the Apostolical Churches (besides those I have named) reckons *Alexandria, Ephesus, Ancyra, Corinth, Thessalonica*, and he might have added *Philippi, &c*

(De Concordiâ Sacerd. & Imperij, lib. 7. cap. 4. §. 7. Tom. 2. p. 224.) for *Tertullian* adds it in the place next cited. (r) *Age jam qui voles Curiositatem melius exercere in negotio salutis tuæ, percurre Ecclesias Apostolicas, apud quas Ipsæ adhuc Cathedræ Apostolorum suis locis Præsidentur; apud quas Ipsæ Authenticæ Literæ eorum recitantur, sonantes vocem, & repræsentantes faciem uniuscujusque. Proxima est Tibi Achaia, habes Corinthum: Si non longe es à Macedoniâ, habes Philippos, aut Thessalonicenses. Si potes in Asiam tendere, habes Ephesum: si autem Italiæ adjaces, habes Romam, &c.* Tertullian. de Præscript. cap. 36. p. 338. Edit. Pamelij, 1662.

cal *Churches*, such as *Corinth, Ephesus, Thessalonica, Philippi, Rome, &c.* and tells us, *That Cathedra Apostolorum*, the Chairs of the *Apostles were then in those Apostolical Churches*; *That Bishops presided in them*; *that if they had great Curiosity and Care of their Salvation, they should make their Address to those Apostolical Chairs and Churches*. *He sends them not all to* Rome, *and* Peter's *Chair there*: *But* (saith he) *if thou art near* Macedonia, *thou hast* Philippi *and* Thessalonica *to go to*; *If in* Asia, Ephesus; *If in* Achaia, Corinth; *If thou art near* Italy, *thou hast* Rome *to Address to*. He knew no Supremacy or Infallibility annex'd to *Peter's* Chair at *Rome*, more than to *Paul's* at *Corinth*, or *Philippi*. He directs them to that Apostolical Chair and Church which was next them, and Judged that sufficient, without going to *Rome*. The Bishop of *Rome* in those days, pretended to no more Supremacy or Infallibility in the Apostolical Church and Chair at *Rome*, then the Bishop of *Ephesus* or *Corinth*, in the Apostolical Chairs and Churches of those Cities. If *Sedes Apostolica*, and *Cathedra Apostolica* be a sufficient ground to infer and prove Supremacy; then either all such Churches must be Supream, (which is impossible) or none at all, which is certainly true.

5. But they say; *The Bishop of* Rome *is* Peter's *Successor, and on this they principally and generally ground his Supremacy*; *as derived to him*, (f) Jure Successionis, and (t) Jure Divino *too*; *by Divine Right and Succession*. Now if this be true; if Succession to *Peter* carry Supremacy with it, Then seeing they constantly say, 1. *That* Peter *was* (u) *seven years Bishop of* Antioch *before he was at* Rome. 2. *And that* (x) Euodius *was his Successor there*.

(f) *Ecclesiæ Rom. specialius in Petro, Cœli Terræque retinet habenas.* Gratian. Can. Si Papa. 6. Dist. 40.

(t) *Jus Successionis, Pontificum Romanorum in eo fundatur; quod Petrus Sedem suam, Jubente Domino, Romæ Collocaverit.* Bellarm. De Rom. Pont. l. 2. c. 1. §. 1.

(u) *Ecclesia Antiocheia hoc Anno* (Christi, 39.) *à Petro Instituta, & 7.*

Annis ab eodem administrata. Baron. ad An. Christ. 39. §. 9. Tom. 1. p. 269. Edit. Antverp. 1612.
(x) Baron. Ibid. §. 18. p. 272. and in their present Roman Breviary, Antverp. 1650. They have a Holy-day for St. *Peter's* Installment at *Antioch*; *In Cathedrâ Sancti Petri Antiochiæ*, (so they call it) *In parte Breviarij Hiemali, ad diem 22. Februarij*. And we are there told, that that Festival was call'd *Cathedra Petri*; *Quia Primus Apostolorum Petrus hodie Episcopatus Cathedram suscipisse referatur*. Ibid. Lect. 3. p. 760. Col. 2. And for this they cite St. *Augustin* De Sanctis, Serm. 15. a known suppositicius and spurious scrap, unworthily father'd on St. *Augustin*.

I desire to know, why the Supremacy did not descend to *Euodius*, his first and immediate Successor? For admit, that *Peter* had such Supremacy, and that it was not Personal, but to be transmitted to some Successor; (both which are manifestly untrue) yet seeing such Transmission of his Supremacy, must be done either, 1. By some Act of our blessed Saviour. Or, 2. By some Act of *Peter*, transmitting his Supremacy to his Successor at *Rome*, and not to *Euodius* at *Antioch*: it will concern our Adversaries to shew such Act of our blessed Saviour, or *Peter*. For if they can, we will submit, and give the Cause; but if they cannot, then seeing, *idem est non esse & non apparere*; they must pardon our unbelief, if we assent not to that, which they cannot prove. I say, cannot prove; there being not one syllable in Scripture or Antiquity for Six hundred years, (I might give more) either expresly affirming, or from which it may (by good Consequence) be deduced, that either our *blessed Saviour* or *Peter* did transmit such a Monarchical Supremacy and Infallibility to the Bishop of *Rome*, more then to the Bishop of *Antioch*. If any man think otherwise, let him give us good proof of the contrary, and we will give him thanks and the Cause. 2. But admit that the Pope succeeds *Peter*, and really sits in *Cathedrâ Petri*, as his Successor, (which is evidently untrue) yet this will not prove his Monarchical Supremacy; if it do appear that any other Apostle succeeded our blessed Saviour (before *Peter* was Bishop any where) and by his own Appointment, sate in our blessed Saviour's Place and Episcopal Chair, as his Successor; I say, if this appear, then as our blessed Saviour is far greater then *Peter*, so his Successor will be greater then the **Pope**, and have a fairer pretence for the Supremacy, as our blessed Saviour's immediate Successor, then the Pope can possibly have, as *Peter's*. Now for this, let our Adversaries consider what *Epiphanius* says, Thus; (y) James *the Brother of our Lord was the first Bishop, when our blessed Saviour concredited and resign'd to him, before all others, his Throne or Episcopal Chair on Earth.*

(y) ΠρῶτΘ ὁὗ- τΘ εἴληφε τὴν χα- θέδραν, &c. *Hic primus Episcopalem Cathedram capit, cum ei Ante Caeteros Omnes, Suum ei in Terris Thronum Dominus tradidisset.* Epiphanius adversꝰ Hæres. l. 3. Tom. 2. Hæres 78. §. 7. pag. 1039. B.

Earth. And here let it be consider'd, 1. That in Scripture our blessed Saviour is call'd (z) *a Bishop, Universal Bishop of the Church*; with (a) *Monarchical and Kingly Power*. 2. He was in a particular and peculiar way *Bishop of the Jews*; he had Ἐπισκοπὴν, a peculiar Oversight and Cure of them. He was sent (in Person) *only to* (b) *them*: He constituted a Church amongst them, Ordain'd Apostles, and Seventy other (c) Inferior Ministers, whom he sent to Preach and do Miracles in Confirmation of their Doctrine; he constantly preached the Gospel amongst them, and did all those Acts a Bishop should do in his Diocese. 3. And *Jerusalem* being the Metropolis of the Jews, *Epiphanius* tells us, that it was (*on Earth*) his Throne, (Thronus suus) his Episcopal Seat, or Chair; where he usually was, preach'd and did Miracles. 4. He says, *That our blessed Saviour chose* James, *before all the rest*, (*even before* Peter) *and concredited and resign'd to him*, Thronum suum, *his Episcopal Seat, and that* James *was Bishop of* Jerusalem, *is attested by all Antiquity*. And this probably was the Reason, 1. Why *Paul* (d) names *James* (as Bishop of *Jerusalem*) before *Peter*. 2. Why in the Council of the Apostles, *James* (and not *Peter*) gave the definitive (e) Sentence. So that these things seem to me certain, 1. That our blessed Saviour, though Bishop of the Universal Church, yet he had a particular Episcopal Cure, and Charge of the Jews, as his Father was King of all the World, yet particularly of the Jews. (*f*) 1 Sam. 12. 12. it was (g) Θεοκρατία. 2. That *James* was his Successor in that Cure. 3. And (if *Epiphanius* say true) our *blessed Saviour* himself appointed him his Successor. Let our Adversaries (by so good Authority) shew; that *Peter* was our blessed Saviour's Successor, either at *Rome*, (as some of them, before-mention'd, only pretend) or any where else; and (for my part) let them take the Cause. Otherwise, if they cannot, then we may evidently conclude, That if *James* never did, nor could pretend justly to a *Monarchical Supremacy* over the whole Church,

(z) 1 Pet. 2. 25.
(a) Rev. 17. 14; & 19. 16.

(b) Matth. 10. 6. & 15. 24. Rom. 15. 8.
(c) Luke 10. 12.

(d) Gal. 2. 9.
(e) Act. 15. 13. 19. 20.
(f) *God your King*: (so *Samuel* tells them) and so 1 Sam. 8. 7. and cap. 10. 19.
(g) So *Josephus* and *Philo* call the Jewish Government, from *Moses* to *Saul*. God was personally their King. 1. He himself personally did give them all their Laws. 2. He personally sent his Vice-Roys, *Moses, Joshua*, and all the Judges. 3. He received and personally answered all their last Appeals, which are evident Characters that he was their Supream Power, their King.

though

though our blessed Saviour's Successor; much less may the Pope for succeeding *Peter.* *Q. E.D.*

4. But the Pope (they say) is *Christ's Vicar*; and that he is, or should be so, we grant. But we further say; that many thousands (besides him) are *Christ's Vicars* as well, and as much as he. This has been manifestly proved before. I shall only add; that the *Trent Fathers* (who, say they, (h) *were inspired* by the Holy Ghost, and so surely Infallible) expresly say, and Synodically define, *That our blessed Saviour before his Ascension, left all Priests his* (i) *own Vicars, to whom, as to Presidents and Judges, all Mortal sins were to be Confess'd.* And (k) *Aquinas*, (and their Schoolmen) say; That in the Church, *the Bishop is Christ's Vicar*; and they prove it well, from the express and plain words of the (l) Apostle; and they might have added also 2 *Cor.* 5. 20. And *Henry Holden*, a Learned *Sorbon Doctor*, in his Annotations upon those Texts, says the same thing. And now if to be *Christ's Vicar*, give any ground or pretence to Supremacy, then all Bishops and Priests (who are confess'd to be *Christ's Vicars*) may pretend to Supremacy as well as the Pope. And they being *Christ's Vicars* as to the Power of Absolving and Retaining Sins, (m) *every poor Priest has as much power to absolve the Pope, as he him.* So that any Argument drawn from this Title, that he is *Christ's Vicar*, to prove the Popes Supremacy, is not only inconsequent but impertinent, and indeed ridiculous: And yet upon this ground, and another as insignificant, Pope *Innocent* the Fourth, in their General Council at *Lions*, Excommunicates and Deposes the Emperor *Friderick*; *Seeing* (says the Pope there) *we are Christ's* (n) *Vicar on Earth*;

(h) *Synodus à Spiritu Sancto, qui est Spiritus Sapientiæ & Intellectûs Edocta declarat*, &c. Concil. Trid. Sess. 21. de Communione, cap. 1. And yet what it declares there is most evidently untrue.

(i) *Christus à Terris Ascensurus ad Cœlos, Sacerdotes suis suos Vicarios reliquit tanquam Præsides ac Judices, ad quos Omnia Mortalia crimina diserantur.* Conc. Trid Sess. 14. *De Pœnitentiâ,* cap. 5. *De Confessione.* vid. Aquinat. Par. 3. Quæst 8. Art. 6. in Corpore.

(k) Aquin. 2. 2. Quæst. 88. Art. 12. *Prælatus gerit Vicem Christi.*

(l) 2 Cor. 2 10.

(m) *Si periculum mortis immineat, approbatúsque desit Confessarius, quilibet Sacerdos potest à quibuscunque censuris & peccatis absolvere.* Rituale Romanum Pauli Papæ 5. Jussu Editum Antverp. 1652. De Sacramento Pœnitentiæ pag. 61. & 62. (n) *Cum Jesu Christi Vices teneamus in Terris, Nobisque in Petri personâ dictum sit, Quodcunque Ligaveris,&c. Memoratum Principem Omni Dignitate privatum denunciamus, & Sententiando privamus; Omnésque ei Juramento Fidelitatis astrictos, à juramento absolvimus; inhibentes ne quisquam de Cætero ei, ut Imperatori pareat; & qui ipsi favorem aut auxilium præstiterint, sint ipso facto Excommunicati.* Cap. ad Apostolicæ, 2. Extra de Sent. & re judicata. vid. Cap. Quanto 3. Extra de Translatione Episcopi.

and

and it was in the Person of Peter *said to us*, *Whatsoever thou binds on Earth, shall be bound in Heaven* ; *we declare and denounce the said* Friderick *deprived of all his Honour and Dignity, absolve his Subjects from all* Oaths *of Allegiance, and Excommunicate all who shew him any favour, or obey him as Emperor.* And to the same purpose their *Trent Catechism* tells us; (o) *That the Pope has* (*by Divine Right,* (*not by any Human Constitutions*) *that Supream degree of Dignity and Jurisdiction, over the Universal Church, as* Peter's *Successor, sitting in his Chair,* **and as** *Vicar of Christ.*

(o) *Cum in Petri Cathedrâ Sedeat, summum in eo Dignitatis gradum, non ullis humanis constitutionibus, sed divinitùs datum agnoscit.: Estque Moderator universalis Ecclesiæ, ut Petri Successor, & in terris verus Christi Vicarius.* Ita Catechis. Tridenr. part. 2. cap. 7. de Ordinis Sacramento, §. 28. vid. etiam Bullarium Romanum, Tom. 1. pag. 347. Col. 1. §. 6. where Alexand. Papa. 6. gives all the *West-Indies* to the King of *Spain*, as Vicar of Christ.

5. But that which they press with most noise and confidence, is, *That our blessed Saviour gave* Peter *the Keys of the Kingdom of Heaven.* They seem to be in love with these words, *Dabo Tibi Claves, &c.* For in their (p) Offices, for only two of St. *Peter*'s Festivals, they are repeated almost Twenty times. But how impertinent this is, to prove any Supremacy (much less their Papal Monarchy) will evidently appear, in that this Power of the Keys, which they would appropriate to the Pope, was given to the rest of the Apostles, as well as to *Peter* (as is proved before) nay to every Bishop and Priest in the World. For, 1. so their own *Roman Breviary*, published by the authority of Pope *Pius* the Fifth, and afterwards revised by *Clement* the Eighth, and *Urban* the Eighth expresly says ; for having told us, *that our blessed Saviour gave the Keys to* Peter : it follows ; (q) *That this power did pass to the other Apostles and Princes of the Church.* 2. Their *Trent Catechism*, having (r) spoke of the Power of the Keys ; afterwards tells us, to whom our blessed Saviour gave and concredited that Power before he Ascended into Heaven ; And it was *To the* (s) *Bishops*

(p) Vide Breviarium Romanum, in Cathedrâ S. Petri Antiochiæ. Febr. 22. & in Festo Cathedræ S. Petri qua Romæ primum Sedet. Jan. 18. Breviarij parte Hiemali.

(q) *Petro dedit Claves ; transivit quidem etiam in alios Apostolos vis potestatis illius, & in omnes Ecclesiæ Principes.* Breviar. Rom. in Festo Cathedr. S. Petri Antioch. Febr. 22. Lect. 9. Part. Hiemali. pag. 762. Edit. Antverp. 1660.

(r) Part. 1. cap. 11. §. 4.   (s) *Eam potestatem Episcopis & Presbyteris concessit.* Ibid. §. 9.

and

and *Presbyters*. So that *Catechism*, publish'd according to the Decree of the Council of *Trent*, by Pope *Pius* the Fifth. And, 3. Their *Roman Pontifical* gives the Authentick Form how they Ordain a Priest; in which the Power of the Keys is given to *every Priest*, in the very same (*t*) words our blessed Saviour did give it to the Apostles———(*u*) *Receive the Holy Ghost, whose sins you remit, they are remitted; And whose sins you retain, they are retained.* 4. Lastly; The *Trent Fathers* are yet (if that be possible) more express; For speaking of the Sacrament of Pennance and Absolution, *They* (x) *declare all their Opinions to be false and erroneous, who think that the Exercise of the Ministery and Power of the Keys, belong to any, save the Bishops and Presbyters; and who think those words* ——— *Whatsoever you shall bind on Earth, &c. And those sins you remit shall be remitted, &c. to be spoken indifferently to all the Faithful; and so think that any of the Faithful may bind and loose, remit and retain sins.* In which words the Council does (I suppose) Infallibly Declare (at least in our Adversaries Opinion) 1. That those two (y) Texts (which are cited in the Margent of the (z) Council) are to be understood of the Power of the Keys; though in one of them (that of *John*) the Keys be not expresly named. 2. That the Exercise of that Power of the Keys belongs *To the Bishops and Presbyters*, but to none else; neither to Lay-men nor any Inferior Orders.

By the Premisses, I think it evident, (and confess'd by our Adversaries) that every Apostle had the Power of the Keys, as well as *Peter*, and (since they left the World) every *Bishop and Priest*, as well as the Pope. Whence it further (and manifestly) follows; *That 'tis impossible that the Bishop of Rome, or any of his Party, should (as they vainly indeavour) prove his Supremacy from his power of the Keys;* which is common, and really possess'd by so many thousands beside himself. For this is just as if *Titius* should brag, that he is far richer then *Sempronius*, because he has Five hundred
pounds

(*t*) Joh. 20. 22. 23.

(*u*) Pontif. Romanum jussu Clement. 8. restitutum Rom. 1511. p. 52. *Accipe Spiritum Sanctum quorum remiseritis peccata, remittuntur eis; & quorum retinueritis, retenta sunt.*

(X) *Declarat Synodus, falsas esse Doctrinas Omnes, quæ ad alios quosvis præter Episcopos, & Presbyteros, Clavium Ministerium extendunt. Putantes verba illa, quodcunque Ligaveris, &c. & quorum remiseritis peccata, remittentur, &c. ad omnes fideles indifferenter dicta, &c.* Concil. Trid. Sess. 14. De Pœnitentiâ, cap. 6.

(y) Matth. 16.19. & Joh. 20.23.

(z) Conc. Trid. Antv. 1633. p.152.

pounds *per Annum*; when *Sempronius* has an equal Estate, and of the very same value. Or as if *Sejus* should say he had far greater Power then *Cajus*, when the Power given them by the Emperor was equal and the same. And yet such is the vanity and folly of their pretended Infallible Judges, that in their Bulls, and Papal Constitutions, received into the Body of their Canon Law, *Dabo Tibi Claves*, this Power of the Keys, is laid as a (sandy and insignificant) Foundation, on which they build the vast and Insupportable Fabrick of their Supremacy. I shall instance only in two (though I might in many more,) 1. In that famous Decretal of *Innocent* the Third (before cited) wherein he impiously and ridiculously indeavours to prove, that the *Papal Dignity*, is as much (a) *greater than the Imperial*, as the *Sun is greater than the Moon*: And amongst other wild and ridiculous Arguments to prove his equally wild and extravagant Position, he comes at last to this, *Dabo Tibi Claves*, to the Power of the Keys, as the *most known* ground of his Supremacy. 2. The second Instance, is that of Pope *Innocent* the Fourth, in his Impious Excommunication and Deposition of the Emperor *Friderick*, (who had been before Excommunicated by his Predecessor *Gregory* the Ninth) in the Council of *Lions*. It is (b) Extant in the Canon Law, and two things there prefix'd to that most Impious Decretal. 1. *That he depos'd* Friderick *in the Council, for a perpetual* (c) *memory of it*. And so it stands for a perpetual memory of his Antichristian Pride and Impiety. 2. *That the Pope can Depose the* (d) *Emperor for lawful Causes*. And then, in that Impious Decretal, he grounds his Power to Depose the Emperor principally upon the *Power of* (e) *the Keys*; which (he says) was given to him in *Pe-*

(a) Vide Cap. Solicit. 6. Extra de Major. & Obedientia. Where the *Lemma* or Title prefix'd to that Decretal is thus ———*Imperium non præest Sacerdotio, sed subest, & ei Obedire tenetur.* This he indeavours to prove by several ridiculous Instances; and then comes with *Dabo Tibi Claves, & quodcunque Ligaveris*, as a most known ground of his Supremacy. *Illud tanquam Notissimum omittamus, quod Dominus dixit Petro & in) etro ad Successores ipsius; Quodcunque Ligaveris, erit ligatum in Cœlis, &c. Nihil excipit, qui dixit quodcunque, &c.* And a little before he tells the Emperor of *Constantinople*, (to whom he writes) *Quanta est inter So-*

lem & Lunam, tanta inter Pontifices & Reges, differentia cognoscatur. (b) Cap ad Apostol. 2. De Sent. & re Judicata. In. 6. (c) *Innocentius Sacro præsente Concilio in Memoriam Sempiternam.* (d) *Papa Imperatorem deponere potest ex causis ligitimis.* (e) *Cum à Christo Nobes in Petri persona dictum sit; Quodcunque Ligaveris super Terram, Ligatum erit in Cœlis, &c. Memoratum Principem, suis Ligatum peccatis, Omni Dignitate privatum denunciamus, sententiamus & privamus; Omnesque ei Juramento astrictos, à Juramento perpetuo absolvimus; Inhibentes ne quisquam sibi de Cætero, tanquam Imperatori pareat.*

ter, when our blessed Saviour said, *Whatsoever thou shalt bind on Earth, should be bound in Heaven*, &c. so he, (and his Predecessors and Successors generally for this Six hundred years last past) applies that *Power of the Keys* (which is purely *spiritual*) to carnal and temporal ends, and impious purposes. And here it seems to me, considerable, (and I believe will seem so, to pious and dis-interessed Persons) that in former (*f*) *Roman Breviaries* (as also in our *Portiforium* or (*g*) *Breviary of Sarum*; and in the (*h*) *Missals of Salisbury* and (*i*) *Hereford*, we have this Prayer;

(*f*) Vid. I. Breviarium Romanum, by Card. *Quignonius*, approved and highly commended by *Clement* the Seventh, and *Paul* the Third, and often printed at *Paris*, Ann. 1536. Again, Ann. 1537. and at *Lions*, Ann. 1543. and at *Lions*, 1546. and, 1548. and again at *Lions*, Ann. 1556. and at *Antverp.* 1566. and though it be the best Breviary *Rome* has had this Six hundred years; yet 'tis damn'd by *Pius* the Fifth, Bullâ Romæ dat. 7. Idus Julij, 1568. 2. *Breviarium Romanum*, ex Decreto Concilij Trident. Jussu Pij 5. Antverp. Editum, 1568. & iterum, 1585. (*g*) Portiforium Salisf. Lond. 1555. Part. Hieman. in Festo Cathedr. S. Petri, Febr. 22. (*h*) Missale Secundum usum, Sarum, Paris. 1555. eodem festo & die. (*i*) Missale secundum usum Hereford Rothomagi, 1520. eodem festo & die.

1. *Deus qui Beato Petro Apostolo tuo, Collatis Clavibus Regni Cœlestis, Animas Ligandi atque Solvendi Pontificium tradidisti; Concede, ut Intercessionis ejus Auxilio*, &c. O God, who by giving the Keys of the Kingdom of Heaven to thy Apostle Peter, hast concredited and delivered to him the Pontifical Power of binding and loosing mens Souls, grant that by the help of his Intercession, &c. Where it is evident that, (in the sense and plain meaning of this Prayer and Scripture too) the *Power of the Keys is spiritual*, to bind mens *souls*, (if impenitent) and (if Contrite and truly Penitent) to loose them. I say *spiritual*, for edification and saving mens *souls*, and not *temporal*, for Deposing Kings and Emperors, and absolving their Subjects from their Oaths of Allegiance.

2. But this Doctrine was not pleasing to the Pope and his Party; And therefore in their late (*k*) *Breviaries* and (*l*) *Missals*, they have left out the word *Animas*, *Souls*;

(*k*) Breviar. Rom. Antv. Ann. 1660. parte Hiemali, in Festo Cathedr. Petri Antioch. Febr. 22. p. 759. & parte æstivâ in Festo Cathedræ Petri Romæ, Jan. 18. ibid. p. 698.
(*l*) Missal. Rom. Antverp. 1619. in Festo Cathedræ Petri Romæ, Jan. 18. p. 331. And they have the same again in Festo Cathedræ Petri Antiochiæ, Febr. 22.

and

and say only, *that God had given* Peter *Peter Power of binding and loosing*; and not mentioning in that Prayer, what it was he had Power to bind and loose.

3. But that we may better know their meaning and reason why they left out the word *Souls*; it follows, a little after in those late Offices ———— ,m) *Tu es Pastor ovium, Princeps Apostolorum*; *Tibi* (n) *tradidit Deus Omnia Regna Mundi*; *& Ideo Tibi traditæ sunt Claves Regni Cælorum.* They all agree, *That the power of binding and loosing is* (as they call it in that Prayer) *Pontificium, the Pontifical or Papal Power*; and having told us, *That God had given All the Kingdoms in the World, to* Peter *and his Successors*; they add, That *Ideo*, Therefore he gave him Pontificium, *the Papal Power of binding and loosing, Superior to all Kingly* (o) *Power*; so that they might, by it, Depose Kings and Emperors, if they were not Obedient to the Pope; for so their Popes (as appears before) have, *in Thesi*, affirm'd, and (in their Bulls, their Publick and Authentick Constitutions) approved, and publickly maintain'd that Doctrine; and (*in Praxi*) to the fatal Mischief and Disquieting of the Western World, the ruin of many Princes, and scandal of Christian Religion, impiously acted according to it, and put it in practise; when they had advantage and opportunity.

(*m*) Dict. **Brev.** Rom Antv. 1660. in Festo Cathedræ Petri Antiochiæ, Febr. 22. In Resp. post Lect. 4. p. 760. Partis Hiemalis. And that it might not be forgotten, (being a Doctrine that makes so much for the Papal Interest) it is repeated again, in Festo Petri & Pauli, Jan. 29. Partis æstivæ, pag. 482. & in Festo Petri ad vincula. Ibid. p. 541.

(*n*) Though I find the word *Animas* left out in some of their older Offices; yet these words *Tibi Tradidit, &c.* I find in none till of late.   (*o*) The Popes Tribunal (they say) is *Supremus Justitiæ Thronus*. So *Pius* the Fifth in this his Bull, §. 3.

By the Premisses, I hope it may (and does) appear, that all those Honorary Titles given to the Pope, or his See, (*Apostolicus, Sedes Apostolica, Cathedra Apostolica, Peter's Successor, Christ's Vicar, the Power of the Keys, Prince of the Apostles, &c.*) having been anciently given to thousands (beside the Pope) who never had, nor dream'd of any Supremacy: Though in these late, and worst Ages, they have been appropriated to the Bishop of *Rome*, and (though old and innocent Titles) made use of, to amuse and deceive the Ignorant, to cover, and give some colour and credit to new Errors, and made Arguments to prove (what

S   he

he never had) the Popes Supremacy; yet 'tis evident that all such Arguments, drawn from such Topicks, are not only inconsequent, but (as I said before, and still believe) impertinent, and indeed ridiculous; and conclude nothing, save that surely they who bring so bad, had no better Arguments. Two other words there are (*Papa* and *Summus Pontifex*) now appropriate to the Bishop of *Rome*, and as generally and impertinently used (as the former) to Insinuate (what they can never prove) the Popes Supremacy. For many Learned men have evidently proved (or confess'd) that anciently, every Bishop was called (p) *Papa*, a *Pope*, and *Summus* (q) *Pontifex* too. *Baronius* a most zealous and partial Assertor of the Popes Supremacy and Monarchy over Kings and Emperors) has, in the *place quoted in the Margent*, confess'd (what without great Impudence he could not deny) that anciently every *venerable Presbyter* was usually call'd *Papa*, or *Pope*. *Afterwards* (he says) *the word* Papa *became common to all the Bishops, though more particularly given to the Bishop of* Rome *; and he further adds, That the name* Papa *continued common to All the Bishops, for Eight hundred and fifty years*; till Hildebrand (Pope Gregory the Seventh) in a Council at Rome, in the Year, 1073. decreed, *That there should be but one Pope* (meaning himself) *in the whole World*. Here we see, that *Hildebrand* that Prodigy of (r) Antichristian Pride and Tyranny) appropriates the name *Pope* to himself and See, which had for Eight hundred years (he might have

(p) Vide Originem Dialogo contra Marcionitas Græco-Lat. per Rad. Westenium, p. 247. & Westenij Notas, pag. 230. 231. Per. Delalande Concil. AntiquorumGalliæ Supplemento, pag. 35. 36. 39. Baronium in Notis ad Martyrologium Rom. ad Diem, Jan. 10. c. p. 35. *Nomen Papæ transit in Dignitatis Nomen, ut Clerici venerandi eo nomine Appellarentur.*

Postea nomen illud cæpit esse peculiare Episcoporum, usque enim ad Annum 850. Nomen commune fuit omnibus Episcopis, inde peculiarius tribui consuevisset Rom. Pontifici, & sequitur, p. 36. *Gregorius Papa 7. in Concilio Romæ habito*, 1073. *Statuit, ut Nomen Papæ Unicum esse in toto Mundo, &c.*   (q) Vide Pet. de Marca de Concord. Sacerdotij & Imperij, lib. 6. cap. 13. § 3. Tom. 2. pag. 126. Col. 1. So *Ruffinus* calls *Chromatius, Pontificem maximum*. Vide Ruffin. Opuscula, Parif. 1580. Epist. ad *Chromatium, Pontificem maximum*, post pag. 194. So *Clemens Romanus* (one of the best and ancientest Popes *Rome* ever had) calls every Bishop Ἀρχιερεὺς, *Summus Sacerdos*, Clemens Rom Epist ad Corinthios, per Patr. Junium, p. 53. Edit. Oxon. 1633.   (r) *Plerique tum privatim tum publice, Hildebrandum Antichristum prædicant, Titulo Christi, negotium Antichristi agitat: in Babyloniâ in Templo Dei Sedit. Super Omne quod Colitur, extollitur, quasi Deus sit, se errare non posse gloriatur, &c.* Aventinus Annal. Bojorum, lib. 5. pag. 352. & lib. 7. pag. 473.

said

said *a thousand*) been commonly given to Bishops and Presbyters, as well as to the Pope. Now I desire to know how this, or any of the aforesaid Honorary Titles or Priviledges, (which were common to all Bishops, and usually given them, for many Ages, as well as to the Bishop of *Rome*); can be an Argument or Ground of the Popes Supremacy, which were confessedly no ground of any such Sepremacy in other Bishops, who had the very same Titles and Priviledges, as well, and as much as he? Suppose twenty Swans (*possibili posito in esse, nil absurdi sequitur*) to have equal whiteness, and the same degree of that Quality; To say that any one of those Swans was, by far, the whitest Swan in the World, when as nineteen others were as white as that one: Or suppose twenty men of Equal Piety, all having the same Degree of Goodness and Vertue; to say, that any one of them, was, by far, the most pious man in the World, when nineteen others were as pious as he; this were certainly irrational, and ridiculous. And yet our Adversaries reason no better, when they say, *The Pope being Christ's Vicar, and having the power of the Keys, has a Monarchical Supremacy over all the Bishops in the World*; when all those Bishops are Christ's Vicars, and have the power of the Keys, as well as he. But enough (if not too much) of this. For were it not for the great noise, number, and confidence of our Adversaries, such miserable inconsequent Reasonings, might deserve Pity and Contempt, rather than any serious Answer.

7. Having made some Observations upon the 'Ἐπιγραφὴ, or Title and Preamble of this Impious Bull; I come now to the Penal part of it, to observe what Punishments and Curses are contain'd in it, and the Persons against whom they are denounc'd. For although in the Title prefix'd to the Bull, 'tis calld', *The Damnation and Excommunication of Queen Elizabeth only*; yet thousands besides the Queen, are concern'd in those Curses, (as will appear anon.) Here then is to be observed,

Observ. 7.

1. That

1. That in this Uncharitable Bull, the Pope Anathematizes and Excommunicates the Queen, as a *Slave of* (f) *Impiety*, as an (t) *Heretick*, *and a Favourer of Hereticks*, *and Cuts her off from the Unity of Christ's Body*.

(f) *Flagitiorum Serva.* Ita § 1. who they are who speak ill of Dignities, (which the Arch-Angel would not do of the Devil) St. *Jude* tells us, in his Epistle, verf. 9. (t) *Apostolicæ potestatis plenitudine declaramus prædictam Elizabeth Hæreticam, & Hæreticorum fautricem, Anathematis Sententiam incurriffe, Effeque à Christi Corpori, unitate præcifam.* §. 3.

2. He depofes and deprives her (fo far as the plenitude of his Ufurped Power and Tyranny could) of *her pretended* (u) *right to the Crown of* England, *and of all*, *and all manner of Dominion, Dignity, and Priviledge*. By the way; what the Pope fpeaks here (notwithstanding his Infallibility) is neither reafon nor fenfe; For if her right to the Crown, was only (as he calls it) *Pretended*; he could not poffibly take it away, no not by his *plenitude of Apoftolical Power* (if he really had it): For, 1. (Notwithstanding all his Excommunications and Curfing) fhe might keep that Right, and as ftrongly pretend a Right to the Crown after, as before his Anathema's. 2. Any if fhe had only a pretended Right, then he could not deprive her of any real Right; it being impoffible to deprive her of a Right fhe had not.

(u) *Quin etiam ipfam prætenfo prædicti regni jure, nec non omni & quocunque Dominio, Dignitate, Privilegióque privatam* §.4. And again; *Dictam Elizabeth. Prætenfo jure Regni privamus.* §. 5.

3. He abfolves all her (x) *Subjects*, and *All Others*, who were bound to her by *Any Oath*, from their Oaths, and all Debt of Fidelity and Obedience, and that *For ever*. Where obferve, 1. That 'tis not only her own Subjects he abfolves from Oaths of Allegiance; but *All Others*, who were bound to her, by *Any Oath* whatfoever. So that if any *French-man, Dutch*, or *Spaniard*, any *Pagan, Jew*, or *Turk* had fworn to pay her Ten thoufand pounds, really (and by the Law of God and Man) due to her; he abfolves them from their Oaths; and fo (if they had not more Honefty and Confcience then he) fhe muft loofe her Money. The Pope, in the mean time, being more kind to *Turks* and *Pagans*, then to (a far better Chriftian then himfelf) Queen *Elizabeth*. 2. He abfolves them from all fuch Oaths *For ever*. So that if

(x) *Item Proceres, Subditos, & populos dicti Regni, ac cæteros omnes qui illi Quomodocunque juraverunt, à Juramento hujufmodi, ac Omni prorfus Dominij, fidelitatis & Obfequij debito. Perpetuo abfolutos, prout nos Authoritate præfentium abfolvimus.* Ibid §. 5.

if the Queen had (y) turned Papist, none of her Subjects (if the Popes Absolution had been valid) were, by an Oath, (unless they took a new one) bound to Obey her as their Soveraign.

(y) Nay, such is their Antichristian Tyranny and barbarous Cruelty to those they call Heretick; that when they are once actually and judicially condemn'd; though they turn good Catholicks; and repent never so sincerely; and though our blessed Saviour Jesus would pardon Penitents, yet Antichrist will not. For by the Popish Law, such Penitents are to be put into Prison, and be immured there, and live and dye in a miserable condition. *Si dicat Hæreticus se velle pœnitere, ac Hæreses abjurare, de misericordia possit recipi, ut Hæreticus pœnitens, & perpetuo immurari.* Nic. Eymericus, Direct. Inquisitorum, part. 3 pag. 516. Col. 1. And *Fran. Pegne* in his Commentary upon *Eymericus* there. Comment. 46. p. 517. Col. 2. Num. 202.

4. Nor does he only Absolve all the afore-mention'd (Subjects and all others) from all Oaths made to the (z) Queen; but also severely interdicts and prohibits them all, to Obey any of her Laws or Commands. That is; he forbids them to do that, to which (by the indispensable Law of God and Nature) they were absolutely bound.

(z) *Præcipimus & Interdicimus universis & Singulis Proceribus, subditis, Populis & Aliis Prædictis, ne ille Ejusve Monitis, Mandatis, & Legibus Audeant Obedire.* Ibid. §. 5.

5. And if any of the Persons mention'd in the aforesaid Particulars, did (a) otherwise, and obey'd any of her Laws or Commands; he pronounces the same Excommunication and Anathema against them. So that, 1. If any *French, Spanish,* or *Italian* Papists lived in *England* in Queen *Elizabeths* days; (after the Bull and Excommunication was publish'd, (as many did, and do, either as Merchants or Travellers) and obey'd the Laws of *England*; (as of necessity they must, and ought to conform to the Civil Laws of the Country where they live) all these, (by this wild Bull) did stand Excommunicate. Nor had they any way to Escape it, but either by Leaving the Kingdom, and all their Trade and Interest in it, to their great loss, and possibly the ruin some: Or by staying here, and disobeying the Queens Laws, (which never was, nor would be permitted) to undergo all the Severity and Penalties of those Laws. 2. But (which is yet much more strange) suppose any *Jews, Turks,* or *Pagans* in *England* in the Queens time; he Excommunicates all those, if they obey the Queen; But surely this rash and

(a) *Præcipimus universis & singulis Prædictis, ne Ejus Mandatis aut Legibus audeant Obedire. Qui secus egerint, tos simili Anathematis Sententiâ Innodamus.* Ibid. §. 5.

and Impious Sentence, was not pronounc'd *è Cathedrâ*; for (which is no good Sign of his Infallibility) he does in this undertake a thing beyond all the Power he did or could pretend to, an absolute Impossibility. For Excommunication being a Seclusion and Depriving a man of Ecclesiastical Communion, a turning out of the Christian Church; it was absolutely Impossible that either *Peter*, or the Pope his pretended Successor, should deprive those of a Communion they never had, or turn them out of a Church in which they never were.

6. He Excommunicates all Papists as well as Protestants, if they obey'd any of the Queens Laws or Commands. So that their Case was this; If they obey'd the Queen, their Sovereign, (to whom they ought a natural and sworn Allegiance) the Pope Curses and Damns them; and if they did not obey her, (as St. (*b*) *Paul* assures us) God himself *would condemn them*. Certainly, all pious and considering Persons will think this an easie choice; and that it is better *rather to Obey God than Men*, and believe St. *Paul* rather than the Pope, and yet such is the Power of Error and strong Delusion, that the generality of the Papists, (I do not say all) choose to obey the Pope; as shall appear evidently anon, by their many open Rebellions, and continual Plots and Conspiracies to disquiet the Government, and their Indeavours (by Pistol or Poyson) to Assassinate and take away the Queens Life. 2. That all Papists who gave any Obedience to the Queens Commands or Laws, were Excommunicate, as well as Protestants, is evident by this: That the Popish Party (*c*) petition'd Pope *Gregory* the Thirteenth, Ann. 1580. *Elizabeth* 13. *That he would declare, that the Bull of Pius the fifth should always bind the Catholicks, as matters then stood; but hereafter, when Publick Execution of the Bull may be had.* The Answer was, *These graces the highest Bishop hath granted* to Rob. Parsons *and* Ed. Campian (*who are now coming into* England) *the Seventeenth day of* April, 1580. *in the Presence of Father* Oliver Manark *Assistant*. Cambden in his History of Elizabeth. ad Ann. 1580. Elizabeth 23. pag. 217. Edit. Angl. Lond. 1635.

(*b*) Rom. 13. 4.

(*c*) Their Petition was, That *their most holy Lord* Gregory *the Thirteenth, would give a Declaratory Explication of* Pius *the Fifth's Bull, against Queen* Elizabeth, *and her Adherents; that it might be understood so, as always to bind her and the Hereticks; but not the*

Queen, and all *Hereticks*, *but not the Roman Catholicks*, *As Things then stood*; *but hereafter only*, *when That Bull might be put in Execution*. They were willing to Obey the Pope, and Disobey their Queen, when they had an Opportunity; They Petition the Pope to give them leave to do, what God (by Divine Law, Natural and Positive) had Commanded them to do; that is, **to obey their Lawful Sovereign**, and that they will Obey no longer, than till they have a Power and Ability, (with Security to themselves and Estates) **to Disobey**.

7. It is a certain Rule of Law and Justice, that before any Judge can Legally Condemn any; Two things are necessary to proceed; 1. *Cognitio* (d) *Causæ*, a Convenient Knowledge of the Cause; What Accusation the Actor or Plaintiff brings; what Answer and Defence the *Reus*, or Defendant makes. 2. That the Proofs and Evidence be such, as may be a just ground for a Damnatory Sentence, either the Judge or Sentence, (or both) are unjust.

(d) The necessity of these things ariseth from the Infirmity and Fallibility of all Human Judges; which is attested by Pope *Innocent* the Third, in the Canon Law; *Judicium Dei veritati, semper inititur, Judicium autem Ecclesiæ, nonnunquam opinionem sequitur,*

Qui aliquid Statuit, parte inaudita alterâ,
Æquum licet Statuerit, haud æquus fuit.

quam & fallere Sæpe contingit, & falli; propter quod contingit interdum, ut Qui Ligatus est apud Deum, apud Ecclesiam sit solutus; & qui liber est apud Deum, Ecclesiastica sit Sententia innodatus. Innocent 3. Cap. A Nobis 28. Extra. De Sententia Excommunicationis. It is Pope *Innocent* the Third who says this; and if he was Infallible, (as the Jesuits, Canonist, &c. pretend) then the Church of *Rome* does (*Sæpe*) often err in her Excommunications; and if he was not Infallible, then both he and his Successors may err.

And hence it was that a *Pagan Judge* could truly say, *It is* (e) *not the manner of the* Romans *to deliver any man to Dye, before he who is Accused have the Accuser face to face, and have Licence to Answer for himself.* Such was the Justice of Pagan *Rome*. But as Christian (or, I fear, Antichristian) *Rome*, the Case is alter'd. *Pius* the Fifth, the pretended Vicar of Christ (our blessed Saviour) Anathematizes and Damns many hundred Thousands, even

(e) Act. 25, 16.

Two

Observations on the Pope's Bull

(f) Gen. 18. 20, 21. *The Cry of the Sins of* Sodom *was great; but before* God *did destroy them, I will go down And See, whether they have done Altogether according to the Cry of it,* which *is come to me; and if not, I will know.* Si Judicas Cognosce.

Two whole Kingdoms at once, *Causâ Indictâ* (f) *& inauditâ*. An Action so prodigiously Impious, as hath no ground or pretence for it in Nature or Scripture, or any Precedent amongst Pagans or Christians for a Thousand years after Christ; till *Hildebrand*, one of the worst in the Papal Catalogue (to the Scandal of Christianity, and fatal Disturbance of Christendom) unhappily Introduc'd it, and his Successors since, have (with like Antichristian Pride and Tyranny) impiously practis'd it.

God gives us an Example, that we ought to be sure of the sin, which deserves it, before we pass Sentence to punish it. But the Pope here, Curses two Kingdoms, without any Hearing or Cognizance of the Cause, or possibility to know (notwithstanding the Cry might come to *Rome*) that every one whom he Cursed, deserved it. 2. God would have spared *Sodom* and *Gomorrah* for ten righteous men, Gen. 18. 32. But the Pope Curses two Kingdoms, though he neither did, nor possibly could know, but that there might be in them Ten thousand pious Persons who deserved it not: Nay, he Excommunicates them for their Piety to God and their Prince, in Obeying the Commands of both, to which by the Law of God and the Land, they were indispensably obliged.

Observ.

(g) Vide Bullarium Romanum Romæ, 1638. & ibi Excommunicat. Frideric. 2. à Gregor. 9. Const. 13. Tom. 1. p. 89. & Excommunicat. Hen. 8. à Paul 3. Tom 1. p. 514. &c.

(h) *Gregory* the Thirteenth, and *Sixtus* the Fifth, renewed the Bull of *Pius* the Fifth. Camden's History of Q. Elizabeth, Ad Ann. 1588. p. 360 361. Edit. Anglicanæ.

8. Seeing it appears by this Bull of Pope *Pius* the Fifth, (as by many more such, published by his (g) Predecessors and (h) Successors) that the Bishops of *Rome* Usurp and Exercise such a vast extravagant Power, to Excommunicate Kings and Emperors, to Depose and Deprive them of all their Dominions, Honour, and Dignity; to Absolve their Subjects from their Oaths of Allegiance and Fidelity: To Inhibit and Interdict them (against the Laws of God and Man) to give any Obedience to their Lawful Sovereigns; and if they do, to Anathematize and Curse them for so doing; and lastly, to Excommunicate whole Kingdoms at one (*Causâ indictâ & inauditâ*) if they do their Duty, and give any Obedience to their Prince, when they forbid them, &c. I say for this, (and many other Reasons) I believe the Bishop of *Rome* has the fairest Plea, of any in the World, to be *that Man of Sin*, and the *great Antichrist* spoken of in the Gospel. It is neither my intention or business now, fully to dispute that Question. *Whether the Pope be Antichrist?* (many have with great success already done it) I shall only (in short) give the Reader

two

against Queen Elizabeth.

two or three Arguments or Motives, which (at present) Induce me to believe that the Pope is Antichrist; And those Motives, either grounded on Scripture, the Confessions of our Adversaries, the Testimonies of many and great men before, or the concurrent Consent of the Reformed Churches since *Luther*. Here consider,

1. That it is not only (*i*) Confess'd by our Adversaries (in their Commentaries on 1 *Pet.* 5. 13. *The Church of* Babylon *salutes you*) but indeavour'd to be proved by many Arguments they bring, *That* Rome *is that* Babylon, *St.* John *speaks of, in the* Revelation; *which he calls the Great Whore, Mother of Harlots, and Abominations of the Earth, and* (in more plain terms) *The* (*k*) *Great City which reigns over the Kings of the Earth*; which cannot possibly be meant of any but *Rome*, that being then the only great City, which Reigned over the Kings of the Earth. I know that some of them would have (*l*) *Pagan Rome* meant: but this evidently untrue; for, 1. It must be *Apostatical Rome*; (as indeed it is) for the Apostle expresly tells us; *That Antichrist will not come, till an* (*m*) *Apostasie and falling from the Faith come first*: which cannot be meant of *Pagan Rome*; it being impossible they should fall from the Faith, who never had any. 2. It is meant of that *Babylon*, or *Rome*, which St. *John* calls the (*n*) *Great Whore, and Harlot*: but in Scripture,

(*i*) See the Annot. on 1 Pet. 5 13. & *Tirinus* the Jesuit says,(in his Comment. on the same Text) *unanimiter asserunt Patres & Doctores Orth. dixi, Citati apud Bellarm. Ribeiram, Viegam, Pererium, Alcazar. &c. per Babylonem, Rom. intelligi.* And so Corn. A Lap. on the same place: the same A Lapide upon Rev. 17. 15. on these words —— *Hi odient fornicam, scilicet, Babylonem, i. e. Romam.* Vide Hen. Valef. in Notis ad lib. 2. Euseb. Hist. cap. 15. Notarum p. 33. Col 2. Riberam in Apocal 14.8.§.25,

(*k*) Rev. 17.18.

(*l*) Pamelius Annot. ad lib. 3. Tertul. adversus Marci-

onem, num 98. pag 687. (*m*) 2 Thess. 2.3. vid. 1 Tim 4.1. Ἀποστασίαν τῆς πίστεως, An Apostacy from the Faith. (*n*) Rev. 17.1,5. And so *Hier.* calls her (alluding to this Place, *Cum in Babylone versarer* (says he) *& Purpuratæ Meretricis essem Colonus, & Jure Quiritum viverem,* &c. in præf. ad Did. Alex. de Sp. S. T. 6. p. 217. And again, l. 2. Adv. Jovin. Sed (Hier. T. 2. p. 379, 380. in calce Libri) *ad Te loquor, qui scriptam in fronte blasphemiam, Christi Confessione delisti. urbs Orbis Domina, Maledictione. quam Tibi Salvator in Apocalypsi Comminatus est, potes effugere per pœnitentiam,* &c. Mar. Victor. in Not. ad dict. Lib. & Loc. num. 58. says he means *Pagan Rome.* But 'tis certain (which I only cite him for) that *Babylon* in the *Revelation* (in *Hierom's* Opinion) is *Rome.* Sure I am, that *Tertull.* is of the same judgment; (Lib. Adv. Jud. c 8. p. 142. num. 106.) *Sic & Babylon apud Johan. Rom. urbis figuram portat, proinde & Regno superbæ, & sanctorum debellatricis.* And he has the same words again, (Lib. 3. adv. Marcion. c. 13. n. 98. p. 674.) where *Pamelius* in his Notes on those places, 1. Would have *Pagan Rome* meant. However, by *Babylon* in the *Revelation* (in *Tertullian's* Opinion, as well as *Hieroms*) *Rome* is meant. 2. He would have those words, (*Babylon Roma*) which were in the Margent of a former Edition of *Tertul.* blotted out; that men might not be put in mind that *Rome* was the *Mystical Babylon, more Romano,* corrupting Records, and blotting out whatever makes against them.

T

none but Apostates from the Faith, and true (*o*) Religion, are call'd so; nore but she who was once a Wife, and afterwards falls into Spiritual Whoredom; which of *Pagan Rome* neither is, nor can be true. 3. The Actings of Antichrist are call'd (*p*) *Mysterium, a Mystery, things hard to be understood*: but that Pagan Idolaters should persecute and oppress Christians, and *be drunk with the Blood of the Saints*, this is no Mystery. But that all this should be done in pretence of the only True and Catholick Religion, in Honour of Christ, and by his Vicar; this is indeed a Mystery, not easily understood. So that it is evident, and confess'd, *That Rome is Babylon*, (*Mystical Babylon*) call'd so, (as she is call'd (*q*) *Sodom* and *Egypt*) in respect of that Analogy and Similitude between the Literal and Mystical, the Pagan and Antichristian *Babylon*, (*Babylon Chaldæa & Italia*.) Some of the Particulars wherein that Similitude consists, are here in the (*r*) Margent; and he who considers what St. *John* says of the *Mystical*, and what *Isaie* and *Jeremy* of the *Literal Babylon*, may find more. I take it then for a manifest Truth, (and confess'd by our Adversaries) *that by* Babylon *in the* Revelation, Rome *is meant, and that it is the Seat of Antichrist*. The next Query will be, *Who that Antichrist is, whose Seat is to be at Rome?* And this will best appear by the Description and Characters of him in Scripture.

(*o*) See Hof.1.2. &c. and Hof.2.2.

(*p*) 2 Thef. 2. 7. Rev. 17. 5, 7.

(*q*) Rev. 11. 8.

(*r*) The Similitude between the *Pagan Babylon*, in the Old, and the *Antichristian* in the New Testament, may appear in this; 1. They were both very great Cities. (Isai. 13. 19. Rev. 16. 19.) 2. They were both Impious and Idolatrous. Isai. 46. 1. Rev. 9. 20.) 3. They were both Oppressors of the Church of God; the *Literal and Pagan Babylon*, of the Jews, (Jer. 50. 11.) *the Mystical Babylon of Christian Church*. (Rev. 17. 6.) They both propagated their Impiety, and made other Nations to sin with them. (Jer. 51. 7. Rev. 13. 16. &c. Rev. 17. 2.) 5. In the *Pagan Babylon* God had some Saints and Servants, and they were Commanded to come out of her. (Jer. 50. 8. & 51. 6.) And so in the *Mystical Babylon*. (Rev. 18. 4.) 6. The destruction of both is denounced in the same words, of *Pagan Babylon*, Isai. 21. 9. Jer. 51. 8.) and of *Mystical Babylon*. (Rev. 14. 8. & 18. 2.)

2. One Characteristical Note and Mark of Antichrist, is given by (*s*) St. *Paul*; That he is an *Enemy*, an *Adversary* to Christ (our blessed Saviour), so the word in St. *Paul*

(*s*) 2 Theff 2. 4. ὁ Ἀντικείμενος.

Paul properly (*t*) signifies; so their Authentick Vulgar Latin (*u*) translates it, and their Learned (*x*) Commentators prove it. So that we are agreed on this; *That Antichrist (whoever he be) is an Adversary to our blessed Saviour;* and though he may pretend (as we know he does) to be *Christ's Vicar,* and Act by his Authority, and for him; yet he is really his Adversary, and acts in Opposition, and Contradiction to him. Now if this be a true Character of Antichrist (and it is St. *Paul's*) then the Pope has a fairer Plea to be that Beast, than any man in the World. For under the Name and Notion of *Christ's Vicar,* and by a vainly pretended and usurped Power from him, he acts contrary to Christ, and the express Commands of the Gospel. I shall (of many) give two or three Instances, 1. Our blessed Saviour, at the Institution of the Eucharist, expresly commands his Disciples (and so all Christians, who are of Age and rightly qualified) (*y*) *Drink ye All of this:* And another Evangelist tells us, *that they obey'd,* and (*z*) *Did All Drink.* But the Pope, in Contradiction to this, (*a*) absolutely forbids all (save the Priest who Consecrates) to drink the Eucharistical Cup; and so (in Contradiction to our Saviour's Command) deprives them of half that Sacrament. And this they do with a blasphemous Impiety, forbidding all *Laicks* to have the Communion in both kinds, *Notwithstanding the* (*b*) *Institution of Christ,* and notwithstanding that in the (*c*) *Primitive Church it was Received in both kinds:* and they further

(*t*) Ἀντικεῖσαι, ἐναντίος κεῖται. Hesychius. Ἀντικείμενος, Adversarius. Glossæ veteres in Calce Cyrilli. Etymolog. Magnum, in verbo Ἀντιάνειρα, which he renders πολεμικη; and then add; ὥσπερ Ἀντίχριστον φαμὲν κ᾽ ἀντίπαλον.

(*u*) Filius perditionis, qui *Adversatur.*

(*x*) Corn. A Lapide in 2 Thes. 2. 4.

(*y*) Match. 26. 27.
(*z*) Mark 14. 23.
(*a*) Concilium Constantiense, Sess. 13.

(*b*) *Licet Christus post cœnam, Instituerit, & Discipulis sub utráque Specie panis & vini administra-*

verit: Hoc non Obstante, &c. Ibid. (*c*) *Licet in Primitivâ Ecclesiâ hoc Sacramentum reciperetur à fidelibus sub utráque Specie, tamen Consuetudo ab Ecclesiâ introducta, pro lege habenda est.* Ibidem. By the way, let the Intelligent and Impartial Reader consider, with what contradiction to truth and right reason the Fathers at *Constance,* establish their half Communion. They reject the uninterrupted perpetual Custom of the Universal Church, (both Greek and Latin, Eastern and Western) for above one thousand two hundred years, for receiving the Communion in both kinds: and yet tell us, That a late Custom of the Roman Church only, and that in some places only (for it was not a general Custom in the Roman Church to receive only in one kind, till *Ann.* 1414. the Council of *Constance* met and defined it) must be a Law to oblige all to receive only in one kind.

declare them (d) *Hereticks*, *who think otherwise*; and Command, *that no Priest shall administer it in both kinds to any Lay-man*, *under pain of* (e) *Excommunication*. By the way; it is observable, **That it is confess'd by our Adversaries** (f) Lindanus, *Cardinal* (g) Bona, &c.) *that the whole Church of God (Lay and Clergy) for about One thousand two hundred years, Received in both kinds, even the Church of* Rome *her self:* And after that, in (h) *Aquinas* his time, it was but in *some* (i) *Churches*, that the Cup was deny'd to the *Laity*. The sum is this; He who acts in Opposition and Contradiction to our blessed Saviour's Commands in the Gospel, abrogates them, (so much as in him lies) calls them Hereticks, and Excommunicates those who obey them, and incourages those who disobey Christ, and obey him; he (I say) is an Adversary to Christ and Antichrist. But (by the Premisses) it appears, that the Pope does all this, more signally in taking away the Cup in the Eucharist then any (who pretends to be a Christian) in the whole World; *Ergo*, he is Antichrist. 2. The next Instance whereby it may appear, that the Pope is ’Ἀντικείμενος, an Adversary to our blessed Saviour, and so has one Character of Antichrist, is this; St. *Paul* in his Epistle to the (l) *Corinthians*, tells them, (and he says they are the (m) Commandments of Christ he writes) 1. *That it is the Commandment of our blessed Saviour, that in their Assemblies all things be done to* (n) Edification. 2. *That speaking in an* unknown Tongue, *does not* (o) *Edifie or* (p) *Profit the Church to which he speaks*; (q) *because they understand not what he says*. 3. *He absolutely forbids all speaking in their Assemblies (if there be none to Interpret) in any* (r) unknown Tongue. Now whether the Pope be not ’Ἀντικείμενος, an Adversary to Christ, let the Reader Judge, by that which follows. Our blessed Saviour expresly Commands, that in the Assemblies of Christians all things should be in a Tongue understood by the People, for their Edification, (and the Apostle

(d) *Pertinaciter afferentes oppositum, tanquam Haeretici arcendi sunt & graviter puniendi.* Ibidem.

(e) *Nullus Presbyter sub poenâ Excommunicationis, Communicet populum sub utrâque specie.* Ibidem.

(f) Lindanus in Panoplia, lib. 4. cap. 55. pag. 322. Edit. Colon. 1575.

(g) Card. Bona de rebus Liturgicis, lib. 2. cap. 18. pag. 491. 492. Parish. 1672.

(h) *In quibusdam Ecclesiis observatur, ut populo Sanguis Sumendus non detur.* Aquinas part. 3. Quaest. 8. Art. 12. in Corpore.

(i) Which was about the year of Christ, 1265. Bellarmine de Script. Ecclesiasticis, in Tho. Aquinat.

(l) 1 Cor. 14.

(m) Ibid. vers. 37. *The things I write unto you are the Commandments of the Lord*.

(n) Ibid. vers. 26. and vers. 12.

(o) Ibid. vers. 17.

(p) Ibid. vers. 6.

(q) Ibid. vers. 2. 9. 14. 15. 16.

(r) Ibid. vers. 28.

thinks

thinks it (*f*) madness to do otherwise) that they might know his Precepts and gracious Promises; and so their Duty, and Incouragements to do it. But the Pope (as all know) in contradiction to this, absolutely forbids what our blessed Saviour expresly Commands; and prohibits all publick Prayers in any Vulgar Tongue; nay, the *printing, reading*, or *having their own* (t') *Roman Missal in French* (u), into which it was faithfully Translated, (not by any *Hereticks*, but by good *Roman Catholicks*.) This evidently appears by the Authentick Bull of Pope *Alexander* the Seventh, and some of his words cited in the Margent. And he there tells us, *That the Translators and Publishers of that Missal, were Studiers of Novelties, to the* (x) *ruin of Souls; Contemners of the Sanctions and Practise of the Church*; and that they were *Sons of Perdition*. But in this, I think his Holiness was not well advised. For if the Apostles (y) Character of Antichrist be true, he himself has a better claim to that Title, and really is (what he calls them) *The Son of Perdition*. What they say in Answer to St. *Paul*, and the clear Text against all praying to, or praising God in an unknown Tongue, is most irrational; and indeed impertinent. It is not my business or intention (in this place and time) particularly to Examine it; but refer the Reader to their (z) Learned Writers for their Latin Prayers, where he may see what they say; and if he be intelligent, and an impartial Seeker and Lover of truth, he will find that St. *Paul* condemns all Prayers to, and Praises of God in an unknown Tongue. Sure I am, a very Learned *Sorbon Doctor* in his (a) Notes on that place in St. *Paul* (convinc'd with the evidence of the Text and Truth) does acknowledge it, and explains St.

(*f*) Ibid. vers. 23.
(t) *Cum quidam Missale Romanum, ad Gallicam vulgarem linguam convertere tentaverint: Nos Novitatem istam Ecclesiæ decoris deformatricem, detestamur; & Missale prædictum Gallico Idiomate conscriptum, damnamus, ac Interdicimus, sub pœnâ Excommunicationis latæ Sententiæ, ipso Jure incurrendæ. Mandantes, ut quà illud habuerint tradant Ordinariis, aut Inquisitoribus, qui sine Morâ, Exemplaria igne comburant.* Bulla Alexand. 7. dat. Romæ, 12. Jan. 1661. Pontificatûs Ann. 6.

(u) Vide Bullam Clement. 9. Rom. 9. April, 1668. It was to be burnt by the Bishop or Inquisitors, even their own Missal in French.

(x) *Quidam Perditionis Filij in perniciem Animarum novitatibus studentes, & Ecclesiasticas Sanctiones, & prax-*

in contemnentes, ad eam nuper Vesaniam pervenerint, ut Missale Romanum in Gallicam vulgarem linguam convertere tentaverint. So it is in the said Bull. (y) 2 Thess. 2. vers. 3.4. (z) Vid. Corn. A Lapide in 1 Cor. 14. Costeri Enchiridion. Cap. 17. De precibus, Latine Recitandis, pag. 502. &c. Johan. Eckij Enchiridion adversus Lutherum, pag. 392. Colon. 1565. vide Azorium Instit. Moral. Part. 1. lib. 8. cap. 26. (a) Hen. Holden. Theologus Parisiensis, in Annot. ad 1 Cor. 14. Parif. 1660.

Paul.

Paul as I have done. If they damn and burn their own Offices in any Vulgar Tongue, (which deserve to be burnt for many other better Reasons) we may easily guess (when they have power to do it, which I pray and hope they never will) what they will do with ours. 3. But that which is the highest and most evident Instance, that the Pope is Ἀντίχριστος, an Adversary and Enemy to our blessed Saviour Christ, and true Christianity, is; That whereas the Gospel was writ to be read and studied (by all who had ability) as the great means of their Salvation; and accordingly was Translated into all Christian Languages, and all permitted to have and read it; that they might (for their direction and comfort) know the holy Precepts and gracious Promises contain'd in it; and continued so to this Day in all Christian Churches (except *Rome*) and in that too, for many hundred years after Christ, while Latin was their Vulgar Tongue. But when the Impiety and Tyranny of the Bishops of *Rome* unhappily prevail'd, the Gospel it self, and the whole Book of God, was reckon'd amongst *Damned Books, and Authors*, and not permitted to be (b) read in any Vulgar Tongue; no not so much as any *Summary* or *Historical Compendium* of it. And further, amongst the Rules of the *Index Expurgatorius*, publish'd by the command of the *Trent Council*, we are told, (with great Impiety and Blasphemy) *That by permitting the Scripture to be commonly read in Vulgar Tongues, there comes* (c) *more Mischief than Benefit*. Pope *Urban* the Eighth says (d) the very same, (with as much Impiety as his Predecessors) and further adds; *That all who have any prohibited Books*, of which number it is evident the Bible in any Vulgar Language is one) *they must bring them to the Bishop or Inquisitor, and they must burn them presently, by the hand of the Hangman, or some such Officer*; (for I suppose they are not to

(b) *Nulla conceditur facultas Legendi vel retinendi Biblia vulgaria, aut alias Sacræ Scripturæ partes, quavis Vulgari Linguâ Editas, & Insuper Summaria & Compendia etiam Historia Sacræ Scripturæ, quocunque vulgari Idiomate conscripta; quod Inviolate Observandum.* Vide Observat. ad Regul. 4. Indicis, in Calce Concilij Trident. Antverp. 1633. & Indicem Expurg. Alexand. 7. Rom. 1667. pag. 14. verbo. Biblia, & Bibliorum.   (c) *Plus inde ob hominum temeritatem, Detrimenti quam utilitatis Oriri.* Ibid. Reg. 4. in Indice Alexand. 7. pag. 4.   (d) *Librorum prohibitorum Lectio, magno sinceræ fidei cultoribus detrimento esse noscitur.* Urban. 8. Constit. 114. Bullarij Rom. Tom. 4. §. 1. p. 119. Edit. Rom. Anu. 1638.

do it themselves). And we have a late and further Instance of this Antichristian Impiety, in a Bull of Pope *Clement* the Ninth. The New Testament (as appears by the Bull) was Translated into *French*, and printed at *Lions*; The Pope (*Animus meminisse horret*) (e) Damns and prohibits it, under the very Name, *The New Testament of our Lord Jesus Christ*; and Excommunicates all, of what Dignity soever, who shall print, sell, read, or have it; and commands (under pain of Excommunication) that they who have it, bring it to the *Ordinary* or (f) *Inquisitors*; and what they must do, with it, the Bull of *Urban* the Eighth, (but now cited) will tell you; they must *burn it*, and (as a damned Book) abolish it. So *Clement* the Ninth commands the (g) *Roman Ritual* in *French*, to be burnt. But that which makes their Error and Impiety more evident, is; That even then and there, where they absolutely prohibit the Gospel in any Vulgar Tongue, and Damn it to the Fire, *they permit the* (h) *Turkish Alcoran* in a Vulgar Tongue, with leave had from the Inquisitors, who yet could give no leave to any (as appears before by the Rules of their Expurgatory (i) Index) to have the Gospel, or any part of it, in any Vulgar Tongue. Prodigious Impiety! The *Turkish Alcoran* (the contrivance of a Monstrous Impostor, and Enemy to Christ and Christianity) is permitted; and the Gospel of our blessed Saviour is *absolutely prohibited and damn'd*. And though in doing this, they Act very Impiously, yet (in their Generation and Circumstances) very wisely. For neither the *Alcoran*, nor any Book in the World, is so fatal to their miscall'd Catholick Religion, as (when truly understood and believ'd) the Bible. That Book evidently disco-

(e) *Liber Versionis Gallicæ Novi Testamenti, cui Titulus est Le Nouveau Testament de nostre Seigneur Jesus Christ, &c. Nos Librum hujusmodi tanquam temerarium, Damnosum, à vulgata Editione deformem damnamus, & prohibemus: ita ut nemo cujuscunque Conditionis sub pœnâ Excommunicationis, illum legere aut retinere audeat, sed Ordinariis aut Inquisitoribus desferat, &c.* Ita Clem. 9. Bulla data Rom. 20. Apr. An. 1668.

(f) *Ii qui Libros prohibitos habuerint, eos ad Episcopum ant Inquisitores deferant, qui eos quantocyus comburere debeant.* Ibid. §. 3.

(g) In his Bull 9. Apr. 1668. Pontificatus sui Ann. 1. *Damnamus*

mandantes, ut quicunque librum illum Ritualem habuerint vel habebunt, locorum Ordinariis, vel Inquisitoribus statim tradant, qui nullâ interpositâ mora, igni comburant, aut comburi faciant, &c. (h) *Item Alcoranus Mahometis in Linguâ Vulgari, ex Concessione Inquisitorum haberi possit.* Index Librorum prohibitorum. Alexandr. 7. Edit. Rom. 1664. pag. 3. (i) *Biblia quocunque Idiomate Vulgari conscripta.* Ita Index Librorum prohibitorum, Alexand. 7. Jussu Editus Romæ, 1667. verbo Biblia, p. 14.

vers,

vers, and condemns their Errors; and therefore they are concern'd to keep it from the People, lest they should find (as by that Divine Light they easily might) and forsake their Errors. The Premisses consider'd, let the Reader judge, Whether the Pope have not this Mark of the *Beast*, and Character of *Antichrist*, that he is, ὁ Ἀντίχριστος, the *Adversary* of Christ, and that Religion establish'd by him; who prohibits the having and reading (and so the Understanding) of the Gospel, Damns it to the Fire, and burns it; and yet at the same time permits the *Alcoran*.

3. Another Characteristical Note or Mark of *Antichrist* given by St. *Paul*, is; *That he Exalts himself above all that is called God or Worshipped*; So our English Translation; so their Authentick Vulgar (*k*) Latin; and their own Learned (*l*) Commentators justifie it. The word in the Text properly (*m*) signifying, *Id quod Colitur*, any thing or person, which is the Object of Honour and Veneration. So that thus far we are agreed, *That Antichrist will Exalt himself above all that is called God*, (as all Magistrates Subordinate and Supream, Kings and Emperors in Scripture are) *or worshipped*. This then (*in Thesi*) being granted, we must next (*in Hypothesi*) inquire, *Whether this Caracteristical Note and Mark of Antichrist, may be truly affirm'd of the Pope, and be really found in him*; In Answer to which Query, I say, I hope it may, and does appear by the Premisses, That the Pope does Exalt himself, far above all Kings and Emperours, more then any man in the World ever did, or (Antichrist excepted) ever will; and therefore I shall only add two or three things in Confirmation of the Premisses. 1. Then, his Favourers and Flatterers give him (and he approves and assumes it) *The* (*n*) *Title of Em-*

(*k*) *Extollitur super omne quod dicitur Deus, aut quod Colitur.* Clem. 8. in Bibliis, 1592.

(*l*) Corn. A Lapide in 2 Thess. 4. §. 27.

(*m*) Σέβω, συβάζω, Colo, veneror. Σέβας, Τιμὴ (Suidæ & Hesychio) Σέβασμα, Colendum, venerandum, Id quod veneratur. Athanasius Orat. contra Gentes, (ex sapientiâ Sirach, c. 14. 17.) Τὸν πρὸ ὀλίγῳ πηχθέντα ἄνθρωπον, νῦν σέβασμα ἐλογίζοντο· ubi σέβασμα Numen, Deum significat. Sic Act. 17. 23. Σεβάσματα Sacra Gentilia, quæ venerabantur, seu Numina, Altaria, Templa, &c. Hinc Cæsares Σεβασοὶ, Augusti; Hesychio, προσκυνητοὶ, Τιμητοί. (*n*) *Sanctiss. Urban. 8. Universi Imperator: Angelus* Maria Cherubinus, in Calce. Tom. 4. Bullarij Romani, Rom. 1638. pag. 120.

peror

peror of the *Universe*. Upon this account, That the *Pope is Emperor of the Universe*, of the whole World; it follows, That all Kings and Emperors are his Subjects, and he their Supream Lord and Soveraign, and so, far greater in Power, then any one, or all of them together And least we should mistake, and undervalue his Papal Greatness; Pope *Innocent* the Third told the Emperor of *Constantinople*, (and has told us in the Body of their approved and received Law) *That the Pope is as much greater than the Emperour, as the* (o) *Sun is greater than the Moon*. And here the Author of the Gloss, (*Bernardus de Botono*, a great Lawyer, but no good Astronomer) tells us, *That the Sun is* 47. *times greater than the Moon*; and so (by that Computation) *the Pope is* 47. *times greater than the Emperor*. This is pretty well, and gives so vast a Magnitude to the Pope above the Emperor, that a man would think it might satisfie his Ambition, so that he needed not ask, nor his greatest Flatterers give him more. Yet they do give much more. For in a Marginal Note on the said Chapter, (in their most (p) Correct Editions of their Law) we are told, *That the Sun is greater than the Moon*, Quinquagies Septies, 57. *times; and so the Pope so much greater than the Emperor*. But this is not all. *Laurentius* (a Canonist) in the *same* (q) *place*, tells us; *That it is evident, that the Sun is* $7744\frac{1}{2}$ *greater than the Moon; and so the Pope (omitting the Fraction) Seven thousand, seven hundred, and forty four times greater than the Emperor*. This is so prodigiously erroneous and impious, as none, save their most Holy and Infallible Guide, could be guilty of such Error and Impiety. But a Learned *Roman* (r) *Catholick* (who understood Astronomy, and the Magnitude of the Sun, (much better than the Pope, or his Parasites) seriously tells us, *That the Sun is greater than the Moon* 6539. *times*. And so by the Popes Logick and Decretal Definition, and the Computation of his best Artists, he must be 6539. times greater than the Emperor. Monstrous Pride and Ignorance! which is so far from proving him to be our blessed

(o) Vid. Cap. Solicit 6. Extra. de Major. & Obed. *Quanta est inter Solem & Lunam, tanta inter Pontifices & Reges differentia cognoscatur.*

(p) Vide Corpus Juris Canon. cum Glossis. Parif. 1612.

(q) *Palam est, quod magnitudo Solis continet magnitudinem Lunæ* $7744\frac{1}{2}$. Vide Addit. ad Gloss. verb. Inter Solem. Ad dictum c. 6.

(r) Clavius Comment. in Johan. de Sacro Bosco. p. 189.

sed Saviour's Vicar, that it evidently proves him, to be that (*s*) *Man of Sin*, the great Antichrist, who exalts himself (ὑπὲρ πάντα λεγόμενον Θεόν) above all Kings and Emperors. Certainly Antichrist cannot exalt himself more, then to declare to the World, (as the Pope here does) in his publick Laws and Constitutions, that he is 6539. times greater then any King or Emperor. So that although St. (*t*) *Paul*, and (*u*) *Peter* too, acknowledged the *Emperors Power Supream*, and required that all men (even the Pope if he were a man) should conscienciously obey them ; though St. *Paul* (x) *appeal* (not to *Peter*, but) to *Cæsar*, as Supream: Though *Athanasius* say, *That there lay no* (y) *Appeal from the Emperor, but to God*; and though (z.) *Tertullian* say, *That the Emperor was, Solo Deo minor*; and the Bishops of *Rome*, for almost One thousand years after our blessed Saviour, acknowledged the Emperors their Sovereign Lords, yet *Hildebrand* and his Successors, have (as above) *exalted themselves far above all that is call'd God*, and have that indelible Character of Antichrist, *Q. E. D.* 2. And they further say, *That this Universal Monarchy is given him by God himself*; and so he has it, (not by any Human Right or Injust Usurpation, but *Jure Divino*) by the Law of God, and a Right derived from him ; and this is said, not once only, nor by any private (*a*) Person, (whose Authority might be question'd) but many times in their Authentick *Roman* (b) *Breviary*, restored according to the (c) *Decree of the Council of Trent*, and revised and publish'd by the Authority and Command of (*d*) three Popes successively; so that we may be sure they approve it. That *Breviary* has it thus, (speaking of *Peter*) ———— *Thou art*

(*s*) 2. Thess. 2. 4.

(*t*) Rom. 13. 1.
(*u*) 1 Pet. 2. 13.
(*x*) Act. 25. 11.
(*y*) Athanasius in Apologia, ad Constantium Tom. 1. p. 680. D.
(*z*) Tertul. ad Scap. cap. 2. & Apolog. c. 30.

(*a*) Τῦ εἶ Pastor Ovium, Princeps Apostolorum; Tibi Tradidit Deus Omnia Regna Mundi: Breviar. Roman. Antv. 1650. part. Hiemali, in Festo Cathedræ S. Petri Antiochiæ, in Resp. post Lect. 4. pag. 760.   (b) Ibid. parte Hiemali in Festo Cathedræ S. j. Petri Romæ, ad diem Jan. 18. pag. 700. Col. 1. & in dicti Breviarij Part. Æstiva, pag. 482. In Festo Petri & Pauli, Jun. 29. & ibidem rursus pag. 541. In Festo S. Petri ad vincula.   (c) The ἐπιγεφη or Title of that Breviary, is thus ———— *Breviarium Romanum, ex Decreto Sacro-Sancti Concilij Tridentini restitutum, Pij 5. Pont. Max. Jussu Editum, & Clement. 8. primum, nunc denum Urbani P. 8. Authoritate recognitum*. Antverp. 1660.   (d) Pius 5. Clem. 8. Urban. 8. as above.

Prince

Prince of the Apostles; *And God hath Given Thee All the Kingdoms of the World.* These are the words of that *Authentick Breviary*, approved and confirm'd by the Authority of those three Popes before-mentioned, (as appears by their Bull prefix'd to the Edition) and is now in publick use in their Church. So that he Exalts himself, as Universal Monarch, over all the Kings and Kingdoms in the World; and that (as he impiously pretends) by a Divine Right, and the Donation of God himself; And hence it is, *That not only the Canonists* (the constant and great Parasites of the Pope) *but even the Learned Divines of the Roman Church, give the Pope* (and he approves and assumes) *such Extravagant and Blasphemous Titles, as none but the Man of Sin, who Exalts himself above all that is called God, would approve.* To pass by many hundreds of the like nature, I shall instance only in one. *Stapleton* (an English-man, and a very Learned Professor of Divinity at *Doway*) in his Dedicatory Epistle to Pope *Gregory* the Thirteenth, calls that Pope (e) ———— *The Highest Top and Prince of the Catholick Church, The Master of the whole World, and on Earth The Supream God or Deity.* Certainly, he who approves and admits such Titles to be given him, *Exalts himself above all that is called God,* and so has the Character of Antichrist mention'd by the Apostle, 2 *Thess.* 2.4. And here (though I intended it not) I shall crave leave to add two or three Passages more, which casually come in my way and memory, and are very pertinent to our present purpose. 1. The Gloss on their (f) Canon Law tells us, *That the Pope is neither God nor Man, but something more then Man.* And though this Impious and Blasphemous Gloss was (g) Censured to be left out, by the Master of the *Sacred Palace.* Yet (h) *Clement* the Eighth thought otherwise; and those words are still in the best Edition of the (i) Canon Law; only with this Note in the Margent, *Hæc verba sunt sane modo intelligenda, prolata enim sunt, ad Ostendendum Amplissimam Pontificis Rom. Potestatem.* But this Gloss is something modest, though it make the *Pope* more then

(e) Stapleton in Academiâ Duacenâ Theol. Professor, in Epist. Greg. 13. Princep. Fidei Doctrin. Demonstrationi præfixa; Papam appellat, *Catholicæ Ecclesiæ Verticem Coruphæotatum, Totius Orbis Magistum & Supremum in terris Numen.*

(f) *Nec Deus es, nec Homo, quasi neuter es, inter utrumque.* Glossa ad Prooemium Clement. verbo, *Papa.*

(g) Vide Censuram in Glossas Jur. Can. per Tho. Manrique, Colon. 1572. p. 13.14.

(h) Vid. Indicem Expurg Olysipone, 1624. p. 350.

(i) Paris. 1612.

then Man; and being in Verse, may have some Poetical Licence allow'd. 2. But another Gloss in plain Prose expresly says, *That it is* (k) *our Lord God the Pope*. For although in some (l) Old Editions of the Canon Law, it was only *Our Lord the Pope*; yet now in the most (m) Correct Editions of that Law, confirmed by *Gregory* the Thirteenth, it is (without any Qualification in the Margent) *our Lord God the Pope*. 3. And to make the Blasphemy full, and evidently Antichristian, *Ant. Fuccius* in an Oration made by him in their General *Lateran Council*, speaking to Pope *Leo* the Tenth, says, (n) *That the Rays of his Divine Majesty did dazle his Eyes*. Impious and Antichristian Pride and Blasphemy! yet approved at *Rome*, and by themselves (to their shame) published to the World. Nor is this all: He pretends to, and assumes an Infallibility, and that of so high a Nature, that all his Definitions and Determinations of Doubts (whether *è Cathedrâ* or *not*; whether in a *General Council*, or out of it; *to be the Word of God*. So a Learned Popish (o) Author tells us; *That the Word of God is threefold*; 1. *His written Word, the Scriptures*: 2. *His unwritten Word, Traditions*: 3. *His explained or declared Word*; *when Scripture or Traditions are declared and explained by the Pope*; *whether in or out of a Council*. And he says, (p) *That this last Word of God*, (the Popes Definitions and Explications) *is the most approved, and most men do with greater pleasure acquiesce in it*. Though this be much, yet not all. For the Pope does not only pretend to, and assume to himself an Universal Monarchy, over all the Kingdoms of the World; but such an Absolute Power to dispose of them; that he can (*parte inconsultâ*) give away Kingdoms (*pro Arbitrio*) to whom he pleases. A memorable, and (for Papal Pride and Injustice) a Prodigious Instance we have of this, in Pope *Alexander* the Sixth, who at one

(k) *Credere Dominum Deum nostrum Papam non posse sé statutere, Hæreticum Censetur.* Glossa ad Cap. cum inter 4. verbo. Declaramus De verborum significatione. Extravag. Johan. 22.

(l) Edit. Parif. 1519.

(m) Edit. Parif. 1612.

(n) *Divinæ Majestatis tuæ conspectus, rutilanti cujus fulgore oculi mei Caligant, &c.* Crab. Concil. Tom. 3. Conc. Lateran. Sess. 9. pag. 648. Col. 2.

(o) *Verbum Dei est triplex*: 1. *Scriptum, scilicet Scriptura sacra.* 2. *Non scriptum, Traditio.* 3. *Explicatum; cum dubia in verbo scripto vel non scripto Explicantur, & determinantur: & hoc et præsertim per summum Pontificem, sive Extra Concilium, seu in Concilio.* Lud. Bail. in Apparatu de triplici verbo Dei, Tom. 1. Summæ Concil. Præfixo.

(p) *Iste Modus ultimus* (the Popes determinations of doubts) *Magis Probatus est, & cum majore suavitate si Plures acquiescunt*. Ibidem in principio dicti Apparatus.

Clap,

Clap, gave to (q) *Ferdinand* and *Elizabeth*, (King and Queen of *Castile*) and their Heirs for ever, *All the West-Indies, from Pole to Pole, and all the Isles about them* (which lay *One hundred Leagues Westward from* Cape Verd, *and the* Azores) *with all their Dominions, Cities, Castles, Villages, all the Rights and Jurisdictions belonging to them.* And this, he says, he gives, *of his own meer Liberality, by Power deriv'd from Peter, and as Vicar of Christ.* Then he Excommunicates all of what degree soever, Kings and (r) Emperors (by name) who shall dare to trade into the West-Indies (given to Ferdinand by him) *without the leave and licence of the said* Ferdinand. Here we see, the Pope gives away almost half the World, from the true Owners, *Causa incognita, inaudita, indicta*; the Persons and their Quality being utterly unknown to him. If it be said, *They were Pagan Idolaters:* Grant that. Yet, 1. What they all were, he neither did, nor could know. 2. If they really were such, (as probably they were) yet *dominium non fundatur in gratiâ*; a Pagan and Idolater may (*jure naturæ*) have as just a Temporal Right to his Estate, as a Christian. *Cæsar* was a *Pagan* in our blessed Saviour's time; and yet he Commands them to (*s*) *give to Cæsar the things which are Cæsars*, Some things were *Cæsars* in which he had a propriety, and to which he had a right, and his Subjects an Obligation to pay him tribute, and other things (*t*) due to him. But I hope this will not be deny'd: For if none, but pious men, and true Christians have any just Right to what they possess, it will (I fear) go hard with his Holiness, and he will have no Propriety in St. *Peters* Patrimony, or any other thing he does possess. And therefore (if he impartially consider it) he may find some

(q) *De nostra merâ Liberalitate, omnes Insulas & Terras firmas inventas & Inveniendas, versus Occidentem & Meridiem, fabricando unam Lineam à Polo Arctico ad Antarcticum, quæ Linea distet à qualibet Insularum quæ Vulgariter dictæ sunt, De los Azores y Cabo Vierde, Centum Leucis versus occidentem, Cum Omnibus illarum dominijs, Civitatibus, Castris, Villis, Juribus, & Pertinentiis universis, vobis, hæredibus & successoribus in perpetuum donamus.* Constit. 2. Alexandr. 6. §. 8. in Bullario Rom. Tom. 1. p. 347.

(r) *Ac Personis cujuscunque Dignitatis, etiam Imperialis, Regalis, & sub Excommunicationis latæ Sententiæ pœnâ, districtius Inhibemus, ne ad Insulas aut terras dictas, pro mercibus habendis, vel causâ aliâ quavis, accedere præsumant, absque veniâ vestrâ, aut Hæredum Speciali Licentiâ.* Ibid. §. 8.

(s) Matth. 22. 21.
(t) Rom. 13. 7. The Apostle commands the Romans to pay Tribute to whom it was due, that is, to *Cæsar*; for to him only they were Subjects, and to him only Tribute was due from them. Our blessed Saviour (as man, born in the Roman Empire) was subject to *Cæsar*, and paid him Tribute. Matth. 17. 25. And that (as *Cajetan* and *Lucas Burgensis* on that place, truly say; That) he paid that Tribute, not *de facto* only, but *de debito*.

reason

reason, if not for Truths sake (which with him is not always a prevailing Motive) yet for his own, to be (in this) of my Opinion: by the Premisses, I hope it may, and does appear, *That the Pope Exalts himself above all that is called God, or worshipped*; and so really has the Characteristical Note and Mark of the Beast, that *Man of Sin*, and is indeed that *great Antichrist* described and foretold in Scripture.

4. Nor am I singular in this Opinion; many Excellent Persons (both for Learning and Piety) have said as much: and some have given us a Catalogue of their (*u*) *Testimonies*. I shall say nothing of the Fathers; many of which make *Rome Babylon* in the *Revelation*, some of them I have cited before, and *Schardius* (in the Place last Quoted) has more. Nor shall I say any thing of the poor persecuted *Waldenses* and *Wiclifists*, or the Reformed Churches since *Luther*; who both believ'd and constantly affirm'd and prov'd the Pope to be Antichrist; especially the Church of *England*, as appears, both by her ablest Writers, and her *Authentick* (*x*) *Homilies*, confirmed by the Kings Supream Authority in Convocations and Parliaments. Omitting all these (which yet were abundantly sufficient to shew, that I am not singular in this Opinion) I shall only (of very many more) give a few evident Instances and Testimonies of those who lived and died in the Communion of the Church of *Rome*. And here,

(*u*) Vide *Testimonia ex variis Authoribus Collecta Romam Babylona esse, Ejusque Episcopum jure Antichristum dici*; per Simon. Schardum, in calce Epistolarum Petri de Vincis. Basil. 1566.

(*x*) See the third part of the Homily of Good Works; in the first part of the Homilies, p. 38. and the sixth part of the Homily against Rebellion, in the second part of the Homilies, p. 316. where the Pope is call'd the *Babylonical Beast of Rome*.

1. The Emperor *Frederick* the Second, in a Letter to the King of *France*, complaining of the Prodigious Pride and Tyranny of the Pope, and his Impious Practices to divide the Empire, and ruin him; he says, *That he Indeavour'd to build the* (*y*) *Tower of Babylon against him*. And that we may know what and whom he meant *by Babylon*, in another Epistle to the King and Nobility of

(*y*) *Novissime ad Supplantationem nostram aspirans, ut adversus David, turrem Construeret Babylonis, &c.* Apud Pet. de. de Vineis, Epist. Lib. 1. cap. 13. pag. 129.

France; he complains of the horrid Injuries and Injustice done him by the Pope and his Party, he calls them (z) the *Elders of Babylon*, &c.

(z) *Videte Orbis generale Scandalum, dissidia gentium, generale justitiæ dominium videbantur,*

leatis Excidium, exeunte Nequitia A Senioribus Babylonis, qui populum hactenus Regere videbantur, &c. Apud eundem, lib. 1. cap. 21. pag. 152.

2. A faithful Historian (speaking of Pope *Hildebrand*, or *Gregory* the Seventh, and his Prodigious Tyranny and Impiety) tells us, (a) *That in those times, Most Men, both privately and publickly, curs'd* Hildebrand, *call'd him* Antichrist: *that under the Name and Title of Christ, he did the work of Antichrist; that he sat in Babylon, in the Temple of God; and (as if he had been a God) Exalted himself above all that is worshipped, &c.* And much more to the same purpose; abundantly Testify'd by the Historians of those times, who were neither *Lutherans*, nor (by the *Roman Church*) then reputed *Hereticks*. And afterward (speaking of the same *Hildebrand*) we are told ―― (b) *That he laid the Foundation of the Kingdom of Antichrist One hundred and seventy years before that time* (when that was said) *under a colour and shew of Religion; He began the War with the Emperor: which his Successors continued to that Day*, (till the the time of *Frederick* the Second, and Pope *Gregory* the Ninth) where we have many things more, concerning the Prodigious Pride, Impiety, and Tyranny of the Pope, to prove that he was Antichrist. The same Historian also tells us; *That almost All Good, Just,* and (c) *Honest Men did in their Writings publish to the World, that the Empire of Antichrist begun about that time,* (the time of *Hildebrand* he means) *because they Saw those things then come to pass, which were foretold long before.*

(a) *Plerique tum privatim, tum Publicè indignum facinus clamitant, Pro Concione Gregorio Maledicunt,* Hildebrando *malè precantur;ipsum Antichristum esse prædicant, Titulo Christi, negotium Antichristi agitati in Babylonia, in Templo Dei Sedet; super Omne id quod colitur, extollitur; quasi Deus sit, &c.* Joh. Aventin. Annal.Bojor. lib.5. p. 352.Basil.1615.vid. plura Ibid. p.363.

(b) Hildebr. *ante Annos 170. primus specie Religionis Antichr.Imp.fundamenta jecit. Hoc bellum nefandum primus auspicatus est,quod per Successores huc usque continuatur.――Flamines illi* (Papas Rom. Intelligit) *Babyloniæ Soli regnare cupiunt: ferre*

*parem non possunt, in Templo dei Sedeant, extollantur supra omne id quod Colitur: Ingentia loquitur perditus homo ille,quasi Deus esset,&c.*Aventine Ibid. lib. 7. pag. 420, 421. Vid. plura Ibid. p.444.
(c) *Plerique Omnes Boni, justi, ingenui, simplices, tum Imperium Antichristi cœpisse, quod ea quæ Christus tot Annos Ante nobis Cantavit,evenisse cernebant, memoriæ Literarum prodidere.* Joh Aventinus,Ibid.lib.5 p 363.Edit.1615.& Edit 1580. p. 470. And the Learned Marc. Ephesius in the Council of *Florence*,call'd *Rome Babylon.* Binius Concil.Tom.8.p.580.Edit.Paris.1636.

3. But

3. But this is not all. We have further Testimonies of this Truth. 1. *Robert Grosthead*, who (both for Learning and Piety) was Inferior to none in his Age: He (on his Death-bed) having spoke of *many horrid Enormities* of Rome, *and loss of Souls by Papal Avarice*; he adds———
(d) *Is not such a one deservedly call'd Antichrist? Is not a Destroyer of Souls* (the Pope he means) *an* (e) *Enemy of God and Antichrist?* And after a long List of Papal Tyranny and Impieties, he calls *Rome Egypt*; (so Saint *John* calls it (f) *Spiritually Sodom and Egypt*) and concludes *that the* (g) *Church will never be deliver'd from that Egyptian Servitude, but by the Sword.* 2. Nor is this all: we have great Councils of whole Nations, in their Publick Edicts and Constitutions, expresly declaring the Pope, to be that Antichrist, *who Exalts himself above all that is called God.* We have a Publick Edict, published by *Ludovicus Bavarus* Emperor, and his Counsel; wherein Pope *John* the Two and twentieth is call'd (h) *Antichrist, the Disturber of the Peace of Christendom, and the Bishops and Clergy who adhered to him, Messengers of Antichrist.* And not long after, the same Emperor, in a Diet or Counsel of the Bishops and Nobility of *Germany* and *Italy* too, and with their joynt Consent, publishes an Edict, in the Year 1328. wherein we have a long Catalogue of the Prodigious Impieties and Tyranny of the Pope, and then and there they call him——— (i) *A Personated Pastor,* (one who would seem to be a Pastor of the Church) *but was indeed, That Mystical Antichrist.* And in the same great Counsel, they publish another Imperial Decree or Constitution, wherein having set down that Character of (k) Antichrist, *That he should Exalt himself above all that is called God, or worshipped,* and assume a Power and Domination over the whole World:

(d) *Episcopus dolens de jactura Animarum per Papalis Curiæ Avaritiam, suspirans ait: Obstus devenit, ut animas Lucraretur. Ergo, qui animas perdere non formidat, nonne Antichristus merito dicendus est?* Matth. Paris. in Hen. 3. ad Ann. 1253. p. 875.
(e) *Nonne ergo Animarum destructor inimicus Dei & Antichristus censetur?* Ibidem.
(f) Rev. 11. 8
(g) Ibid. p. 876. Edit. Watsij. *Nec liberabitur Ecclesia ab Ægyptia servitute, nisi in ore Gladij Cruentati.*
(h) *Qui se Mystas Christi ferunt, sunt Nuncij Antichristi*———*Nec per hunc Antichristum, licet Christianis pacem à Deo datam servare.* Joh. Aventinus Annal. Bojorum, lib. 7. p. 469. Editionis Basil. 1615. (i) *Sicuti Pastor es Personatus, ita Mysticus est Antichristus.* Ibidem, pag. 473. vid. Epist. Ecclesiæ Leodiensis ad Paschal. 2. apud Binium, Tom. 7. part. 2: p. 518. (k) *In Templo Dei, hoc est, Ecclesia, quasi Deus, Sedebunt, & super Omne illud quod usquam Gentium, aut Colitur, aut cultum est, extollentur. Dominationem, turbi orbique Terrarum, rejecta Cruce Christi, arripient, &c.*

They

against Queen Elizabeth. 137

They add, *That by many* (l) *Experiments, they saw these Predictions, come to pass, and* (*unless they were as stupid as Asses*) *they must be sensible of them*; And then (m) Declare, *That all who adhere to, and follow the Pope, are Antichristians, and He Antichrist.* I know that the *Roman* (n) *Inquisitors* have call'd *Aventine, Author damnatus,* an Author damn'd by them; and have noted all these places, I have Cited, to be Expunged; (I have the *Inquisitors* own Book, wherein all the Places in *Aventine* are to that purpose, *Uncis inclusi,* and to be left out in all following Editions of *Aventine*). But the World knows, that they have (with great Impieties and Impudence) corrupted thousands of Authors, putting out whatever makes against their Errors, and putting in, what makes the Author say, what he never meant. But their Damnation of what *Aventine* says, out of the Imperial Constitutions, is no refutation of it; nor are those things untrue because they would have them Expunged: as the Second Commandment is no less Divine, and a part of the Decalogue, because they leave it out. But enough of this; The Case is too plain, to need more proof.

nish Index Expurgat. Madriti, 2612. & p. 449. and at Madrid, 1667. down particularly, all the passages to be Expunged.

But some say, *That Antichrist is not yet come; nor will come till towards the end of the World.* And (o) *Bellarmine* says, *That this is the Opinion of Catholicks.* And some Learned Protestants (as *Grotius* and Dr. *Hammond*) say, *That Antichrist is both come, and gone,* 1600 *years ago.* For *Caius Caligula* (*Grotius* his Antichrist) died (p) *Anno Christi,* 43. And *Simon Magus* (who by Dr. *Hammond* is supposed to be Antichrist) died (q) *Anno Christi,* 68. So that both *Caius* and *Simon Magus,*(who are their supposed Antichrists) are dead above a thousand six hundred years ago. Whence it will follow, That the Pope neither is, nor ever was, or can be Antichrist. For if either *Caius* the Emperor, or *Simon Magus* were then, when they lived, Antichrist, then

(l) *Quæ ideo vates viridici, Nobis ante cantarunt, verissima esse experimentis animadvertimus; & nisi plane Asini simus, Sentimus, &c.*

(m) *Qui contra obstrepere ausit, tanquam Reipubl. hostis. inimicus Pietatis & Satelles Antichristi, ultimo Supplicio Parricidium luat.* Conditum est hoc Decretum An. 1338. Extat apud Aventinum, Annal. Lib. 7. p. 479.

(n) The Portugal Index Expurgatorius. Olysipone, 1624. pag. 29. damn; *Aventine,* in General only. But the Spanish p. 562. Col. 2.

Dubium.
(o) Bellarm. de Rom. Pontif. lib. 3. cap. 3. §. 1.

(p) Baronius Annal. Tom. 1. ad Ann. 43. §. 1.
(q) Item Tom. 1. ad Ann. 68. §. 15. 17.

the Pope was not; (neither of them being Bishop of *Rome*) and both of them being (so many Ages since) dead; the Pope neither is, nor ever can be Antichrist, unless you will have two great Antichrists; which no man yet ever did, or (with any Reason or Sense) can say.

In Answer to this, I shall say a few things: And, 1. For *Bellarmine* (who says, *That the Catholick Opinion is, That Antichrist is not yet come*) I confess he, and all his Party are highly concern'd to say so. For if Antichrist be Actually come, then the Pope must be that *Man of Sin*: He (and none in the World but he) having all the Characters and Marks of Antichrist mention'd in Scripture, so plain, that he who runs may read them. 2. Though *Bellarmine* say, *'Tis the Catholick Opinion, that Antichrist is not yet come*; yet it evidently appears (by the many Authentick Testimonies before Cited, and the Authors were Papists) That Antichrist is come Six hundred years ago, and that the Pope was he, *Plerique Omnes Boni, &c.* (says the Historian before cited) *Most Good Men believed* Rome *to be* Babylon, *and the Pope Antichrist.* 3. *Bellarmine* (r) Cites one, (and he Bishop of *Florence*) whose (s) Opinion was, *That Antichrist was then come*, (almost (t) Six hundred years ago) and was severely rebuked for it by Pope *Paschal* the Second, in a Synod call'd by him at *Florence*. But *Bellarmine* might have named Five hundred more, (which he wisely conceal'd, because they were against him; and he neither had, nor could have any just Answer to so many, and so evident Testimonies) I shall only add (besides those before mention'd) one signal Testimony more, to shew, That even at *Rome* it self, it was believ'd, that Antichrist should come in the end of the Tenth Century. I have seen (and the Book, if any desire it, is still to be (u) seen) a very Ancient and Excellent MS. Missal, belonging anciently to the Church and City of *Rome*, (for there are some particular Services in it, to be said in some of the chief Churches in *Rome*.) In this MS. Missal, in the begin-

Sol. I.

(r) Bellarm. de Rom. Pont. Lib. 3. cap. 3. §. Refert. B. Augustinus.
(s) *Concilium Florentinum, Episcoporum 340. Præside Paschal. 2. contra Fluentinum illius Loci Episcopum, qui Motus Quotidianis Portentis, quæ tunc Accidebant, dicebat jam tum natum esse Antichristum.* Genebrard. Chron. lib. 4. ad An. 1105. p. 355.
(t) Since that Council wherein he was censured, (Ann. 1105.) are 574 years pass'd.
(u) In *Bodley's* Library in Oxon. Cod. 76. super D. Art:. The MS. was given to St. *Peter's* Church in *Exester*, in *Edward* the Confessor's time, by *Leofricke*, first Bishop of *Exon*; as appears by his own hand, in the beginning of that Manuscript.

ning

ning of it, there is a Chronological Table, in which (amongst other things) we are told, That *à Christo ad Antichristum sunt Anni* 999. So that it was believ'd then at *Rome*, that Antichrist should come in the last year of the tenth Century: and if he d d so, (and so it was believed then) *Sylvester* the Second (a *Prodigious* (*x*) *Villain* was then Pope, *who was a famous* (or rather infamous) *Magician*, *and obtain'd the Popedom by the help of the Devil*, as their own *Platina*, and *Johan. Stella* tell us. I know their Writers and the Popes Parasites since *Luther*, do (but without any just reason) question the truth of what *Platina*, *Stella*, and others more ancient have said of this *Sylvester*; so (*y*) *Onuphrius*, *Papirius*, (*z*) *Massonus*, and others, who against Truth, and the Faith of all former Historians, indeavour (*Æthiopem lavare*) to quit *Sylvester* of all these Crimes, and make him (what he was not) an Excellent Person.

(*x*) *Malis Artibus Pontificatum adeptus est —— Ambitione & Diabolicâ dominandi cupiditate Impulsus, Archiepiscopatum Rhemensem, dein Ravennatem, postremò Pontificatum, Adjuvante Diabolo, consecutus.* And a little before, *Relicto Monasterio. Diabolum secutus, cui se Totum tradiderit, &c.* Plat. in vitâ Sylvest. 2. See the Hist. of Magick by *Gabr. Naudæus*, c. 19. pag. 255. & Johan. Stella de vitis Pontificum, (*opus revisum & correctum sub Julio* 2. as we are told in the last page save one) Basil. 1507. in vita Silvestri. 2. (*y*) In Annotat. ad vit. Silvest. 2. apud Plat. Edit. 1526. (*z*) In vitâ Silvest. 2.

2. For (*a*) *Grotius*, who would have *Caius Caligula* to be Antichrist, and Dr. *Hammond*, who thinks, that *Simon* (*b*) *Magus* and his *Gnosticks* better deserv'd that Name: I confess they were very Learned and Worthy men, but men; and had (as the best have) their Errors. *Optimus ille non qui nullis, sed minimis urgetur*. Certainly it is as lawful for me (and not more immodestly) to contradict them, as it was for them to contradict all (Ancient and Modern) who ever writ on those Passages in the Second to the *Thessalonians*, concerning Antichrist. I had, and have great respect and reverence for their Persons, and Memory, but more for Truth; and therefore, the Apology of *Aristotle* (concerning the Errors of his Master *Plato*) may, and shall be mine. *Amicus Plato μᾶλλον δ᾽ τ᾽ἀληθής*. He (whoever he be) who out of Reverence and Respect to any men (how great soever) either imbraces; or (when he knows them) conceals their Errors, wants Charity to himself

(*a*) Grot. in 2. Thess. 2. 4, 5.
(*b*) Dr. *Hammond* on the same place, and more largely, contra D. Blondellum Dissert. 1. Prooemialis. De Antechristo.

self and others; who possibly (if he had not conceal'd them) might have avoided those Errors, and gain'd the knowledge of Truth. In short then, I consider

1. That it is evident in the Apostle, that Antichrist was not come when St. *Paul* writ that Epistle; for he tells them, (e) *That an Apostacy must first come, and that which hindred the Appearing of Antichrist, must be taken out of the way,* (neither of which was done, when he writ that Epistle) *Grotius* saw this, and therefore (unless he would contradict Truth and the Apostle) he could not make *Caius* Antichrist, unless the Epistle were so dated, that it was writ before *Caius* appear'd. For this purpose, he tells us, *That Paul writ the Epistle,* Anno (d) Christi, 38, or 40. *in the Second year of* Caius Caligula; *and* (he says) *that although* Caius *was Emperor before St. Paul writ this Epistle, yet his Impiety did not appear till afterwards; He in the beginning of his Reign carrying himself like a good Prince.* So that the main Hinge on which *Grotius* his Opinion turns, is this date of *Paul's* Epistle: For if it was not writ before *Caius* appeared, (or the year 40.) then 'tis evident that *Caius* cannot be Antichrist, nor *Grotius* his Hypothesis true. Now that this Epistle was writ in the Second year of *Caius Caligula* (which *Grotius* affirms) is so far from being true, that (by the Judgement and Consent of the most Learned Chronologers (Papists and Protestants) it was writ at least Seven or Eight years after *Caius* was dead. Such, I mean, as the late Lord Primate of *Ireland* Dr. (e) *Usher,* (f) *Baronius,* (g) *Simpson,* (h) *A Lapide,* (i) *Calvisius, &c.* all of which Authors (and many more) say, and prove, that it could not be writ before the year of Christ, 50. and some of them, that it was writ *Anno Christi,* 53, or

(c) 2. Thess. 2. 6, 7.

(d) Secundum Computum Dionysij vu'gat 38 sed Ann. Christ. 40. secundum verum Computum. *Collegi* (inquit Grotius) *scriptam hanc Epistolam Anno Altero Caiani Principatus.* Grotius in Prolog. ad 2. ad Thess.

(e) Usserius Annal Part. posteriori. Ætat. Mundi. 7. ad Ann. 54. p. 667. in which year he says, and proves this Epistle to be writ. (f) Baronius Annal. Tom. 1. ad Ann. Christ. 53. §. 1. p. 408. in which year he says this Epistle was writ. (g) Ed. Simpson Chronici Cathol. part. 7. ad Ann. 51. p. 36. hoc Ann. 2. ad Thess. Epist. scriptam putat. (h) Corn. A Lapide in Argumento ad. 2. ad Thess. & in Chronolaxi Actuum Apostolorum ad Ann. Christ. 53. pag. 4. quo Ann. 2. ad Thess. Epist. esse Scriptam asserit. (i) Calvisius ad Ann. Christ. 50. hoc Ann. 2. ad Thess. scriptam vult.

54. So that the Learned Primate of *Ireland* (Second to none in Exactness in Chronology) speaking of *Grotius* his date of this Epistle, says, (k) *That* Grotius *erred exceedingly, when he said this Epistle was writ in the time of* Caius Caligula. 2. But that it may evidently appear, that St. *Paul* did not write this Second Epistle to the *Thessalonians* Anno Christ. 40. (as *Grotius* says) but at least Ten or Eleven years after; let it be consider'd, 1. That it is a received Truth, that *Paul* was Converted *Anno Christ*. 34. 2. 'Tis certain in the Text, that *Paul* had been at (l) *Thessalonica*, before he writ his First Epistle to them. The Query then will be, When he came to *Thessalonica*: For if he had not been there, before the year 40. *Grotius* his Hypothesis will be evidently untrue. And that he was not, will appear from that Account Scripture gives of him, after his Conversion; Thus, 1. He himself tells us, that immediately after his Conversion, he (m) went into *Arabia*, and returned to *Damascus*; and then (n) after three years, he went to *Jerusalem* (which was *Anno Christ*. 37. and (o) fourteen years after, he and *Barnabas* went up to *Jerusalem* (*Anno Christ*. 51.) 2. He and *Barnabas* (sent from *Antioch*) went to *Jerusalem*, and were at the (p) Council of the Apostles there; which Council was held, *Anno Christ*. 47. says (q) *Simpson*; *Ann*. 48. as the (r) *Magdeburgenses* think; *Ann*. 50. says (s) *Helvicus*; *Ann*. 51. so (t) *Baronius*, (u) *Funccius*, (x) *A Lapide*, (y) *Bellarmine*, &c. *Anno Christ*. 52. says (z) Archbishop *Usher*. Now let the Council be held which of these years you please, it will utterly overthrow *Grotius* his Hypothesis. For, 3. It is evident in the Text, that *Paul* at the time of that Synod, had not been at *Thessalonica*, and so had writ no Epistle to them; seeing he says, (a) that he had been with them before he writ his First Epistle. That he had not been at *Thessalonica* at or before the time of the Council, appears by what *Luke* says of him after the Synod: who tells us, that he went to (b) *Antioch*; then through (c) *Syria* and *Cilicia*; then to (d) *Derbe* and *Lystra*,

(k) Annal.part. posteriori, Ætate Mund. 7. ad Ann. Christ. 54. p.668. *Toto Cœlo erravit Grotius, cum hanc Epistolam sub Caio exaratam existimabat.*
(l) 1 Thess.i.5.

(m) Gal.1.17.
(n) Gal.1.18.
(o) Gal.2.1.
(p) Act 15.2.
(q) Chron. Catholici, part. 7. ad Ann.47 p 34.
(r) Centur.1.lib.2.cap.9.p.420.
(s) Theatro Hist. ad dictum Annum.
(t) Tom. 1. ad Ann.51.§.6.
(u) Chronol ad dictum Ann. p.93.
(x) In Chronotaxi, ad Ann.51.
(y) In Chronor. sua ad dictum Ann.
(z) Usserius Annal.part.2. ad Ann. 52. pag.660.
(a) 1 Thess. 1.5.
(b) Act.15.30.
(c) Ibid. ver.41.
(d) Act.16.1,2.

Lystra, Circumcised *Timothy*, and took him along with him. Then he went through (*e*) *Phrigia, Galatia*, and *Mysia*, and so to *Troas*. And (in a Vision) being call'd to (*f*) *Macedonia*, he went to *Neapolis* and *Philippi*: and having pass'd through *Amphipolis* and *Apollonia*, he came to (*g*) *Thessalonica* (the first time he ever was there; but, as yet, had never writ to them.) Thence he went to (*h*) *Berea*, (*i*) *Athens*, and (*k*) *Corinth*; At *Corinth*, *Aquila* and *Priscilla* (banish'd from *Rome*, as all Jews were, by *Claudius*) came to him: and this was the Ninth year of *Claudius*, (that is, *Anno Christ.* 51.) as *Josephus, Orosius, Baronius*, and all *Chronologers* testifie, as a very Learned (*l*) Historian tells me: And he himself confesses, that *Paul came into* Greece (*m*) *Anno Claudij.* 9. that is, *Anno Christi*, 51. And yet *Paul* had writ no Epistle to the *Thessalonians*, till *Timothy* (whom he left at *Thessalonica*) came to him into (*n*) *Greece*, (as he himself tells us) so that by the Premisses, I think it may, and does appear, that the First Epistle to the *Thessalonians*, was not only writ after the Synod of the Apostles, *Act.* 15. but after *Paul* had pass'd through and preach'd in all those Countries before mention'd, after he had been at *Thessalonica*, left *Timothy* there, came into *Greece*, met *Aquila* and *Priscilla* come from *Rome*, (which was *Anno Christ.* 51.) and *Timothy* was returned to him; then (and not till then) he writ his First Epistle to the *Thessalonians*; and therefore it is impossible *Caius Caligula* should be Antichrist, who was not come (as (*o*) St. *Paul* tells us) when he writ his Second Epistle, who yet was come and dead, at least Seven or eight years before he writ the First. 3. And Dr. *Hammond* confirms what I have said; who grants, that the Second Epistle to the (*p*) *Thessalonians* was writ *Anno Christ.* 51. which was at least Seven or Eight years after *Caius* (*Grotius* his Antichrist) was (*q*) dead and gone. So that (by (*r*) Dr. *Hammond*'s Principles) *Grotius* his Hypothesis is utterly overthrow,

(*e*) Ibid. vers. 6.
(*f*) Ibid. vers. 11, 12.
(*g*) Act. 17. 1.
(*h*) Ibid. vers 10.
(*i*) Ibid. vers. 15.
(*k*) Act. 18. 1.
(*l* Orosium secuti sunt Omnes deinceps Chronographi, & Baronius, &c. Hen. Valesius in Notis ad cap. 18. lib. 2. Eusebij p. 37.
(*m*) Paulus Anno demum Claudij. 9. venit in Græciam. Ibid. Col. 2. B.
(*n*) 1 Thess. 3. 2, 6. vid. Hen. Holden Theolog. Parisiensem in Tabula Gestorum Pauli, In Calce N. Test. à se, cum Annotat. Edit. Paris. 1660. p. 883, 884. ubi hæc Omnia sinnat.

(*o*) 2 Thess. 2. 6, 7.

(*p*) Dr. *Hammond* in the Prologue to his Annotat. on the Second to the *Thessalonians*.
(*q*) Baronius Annal. Tom. 1. ad Ann. Christ. 43. §. 1. In which year 'tis certain *Caius* died. (*r*) Dr. *Hammond* Annot. p. 718. Col. 2. ex Professo proves that *Caius* could not be Antichrist.

overthrown, and *Caius* the Emperor cannot possibly be that Antichrist St. *Paul* speaks of; who was not come, when he writ that Epistle.

2. And by the same Principles, Dr. *Hammond* has evidently Confuted his own Opinion, and Excluded *Simon Magus* from all possibility of being Antichrist. For that Doctor expresly affirms two things; 1. That the Second Epistle to the *Thessalonians*, was writ, in the year of our blessed Saviour, 51. 2. That then Antichrist (when that Epistle was writ) was not come or reveal'd: which two things being granted, (as they must, for the Doctor says the one, and the Apostle the other) it evidently follows, that *Simon Magus* neither was, nor could be that Antichrist the Apostle speaks of in that Epistle. For it is certain, that *Simon Magus* was come, and his Heresie and Prodigious Impiety discovered many years before. For, 1. It is certain, that when *Peter* and *John* were sent to (*f*) *Samaria*, they met *Simon Magus* there; who though he had been (*t*) baptiz'd by *Philip* the Deacon, was no better for it, and Impiously offer'd (*u*) Money to purchase Power to give the Holy Ghost; *Peter* (cursing both (*x*) him and his Money) told him, *That he was in the* (*y*) *Gall of Bitterness, and the Bond of Iniquity*. 2. Now this was done, in the year of our blessed Saviour (*z*) 35. which was Fifteen or Sixteen years before, the Second Epistle to the *Thessalonians* was writ, or Antichrist come and revealed, (according to Dr. *Hammond*'s own Computation) And therefore it is impossible that *Simon Magus* should be that Antichrist, the Apostle speaks of. For that from the year 35. till after 51. (for Sixteen years together) he should not discover, but conceal his Impiety, (who as a Magician and an Impious Villain before, and then declared by *Peter*, to be in *the Gall of Bitterness, and Bond of Iniquity*) is utterly Incredible. Sure I am, that (*a*) *Baronius* and (*b*) *Nicephorus* (to name no

(*f*) Act. 8.
(*t*) Ibid. ver. 13.
(*u*) Vers. 18.
(*x*) *Thy Money perish with thee*, ver. 20.
(*y*) Ibid. ver. 23.
(*z*) Baronius Annal. Tom. 1. ad Ann. 35. §. 9. Ita etiam Hen. Holden Dr. Theol. in Tabulâ Gestorum Petri, in Calce N. Test. cum Annot. suis Edit. Parif. 1660. p. 881.
(*a*) *Magus cum inde recessissent Apostoli, contra eos obniti, eorumque Doctrinæ adversari non dubitaret: & qui olim Samaritas dementarat, Judæos iisdem Artibus aggressus, quos Apostolis Infensos videat, se esse Dei Fi-*

lium, illis Suadere Conatus est. Baronius Annal. Tom. 1. ad Ann. 35. §. 20. &c. *Itaque hinc Simon Magus æmulatione percitus, contra Apostolos, eorumque Doctrinam si Arma-vit*. Nicephor. Histor. Eccles. Lib. 2. cap. 6. p. 141. (*b*) Καὐτὸς ὁ *Doctrinam si Arma-*

more)

more) tells us, That after the Apostles were gone from *Samaria*, *Simon Magus* set himself against our blessed Saviour and his Apostles, (whom he thought only better Conjurers than himself) and by his Magick and Diabolical Arts seduced many Samaritans and Jews, and made them believe that he was the Son of God, &c. So far was he from Concealing his Impiety, till after the writing of that Second Epistle to the *Thessalonians*, and the year 51. That by all the Magick and Malice he had, he publickly seduc'd both Jews and Gentiles, long before that time; and so could not be that great Antichrist St. *Paul* speaks of. 2. But I neither shall, nor need bring any further proof of this Particular, (that *Simon Magus* had before the year 51. discovered himself to be an Adversary to our blessed Saviour, and his Apostles and Christianity) because Dr. *Hammond* himself (though in Contradiction and Evident Confutation of his own Hypothesis) doth both Confess, and *ex professo*, prove it. For he tells us ———— (c) *That after he was baptiz'd*, Act. 8. *he went on in his way of deceiving the People by Sorceries, as appears, by his desiring to buy the Power of working Miracles from the Apostles, and being deny'd that, Soon after he set up, and opposed himself against Christ, and accordingly is here call'd ὁ Ἀντικείμενος, the Adversary, &c.* where Dr. *Hammond* tells us, *That soon after Simon's being with the Apostles at* Samaria, *he discovered himself to be an Adversary to Christ, our blessed Saviour.* Now 'tis certain, that his meeting the Apostles at *Samaria*, was *Anno* (d) *Christ*. 35. and so (by Dr. *Hammond's* Computation, who says *that Epistle* (the Second to the *Thessalonians*) *was writ Ann.* 51. that is, Fifteen or Sixteen years before Antichrist came, and therefore it is impossible *Simon* should be that Antichrist *Paul* speaks of, who was not come when he writ that Epistle, unless you will say, (which is highly irrational) that Antichrist came Fifteen or Sixteen years, before St. *Paul* says he was to come. 3. Nor is this all; for the same Learned and Reverend (e) Doctor tells us, out of (f) *Eusebius*, *That* Simon Magus

---

(c) Dr. *Hammond* in his Annotat. on 2 Thess. 2.3. Lit. E. p. 719. Col. 1.

(d) Baronius Annal. Tom. 1. ad An. Christ. 35. §. 9.

(e) Dr. *Hammond* Annotat. on 2 Thess. 2.3. litera d. p. 718. Col. 2.

(f) Eusebius Hist. Ecclesiast. lib. 2. c. 12. in the Latin; but 13. in the Greek.

Magus *came to* Rome, *in the beginning of* Claudius *his Reign*; *where he did such Miracles by the help of the Devil, that he was taken for a God, and had a Statue erected for him. And almost all the* Samaritans, *and some of other Nations confess'd him to be the first and Principal God, and worshipped him with all sorts of Sacrifices,* &c. These are his words, by which it is evident (in the Doctors Opinion) that *Simon* was at *Rome*, In the Beginning of *Claudius* his Reign, and sufficiently revealed to be an Adversary to our blessed Saviour and the Gospel, and prevailed so far, that (as (*g*) *Hierome* tells us) *Peter* went to *Rome, Anno Claudij* 2. (which was *Anno Christ*. 44.) to oppose *Simon* and defend the Gospel. Now all know, that *Claudius* began his Reign, *Anno* (*h*) *Christ.* 43. which was at least Seven or Eight years (in Dr. *Hammond*'s own Computation) before the Second Epistle to the *Thessalonians* was writ, or Antichrist come; And therefore *Simon Magus* could not be that Antichrist *Paul* speaks of, who was not come or reveal'd, when that Epistle was writ; whereas *Simon* was both come and reveal'd some years before.

3. Many things are said of Antichrist in Scripture, which cannot be applied to *Caius*, or *Simon Magus*, with any truth or probability. 1. Antichrist was (by Usurpation) to have a *Supream Power* and Authority, (as our (*i*) Adversaries confess) and should make war with, and persecute the Servants of Christ, and (as to killing the Body) overcome (k) them, *till he was drunk* (l) *with the Blood of the Saints.* This neither *Caius* nor *Simon Magus* did. *Caius* (though he had a Supream Power) was no persecutor of Christians; much less so far, as to be *drunk with their Blood. Nero* (*m*) was the first Roman Emperor who persecuted Christians; three and twenty years after *Caius* (*n*) was dead: And as for *Simon Ma-*

(*g*) Hierome De Scriptor. Eccles. in Petro.

(*h*) Baronius Annal. Tom. 1. ad Ann. 43. §. 1.

(*i*) Vide Hen. Holden. Dr. Parisiens. in cap. 13. vers. 1. Apoc. *vidi Bestiam*; i.e. *Antichristum, habentem Cap.* 7. i.e. *Authoritatem Supremam, & Cornua.* 10. *id est, potestatem Maximam.* Vid. Grotium in dictum locum.

(*k*) Apoc. 13. 7.
(*l*) Apoc. 17. 6.

(*m*) Euseb. Hist. Ecclef. l. 2. c. 25. πρῶτος αὐτοκρατόρων, &c. Nero Rom. Imperat. primus Hostis, &c. Ita Tertullianus —— *Neronem primum in sectam nostram gladio ferocisse.* Euseb. in Chronico ad Ann. Christ. 70. (*n*) *Caius* died *Anno Christ.* 43. and the first Persecution under *Nero* was *Anno Christ.* 65. Baronius Tom. 1. ad Ann. 43. §. 1. & ad Ann. 65. §. 9.

gus (a despicable and beggarly Magician) he never had any Power of the Sword, nor ever did, or could make War against the Christians, much less overcome them, and be drunk with their Blood. 2. But (that I may not trouble the Reader, nor my self, with any more Particulars) I say (and think it an Evident Truth) that there is nothing said in Scripture, or in the Works of the Fathers, or in any Writings of Ecclesiastical Authors, for Sixteen hundred years after our blessed Saviour, from which it may but probably be concluded, that *Caius* the Emperor, or *Simon Magus*, was that great Antichrist mention'd by St. *Paul* and St. *John*; But πᾶν τοὐναντίον, on the contrary, it does appear both by Scripture and the Consent of Christendom, for Sixteen hundred years, that neither of the two was, or possibly could be that great Antichrist. For,

1. It does appear (by what is above said) that what St. *Paul* says of Antichrist, 2 *Thess.* 2. cannot be meant of *Caius* or *Simon Magus*; because St. *Paul* in that place says expresly, that when he writ that Epistle, the *Man of Sin*, and Son of Perdition *was not come and reveal'd*. And yet that Epistle being writ (as Dr. *Hammond* Confesseth) *Anno Christ.* 51. *Caius* was both come and dead at least Seven or Eight years before the year 51. and therefore could not possibly be that Antichrist who was not come till after it. And for *Simon Magus*, he was (as Dr. *Hammond* grants and proves) both come and reveal'd as many years (as *Caius* was dead) before St. *Paul* writ that Epistle; and consequently before Antichrist was come or revealed. And so he (who was come and reveal'd) could not be that Antichrist, who (as St. *Paul* assures us) was not then come or revealed.

2. St. *Paul* elsewhere gives us some Characters of Antichrist, and his Adherents; as (*o*) *men giving heed to seducing spirits, speaking lies in Hypocrisie, forbidding to marry, and commanding to abstain from meats, which God had created to be received, &c.* Where I observe, 1. That in the

(*o*) 1 Tim. 4.1, &, 3.

the former place, (but now (*p*) spoken of) he told the *Thessalonians*, that an Apostasie must precede the coming of Antichrist; and he tells us, what kind of Apostasie it must be; (*q*) *A departing or falling from the Faith.* 2. That these two Marks of Antichrist (*forbidding Marriage, and commanding to abstain from Meats*) are such as none but the Pope can pretend to; who so severely forbids the Marriage of the Clergy (Secular and Regular) *that it is a* (*r*) *greater sin* (with them) *for a Priest to marry* (though God Approves and Commands it) *in such as otherwise have not the Gift of Continence*) *then it is for him to commit Fornication, and keep a Concubine.* Nay they say, *that a Priests marriage is* (*s*) *Incestuous, Sacrilegious, and worse than All Adulteries.* Nor is this Abominable Doctrine, the Opinion of any *private Doctor* only, but is approved as *Orthodox*, by (*t*) *several Universities.* So that in both these [*forbidding to marry, and commanding to abstain from meats*] what God in his Word expresly approves, the Pope condemns; and what God Commands, he Impiously Contradicts; and so evidently proves himself to be, *That Man of Sin, who Exalts himself above all that is called God.* 3. What the Apostle in this Epistle speaks of the Apostasie and Antichrist which followed, is not of things past or then in being, but of things to come afterwards. For he expresly says ——— (*u*) *That in the Latter Times some should depart from the Faith, &c.* Neither *Apostasie* nor *Antichrist were then come*; but afterwards, *in the Latter times, should come.* 4. Now he writ this we have, 1. The Approbation of the University of *Mentz*; and they say, they had read it diligently; *Dignissimùmque judicasse quod in publicum prodiret, manibúsque Studiosorum Assiduè tereretur.* 2. The University of *Colon* : *Approbat, Omnibúsque veritatis amantibus Plurimum Profuturum testatur.* 3. The University of *Lovan* :——— *Dignum judicat, quod adversus pestilentes nostri Temporis Sectariorum errores, Catholicorum manibus teratur.* 4. The Divines of *Triers*:———*Enchiridion Costeri, quia & eruditè & Orthodoxè per Omnia Scriptum, Summa Cum utilitate legi possit.* (*u*) 1 Tim. 4. 1. ἐν ὑστέροις καιροῖς.

(*p*) 2 Thess. 2. 3.

(*q*) Ἀποστασίαι προς τῆς πίστεως 1 Tim. 4. 1.

(*r*) *Gravius peccat Sacerdos, si Matrimonium contrahat, quam si fornicetur, & domi concubinam foveat.* Vid. Costeri Enchiridion, cap. 15. Propos. 9. p. 459. Edit. 1587.

(*s*) *Hæreticorum Ministri Sacerdotium Incestis Nuptiis fœdant; quæ non sunt Nuptiæ, sed Pejora Omnibus Adulteriis Sacrilegia.* Idem Ibid. p. 460.

(*t*) See the Approbations of *Coster*'s *Enchiridion* in the Beginning. Edit. Colon. 1587. & Edit. Turnoni, 1591. Where

148 Observations on the Pope's Bull

(x) So Ed. Simpson Chronol. Cathol. Part.7.ad Annum 54.p.37.
(y) So Baronius Annal. Tom. 1. ad Annum 57. Num. 189. So Ger. Mercator Atlant. Minoris Arnhemij, 1621. p. 676. In Itinerario Pauli. And so Corn. A Lapide in Chronotaxi, ad Annum 57. *(z) Jac. Userius Armachanus Annal. Part. 2. ad Annum Christi 65. pag. 688.*

Epistle, as some (x) think, *Anno Christi* 54. or as some (y) others (and they far more) *Anno* 57. or (as the most Exact (z) Chronologer) *Anno Christi* 65.

Now let my Adversaries choose which Computation they will, for the date and time of writing this Epistle; let it be (if they please) the year 54. which is furthest from Truth, yet most favourable to their Opinion. I say, admit that this first Epistle to *Timothy* was writ by St. *Paul*, *Anno* 54. yet it will appear by the Premisses, 1. That Antichrist was not then come, nor revealed, because St. *Paul* says so. 2. And therefore, that neither *Caius* nor *Simon Magus* could be Antichrist; Because *Caius* was both come and dead ten or eleven years before; and *Simon Magus* was come, and his Heresie and Impieties revealed (as Dr. *Hammond* grants and proves) long before that time.

(a) In his Second to Tim. 3.1.2.2. &c. which Epistle was writ, says Baronius, Anno Christi 59. Annal. Tom. 1. ad Ann. 59. Num. 19. And Archbishop Usher says it was writ Anno Christi 66. Annal. Part. 2. ad dictum Annum, p. 691. (b) 2 Tim. 3.1. (c) 2 Thess. 2.3.

3. After (a) this, St. *Paul* speaks of this *Apostasie* from the Faith; but still as of a thing not yet come, but to come in future (b) times; ἐσχάταις ἡμέραις, *in the last times*; so that if St. *Paul* say true, that great Apostasie (which was to (c) preceed the coming of Antichrist, was not come when he writ that Epistle, which was (as the Learned Primate of *Ireland* Dr. *Usher* thinks) *Anno Christi* 66. or (as *Baronius*) *Anno Christi* 59. And therefore it is impossible that *Caius* or *Simon Magus* should be Antichrist, both come, and their Villanies revealed long before.

(d) 2 Pet. 1.14. ταχινή ἐστιν ἡ ἀπόθεσις τοῦ σκηνώματός μου, velox est depositio tabernaculi mei. Versio Vulgata.

4. St. *Peter* writ his Second Epistle a little before his Martyrdom; for so he himself says ——— (d) *Knowing that I must shortly put off this Tabernacle*, (or that my death hastens).

haftens) now an Exact (e) Chronologer tells me (and proves) that he died *Anno* 67. and writ this (f) Epiftle *Anno Chrifti* 66. I do know that fome (g) fay he writ it *Anno Chrifti* 67. and *Baronius* fays (h) he writ it *Anno* 69. But, 2. which of thofe years foever it was writ in, the great Apoftafie (which preceeded the coming of Antichrift) was future and afterwards to come. So he himfelf tells us, (i) *But there were falfe Prophets among the People, even fo (ἔσονται) there fhall be falfe Teachers among you, who privily fhall bring in damnable Herefies, &c.* Thefe falfe Prophets and the great Apoftafie were (when he writ that Epiftle) future and to come. And therefore 'tis certain *Caius* or *Simon Magus* could not be Antichrift. For it was writ in the Year 66. *Caius* was come, dead and gone three and twenty years before; and *Simon Magus* his Herefies and Impieties publickly reveal'd and known, and is afore proved, even by Dr. *Hammond* himfelf.

5. In the *Revelation*, St. *John* does more fully defcribe Antichrift; That (k) *he rofe out of the Sea, with feven Heads and ten Horns, and on his Horns ten Crowns, &c. That he fhould make War* (l) *with the Saints, overcome them, and be drunk with their blood*; *That his Seat fhould be* (m) Rome, *myftically, or* (n) *fpiritually call'd* Egypt, Sodom, *and* Babylon; *That ten* (o) *Kings fhould give their Power to that Beaft, aid and affift him in his Tyranny and Impieties*; *That thofe Kings fhould at laft forfake him, and utterly deftroy* (p) *him, and burn and utterly deftroy* (q) Babylon (*or* Rome) *his Seat, never to be inhabited any more*: Which is fuch a Defcription of the great Antichrift, as never can (with any truth or probability) be attributed to *Caius Caligula* or *Simon Magus*. 2. But that which here, I more particularly prefs, is, 1. That St. *John* in the *Revelation* fpeaks of *Antichrift*, (not as paft, or prefent, but) as future, and yet to come, when he writ that Book (as is evident in the Text, and is, and muft be confefs'd. 2. And it is as certain, and generally agreed upon, that he writ the *Revelation* in (r) *Patmos*

(e) Jac. Uflerius Armach. Annal. Part. 2 ad Ann. 67. p. 691. vide Lyranum in Gloffa ad Prologum Hieron. in 7. Epift. Canonicas, & Hieronym. De Illuft. Ecclef. Doctoribus, c. 1.

(f) Idem Ufferius ibid. p. 691.

(g) Simpf. Chron. Cathol. Part. 7. ad Annum 67. p. 44.

(h) Baronius Annal. Tom. 1. ad Annum 69. §. 1.

(i) 2 Pet. 2. 1.

(k) Rev. 13. 1.

(l) Rev. 17. 6.

(m) Rev. 17. 18.
(n) Rev. 11. 8.
(o) Rev. 17. 12. 13.

(p) Ibibem verf. 16. 17.
(q) Rev. 18. 2. 21.

(r) *Patmos* (whether he was banish'd by (*s*) *Domitian*) *Anno* (t) *Christi* 97. The Premisses being granted, (as they ought and must) being built upon better Authority, then any is, or can be for the contrary, 1. That Antichrist was future and to come, when St. *John* writ the *Revelation*. 2. That he writ it *Anno Christi* 97. It will evidently follow, that it was impossible, that either *Caius* the Emperor, or *Simon Magus*, should be that great (*u*) Antichrist. *Caius* being dead four and fifty, and *Simon* (*x*) *Magus* nine and twenty years before St. *John* writ the *Revelation*, and so before Antichrist was to come. I know that the Reverend Dr. (*y*) *Hammond* indeavours to prove, that *John* was in *Patmos*, and writ the *Revelation* there in the time, and about the ninth year of *Claudius*, which was *Anno Christi* 51. which was six and forty years before the time I have assigned for St. *Johns* being in *Patmos*, and writing the *Revelation*: Now for his Opinion, Dr. *Hammond* neither has, nor pretends to any Testimony of Antiquity, save only that of (*z*) *Epiphanius*; who in that particular is miserably mistaken, (as he is in many more) as is (*a*) confess'd and prov'd by Learned men, and they such, who have a due Reverence for the Fathers, and particularly for *Epiphanius*. 2. That St. *John* should be banish'd, and write the *Revelation* under *Claudius*, (which only Dr. *Hammond* and (*b*) *Grotius* say (out of *Epiphanius*) to give some Colour to their new and contradictory Hypothesis) is evidently against the concurrent Sense and Testimonies of Ancient and Modern Authors. For besides *Irenæus*, *Clemens Alexandrinus*, *Eusebius*, *Acta Martyrij*

(r) Rev. 1.9.
(s) *Johannes Apocalypsin viderat, pene sub nostro seculo, ad finem Domitiani Imperij*. Irenæus adverf. Hæres.lib.5. pag.259. Col.2. Edit. Erasmi. So Eusebius Hist. Eccles. lib 3. cap. 23. where he cites *Clemens Alexandr*. for the same purpose. So the *Acta Martyrij Timothei*, apud Photium Biblioth. Cod. 254. p.1402.1403. So Orosius Hist. l. 7. c. 10.11. p. 594. And so Hierom, de Doct. Ecclesiæ Illust. c. 9. ad Ann. 97.

(*t*) Baronius Annal. Tom. 1. ad Annum 97. §. 1.

(*u*) The *Revelation* was writ *Anno Christi* 97. *Caius* died *Anno* 43. (Baronius Annal. Tom. 1. ad Ann. 43. §. 1.) and so was dead 54 years before Antichrist came.

(*x*) *Simon Magus* died *Anno Christi* 68. (Ita Baronius ex Eusebio, Epiphanio, &c. Tom. Annal. 1. ad Annum Christ. 68. §. 17. 18.) which was Nine and twenty years before the *Revelation* was writ, or Antichrist come, if St. *John* says true. (*y*) Dr. *Hammond* in his Premonition to his Annotat. on the *Revelation*, pag. 906. & 907. (*z*) Epiphanius Hæresi. 51. §. 12. & 33. (*a*) Baronius Annal. Tom. 1. ad Annum 99. §. 2. Dionysius Petavius in Notis ad Epiphan. Hæresin. 51. Num. 33. & Baronius Ibid. ad Ann. 93. §. 9. D. Blondellus de Sybillis, lib. 2. cap. 2. Possevin. in Apparat. verbo Johannes Apostolus, pag. 814. &c. (*b*) Grot. in Apocalyp. 1. 9.

Timothei

Timothei apud Photium, Hierome, and *Orosius* (before-cited) *Johan.* (d) *Malela Antiochenus*, (e) *Haymo*, (f) *Arethas*, *Ado* (g) *Viennensis* (and many more) constantly say; That *John* was banish'd into *Patmos*, not by *Claudius*, but by *Domitian*, and writ his *Revelation* there. 3. But I shall not go about any further proof of this; For Dr. *Hammond* has saved me the Labour, and confess'd it; For it is certain from the Text, that *Antipas* had suffer'd Martyrdom, before *John* writ the *Revelation*; *John* himself telling us (h) so, *Thou hast not deny'd my Faith, when* Antipas *my faithful Martyr was slain among you*. So that 'tis Evident, *Antipas* had suffer'd Martyrdom before *John* writ his *Revelation*. Now *Antipas* suffer'd, and was slain by *Domitian*, in the Second Persecution of the *Christians*, which was *Anno Domitiani* 10. *Christi* 92. So the Old *Roman* (i) *Martyrology*, and (k) *Baronius* assures us; and Dr. (l) *Hammond* confesses it, *That* Antipas *suffer'd Martyrdom under* Domitian. Whence it evidently follows, That St. *John* speaking of *Antipas* his Martyrdom, as a thing past when he writ his *Revelation* (and that in *Domitian's* time) he could not write it in *Claudius* his time, who was dead (m) *eight or nine and twenty years before* Domitian *came to the Empire*. So that *Antipas* being put to death, in *Domitian's* time, (as Dr. *Hammond* affirms) and St. *John* in the *Revelation*, mentioning his Martyrdom as a thing past, when he writ; 'tis Evident, that he writ that Book after the death of *Antipas*, and so in, or after *Domitian's* time, and not in the time of *Claudius*.

(d) Joh. Malela in Domitiano MS. in Bibliotheca Bodleiana Oxon. pag. 161. alias 171.
(e) Haymo Hist. lib. 3. cap. 15. pag. 55.
(f) Arethas in Apocalyps. cap. 1. 9.
(g) Ado Viennensis in Chronico, ad Annum Christ. 84. apud Laurent. de la Barre, pag. 493.
(h) Rev. 2 13.
(i) Martyrologium Romanum ad diem Apr. 11.
(k) Baronius Annot. ad Martyrologium Roman ad dictum diem April 11. & Annal. Tom. 1. ad Ann. Christ. 93 §. 9.
(l) Dr. *Hammond* in Annotat. ad Apocal. 2. 13. lit. i. pag. 927. Col. 1.
(m) Moritur Claudius An: Christ. 55. seu 56. Baronius ad Ann. Christ. 56. §. 42. & §. 1. And hence it

Domitianus Imperium adiit Anno Christi 84. *Baronius* ad dictum Annum. appears that *Claudius* died either {84/55/29} Twenty nine, or {84/56/28} Twenty eight *years before* Domitian *came to the Empire*.

5. St. *John* in his first (n) Epistle, speaks of Antichrist *as then to come*, when he writ that Epistle. *It is the last time* (saith he) *and as you have heard that Antichrist shall come,*

(n) 1 Joh. 2. 18. & cap. 4. 3.

even

even now there are many Antichrists, &c. Here two things (I conceive) are *Evident*; 1. That νῦν, *nunc*, when St. *John* writ this Epistle; there were *many Antichrists*; that is, *many* (o) *false Prophets and Hereticks* forerunners of Antichrist, who made way for him. 2. And that the great *Antichrist*, ὁ Ἀντίχριστος, *was to* (p) *come*, when St. *John* writ. This *Oecumenius*, *Bede*, *Estius*, and generally all *Commentators* (Ancient and Modern, Protestant and Papist) which I have yet met with, constantly affirm. 'Tis true, that when St. *John* says (q) afterward, that Antichrist was *Now in the World already*: they truly Explain it, that the meaning is, That he is *now* in the World; *Not* (r) *personally, but in respect to his Forerunners* (*false Prophets and Hereticks*) *who make way for him*. I take it then for a certain truth, that when St. *John* writ this Epistle, ὁ Ἀντίχριστος, *The Antichrist*, or (as Venerable *Bede* calls him) *Maximus ille Antichristus*, was *future*, *and to come*. And (which is something strange) *Grotius* confirms what I have said (which makes much for mine, but little for his purpose) For, 1. He *grants*, that this Text (1 *Joh*. 2. 18.) speaks of (ſ) Antichrist, as *future*, and *to come*. For though the *word here* (and cap. 4. verſ. 3.) be ἔρχεται, in the *Present Tense*, yet *Grotius confesses*, that it must *be taken in the* (t) *future*; *Veniet Antichristus*, Antichrist *will come*. 2. He says, that amongst those many Antichrists St. *John* here speaks of, there shall be one (u) *more Eminent*, which he says was *Barcochebas*, *who appeared not* (he says) *till the Emperor Adrian's time* (which was (x) *long after St. John writ this Epistle*). And he further says, (in Confirmation of what is aforesaid) (y) *That the false Christs, Hereticks, and false Prophets*, (which

---

(o) *Nunc multi sunt Antichristi λέγοι δὲ Κλεινθὸν κ) τῆς ὁμοίας) qui suam illum praecedant, iterque illi parant: προςδοτωσι ὄντων τῶν πολλῶν Ἀντίχρείσων τῷ ἑνί. Oecumenius* in 1 Johan. Epist. κεφ. γ. p 573 C D. So *Beda*, *Estius*, &c. in 1 Joh. 2. 18. So *Gagnaeus*, Ibid. &c.

(p) Τὸν Ἀντίχριστον ἐν ἐσχάτοις καιροῖς προσδοκῶμεν. Idem Ibidem. *Nunc multi sunt Antichristi, qui Omnes Maximo illi Antichristo in Finem Seculi Venturo, quasi suo Capiti, Testimonium credunt.* Beda in 1 Joh. 2. 18.

(q) 1 Joh. 4. 3. Ἀντίχριστος κ) νῦν ἐν τῷ κόσμῳ ἐστὶν ἤδη.

(r) *Jam in Mundo est; ἃ Σωματικῶς ἀλλὰ διὰ τῶν προσδοποιούντων* τῶν πολλῶν Ἀντιχρείσων τῷ ἑνί· Oecumenius ibidem κεφ. δ. pag. 587. D. (ſ) Vide Grotium in 1 Joh. 2. 18. (t) Ἔρχεται, *est sono praesens, sensu futurum*. Grotius in 1 Joh. 4. 3. (u) *Inter Antichristos, unus futurus erat Caeteris Eminentior, ad quem Locus* 1 Joh. 4. 3. *pertinet, is vero non alius fuit quam Barchochebas.* Grotius in 1 Joh. 2. 18. (x) *Apparuit Barchochebas* Ann. Christ. 130. Adrian. 11. apud Baronium, Annal. Tom. 2. ad Ann. 130. Num. 4. 5. (y) Grotius in 1 Joh. 4. 3. *Talis Prophetia* (he speaks of the Prophecies of false Christs, and Prophets) *viam struit Magno Ipsi & Eximio Antichristo.*

John

John calls Antichrists) *do make way for that Great and Eminent Antichrist.*

I take it then for certain, (and confess'd by *Grotius*) that the *great Antichrist was not come*, when St. *John* writ this Epistle. The next thing to be inquired after, is, *When this Epistle was writ?* for if it was writ after *Caius Caligula*, and *Simon Magus* were dead, then it will be undeniably Evident, that neither of them could be that *great Antichrist*, of whom St. *John* speaks; who (when he writ this Epistle) was *future*, and *to come*. Now here it is to be considered,

1. That 'tis a common and received Opinion amongst Learned men, that St. *John* writ this Epistle *Anno* (z) *Christi* 99. or at least after (*a*) *the death of Domitian* (which was *Anno Christi* 95.) So *Baronius*, *Gavantus*, *Lyranus*, (in the places cited) and many others. Now if this Computation be true, (as in the Opinion of very Learned men it is) then *Grotius his Antichrist*, (the Emperor *Caius Caligula*, who died *Anno Christi* 42. was dead Seven and fifty years before *John* writ this Epistle; and therefore Seven and fifty years before Antichrist came; for St. *John* Says, *he was future, and to come when he writ*. And for *Simon Magus* (Dr. *Hammond*'s Antichrist) it is (*b*) certain, he died *Anno Christi* 68. and so One and thirty years before Antichrist was come.

(z) So Baronius Annal. Tom. 1. ad Annum Christi. 99. Num. 7. Bart. Gavantus Comment. in Rubricas, Breviarij Rom.Sect. 5. p. 84.

(a) *Johannes vero nullum post Evangelium & Epistolas Scripsit; Scilicet post mortem Domitiani; quia reversus de Exilio invenit Ecclesiam per Hæreticos perturbatam,&̩ tunc,*

Scripsit Evangelium & Epistolas contra Ipsos. Lyranus in Glossa ad Prologum Hieronymi in septem Epist. Canonicas. (*b*) Baronius.Annal. Tom. 1. ad Ann. 68. Num. 16.17.&c.

2. But *be this as it will*; I shall not (*though I might*) stand upon it; but take the Computation which both (*c*) *Grotius*, and Dr. (*d*) *Hammond* approve; for they both agree in this, that St. *John* writ this Epistle *a little before the destruction of* Jerusalem; and (in the places cited) indeavour to prove it. 2. This being granted; it is further certain, that the *Excidium Hierosolymorum*, was in writ a little before the great destruction which befell the *Jews, &c.* Dr. *Hammond* in his Prologue to his Annot. on the first of *John*:

(c) *Puto Scriptam hanc Epistolam non multo. ante. Excidium Hierosolymorum.* Grotius Annor. In 1. Johannis, in Principio.

(d) *This Epistle seems to have been*

the

the *Second year of Vespasian*; that is, *Anno Christi* 72. That this is so, (*e*) *Josephus*, (*f*) *Eusebius*, (*g*) *Jac. Usserius Armachanus*, (*h*) *Baronius*, &c. assure us. 3. And hence it evidently follows, That both *Caius Caligula* and *Simon Magus* were dead before the year 72. when Antichrist (as St. *John* assures us) was not come. *Caligula* being dead Thirty, and *Simon Magus* Four years before that time.

By the Premisses (I believe) it may, and *does appear, that in Scripture, Antichrist (the great Antichrist) is never spoken of, but as future and to come*: and therefore it is impossible by *Scripture*, (and there is *no other Medium* can do it) to prove that Antichrist *was come*, in any part of that time *in which Scripture was writ*. 2. And as the *Apostles believed and writ*, that in their times, (even in St. *John's*, who lived (*i*) longest) Antichrist *was not come*. So the *Fathers*, and *Ecclesiastical Writers* after them, for about a Thousand years generally, (if not universally) speak of Antichrist as still *future*, and (in their several times) *to come*. I know that some (*k*) anciently (and wildly) thought, that *Nero* was Antichrist, and as much might be said for him, as *Grotius* has said for *Caligula*) but they said, that he was to rise again, and come *Sub Seculi Finem*, and Act as Antichrist. But I never yet read or heard of any, besides the Learned *Grotius* and Dr. *Hammond*, who (in *Sixteen hundred years after our blessed Saviour*) ever seriously *affirm'd*, that *Caligula*, or *Simon Magus* was *Antichrist:* The two Learned Persons (before-mention'd) are the first, and they *Contradict each other*, *themselves*, the *received Opinion* of the *Christian World*, and *gratifie Rome*; whilst they indeavour (which neither they, nor any body else can do) to free the Pope from being the great *Antichrist*. For if

(*e*) Josephus de Bello Judaico, l. 7. c. 47. p. 969.
(*f*) Eusebius in Chronico ad Ann. 72.
(*g*) Usserius Annal. part. 2. p. 698.
(*h*) Baronius Annal. Tom. 1. ad Ann. 72. Num. 29.

(*i*) Hieron. de Illust. Eccles. Doctoribus, c. 9. says St *John* liv'd 68 years after the Passion of our blessed Saviour, to which if we add 34. (the year of the Passion) it will appear that St. *John* died *Anno Christi* 102. Trajan. 2. vel 3.
(*k*) Vide Baronium Annal. Tom. 1. ad Ann. Christi 70. Num. 3. 4. ex Augustino, De Civitate Dei, lib. 20. c. 19. where he says, That by those words (2 Thess. 2.

7.) *Mysterium iniquitatis jam operatur*, *Neronem voluerit Intelligi: cujus jam facta velut Antichristi videbantur.* So *Athanasius* tells us, that *Constantius* (the *Arian* Emperor) acted all those things, which are spoken of Antichrist, but was not *that Antichrist* spoken of in Scripture, (for he was future, and to come, says *Athanasius*) *Quid igitur hic* (Constantius) *quod Antichristi est, omisit? aut Quid ille ubi Venerit, plus committere poterit?* Athanasius Epistola ad Solit. vitam Agente. p. 236.

either

either *Caligula*, or *Simon Magus* (who have been *dead this Sixteen hundred years and more*) be *that Antichrist*, then (unless you will *have two or three such Antichrists*) The *Pope is secure*, and (wrong'd by those who call him so) mis-call'd Antichrist. *Sed salva res est*, there is little danger from such extravagant Opinions; they will neither be beneficial to the Pope, nor prejudical to his Adversaries, **to** believe and prove him to be Antichrist. That *Caligula*, or *Simon Magus*, was that great Antichrist, *none*, or (if any) *very few believe*. The *Reformed Churches* say, that the *Pope is Antichrist*, and have great reason to say so: many **of** the *Prophecies*, and *Predictions of him* in Scripture, being *now actually fulfilled*, and so the truth of the Prediction made *Evident*, and easie to be *understood by the Event*. On the other side the Popish Party say, *that Antichrist is not yet come*; and so neither Party does believe *Caligula* or *Simon Magus* to be Antichrist; because it is a Novel and Apocryphal Hypothesis (take which of the two you will) without truth or probability. Sure I am, that the Reasons those two Learned Persons bring for their Opinions, are evidently Illogical and Inconsequent. For, 1. If *Grotius* his proofs for *Caligula*, be cogent and concluding, then Dr. *Hammond*'s for *Simon Magus* are inconsequent; and if Dr. *Hammond*'s be Good, those of *Grotius* are not. Whence 'tis evident, that all the proofs of the one Party, (at least) are impertinent, and to prove his Position insufficient. 2. But indeed all the Reasons they do bring, to prove their several Positions, are (as I said) illogical and inconsequent. That this may not be *gratis dictum*; I say,

1. That *both their proofs* are built and rely *upon the same ground*; they take (not all, but) only some of the *Characters and Marks of Antichrist* which the Apostles give him in Scripture.
2. They indeavour to accommodate and apply those Marks to *Caligula*, or *Simon Magus*; and think they make it appear, that such Marks are really found in *Caligula* or *Simon Magus*.

3. And

Observations on the Pope's Bull

3. And hence they Argue and Conclude thus —— *Such Marks of Antichrist are to be found in* Caligula, *or* Simon Magus: Ergo, *They (the one of them at least) are that Antichrist:* Or (which is all one) *Magus* and Antichrist agree in some things; *Ergo*, They are the same.

4. Now such Arguing is *miserably illogical and inconsequent;* and no better then this —— *A Duck and a Goose do agree in many things* (each of them has one Head, two Legs, two Eyes, a flat Bill or Beak, and sometimes Feathers of the same Colour, &c.) *Ergo*, A Duck is a Goose. Or thus —— Sempronius *and* Titius *agree in many things* (*they have the same Father and Mother,* Romans *both, born in the same Hour,* (being Twins) *bread at the same School, both good Scholars, &c.* Ergo, Titius *is* Sempronius. The Reasons those Learned men bring to prove their several Antichrists, prove no more then those I have given ; that is, just nothing.

5. The reason of such inconsequence, in such Arguments, is this; Young Sophisters in the University can tell you, out (l) of *Pophyrie*, *Aristotle*, and their Scholiasts) That *every individual person* or *thing*, is made up, and does consist of such *Properties and Qualifications*, *Quorum Collectio nunquam in aliquo alio Eadem esse potest*. It is certain, that a *Collection* of all the *Properties and Qualifications* which Constitute any *Individual person*, cannot be in any other person whomsoever; though it is *as certain*, that *some of them may*. Now had *Grotius* or Dr. *Hammond* taken a *Collection of all the Characters and Marks of Antichrist*, given *him in Scripture*, and made it *appear*, that all those Marks had been *really found* in *Caius Caligula*, or *Simon Magus*, their proofs *had been Logical and Consequent*, (This they *neither did, nor could*) But their *accommodation and applying only some of the Marks of the Beast*, to *Caius* or *Magus*, and thence concluding that they were Antichrist, such deductions are *evidently Illogical and Inconsequent*. And so much the more Inconsequent, because even *those Marks of Antichrist* which they indeavour

(l) "Ἄτομα δὲ λέγεται τὰ τοιαῦτα, ὅτι ἐξ ἰδιοτήτων συνέστηκεν ἕκαστον, ὧν τὸ ἄθροισμα οὐκ ἐπ᾽ ἄλλου ποτὲ τὸ αὐτὸ γένοιτο. Porphyrius in Isagog c 2. §. 28.

against Queen Elizabeth.

deavour *to prove* to be *really* in *Caligula* or *Simon Magus*, never were in either of them, in *that sense* and *extent*, in which *they were* (and since his *coming are*) to be found in Antichrist. If any man *censure* me (as may be some will) for contradicting those two Learned Persons (Dr. *Hammond* and *Grotius*) all the Apology I shall make, (for it needs none) is only this; It is as lawful for me to contradict them, in defence of evident Truth, as it was for them to contradict each other, and the Christian World, in *defence of a Manifest Error*.

9. The Pope in this his Impious and Lying Bull, declares the Queen to be (*what he really was, and she was not*) a (m) *Slave of Sin*, a (n) *Heretick*, and *a favourer of Hereticks*: And then (with a prodigious Antichristian Pride and Impiety) pronounceth his *Penal Sentence* against her, of *Damnation, Excommunication, Deprivation,* &c. And here it is further to be observed;

1. What this *Papal Power* is (and *whence he has it*) which he pretends to inable and authorize him, to sit Judge and pass such Damnatory Sentences against Princes and Supream Powers, for Heresie.
2. What that Heresie is, and who the Hereticks, who (by the Pope) are so severely damn'd for it.
3. What those Punishments are, which they pretend they may, and actually do inflict upon such Hereticks.

1. For the first, *Pius* the Fifth, in the beginning of this Impious Bull, tells us; that this Papal Power *is Divine*. For he says —— (o) *That our blessed Saviour did constitute* Peter *and his Successors, the Popes of* Rome, *Princes over all Nations, and Kingdoms, with a Plenitude of Power, to Pull up, Dissipate, and Destroy,* &c. Thus he, and so others, in their Damnatory Bulls; but with some variation; and (if it were possible) in such words as are more Extravagant, Erroneous, and Impious. I shall only instance in one; *Paulus* the Fourth, who was next Predecessor (save one) to *Pius* the Fifth,

Observ. 9.
(m) *Elizabetha prætensa Angliæ Regina, Flagitiorum Serva.* Bulla, §. 1.
(n) *Declaramus prædictam Elizabeth Hæreticam & Hæreticorum fautricem.* §. 3.

(o) *Christus Sto Petro, Petrique Successori, Romano Pontifici, in potestatis, plenitudine Ecclesiam tradidit Gubernandam. Hunc unum super omnes Gentes & omnia Regna Principem constituit, qui Evellat, Destruat, Dissipet, Disperdat,* &c. *In dictæ Bullæ Principio*.

Fifth, who in his Bull (*p*) *against Hereticks and Schismaticks and their Favourers*, expresses his Power to damn them, thus —— (*q*) *The Pope of Rome here in Earth is Vicar, or Vice-Roy of God and our Lord Jesus Christ, and has Plenitude of Power over Nations and Kingdoms, and is Judge of All men, and not to be judged by any Man in the World.* And that you may see, that they are not *asham'd to pretend to*, and *usurp such an Antichristian Power* (for none but (*r*) Antichrist ever pretended to it). This Bull of Pope *Paul* the Fourth is referr'd into the (*s*) Body of their Canon Law (almost One hundred years ago) dedicated to Cardinal *Cajetan*; and *lately* publi h'd (*t*) again, as a *part of their Law*, without any *Contradiction* (and therefore with the *approbation*) of the *Pope or his Party*. That this their *Opinion of the Papal Power* is far from truth or probability, I have indeavoured to prove before; *& sic transeat cum cæteris erroribus.*

(*p*) *Hæreticorum, Schismaticorum, torumque fautorum pœnæ.* That's the Title of the Bull.

(*q*) *Romanus Pontifex, qui Dei & Domini nostri Jesu Christi Vices-gerit in terris, & super Gentes & Regna, plenitudinem potestatis, obtinet, Omnésque Judicat, à Nemine in Seculo Judicandus, &c.* In Bulla, 19. Paul. 4. Bullarij Rom. Tom. 1. pag. 602. Edit. Rom. 1638.

(*r*) 2 Thess. 2. 4.

(*s*) Corpus Juris Canonici per Pet. Matthæum, Francofurti, Ann. 1599. Cap. Cum ex Apostolatûs, 9. De Hæret. & Schismat. in 7.

(*t*) In *Corpore* Juris Canonici, Lugduni, 1661.

---

2. As to the second point; *What is Heresie*, and *who is the Heretick*, who is to be persecuted with such *fearful Damnations* and *Excommunications*? I say in short,

1. That it is agreed amongst their (*u*) *Casuists*, and (*x*) *Canonists*, That *Heresie is an Error against that Faith which they ought to believe, joyned with pertinacy; or it is a pertinacious Error in Points of Faith;* and he who so holds such an Opinion, is an Heretick.

2. *And he is pertinacious*, they say, *who holds such an* (*y*) *Opinion, which he does, or might, and ought to know to be against Scripture, or the Church*. By the way; I desire to be inform'd, *how it is possible for their Lay-people and Unlearned, to know* (with any *certainty*, or *assurance*) what *Truths are approved, or Errors damn'd in Scripture*; when they are (*z*) *prohibited* (under pain of Excommunication)

(*u*) Hæresis est Error in Fide, cum pertinaciâ. Card. Toler. Instruct. Sacerd. lib. 1. cap. 29. §. 2.

(*x*) Gratian. Can. dixit *Apostolos*, 29. & Can. Qui in Ecclesiâ. 3. Cauf. 24. Quæst. 3. & Glossa ibidem.

(*y*) *Est autem pertinacia, quando homo scit, aut scire debuit & potuit, aliquid esse contrarium Scripturæ, aut ab Ecclesiâ damnatum.* Cajetan. ibidem.

(*z*) Vide Regulas, Indici librorum Prohibit. ex Decreto Conc. Trid. Confecto, præfixas; Reg. 4. & Observat. Regulæ dictæ annexam.

ever to read, or *have Scripture in any Tongue they understand?* Nor are *Bibles* only, in any *Vulgar Tongue* prohibited; but all *Books of Controversie between Protestants and Papists,* in any Vulgar Tongue, are (a) *equally prohibited.* So that they are *absolutely deprived* of the *principal means to know Truth and Error,* what *Doctrines are Evangelical,* what *Heretical.*

(a) *Libri Vulgari Idiomate, de Controversiis inter Catholicos & Hæreticos nostri Temporis differentes, non passim permittantur; Sed idem de ipsis servetur, quod de Bibliis Vulgari Lingua scriptis, Statutum est.* Ibid. Reg. 6.

3. And although they are pleased sometimes to *mention Scripture* in the *Definition of Heresie*; yet 'tis not really *by them meant.* For (by their received Principles) a man may hold a *hundred Errors,* which he *Does,* or *Might* and *Ought* to know to be *against Scripture* and the *Articles of the Faith,* and yet be no *Heretick.* For thus Cardinal *Tolet* tells us ——— (b) *Many Rusticks or Country Clowns,* having Errors *against the Articles of Faith, are excused from Heresie; because they are ignorant of those Articles, and are ready to Obey the Church.* And a little before ——— (c) *If any man err in those things he is bound to know, yet so, as it is without pertinacy, because he Knows it not to be against The Church, and is ready to believe as the Church believes, he is no Heretick.* So that (by their Principles) let a man believe as many things as he will, contrary to Scripture; yet if he have the Colliers Faith, and implicitly believe, as the Church believes, all is well; he is (by them) esteemed no Heretick.

(b) *Unde multi Rustici, habentes errores contra Articulos fidei, excusantur ab Hæresi; Quia Ignorant Articulos, & sunt Parati Obedire Ecclesiæ, &c.* Card. Toletus Instruct. Sacerd. lib. 4. cap. 3. §. 7.

(c) *Siquis erret in his, quæ tenebatur scire, tamen sine pertinaciâ, Quia nescit esse contra Ecclesiam, paratusque est credere, quod tenet Ecclesia, non est Hæreticus.* Idem ibidem.

4. And hence it is, that they have of late, left the word (d) *Scripture* out of their *definition* of *Heresie*; and they only pass for *Hereticks* at *Rome,* (not who hold *Opinions contrary to Scripture,* but) who *receive not,* or *contradict* what is believed to be *de fide,* by the *Pope and his Party.*

(d) *Non enim ut quisque primum in fide peccaverit, Hæreticus dicendus est. Sed qui Ecclesiæ Authoritate neglectâ, impias opiniones pertinaci animo tuetur.* Catechis. Trid. ex Decreto Concilij Tridentini, Jussu Pij 5. Edit. Paris. 1635. Part. 1. cap. 10. De 9. Symboli Articulo, §. 1. p. 107.

And therefore they plainly tell us; That *None can be an Heretick, who believes that Article of our Creed, The Holy Catholick Church* (you may be sure they mean their own *Popish Church,* not only without, but against all reason) For so their (e) *Trent-Catechism* tells us; not only *in the Text,* but (lest we should not *take notice of it*) in the *Margent* too; where they say, *Versu. 9. Articuli Professor* (that is, he who will believe what their Church believes) *Nequit dici Hæreticus.* That is, he who believes the *Church of Rome,* to be the *Catholick Church in the Creed,* and that Church *Infallibly assisted by the Holy Ghost,* he shall not (we may be sure) be call'd an Heretick at *Rome.* Nay, so far are they in Love with their most *irrational Hypothesis; That to believe as the Church believes, excuses their Laicks and the Unlearned from Heresie*; that they expresly say, *That such men* may in some Cases, (not only *Lawfully, but Meritoriously*) believe an *Error contrary to Scripture,* which (in another more knowing Person, would be a *real* and *formal Heresie.* The Case is this, (as Cardinal *Tolet* and *Robert Holkott* propose it, (f) *If a Rustick or Ignorant Person, concerning Articles of Faith, do believe his Bishop proposing some Heretical Opinion,* he does *Merit by believing,* although it be an *Heretical Error*; because he is *Bound* to believe, till it *appear to him to be against The Church.* So that in the mean time he is no Heretick. For, 1. He *may lawfully do it.* 2. He is *Bound* to do it, to believe his Bishop, and the Doctrines proposed by him. 3. Nay, it is a *Meritorious* action to believe such *Heretical Errors,* though it be contrary to Scripture and the Word of our gracious God. This is *strange Doctrine,* yet *publickly*

(e) *Fieri igitur non possit; ut aliquis se Hæresis Peste Commaculet, si iis fidem adhibeat, quæ in hoc nono fidei Articulo credenda proponuntur.* Catechis. Trident. loco dicto.

(f) *Rursus, si Rusticus circa Articulos Credat suo Episcopo, proponenti aliquod Dogma Hæreticum, in Credendo Meretur, licet sit Error; quia Tenetur Credere, donec ei Constet esse contra Ecclesiam.* Tolet. Instruct. Sacerd. l. 4. c. 3. §. 7. Idem habet Rob. Holcott. in 1. Sentent. Quæst. 1. in Replica. ad 6. Principale: where he tells us, that simple people may erre in many things, *Dummodo velint Credere sicut Ecclesia Catholica credit.* And when he puts the case in an old simple woman, and says ——— *Si audiat Prælatum prædicantem Propositionem erroneam, quam ipsa nescit esse erroneam, & ei credit: Non peccat, sed Tenetur Errare, quia tenetur ei Credere; & Meretur volendo Credere Errorem; & concedo (Inquit) quod ipsa potest adipisci Meritum Debitum Martyri, si ipsa Interficitur pro tali Errore, quem credit Articulum fidei, &c.*

maintain'd by (g) their *Casuists* and *Schoolmen*, and approved by their *Church*. For I do not find it *Condemn'd* in any *Index Expurgatorius*, nor (in any *publick Declaration*) *disown'd* by their *Church*; *& quæ non prohibet peccare, aut errare cum possit, Jubet*. And here, in relation to the Premisses, I shall further propose two things, and leave them to the Judgment of the Impartial Reader.

(g) Especially the Jesuits; In the end of the *Exercitia Spiritualia Ignatij Loyolæ*, *Tolosæ* 1593. there are *Regulæ Servandæ, ut cum Ecclesiâ verè Sentiamus*. The first of which is, *Sublato proprio omni Judicio, tenendus est paratus animus ad obediendum veræ Ecclesiæ*. You may be sure they mean the Church of *Rome*. The Thirteenth Rule is this——— *Si quid quod Oculis nostris Album apparet Ecclesia Nigrum esse definierit, debimus itidem, quod nigrum sit pronunciar.* And to the same purpose *Bellarmine* tells us ——— *Fides Catholica docet, Omnem virtutem esse bonam, & Omne vitium malum. Si autem Papa erraret, præcipiendo vitia & prohibendo virtute, Teneteur Ecclesia Credere vitia esse Bona, & virtutes Malas*———*Tenetur credere bonum esse quod ille præcipit, & malum quod ille prohibet*. Bellarm. de Rom. Pontif. l. 4. c. 5 §. ultima. Ita etiam V. Erbermannus contra Amesium, Tom. 1. l. 3. c. 6. §. 5. p. 401. 402.

1. That seeing it is their *Received Doctrine*, that an *Implicite Faith* in their *Church* and a *profession and resolution* to believe as *she believes*, is enough to *free a Papist from Heresie*, and the *punishment* of it: though otherwise (through Ignorance) he *hold some heretical Errors*, contrary to what his *Church believes*: why may not a Protestants Implicite Faith in Scripture, with a Profession and Resolution to believe every thing in it, as it comes to his knowledge; free him from *Heresie* and the punishment of it; though otherwise (in the mean time) he may believe some things contrary to Scripture? Certainly, if an *Implicite Faith* in the *Doctrines taught by the Pope* and *his Party*, (for they are the *Roman Church*) with a *resolution to believe them all*, when they come to *their knowledg*, be sufficient to free *a Papist from Heresie* and the *Punishment* of it; much more, will an *Implicite Faith in the Doctrines taught by our blessed Saviour*, and his *Apostles* in *Scripture*, with *a Resolution to believe them all*, when they really come to *their knowledge*, be sufficient to free a *Protestant from Heresie* and the *Punishment* of it. Because the Doctrines taught by our blessed Saviour and his *Apostles are Divine*, and in such a *measure and degree* Infallible, as the Doctrines taught

taught by the Pope and his Party, (without great Error and Impudence) cannot pretend to.

2. Seeing it is there *Received Doctrine* (as may appear by the Premisses) that if any Bishop preach to this People, (the Laity and Unlearned Rusticks) some *Heretical Doctrine*, they are bound to believe it, and may not only *Lawfully*, but *Meritoriously* do so, till it appear that their Church is against it. Hence it evidently follows; That if the Bishop preach'd this Doctrine, *That 'tis lawful to kill an Heretical King, who is actually Anathematiz'd, and Deposed by the Pope*; they were *bound to believe it*, and might lawfully and *meritoriously do so*; and then, if it was *meritorious* to *believe such a Doctrine*, then to put it in Execution, and actually *kill such a King*, could *not be unlawful* and vitious. So that we need not wonder, that those *prodigious Popish Villains* who were *hired to Assassinate* our *Gracious King* in the late Conspiracy, undertook such an Impious Imployment, since besides great store of Gold given to incourage them, their *Religion* and *Learned Casuists* afforded them such Principles (which they were bound to believe) to warrant and *justifie their Villany*, so that without scruple of Conscience they might do it. In short, they are Hereticks whom *the Pope and his Party are pleased to call so*; for (by their (*h*) Law and Canons) they are *sole Judges of the Crime* (what Heresie is,) and the punishment due to it. 'Tis true, when they have *passed Sentence* upon *any Heretick*, they deliver him to the *Civil Magistrate*; but he is only their *Executioner*, to *hang* or *burn* according to their Sentence; but has no Power to *reverse their Sentence*, nor so much *as to Examine* whether it be just or unjust; but (right or wrong) must do as they determine. And here (to say nothing of the *Impiety and Injustice* of the *Roman Church*, in condemning those they call (or rather miscall) *Hereticks*; I shall take notice of a strange piece of their Hypocrisie, used by them, when (after Condemnation) they deliver the Comdemned person to the Civil Magistrate, when the Bishop or Inquisitor who delivers him, thus bespeaks the Civil Magistrate

(h) *Crimen Hæresis est Mere Ecclesiasticum.* Innocent. 8. Constit. 10. §. 2. In Bullario Romano, Romæ, 1638. Tom. 1. p. 337. Col. 1. vide Cap. Ad abolendum. 9. Extra de Hæreticis. *Qui aliter docent quam Ecclesia Romana, Excommunicantur.*

giſtrate——(*i*) *Sir, We paſſionately deſire you, that for The Love of God, and in reguard of Piety, Mercy, and our Mediation, you would free this miſerable Perſon, from All Danger of Death or mutilation of Members.* And it is there ſaid, that the Biſhop may do this, (*k*) *Effectually and from his Heart.* But notwithſtanding all this *ſeeming Piety* and *Tenderneſs*, when they have Sentenced an Heretick *to death*; they expect and *require the Magiſtrate to Execute* that Sentence, within (*l*) *ſix days*, upon pain of *Excommnuication, Deprivation*, and *loſs of Authority* and *Offices*. Hence it is, that Pope *Alex.* 4. about the year 1260. gives Authority to the Inquiſitors, to (*m*) *Compel All Magiſtrates* to Execute their Sentence, (be it what it will). And Pope *Innoc.* the Eighth ſays, they muſt neither Examine (*n*) *Nor ſee the Proceſs* againſt thoſe they are *to Execute.* Nor is the matter mended ſince the times of *Innocent* the Eighth, and *Alexander* the Fourth; their Succeſſors are for the ſame *Compulſatory Power.* The Council of *Trent* expreſly ſays —— (*o*) *That All Catholick Princes are to be Compelled to obſerve All the Sanctions and Conſtitutions declaring their Eccleſiaſtical Immunities amongſt which this of puniſhing Hereticks is not the leaſt, &c.* By the Premiſſes (I believe) it may appear, that the Hypocriſie of the *Popiſh Church* is inexcuſable, when ſhe takes God's Name in vain, and prays the Civil Magiſtrate, *For the Love of God, &c.* to do that which ſhe knows (if he were willing) he *neither can* nor *dare do*; nor will *ſhe permit him* to do, having *under pain of Excommunication* (and may *other Penalties*) *abſolutely prohibited him* to do it. I ſay, 'tis not only the *Boſhop* who ſo *interceeds to the Civil Magiſtrate*, but the *Church of Rome* her ſelf, by him. Pope *Innocent* the third is my warrant for ſaying ſo; who (in a Decretal Epiſtle to the Biſhop of *Paris*) tells us; That *when a Condem'd*

(*i*) *Domine Judex, rogamus Vos cum Omni affectu, quo poſſumus, ut Amore Dei, Pietatis, & Miſericordiæ Intuitu, & noſtrorum interventu precaminum, miſerimo huic nullum mortis, vel mutilationis periculum inferatis.* Pontif. Roman. Romæ, 1611. p. 456. & Hoſtienſis in ſummâ. lib 5. De Hæretici; pag. 424. Edit. Ludg. 1517.

(*k*) *Pontifex Efficaciter, & ex Corde, Omni Inſtantiâ intercedit, &c.* Ibidem in Rubrica.

(*l*) *Infra 6. dies, ſint aliqua Proceſſuum Viſioni, Sententias latas promptè exequantur, ſub Excommunicationis pœnâ, aliiſque Cenſuris.* Innocent. 8. Conſtit. 10. in Bullar. Rom. Tom. 1. pag. 337.

(*m*) *Facultas Cogendi quoſcunque Magiſtratus, ſub pœna Excommunicationis & Interdicti, &c.* Alexandr. 4. Conſt. 17. in dicto Bullar. pag. 117. Tom. 1. & Conſt. 18. in Lemmate. Ibid.   (*n*) *Sint aliqua Proceſſuum Viſioni.* Innocent. 8. dicta Conſtit. 10.   (*o*) *Cogantur Omnes Principes Catholici conſervare omnia Sancita quibus Immunitas Eccleſiaſtica declaratur.* Concil. Trident. Seſſ. 25. De Reformat. c. 20. In Lemmate, Edit. Antverp. 1633.

(p) Degradatus propter flagitium damnabile & damnosum, traditur Curiæ seculari; pro quo tamen debet Ecclesia efficaciter Intercedere ut contra mortis periculum, circa eam sententia moderetur. Cap. Novimus 27. Extra.De verb.significatione.

(q) Roffensis contra Lutherum, ad Art. 33. Operum p. 642. Dixit enim Lutherus, Eos dicta Orationis formulâ non Orare, sed ludere.

(r) Ecclesia Hæreticum Excommunicat, & ulterius relinquit eum Judicio Seculari, à Mundo Exterminandum per Mortem. Aquin 2.2. Quæst. 11. Art. 3. Respondeo. Si Judex Ecclesiasticus

Person is delivered to the Secular (p) Judge, The Church must effectually interceed, that he moderate the Sentence so (which she knows he neither dare, nor by their Law can do) that the Condemn'd Person may be in no danger of death. I know that (q) Roffensis, (and other of the Popish Party) do endeavour, with many little shifts to palliate the Hypocresie of their Church, but in vain. For *Omnia cum fecit, Thaida, Thais olet.* Sure I am, that (r) Aquinas (Bannes (s) and others who Comment on that part of Aquinas) tells us, *That the Condemn'd Heretick is deliver'd over to the Secular Power, to this very end, that he may be put to death, and taken out of the World*; and a great and famous (t) Canonist (Hostiensis) says expresly, what I have done; that this *Intercession* of their *Church* to the *Secular Magistrate,* in behalf of the *Condemned Heretick,* is (in the Common Opinion) barely *a Colour,* and *verbal* (u) *only,* not *real.* For thus I finde him cited in *Panormitan* on the Decretals ——*Whatever* (says he) *may be said to the contrary*; yet *To this end, is He Delivered to The Secular Power, That he may be punished with death.* Upon these Premisses, I think it evident, that the *Church of Rome,* in this her *Intercession* to the Secular Power, does (with strange *Hypocrisie*) seem earnestly to desire that of the Magistrate, which she knows he dare not do; nay, which *she herself,* by her *publick Laws,* has Commanded him not to do. How she will

tradat Curiæ Seculari Hæreticum, non potest in aliquo cognoscere secularis; scilicet, An Bene vel Male fuerit judicatum, sed tenetur exiqui omainó. Card. Tuschus Conclus. Pract carum Juris, Tom. 4. Lit H. Concl. 95. §. 4. pag. 166. vide Turrecremaram summa de Ecclesia. Venet. 1561. Part.2.lib. 4. pag. 411. where he cites *Wicliff*'s Opinion, *That the Popish Bishops are like the Pharisees, who having said, Non licet nobis quenquam occidere, Christum Seculari potestati tradiderunt, erant tamen homicidæ Pilato Graviores.* And when the Gloss (*verbo deprehensi. Cap. Excommunicamus,* 15. *Extra de Hæreticis*) made some distinction of Persons deliver'd to the Secular Magistrate; and that *docentes trant ultimo supplicio afficiendi; discentes vero decem Libris auri, &c.* There is this Note in the (b) Margent ——— *Hodie nulla est talis distinctio, nam Magistratus Secularis, Quemcunque Hæreticum, sui à Judicibus fidei traditum, debet ultimo Supplicio afficere.* Cap. ut Inqusitioni de Hæreticis. Lib. 6. (b) In Corpore Juris Canon. cum Glossis. Parif. 1612. (s) Bannes ibidem. Conclus. 3. (t) *Sed quicquid dicatur, Ad Hoc fit ista Traditio ut Puniatur morte.* Vide Panormitan. ad Cap. Novimus 27. Extra. De verb. significat. §.8. (u) *Solet Communiter dici, quod ista Intercessio est Potius Vocalis & Colorata quam Essentialis.* Idem Hostiensis, ibidem.

Answer

Answer God (who Infallibly knows all her Hypocrisie) *& her Adversaries*, objecting it, I know not; *ipsa viderit*. In short; it is (x) confess'd, that all those who will not be Inslaved to *Rome*, and believe as she believes, in *every thing*, are *Hereticks*; and not only so, but *damn'd*, and while they continue so, and do not *intirely believe their*, *New-Trent-Creed*, *they are out of all Possibility of Salvation*. So their (y) Casuists perpetually affirm, and their *Trent Council* (in that *Forma Juramenti Professionis Fidei*, in the Bull of Pope *Pius* the Fifth, extant in the (z) *Constitutions of that Council*) requires all their *Ecclesiasticks*, to *promise, vow, and swear to believe and maintain it to their death*. For in the end of that Creed, the words are —— (a) *This is the Catholick Faith, out of which no man can be saved*. And then, they must (b) *promise, swear and vow to believe and profess it, most constantly as long as they live*. So that although *mens lives* be *exemplary and innocent*, their *Doctrines* which they believe, Ancient and Catholick, yet if they dissent from *Rome in any one thing*, (and that too upon just grounds and evident reason) yet they shall be call'd and used *as Hereticks*. A signal Instance we have of this in the *Waldenses* anciently: and because many perhaps, (I speak not of the Learned) may neither know what it is, nor where to finde it; I shall here crave leave to set it down. (c) *Reinerus*, a *Dominican Frier*, an *Inquisitor*, a *severe Persecutor*, who writ against the *Waldenses*, does (to their great honour, and the shame of *Rome*) give them this signal Testimony. *He tells us of more then Seaventy ancient Heresies*, most of which (he says) in his time, were overcome and vanished; *But* (says he)

(x) *Omnes qui ab Ecclesiâ Rom. hactenus descivérant, pro Hæreticus habiti fuerint.* Honorat. Fabri contra Indifferentes; Dilingæ, 1657. lib. 2. cap. 18. & Mart. Bresserum. De Conscientia, lib. 1. cap. 25. pag. 113. 117. 118. *Qui in uno rejiciunt Authoritatem Ecclesiæ.* p. 117. Col. 1. Lin. ultima & penultima.

(y) *In Ecclesiâ duntaxat Romana homines salvari possunt.* Honorat. Fabri, Loco citato. p. 133. So *Bresserus* and the rest of them not only of late, but above five hundred years ago; (yet after the Devil was let loose, and Antichrist revealed) For an old Collector of their Canons tells us *(Ivo Cornotens. Decret. Part. 1. De fide, c. 38.) Firmissimè tene, & nullatenus dubites, Omnes Paganos,*

Judæos, Hæreticos & Schismaticos, qui Extra Ecclesiam Catholicam (Romanam Intelligit) finiunt vitam, in Ignem Æternum ituros, qui diabolo & Angelis ejus paratus est. This is the Charity of *Rome*, to damn all but themselves. (z) Conc. Trid. Antv. 1633. Sess. 24. De Reform. p. 452. (a) Ibid. *Hæc est Fides Catholica Extra quam, Nemo Salvus esse potest.* (b) *Hanc fidem tenro & profiteor, in Præsenti, & Constantissimè tenere ad ultimum vitæ spiritum spondeo, voveo, juro.* Ibid. (c) Reinerus contra Waldenses, Cap. 4. in Magna Bibliothecâ Patrum. Parif. 1654. Tom. 4. Part. 2. Col. 749. *Sectæ Hæreticorum fuerant plures quam 70. quæ Omnes delitæ sunt.* Cap. 4. Reineri.

of all the Sects that were, or had been, (d) *None was so pernicious to The Church of* Rome, *as the* Leonists, *or* Waldenses: *and that for three Reasons.*

(1) *For the Antiquity and long Continuance of these* Waldenses, *from the time of Pope* Sylvester (who was made Pope *Anno Christ.* 316.) *and some said; or* (as others) *from the time of the Apostles.*

(2) *For the Generality of that Sect; because there was Scarce any Country where they were not.*

(3) *When all other Hereticks* (by reason of their Blasphemies against God) *were abhorr'd by those who heard them: The* Waldenses *had A Great Appearance of Piety; because they Lived Justly Before Men; Believ'd All Things well of God, and All the Articles of the Creed.* (The Twelve Articles of their New *Trent* Creed, were neither then believ'd nor known, no not at *Rome*). Well, if all this be true (and it is their Enemy, who gives them this ample Testimony) what was it, that made this Sect of all others *the most pernicious to the Church of Rome?* Certainly, the *Antiquity* or *generality of this Sect*, the *Piety* of their Lives, their *believing all things well of God*, and all *the Articles of the Creed*; none of these could be *Pernicious* to any *Truth*, or any *True Church*. What was it then; Why, he tells us, in the next words, that it was (e) *only* this; *They Blasphemed,* (or spake ill of) *the Church and Clergy of Rome*; *And* (as he Confesses) *The Multitude of the Laity easily believed them:* which is an evident Argument, that it was neither *incredible* nor altogether *improbable*, which the *Multitude of the Laity so easily believed*. Two things indeed those poor persecuted *Waldenses* said, which were very true, and most pernicious to the Church of *Rome*; (for nothing is more pernicious to darkness and error then light and truth) 1. They said, *That the* (f) *Church of* Rome *was the Whore of* Babylon *in the* Revelation.

(d) *Inter Omnes Sectas quæ adhuc sunt, vel fuerunt, non est Perniciosior Ecclesiæ, quam Leonistarum, & hoc tribus de Causis.* Ibid.

(1.) *Prima est, quia est Diuturnior; aliqui enim dicunt quod duraverit, à tempore Sylvestri; aliqui, A Tempore Apostolorum.*

(2.) *Quia est Generalior; Fere enim nulla est Terra, in qua hæc Secta non sit.* Ibid. cap. 4.

(3.) *Tertia quia cum Omnes aliæ Sectæ immanitate Blasphemiarum in Deum, audientibus horrorem inducunt; Hæc Leonistarum, Magnam Habet Speciem Pietatis; eo quod coram hominibus Juste Vivant; & Bene Omnia de Deo credant, & Omnes Articulos qui in Symbolo continentur.* Ibidem.

(e) *Solummodo Romanam Ecclesiam Blasphemat, & Clerum; cui Multitudo Laicorum Facilis est ad Credendum.* Ibid.

(f) *Ecclesia Romana est Meretrix in Apocalypsi.* Cap. 17. vers. 1. 2. &c. Reinerus loco citato, cap. 5. De Sectis Modernorum Hæreticorum. Errore. 6. pag. 750.

2. That the Pope was the (g) *Head of all the Errors in that Antichristian Church*. And on this Account it was, that the Church of *Rome* did call those poor *Waldenses Hereticks*, and as such, did (with Fire and Sword and the utmost Cruelty) persecute them. For (as is aforesaid) he is an Heretick at *Rome* who *Contradicts* or *disbelieves* the (h) *Canons* and *Constitutions of that Church*; although he do not really disbelieve any Divine Truth contain'd in the Canon of Scripture. Now as it was with the poor *Waldenses*; so we are sure, it has been, is, and will be with all Protestants (Princes and People, Supream or Subjects) they are (at *Rome*) declared *Hereticks*, and liable to all the Punishments of that, which they are pleased to call Heresie; and (when they have opportunity and ability) those Punishments will certainly be Inflicted without any Pity or Mercy. And this brings me to the third Inquiry, What those Punishments are? And here, because the Punishments of Heresie are very many, and very great, it is neither my present business nor purpose, particularly to set them all down, and explain them; Only I shall (in favour to the Ordinary Reader, for to the Learned they are better known) name some Authors, where he may finde a Distinct and full Explication of the Nature of Heresie (according to the Popish Principles) and the Number of its Punishments. And here

(g) *Papa est Caput omnium errorum*, &c. Ibid. Errore. 8. they deny'd also. *Transubstantiation, Purgatory, Invocation of Saints, the Popes Supremacy*. Vide Card. Turrecrematam, in summa de Ecclesiâ. Part. 2. lib. 4. cap. 35. p 407. Edit. Venet. 1561.

(h) *Hæresis est, cum quis non sequitus Doctrinam Christi, vel Apostolorum, vel Ecclesiæ, Eligit sibi novam credulitatem* Card. Tuschus Conclus. Juris. Tom. 4. Lit. H. Concl. 91. verbo Hæresis. p. 164. *Hæreticus est, qui aliquid credit, non obstante quod Ecclesia contrarium decreverit. Debet enim Intellectum captivare Sacræ Scripturæ Sanctæque Ecclesiæ*. (Cado mean their own Christians, as Hereticks.

jet. in sum. verbo Hæresis.) And by Holy Church you may be sure they Roman Church, for they acknowledge none else, but damn all other

1. The Gloss of their Canon Law reduces the Punishments of Hereticks to Four Heads, in the General: *Hereticks* (says the (i) *Glossator*) are to be punished either 1. By *Excommunication*. 2. *Deposition*. 3. *Loss of all their Goods*. 4. *By Military Persecution*: that is, by Fire

(i) *Quadruplex Hereticorum pœna secundum Canones: scilicet, Excommunicatio, Depositio, Bonorum ablatio, Militaris Persecutio*. Gloss. ad Cap. ad Apostol. 2. De Sentent. & re Judicata. In 6. verbo. Hæresis, In additione. Ita Hostiensis in summa. Lib. 5. pag. 424. Edit. Ludg. 1517.

and

and *Sword, by War and armed Souldiers.* This is (*k*) approved by several of their Learned Writers.

2. For the *Body of the Canon Law*, (to pass by *Gratian* and his *Decretum*) those who have a mind and leasure, may consult the Titles *De Hæreticis*, which occur in the (*l*) Decretals of *Greg.* 9. of (*m*) *Bonif.* 8. in the (*n*) *Clementines*, *Extravagantes* (*o*) *Communes* (and in the lately added (*p*) *Seaventh Book of the Decretals*) with the *Glosses*, and *Panormitan*'s large Comment upon them.

(*k*) Reynerius de Pisis, in summa de Hæresi. cap. 4. & F. Reynerus contra Waldenses. c.10.
(*l*) Decretal. Greg. 9. Lib. 5. & Tit. 7.
(*m*) De Hæreticis Lib. 5. Tit. 2. in Sexto.
(*n*) Clement. Lib. 5. Tit. 3. De Hæreticis. (*o*) Extrav. Commun. Lib. 5. Tit. 3. De Hæreticis. (*p*) Septimi Decret. Lib. 7. Tit. 3. De Hæreticis & Schismaticis. This Seventh Book of the Decretals was first printed with the Body of the Canon Law, (dedicated to Cardinal *Cajetan*) at *Francfurt.* 1590. and since at *Lions, Anno* 1661.

3. For the Punishment of Hereticks by the Civil Laws; they who have a mind to know, may consult *Justinians Code. Lib.* 1. *Tit.* 5. *De Hæreticis & Manichæis*, with the *Gloss* there. And especially the *Theodosian Code, Lib.* 16. *Tit.* 5. *De Hæreticis, Manichæis & Samaritanis*, with the Larger and most Learned Notes of *Jacobus Gothofredus*; in the Edition of the *Codex Theodosianus* at *Lions*, 1665. *Tom.* 6. *pag.* 104. To these may be added the Severe Laws of the Emperor (*q*) *Friderick* the Second, made in pursuance of the (*r*) *Lateran Council*, and (though he had little reason for it) to gratifie the Pope in his barbarous designs to ruin all those he call'd (generally miscall'd) *Hereticks*: which *Laws* (as we may be sure they would) the (*s*) Pope and his party did highly approve. And have referr'd them into the Body of their Canon Law. 7. *Decretalium. Lib.* 5. *Tit.* 3. *Cap.* 1. 2. *In Edit. Corporis Juris Can. Lugduni, Anno* 1661.

(*q*) Leges Frider. 2. extant in Corpore Jur. Civilis cum Gloss. Lugd. 1618. in Calce lib. 2. Feudorum. Tom. 5. pag. 137. 138. &c.
(*r*) Concil. Laterani sub Innocent. 3. Ann. 1215. & præcipuè Canonis. 3. de Hæreticis.

(*s*) *Nos Honorius, Servus Servorum Dei, has leges à Friderico, pro utilitate Omnium Christianorum* (pro Pernicie Waldensium) *Editas, Laudamus, Approbamus, & Confirmamus, tanquam in Æternum valituras. Ita Honorius Papa* 3. *in Calce dictarum Legum.*

4. And for a full and particular Explication of those Laws, and the Quality of the Punishments of Hereticks Inflicted by

by them, their Casuists and Canonists may be consulted: Amongst many others, such as these ; (*t*) *Fillincius*, (*u*) *Durantus*, (*x*) *Antonius Archiepiscopus Florentinus*, (*y*) *Azorius*, *Paul* (*z*) *Layman*, (*a*) *Raynerius*, *Johan de* (*b*) *Terrecremata*, Cardinal (*c*) *Hostiensis*, and *Antonius Augustinus Archiepiscopus Terraconensis* (a most Learned Canonist, and a very useful Book) has given us a Catologue of their (*d*) Canons *De pœnis quæ sunt Hæreticis Constitutæ*. In short, whoever has a mind, opportunity and ability to Consult the aforemention'd Authors, (or such others) may easily find the Number and Nature of those Punishments, which (by their Impious Papal Canons and Constitutions) are to be Inflicted on those (better Christians then themselves) they are pleased to call Hereticks.

(*t*) Moral Quæst. Tract 32. cap. 7. *De Pœnis Hæreticorum.*
(*u*) Speculi. Lib. 4. Part 4. *De Hæreticis.*
(*x*) Summæ. Pare. 2. Tit. 12. Cap. 4. *De Hæresi*, & *Hæreticorum Pœnis.*
(*y*) Instit. Moral. Tom. 1. Lib. 8. Cap. 10. 11. 12.
(*z*) Theol. Moral. Lib. 2. Tract. 1. c. 15. p. 202.
(*a*) Summæ. Tom. 2. lib. 4. cap. 1. &c.
(*d*) Epitome

1. *De Hæresi.* p. 1017. Venet. 1585. (*b*) Summæ de Ecclesiæ. Part. (*c*) Hostiensis in summæ. Lib. 5. *De Hæreticis.* p. 422. Edit. Lugd. 1517. *Juris Pontificij Veteris.* Lib. 34. Tit. 3. & Lib. 38. & Lib. 11. Tit. 53. Part. 1. & 2. &c.

10. Concerning this Impious Bull, containing the Damnation (as he calls it) and Excommunication of Queen *Elizabeth*, by Pope *Pius* the Fifth ; it is further to be observed, That it is no new things. For Queen *Elizabeth* was actually Excommunicate before, 1. In their famous (*e*) *Bulla Cœnæ Domini* (take *famous* in which sense you will, the worst is good enough) wherein they do (at *Rome*) *Anathematize* and (*f*) *Curse* all *Protestants* (both Kings and Subjects, Princes and Common People) It is called *Bulla Cœnæ Domini*, because it is published every year on *Maundy Thursday*, the Day in which our blessed Saviour Instituted (*Cœnam Domini*) the Sacrament of his last Supper. And here, (by the way) we may observe the difference *between Christ*, and (his pretended Vicar) Antichrist. 1. On that day our blessed Saviour Institutes that Sacrament, as a blessing and seal of the mutual Love between him and his Church, and of the Communion and Charity of Christians amongst themselves ; but the Pope (far otherwise and unlike him whose Vicar he pretends to be) one the very same Day, (without and against Chri-

Observ. 10.

(*e*) Vide Constit. 63. Paul. 5. in Bullo Romano. Rom. 1638. Tom. 3. pag. 183. *ubi omnes istiusmodi Bullæ, quæ dicto Bullario occurrunt Notantur.*

(*f*) *Anathematizamus quoscunque Hussitas, Wickliffistas, Lutheranos, Suinglianos, Calvinistas, Hugonottos.* §. 1. *dictæ Bullæ.*

stian

stian Charity) Anathematizes and Curses the greatest part of Christians. 2. Our blessed Saviour was that Day ready to *Dye* for the Salvation of *Sinners*; but his pretended Vicar is ready, (on the same Day) and (so far as he is able) does *actually damn* the greatest part of the Christian World, and has been drunk with the blood of the Saints. 3. Nor did Queen *Elizabeth* stand Accursed (before *Pius* the Fifth.'s Excommunication of her) only in that *Bulla Cænæ*, but in several other Papal Bulls. I shall only name one; and (because it is of signal Consequence, and to our present purpose) give some short Account of the Contents of it. The Bull I mean, is that of Pope (*g*) *Paul* the Fourth, next Predecessor, (save one) to *Pius* the Fifth, and is (*h*) dated eleven years before that of Pope *Pius* the Fifth. Now concerning this Bull, I observe,

(*g*) Vid. Paul 4. Constit. 19. In dicto Bullar. Tom. 1. p. 602.
(*h*) Bulla Paul 4. data Romæ, 15. Cal. Mart. Ann. 1559. Bulla autem Pij 5. data Rom. 5. Cal. Maij 1570. Eliz. 13. In dicto Bullario Tom. 2. p. 229.

1. That it was no *rash Act* of that Pope, but (if he say true) made with (*i*) *Mature deliberation*, by the *Counsel and unanimous Consent of himself and the Cardinals.*
2. And it is further (*k*) *Confirmed* by his Successor, *Pius* the Fifth, *who Approves and Commands it to be Inviolably kept and observed.* Nor is this all; but (that we may see how such Doctrine is approved at *Rome*). This Bull of *Paul* the Fourth, and that of *Pius* the Fifth, which so fairly confirms it, are now both of them reserv'd into the Body of their (*l*) Canon Law.

(i.) *Habita deliberatione Maturâ, de Cardinalium Consiliis & unanimi assensu.* Bullæ dictæ §. 2.
(*k*) *BullamPaul. 4. &c. Renovamus Confirmamus, illamque Inviolabiliter, & ad unguem Observari volumus & Mandamus.* Constit. Pij 5. 22. §. 3. dicti Bullar. Tom. 2. p. 151. (*l*) Vid. cap. 9, 10. Decret. 7. De Hæreticis & Schismaticis. In Corpore Juris Canon. Lugd. 1661.

Now in this Bull of Pope *Paul* the Fourth, thus confirm'd, approved, and received into the Body of *their Law.*

(m) *Omnes & singulas Excommunicationis, Privationis, &c. & Quasvis alias Censuras & Pænas à Quibusvis Rom. Pont. aut Pro Talibus Habitis, in Constitut. contra Hæreticos Quomodolibet Latas, Approbamus, Innovamus, ac Perpetuo observari, ac in Viridi Observantia esse debere decernimus.* §. 2.

1. He does (*m*) *Approve, Innovate,* and *Confirm All the Cen-*

sures

sures and *Punishments due to Hereticks and Schismaticks*, by any *Constitution of any former Pope*, or *those who were reputed Popes*, *Howsoever those Constitutions were made and promulgated*, and Commands them *to be kept in fresh Memory, and perpetually Observed.*

2. And then he (n) declares (with as little Charity as Infallibility) *that all Hereticks which are, or For the Future shall be, do Incurr All these Censures and Punishments, and 'tis his express Will and Decree they should do so.* And that we may not mistake his meaning, as if All those Censures and Punishments were by him Inflicted and Denounced only upon and against some Inferior Persons and Hereticks, he does seven or eight times expresly name *Counts, Barons, Marquesses, Dukes, Kings and Emperors*: And further says; *That as Heresie and Schism in them is more Pernicious to others*, *so ought their Punishment to be more severe*; and then (*by his Constitution, which he declares to be* (o) *perpetually and for ever Obligatory*, he actually and totally (p) *Deprives them of their Counties, Baronies, Marquisats, Dukedoms, Kingdoms and Empires*, and leaves them *to the Secular Power*, to (q) *receive Due Punishment*, that is, *Death*; as is evident by the Consequents in that Constitution). Nor is this all; He damns them to an (r) *Incapacity* and *Perpetual Inability* of being *restored to their Honours or Possessions*; No, not if they *seriously and truly repent*, and become good Catholicks. For in that case of their true Repentance and forsaking their Heresie, they shall save their Lives; yet they must be (ſ) *Cast into Perpetual Prison, and there be fed with Bread of Sorrow, and Water of Sadness*, *and to have no Comfort or Humanity shew'd them by any, no not by Kings or Emperors*. And though this be the height of Impious and An-

(n) *Necnon Quoscunq; qui hactenus à fide Catholicâ deviasse, aut in Schisma aut Heresin incidisse deprehensi sint, seu in Posterum incident, cujuscunq; Conditionis, Gradus, seu Praeeminentiae existant, etiamsi Baronali, Ducali, Regali, & Imperiali excellentia profulgeant, & eorum Quemlibet, Censuras Poenas praedictas incurrere Volumus ac Decernimus.* Ibidem §. 2.

(o) *Hac nostra Constitutione in Perpetuum Valiturâ, sancimus, statuimus, definimus, &c.* §. 3.

(p) *Comitatibus, Baroniis, Marchionatibus, Ducatibus, Regnis & Imperiis penitus, &, in Totum Perpetuò Privati sint, &c.* Ibidem.

(q) *Secularis* relinquantur arbitrio Potestatis, animadversione Debitâ puniendi, habenturque Pro Relapsis. Ibid. §. 3. (r) *Ad illa de Caetero sint Inhabiles & Incapaces; nec Restitui aut Rehabilitari possint.* Ibidem. (ſ) *Apparentibus verè Poenitentiae Judiciis & Condignis fructibus, in loco aliquo Regulari, ad Peragendum Perpetuam in Pane Doloris & Aquâ Moestitiae poenitentiam, Detrudendi sunt —— & evitari Omnique Humanitatis Solatio destitui debent.* Ibid.

tichristian *Tyranny*, yet (t) it must be Imputed (as he tells us) to the Popes *Clemency and Benignity*. By the Premisses it may evidently appear, That Queen *Elizabeth* was (by many Papal Bulls, and Damnatory Constitutions) actually Excommunicate, before this Bull of *Pius* the Fifth. I desire then to know, Whether those Anathema's of former Popes, (which they Declared and Commanded to be in force against all Hereticks *For ever*, and *Perpetually* Obligatory) were *valid* and did Actually and (as they intended) *Effectually Exclude that Queen out of their Church*, or not? If not; then 'tis certain, the Pope has not that Supream Power he pretends to. For when so many Popes, in their Damnatory Bulls, (and that *Ex Plenitudine Potestatis Apostolicæ*) declare the Queen, and all such Hereticks, Excommunicate, and (as their Phrase is) *cut* (u) *off from the Unity of the Body of Christ*, and Eternally damned : If this be not Effectually done, then all those Bulls are *Bruta Fulmina*, Inefficacious, Null and Insignificant. But if those Anathema's and Excommunications of former Popes, were valid, and the Queen by them, Actually put out of the Church, (as will, I suppose, and must (by them) be granted) then *Pius* the Fifth his Excommunication is a nullity, and indeed a ridiculous Impossibility. It being impossible, he should take from her what she had not ? and deprive her (by any Excommunication) of that Ecclesiastical Communion, of which she stood Actually deprived before by his Predecessors; especially by Pope *Paul* the Third, who Excommunicates and Curses not only *Henry* the Eighth, but particularly all (x) his *Children, Male and Female, born or to be born* of Ann Bolen (Mother of Queen *Elizabeth*): declares them deprived of all *Power and Dominion, and of all their Goods and Patrimony, and Incapable of restitution to that Power and Patrimony, and of Acquisition of any other for the future*. And that we should not doubt, that this was the Popes meaning, they have added a Marginal Note to that Bull in the Roman Edition, which tells us;

(y) *That*

(t) *Ex Ipsius Sanctæ Sedis Benignitate & Clementia.* Ibid. §.3. N. Eymericus Directorio Inquisitorum, part. 3. pag. 516. Col. 1.

(u) *Esséque à Christi Corporis unitate precisam.* In Bulla Pii 5. §.3. & *Paul* the Third in his Damnation of *Hen.* 8. and all his Adherents, says, *Eisque Anathematis, Maledictionis & Damnationis Æternæ Mucrone Percutimus.* Bulla Paul. 3. 7. §. 7. In Bullario Rom. Tom. 1. p. 515. Col. 2. Edit. Romæ, 1638.

(x) *Henrici Regis ex dicta Annates & nascituros, aliósque descendentes, usque ad gradum in Jure Constitutum, nulla ætatis aut sexús ratione habita, dignitatibus, Dominiis, &c. Privamus, & ad Similia obtinenda Inhabilitamus.* Ibid. dictæ Bullæ. §. 9.

(y) That the Pope (in that Bull) *did deprive the Children of* Henry *the Eighth, and his Adherents, of all their Goods and Dignities, and declared them Incapable of any other for the future.*

By the Premisses, I think it may be, and is Evident, that Queen *Elizabeth* (by most Papal Bulls and Constitutions) stood Actually Excommunicate and Depos'd before this Bull of *Pius* the Fifth. Sure I am, the Popish Party never own'd her as their lawful Sovereign, but call'd her an Usurper of the Crown, to which (as a Declared and Excommunicate Heretick) she had no right at all. And it seems, Pope *Pius* himself was of the same Opinion. For in this very Bull, he speaks of her only as (z) *Pretended* Queen; and of her (a) *Pretended right to the Crown.* And hence we may with Reason and good Logick Infer, That when *Pius* the Fifth in this his Bull *Excommunicates* and *Deposes* her; he does (notwithstanding his Plenitude of Power and Infallibility) ridiculously undertake (what he could not do) an Impossibility. For as it is impossible to turn *Sempronius* out of a House in which he never was; or deprive him of a Dominion which he never had, (turning out of a House, necessarily presupposing his being in it, and deprivation presupposing Right and Possession) so it is a like Impossibility for the Pope, by any Excommunication, to turn the Queen out of the Communion of the Popish Church, in which she never was; (being born, baptiz'd and always bred in the Protestant Church and Religion) or deprive her of those Dignities and Dominions, which (according to their own (b) Principles) she never had any right to, nor ever could have any; being (by their Law, and many Papal Anathema's and Decretals) utterly disabled, and made incapable of any such Dominions or Dignities.

(y) *Filiósque eorum de dignitatibus, Dominiis, &c. & bonis Omnibus Privatos, & Ad Alia de Cætero Obtinenda Inhabiles esse declarat.* Ibid. in Margine.

(z) *Elizabetha Prætensa Angliæ Regina.* Bullæ Pij 5. §. 4.

(a) *Ipsam Prætenso Regni Jure privatam.* Ibidem §. 4.

(b) It is a Resolved Case in the Canon Law, (and Pope *Gelasius* is the Casuist who Resolves it) *Quicúnque in Hæresin semel damnatam labitur, ejus damnatione seipsum invaluit*: Or, (as it is in the *Lemma* prefix'd to that Canon) *Ejus Damnationis participem se facit.* Vid. Can. Achatius 1. Caus. 24. Quæst. 1. And Can. Majores 2. Idem Gelasius eodem modo Statuit. And Pope *Felix* says, *Non ultra in eum procedere oportet, qui in hæresin damnatam incidit.* Ibid. Can. Achatius 3.

Obferv. 11.

(c) Vid. Juſtinianum F. ad Leg. Juliam Majeſtatis; & Statut. 25. Edvardi 3 c.2. in the Statute of Purveyors, Anno Domini 1350.

11. It is evident that the Pope in this Impious Bull, does (by his Uſurp'd Antichriſtian Power) Depoſe and Deprive Queen *Elizabeth* of all her Royal Authority, Dominion and Dignity, and ſo puts her into the Condition of a Poor Private Perſon, without any Power or Juriſdiction over all, or any of her Subjects. Whence theſe damnable Doctrines and Impious Concluſions evidently follow.

1. That if any Jeſuit, any Villanous *Raviliac*, or through pac'd Papiſt had kill'd, or with Poyſon or Piſtol had taken away her Life, (as they often Indeavour'd) it had been no Treaſon. For all know, that Treaſon is *Crimen* (c) *Majeſtatis*, or *Laſa Majeſtas*; a Crime againſt Sacred Majeſty; either Immediately, againſt the Perſon, or Perſons in whom Majeſty reſides; or mediately againſt thoſe who are his nearer Repreſentatives, as the Lord Chancellor, Treaſurer and the Judges, when they are in Execution of their Office. And though there be an Inferior Degree of Treaſon, (as of a Servant againſt his Lord and Maſter, a Wife againſt her Husband) yet no Treaſon ever was (either by the Imperial and Civil, or our National and Common Laws) but againſt a Superior. And therefore the Queen being depoſed by the Pope as an Heretick, and actually deprived, not only of all her Royal Power and Majeſty, but of all Juriſdiction and Superiority over her Subjects (and they abſolved from their Oaths of Allegiance and Fidelity) and ſo a Private Perſon only, without any Power to Command Obedience. I ſay, upon theſe Impious Popiſh Principles, to kill the Queen could not poſſibly have had the Nature or Name of Treaſon. Had they by open War, or privately by Poyſon or Piſtols, taken away her Life (as they intended, and often Indeavour'd, as we ſhall ſee anon) they might have been Murderers, but not Traitors. So that the Pope and his Party believing that the Queen was Actually depoſed and deprived of all her Royal Dignity and Dominion, as a Heretick; they muſt conſequently believe, that the Murdering of her, by any

of

of her former Subjects, neither was, nor could be Treason. But this is not all, For,

2. Admit she had not been deposed, by any Papal Law, Bull or Decretal Constitution; yet any of their Popish Clergy might have murder'd her, and been no way guilty of Treason, though they were English men, and born her Subjects; nay, though they had actually taken their Oaths of Allegiance before they took Popish Orders. The reason of this is evident, and a necessary Consequent, from their Impious and Rebellious Principles. For they say, *That the Clergy* (d) *Are no Subjects of any Prince*; and therefore they themselves conclude (as well they may) that if they Rebel and seek the Ruin of their Prince, yet (in them) it is no Treason. This *Emanuel Sa*, the Jesuit expresly tells us, in a Book (not surreptitiously sent into the World, but) publish'd with his (e) *Name* to it, *Dedicated* to the *Virgin* (f) *Mary*, approved, highly *Commended*, and *Licenc'd* by (g) *Publick Authority*. Thus is this Rebellious Doctrine approved, not only by the *Librorum Censor* at *Antverp*; but in Heaven too; at least in the Opinion of the Author, who otherwise would not have dedicated it to the *Virgin Mary*, and desired her Patronage, and Promotion of it, for the good of Souls. Sure I am, I do not find it Condemn'd in any of their *Indices Expurgatorij* (neither in the (h) *Spanish Index*, nor that of (i) *Portugal*, nor that of Pope (k) *Alexander* the Seventh at *Rome*, &c. Nay, so far are the Inquisitors from Condemning this Rebellious Doctrine of *Emanuel Sa*, that the *Spanish Index* does not so much as name, much less censure him or his *Aphorisms*. But the (l) *Portugal Index*, (in which both the Author and his Aphorisms are expresly nam'd) censures only two Propositions (one about *Pennance*, the other about *Extream Unction*) which the *Inquisitors* (the *Supream* (m)

(d) *Clerici Rebellio in Regem non est Crimen Læsæ Majestatis, quia non est Subditus Regi.* Eman. Sa Aphoris. Confess. verbo Clericus p. 41.

(e) Colon. 1599.

(f) *Ad Beatiss. Dei Matrem. Accipe (Sapientia Divinæ Sacrarium) Libellum hunc; tuoque Præsidio sic tuere & promove, ut ad Multorum proficiat æternam Salutem.* Ibid. pag. 2.

(g) *Hi Aphorismi Docti sunt & Pij, Multámque utilitatem allaturi Confessariis Omnibus.* Ibid. pag. 384. Sylvester Pardo. Eccles. Antverp. Canonicas Librorumque Censor.

(h) Index Librorum Prohibit. Novissimus, Madriti 1667. Eman. Sa non Omnino meminit.

(i) Index Librorum Prohibit. Olysipone An. 1624. p. 543. (k) Index Librorum Prohibit. Alexandr. 7. Romæ, 1667. pag. 41.
(l) Loco dicto. (m) *Ii Aphorismorum Codices deinceps permittuntur, à quibus Expunctæ sunt duæ Sententiæ, quas Ann. 1611. pridie Calend. Mart. Cavendas Rescripsit, Sancta & universalis Inquisitionis Congregatio, per Illustriss. Card. Arragonium.* Index Olysipone, 1624. loco dicto.

Congregation.

Congregation of them at Rome) would have left out; and then approved and permitted all the rest. And so that Erroneous and Impious Aphorism, *That Clergy-men are not Subjects of Kings, and therefore not Capable of Committing Treason, although they actually Rebel against and Murder them.* But the late Index of Pope *Alexander* the Seventh, speaks more fully and home to our present purpose, and expresly, *permits,* and *approves* (for we may be sure they will not permit what they do not approve) all *Editions of those* (n) *Aphorisms,* (*Even at* Rome) *before the year* 1602. In all which this Rebellious Aphorism, we are speaking of, was, and so was approved by them. This does further and (if that be possible) more evidently appear out of these their Approved and Authentick Expurgatory Indices, wherein this Proposition ——(*Priests Are By the Law of God Subject to Princes*) is damn'd as Erroneous and Heretical, both in the (o) *Spanish Index,* and that of (p) *Portugal.* For the Inquisitors finding it in the (q) *Index* of *Chrysostom,* Command it to be expunged and blotted out; Although *Chrysostom* (in the Text) says the very same thing. Hence it evidently follows; That if this Proposition (*Priests (by the Law of God) Are Subject to Princes*) be erroneous and false, as the Pope and his Party say it is, (their Inquisitors Commanding it to be Expung'd, as Erroneous) then the Contradictory (*Priests Are not by the Law of God Subject to Princes*) must of necessity be true, and by them approved and believed. Unless they will say, (which were highly irrational and ridiculous) that Contradictory Propositions may be both false, and they believe neither of them. But this they neither do, nor will say; for their greatest Writers publickly say, and Indeavour to prove, *That Priests are not Subject to Princes.* Nay, (r) Cardinal *Cajetan* expresly says, *That the Clergy are so Sacred, that 'tis impossible they should be Subject to Princes.* When

(n) *Emanuelis Sa Aphorismi Confessariorum Hactenus Impressi, etiam Romæ, ante Ann.1602. post autem tale Tempus Romæ Editi de mandato Magistri Sacri Palatij Permittantur.* Index Alexandri. 7. loco dicto.

(o) *Ex Indice Joh. Chrysostom. Basil.* 1558. *Dele sequentia.* And then (amongst many other evident truths) this Proposition follows; *Sacerdotes etiam Principibus Jure Divino Subditi.* This must be Expunged. Index Libror. Prohib. Madriti. 1667. pag. 703. Col.1.

(p) And the Index of *Portugal,* Edit. Olysipone, Ann.1624. p. 753. Col.1. damns the very same Position.

(q) In Indice Operum Chrysostom. Basil. 1558. ex Officina Frobeniana. (r) *Persona Cujuslibet Clerici est Sancta quoad hoc, quod Non Potest Subjici Potestati Seculari.* Cajetan. In 2. 2. Quæst. 99. §. Ad Quintum Dubium mihi, p. 247. Col. 3, 4.

he says, *It is impossible*, his meaning is, that 'tis (not *naturally*, but) *morally* impossible; because if any Prince should use his Priests and Clergy as Subjects, it were a great Sin, and (in his Opinion) Sacriledge; and therefore Impossible: because, according to the Rule of Law, *Illud solum Possumus quod Jure Possumus*. So we have that great Roman Cardinal expresly approving that Rebellious Doctrine, *That Priests are not Subject to Princes*. Nor (we may be sure) was it any private or singular Opinion of his, which died with him; For when (*f*) afterwards, *Emanuel Sa*'s Aphorisms (wherein the same Doctrine was maintained) were publish'd, as a (*t*) Work *Profitable* and *Necessary* for Divines, and *All who had Cure of Souls*. An Advocate of the Parliament of *Paris* (eminent for Law and Learning) tells us two Things. 1. *That those Aphorisms were approved at* (*u*) Rome. 2. And then passes a just Censure upon them ―― (*x*) *That such Doctrine was the Plague and Ruin of Commonwealths: Royal and Supream Powers being the Ordinance of God, by which All Men are made Subject to the Jurisdiction of Kings*; So that Learned Person. And (to pass by all others) an Excellent Person of great Judgment and Integrity, and a *Roman Catholick*, (I mean Father (*y*) *Paul* of *Venice*) tells us; that in the *Quarrels* between Pope *Paul* the Fifth, and the *Venetians*, a World of Books were writ (by Jesuits and others) to vindicate the Popes Cause, and they (*z*) *All Agreed in this, That the Clergy were Exempt from all Secular Jurisdiction, & quoad Personas & Bona; Secular Princes had nothing to do with their Persons or Purses; nor were they Subject to Princes no not in Cases of High Treason*. Nor was this Rebellious Doctrine maintained only by the Popes Party and Parasites; but the Pope himself (whom the Jesuits and Canonists miscall *Infallible*) approves and justifies it; and in *Decemb*. 1105. tells the

(*f*) R. Patris Emanuelis Sa Aphorismi Confessariorum. Coloniæ, 1599.

(*t*) *Opusculum Theologis Omnibúsque animarum Curam habentibus utile ac Necessarium*. Ibid. in Libri dicti Ἐπιγραφῇ.

(*u*) Vide Librum cum hac Ἐπιγραφῇ, Les Oevures de Maistre *Jacques* Leschasier, &c. Paris. 1652. p. 421. *Libellus Aphorismorum Romæ Probatus*.

(*x*) *Quæ Doctrina* (that the Clergy are not Subject to Princes) *est pestis & eversio Rerum publicarum――Regia potestas vel suprema nihil aliud est, quam Constitutio*

(*y*) Vide Historiam

Dei, quæ Omnes Mortales Jurisdictioni Regum subjiciuntur. Ibidem. riam Interdict Veneti, per P. Sarpium, 1626. Edit. Latina. (*z*) *Omnes, in eo Concordes asserebant, Clericos Non esse Principi Subditos, ne in Crimine quidem Læsæ Majestatis*: pag. 107. dictæ Historiæ & pag. 13.

Venetian Ambassador, That (a) *Ecclesiasticks were not Comprehended in the number of a Princes Subjects, nor could be Puplished By him, though they were Rebels.* A hundred such Passages (out of their School-men, Canonists, Casuists, (especially the Jesuits) and their Canon Law) might easily be quoted; but these, to Impartial and Intelligent Persons, will be sufficient to Evince, That the Pope and his Party do publickly and expresly maintain this Rebellious Doctrine, and (when it makes for their Catholick Cause, and they have Opportunity and Ability to put it in Execution) do also practise it. The Sum of which Damnable Doctrine (repugnant to the clear Principles of Nature and Scripture, and all Religions, save that of *Rome*) is this; If any King be Excommunicate and Deposed by the Pope, then any of his Subjects, Clergy or Laity, (*horresco referens*) may take Arms and Rebel against him, or Murder him, and yet (by this Impious Popish Doctrine) be neither Rebels nor Traytors: And if their King be neither Excommunicate nor Deposed, but stands *rectus in Curia Romana*, and be (as they call it) a good Catholick; yet if any of his Ecclesiasticks (Secular or Regular) Rebel or Murder him, it can be no Treason or Rebellion in them; seeing (according to their Principles) they are none of his *Subjects*, nor he their *Superior*; and Treason or Rebellion against an Equal or Inferior, is (in Propriety of Law) impossible. But this is not all. For,

3. Let it be granted, (which is both Impious and Evidently untrue) That any Popish Assassin or Roman *Raviliac*, had not been Guilty of any Treason, if he had kill'd the Queen, after the Pope had Deposed her, as a Heretick; yet sure they must grant that it was Murder, and an Impious Act, to kill a Person over whom he had no Jurisdiction. No; this they deny: the approved and received Principles of the Popish Church acquit such Prodigious Villains not only from Rebellion and Treason, but from *Murder* too. He who had kill'd the Queen, after Excommunication and Deposition by the Pope,

---

(a) *Ecclesiasticos non Comprehendi inter Subditos Principis, nec ab eo posse pœnis affici, etsi rebelles essent.* They are the words of Pope *Paul* the Fifth to the Venetian Ambassador, in *Decemb.* 1605. in the aforesaid History, p. 13. *Gretser* tells us —— *Clerici non pertinent ad Regis Jurisdictionem.* Considerat. ad Theolog. Venetos 12. pag. 137. Edit. Ingoldstadij, Ann. 1607. And there (besides *Bellarmine* and *Baronius*) he gives us a List of Thirteen or Fourteen Authors, who writ for the Pope in his Quarrel with the *Venetians*, of the same Opinion. Gretser Ibid. pag. 380.

Pope, had been *no Traitor*, nor (which is less) so much as a *Murderer*. We are told in the Body of their Canon Law——(b) *That they are no Murderers, who (out of Zeal to the Church) take Arms against Excommunicate Persons*. So the Title prefix'd to the Canon cited in the Margent; and the Text of the Canon says further; *Those Souldiers so armed,* (c) *Are not Murderers, if out of a burning Zeal to their Catholick Mother* (the Church of *Rome* he means) *they Kill any of such Excommunicate Hereticks*: Thus the Case is deliberately determin'd by their Supream Infallible Judge, Pope *Urban* the Second, a little before the (d) end of the Eleventh Century; and about Twenty years after (by *Ivo Carnotensis*) referred into a (e) Collection of the Roman Canons: And *Gratian* (about Forty years after *Ivo*) Registers it in his *Decretum*, which Pope (f) *Gregory* the Thirteenth approves and confirms for Law; and so it stands confirm'd, and received for Law, (g) in their last and best Editions of that Law, ever since. Whence it may (and does) appear, that this Impious and Rebellious Doctrine, (*That Killing Kings or Queens Excommunicate by the Pope, was no Murder*) has been approved at *Rome* (since (h) the Devil was let loose, and Antichrist appeared) above six hundred years.

(b) *Non sunt Homicidæ, qui adversus Excommunicatos Zelo Matris Ecclesiæ, armantur* Ita Lemma præfixum Can. Excommunicatorum 47. Cauf. 23. Quæst. 5. vide Lemma hujus Can. apud Juonem. Decreti part. 10. cap. 54.

(c) *Non eos Homicidas Arbitramur, quos adversus Excommunicatos, Zelo Catholicæ Matris ardentes, aliquos eorum Trucidasse contigerit*. Ibid. in Canone.

(d) *Ivo Carnotensis Episcopus*; Decret. part. 10. cap. 54.

(e) *Moritur Urban.* 2. Ann. Christ. 1099. (f) Vide Bullam Gregor. 13. dat. Romæ, 1. Jul. 1580. Corpori Juris Canonici præfixam. (g) Vide Edit. Juris Canon. cum Glossis Parif. 1612. & Edit. sine Glossis, Parif. 1668. & Editionem Lugduni, 1661. &c. (h) Rev. 20. 2, 3.

I know that honest Father (i) *Caron* (not so disloyal as most of his Party) indeavours to mollifie this Rebellious Constitution of Pope *Urban* the Second; and tells us, that the meaning of that Canon is only this (k)——*That if any man by Chance and Casually had kill'd an Excommunicated Person,* (*si contigerit trucidasse*) *then he was not A Formal Murderer*: So Pope Urban's *Sentence was not to* (l) *Excuse those*

(i) Remonstrant. Hibernorum part. 5. cap. 13. §. 10. pag. 34.

(k) *Si Contingenter trucidaverit, non esse Homicidam Formalem, &c.* Ibidem.

(l) *Urbani ideo Sententia Non fuit, Excommunicatos vel Hæreticos De Proposito interimi posse.* Ibidem.

from *Murder*, who *Intended*, and *directly Purposed to kill Hereticks* and *Excommunicate Persons*. For (says he) *this were to* (m) *Overthrow all Truth and Fidelity to Princes*. The good man was (God forgive him) a *Roman Catholick*, and believed (though Erroneously) that the Supream Head of his Church, and St. *Peter*'s Successor and Vicar of Christ, could not approve and maintain such a Rebellious and Impious Position and Principle, *That men might lawfully be kill'd, because they were Hereticks or Excommunicate Persons*: which he there truly calls ———— (n) *A Horrible, Cursed and Execrable Principle*. That the Doctrine is *Cursed* and Execrable, is easily believed, and (by me) willingly granted. But that *Urban* the Second did not, in that Canon, approve it, (notwithstanding what Father *Caron* has said to the contrary) I absolutely deny. Sure I am, 1. That Cardinal *Bellarmine* (as is confessed by Father *Caron* in the place cited) expounds that Canon as I have done. 2. So does (o) Cardinal *Turrecremato* too; who says, *That Excommunicate Hereticks may be kill'd*, not only Casually (as Father *Caron* mistakes the Text) *but with an* (p) *Intention and purpose to kill them; and yet they who intend and do kill them, be no Murderers*; but both the *Intention and Act Just and Innocent*. But then their *Intention* must not be to get the *Goods* of those *Hereticks* they kill, but it must be Zelo Matris Ecclesiæ, *to secure the Church from the Mischievous Designs of those Hereticks*. So that in the Opinion of this great Cardinal, and Canonist, (who well knew the opinions and practise of their Church) killing of Hereticks was so far from being *Murder*, that it was no Crime at all; but *sine Reatu* (as he says) *without all guilt*; and therefore (*nulla pœnitentia erat imponenda*) it needed no Repentance. 3. Cardinal *Peron* in his Oration to the Estates of *France*, does expresly (q) affirm, That *all Tyrants by Usurpation*, may lawfully

(m) *Alioquin certe veritatem Omnem & Fidem expugnasset*. Ibidem.

(n) *Horrendum igitur Principium, Maledictum & Execrabile est, Hæreticos, vel Excommunicatos, eo ipso interimi posse, &c.* And again, *Inter damnabilia & Anathemata reponimus*. Ibid. §. 11 p 25.

(o) Turrecremata ad Can. Excommunicator. 47. Cauf 23. Quæst. 5.

(p) *Intentio requiritur, quia licet bonam habuerint voluntatem, potuerant tamen peccare Intentione. Si Interfecerant Hæreticos, quia Insistebant Ecclesiam, in hoc bonam habuerunt Voluntatem; peccaverunt tamen si Intendebant habere Bona Hæreticorum Si ergo bono Zelo & Mandato Ecclesiæ aliquos interfecerunt, non sunt Homicidæ Reatu, nec ulla Pœnitentia est Imponenda*. Turrecremata loco d &o.   (q) *Agnoscit Peronius*, (Orat ad Status, pag. 107.) *Tyrannum usurpatione Licitè interimi posse: atqui Rex Omnis semel à Papa depositus, si post: a administraverit, Rex Usurpatione & Tyrannus est; quia absque Jure Jus usurpat*. F. Caron Remonst. ant. Hibernorum, part 4. c. 1. §. 20. p. 265.

be

be *kill'd*; and such was Queen *Elizabeth*, and all Protestant Kings and Princes now are, (in the Judgment of the Pope and his Party) seeing they all did, and now do stand Excommunicate (at *Rome*) and deprived of all Dominion; and therefore, their medling with the Government, after such Deprivation, is evidently Usurpation (in the Opinion of our Adversaries) and then it follows (on their Principles) that they may lawfully be kill'd, and therefore the killing of them cannot be Murder; it being impossible that a Crime against the Indispensable Law of Nature, should be lawful. 4. But we have greater Evidence to prove, that (at *Rome*) the killing of Protestant Princes, (as Excommunicate Hereticks) is not Murder. For in the year 1648. when the *Parliament* was, (or seemed to be) severe against Papists, as believing and maintaining Principles Inconsistent with our Government: This Question (amongst others) was proposed to some of our English Popish Divines——(r) *Whether the Pope could Depose or Kill Protestant Princes or Magistrates, as Excommunicate Persons?* Some of those Divines met, and (whether out of Love of Truth, or fear of the Parliament, I know not) (s) *Subscribed the Negative;* **That the Pope could not Depose or Kill such Protestants.** But when this was heard at (t) *Rome*, the Pope and his *Sacred Congregation* (as they call it) Condemned that Negative Proposition, as Heretical, and Summon'd the Subscribers to *Rome*, where Prisons and Censures (as Father *Caron* tells us) were prepared for them. Whence it is evident, that to deny the Popes *Power to Depose and Kill Protestant Princes*, is (at *Rome*) declared *Heretical*; and therefore, that he has a Power to *Depose and Kill*, is a part of their Catholick Creed, and believ'd here. Whence it further follows, that they do think such *Killing of Protestants* to be no *Murder*, nor those who kill them, (out of Zeal to the Catholick Cause) *Murderers*. 5. When *Raymundus* (u) *Lullus* (a (x) man fa-

temnat, citatisque Romam Authoribus, Carceres & Censuræ parantur. Ibidem. ab Greg. 11. circa Ann. 1311. Nicol. Eymericus Direct. Inquisit. p. 255. Col. 2. D. Levin. Apparat. in Pet. Remundo.

(r) *An Pontifex Romanus Principes seu Magistratus Protestantium possit deponere, vel Occidere, tanquam Excommunicatos?* Vide F. Caron Remonstrant. Hibernorum part. 1. cap. 4. §. 3. p. 12.

(s) *Convenientibus ergo in hac Causa Theologis Anglicanis, pro Negativâ resolverunt.* Ibid. §. 3. num. 3.

(t) *His Nunciis Romæ receptis, sacra Congregatio resolutionem illam negativam, tanquam Hæreticam mox Con-*

(u) Floruit

(x) Posmous

mous in his time and after it) had said, and in his Writings published, *That it was* (y) *unlawful and impious to kill and murder Hereticks*; (for he had seen and heard, of the bloody Persecutions of the *Waldenses*, and such as at *Rome* were call'd Hereticks, in, and before his time) *Nic. Eymericus* (Inquisitor of *Arragon*) complains of him, and his Writings, to Pope *Gregory* the Eleventh; who (in full Consistory with the (z) Council of his Cardinals) damns the Doctrine of *Raymundus Lullus*, and declares for the *Lawfulness* and *Justice* of *Killing Hereticks*, 6. And Lastly, Pope *Leo* the Tenth in his Oecumenical (so they call it) *Lateran Council* (*Sacro Approbante Concilio*) with the Consent and Approbation of that Council) declares; *That our blessed Saviour* (a) *Did Institute* Peter *and his Successors his Vicars! to whom* (by the Testimony of The Book of Kings) *it was so necessary to yield Obedience, that Whosoever would not* (as no true Protestant ever would or could) *was to be punished with death.* The Pope was not pleased to tell us, what *Book of Kings* (for in their Vulgar Latin Version, there are four Books of that name) nor what Chapter or Verse he meant: and he did wisely to conceal what place in those Books he intended; for had he named any particular place, (though he pretended to *Infallibility*) his *folly* would have much sooner appeared. It is indeed ridiculous, for any man to think, that any thing said in those Books of *Kings*, can prove, that our blessed Saviour Constituted a Vicar General over his whole Christian Church, with power to kill all who would not comply with him, and that *Peter* and his Successors the Popes, were the men: seeing there is not one Syllable of all, or any of this, in any of the four Books of *Kings*; nor any Text from which it may (with any sense or probability) be deduc'd. Nor have the Publishers of that *Lateran* and other Councils (*Peter Crabb, Surius, Binius, Labbe*, &c. supply'd that defect, and told us, what place Pope *Leo* meant, and from which he, or they could prove *the Popes Power to kill all who comply'd not with his Commands.* I know that (b) *Crab*, (c) *Surius*, and (d) *Binius* (though *Labbe* has omitted it,

as

(y) *Interficientes Hæreticos sunt injuriosi & vitiosi in suo Memorari, Intelligere, & Velle, &c.* Eymericus Ibid. p. 260. Col. 2. A.

(z) *Greg. 11. in Consistorio, etiam de Consilio Fratrum, interdixit & condemnavit Doctrinam Raym. Lulli, &c.* Eymericus loco dicto p. 255.

(a) *Christus Petrum Ejusque Successores Vicarios suos Instituit, quibus (ex Libri Regum Testimonio) ita Obedire Necesse est, ut qui non Obediret, Morte Moriatur.* Binius Concil. Tom. 9. pag. 151. Col. 2. E. Edit. Paris. 1636.

(b) Pet. Crab. Concil. Colon. Agrip. 1551. Tom. 2. p. 694. Col. 2. So Turrecremata summa de Eccles. l. 2. cap. 114. Prop. 7.

(c) Laur. Surius Concil. Colon. Agripp. 1567. Tom. 4. p. 681. Col. 2.

(d) Binius Concil. Later. Paris. 1636. Tom. 9. pag. 151. Col. 2. B.

as Impertinent) have, in their Editions of the Councils, cited in their Margents, *Deut.* 17. for a proof of that erroneous and impious Position, (it seems their Infallible Judge mistook *Kings* for *Deuteronomy*, or that they could find nothing in any Book of *Kings* for the Popes purpose.) But they name not the Verse; though (I believe) it is the Twelfth Verse of that Seventeenth Chapter they mean. Where 'tis said, *That he who will not hearken to the Priest or Judge, That Man shall Dye.* This (I say) is altogether impertinent, as to the proof of the Popes Position. For admit (which is (e) manifestly untrue) that by *Priest* here, the *High Priest* only was meant: yet it will neither be consequence nor sense to say, *Whosoever disobey'd the Sentence of the High Priest, in the Jewish Church, must be put to death* : Ergo, *Whoever disobeys the Pope in the Christian Church, must be so too.* This (I say) is inconsequent, for the Priests in the Jewish Church (not only the High Priest, but other Priests and Levites) by the express Law of God, had as Judges in many Cases, power of Life and Death : but in the Gospel, our blessed Saviour left no such power to his Apostles and their Successors; *Excommunication* is the highest punishment, *Peter*, or any, or all the Apostles could inflict, by any Authority from our blessed Saviour in the Christian Church, and this power succeeded Interfection or putting to death in the Judaical Church. So St. (f) *Augustine* expresly tells us, and to him I refer the Reader. By the Premisses, I think it may appear, that, if (after the Popes Damnation and Deposition of Queen *Elizabeth*) any of her Popish Subjects, (Laity or Clergy, Regular or Secular) had by taking Arms publickly, or by Poyson or Pistol, privately taken away her Life, (according to their approved Principles.) it had been no Rebellion, Treason or Murder, but (in their Opinion) an Action Just and Innocent. But this (though too much) is not all; their Error and Impiety rises higher. For,

(e) Vide Grotium & Ainsworth in Deut. 17. vers. 9. 12. &c. Vide 2 Chron. 19. 8. 9. &c.

(f) *Nonnunc Agit in Ecclesia Excommunicatio, quod tunc (ante christum in Synagoga) agebat Interfectio.* Aug. Quæst. super Deuteronomium, lib. 5. cap. 38. And elsewhere; *Phineas Sacerdos Adulteros simul Inventos ferro ultore confixit. Quod utique Degradatio-*

nibus & Excommunicationibus, significatum esse faciendum hoc tempore. Idem Aug. de Fide & Bonis Operibus, cap. 6.

4. Had

4. Had any of Queen *Elizabeths* Subjects (after the Popes Excommunication) kill'd her, that Execrable Fact had been so far from being Murder, that (in their opinion) it had been an Action not only *Indifferent, or Morally good, but Meritorous.* In the year 1586. (which was the Nine and twentieth of *Elizabeth*) in the Colledge of *Rhemes, Giffard,* Dr. of Divinity, *Gilbert Giffard* and *Hodgson,* Priests, had so possess'd the English Seminaries, with a belief of this Doctrine, That *John Savage* willingly and gladly vowed to kill the Queen. The Story is in (*g*) *Cambden* (an Historian of unquestionable truth and fidelity.) *After* (h) *this,* Walpoole, *the English Jesuite, persvvades* Edward Squire, *that it was a Meritorious Act to take away the Queen;* tells him, *it might easily be done, by Poysoning the Pomel of her Sadle;* gives him *the Poyson;* Squire *undertakes it,* Walpoole *blesseth him, and promises him Eternal Salvation, and so (having sworn him to Secresie) sends him into* England: *where (notwithstanding all the Jesuits blessings) he was taken, confess'd all this, and was Executed in the year.* 1598. And *Cambden* (*i*) there tells us, *That a Pestilent Opinion* (as he truly calls it) *was got amongst the Popish Party (even amongst their Priests) That to take away Kings Excommunicate, was Nothing Else, but to Weed the Cockle out of the Lords Field.* It is true, none of those impious and damnable Desigs, had their desir'd Effect; God almighty protecting that good Queen, (it being impossible that any Power or Policy should prevail against his Providence) yet the Matter of Fact (confessed by themselves, or evidently proved by Legal Witnesses) manifestly shews, *that they thought killing the Queen,* (for the benefit of their Catholick Cause) *was a Meritorious Work,* which they designed to do, and (had their Ability been Equal to their Impiety) would have done. 2. Nor was this the *private opinion* of some *Priests and Jesuits* only; but the *definitive Sentence* of several Popes, (their (*k*) Infallible and Supream Judges) Publickly declared, and (that we may be sure they are *obligatory* at *Rome*) amongst other Papal Sanctions (they say) are Divine (Can. sic Omnes. 2. dist. 19.) *as if* Peter *himself had made them.* And no wonder, seeing they tell us, That God by his Holy Spirit, speaks in the mouth of the Pope, *Deus ipse, Spiritu suo, per Ora Pontificum loquitur.* P. Matth. J.C. Lugd. Præf.præfixa Corp. Juris Can. à se Edit. Franc. 1590.

De-

(*g*) *In the English Seminary at* Rhemes, *some there were, who believ'd,* Pius *the Fifth's Bull to be dictated by the Holy Ghost, and they perswaded themselves and others, that it was meritorious to take away the lives of Princes Excommunicate, and Martyrdom to spend a man's life in the cause. These things* Giffard, *Dr. of Divinity,* Gilbert Giffard *and* Hodgson *inculcated so deeply into* John Savage, *that he willingly and gladly vowed to kill Queen* Elizabeth. Cambd. Annals of Q. Eliz. l. 3. p. 301. 202. of the English Edition, (I have not the Latin now by me) Lond. 1635.

(*h*) Ann. Christ. 1598. Eliz. 41. apud Cambdenum Annal. lib. 4. pag. 498. 499. dictæ Editionis.

(*i*) Ibid. p. 499.

(*k*) All the Popes

Decrees refer'd into the Body of *their Canon Law*, confirm'd by *Gregory* the Thirteenth and by their *General Councils* (the *fifth Lateran*, and that of *Trent*) Commanded to be obeyed, *Tanquam Divina Inspiratione Edita, & Tanquam* (l) *Dei Præcepta*. Now the Papal Sentences or Decrees I mean, are 1. That of *Pope* (m) *Nicolas to the French Army*: wherein the Pope tells them, *That if any of them were slain in that War against the Infidels, that is,* (as Cardinal (n) *Turrecremata* explains it) *against the Hereticks, Heaven* (o) *should not be deny'd them*: They should be sure of that. But the *Lemma* or Summary prefix'd to the Canon (p) says, *That those Souldiers who faithfully fought against the Hereticks, if any one of them were slain in the fight, He should merit Heaven.* Murdering Hereticks, was (in the Popes Opinion) a *meritorious Work*, and if the Souldiers could kill them, and take away their Temporal Life here, they should (for that good Service to the Pope) gain to themselves, an Eternal Life hereafter. 2. Pope (q) *Leo* (to the same purpose, and almost in the same words) *Incourages a French Army to* (r) *fight stoutly against the Enemies of the Faith, and of the Church,* (you may be sure he means the Roman Church) *and tels them, that they need not be any way affraid, to kill Hereticks and the Churches Enemies, for God knew, that if any of them died in that Service, it was for the true Faith, for which Heaven should be their Reward.* So the Pope in that Canon. And because some of those Souldiers might fear (as there was great reason they should) that the Persecuting those poor Christians, whom the Pope call'd Hereticks, with Fire and Sword, might rather deserve punishment then a Heavenly Reward; *John Semeca* (the Glossator) tells us, *That the Popes meaning was* (s) *that (being secured from Punishment) Heaven should be their Reward*.

(k) Jul. 2. Conc. Lateran. 5. Generali, approbante Concilio. Sess. 5. apud Binium. Tom. 9. p. 48. Col 1. F. 2. A.
(l) Concil. Trid. Sess. 25. De Reformat. c. 22. p. 624. Edit. Antverp. 1633.
(m) Can. Omnium. 46. Causa 23. Quæst. 5.
(n) Turrecremata ad dictum Canonem.
(o) *Regna illi Cœlestia minime negabuntur.*
(p) *In certamine quod contra Infideles (Hereticos) geritur quisquis moritur Cœleste Regnum meretur.*
(q) Can. Omni Timore. 9. Cauf. 23. Quæst. 8.
(r) *Omni timore Deposito contra inimicos Sanctæ Ecclesiæ viriliter agere Studete, novit enim Omnipotens, si quilibet vestrum moritur, quod pro utilitate fidei mortuus est, & ideo præmium Cœleste consequetur.*

(s) *Hortatur Papa, ut viriliter pugnet contra Inimicos Ecclesiæ; & si qui propter hoc moriatur, Non Pœnam, sed Cœleste præmium consequetur*. Glossa Ibidem.

These, and such other Principles, must (of necessity) be a great Incouragement to the Popish Party, who believe (though without, and in contradiction to Truth and Reason) the vast usurped Papal Power and Infallibility, to Execute

ecute the Popes Damnatory Bulls and Excommunications, and kill all Hereticks (even Kings and Emperors) having Heaven promised for doing it. This is very much, but there are more and greater Promises made by the Pope, for *killing Hereticks.* For,

5. The Pope (out of his great Ability and Bounty) promises such Impious and Bloody Murderers of hereticks, not *Heaven only, but a higher Degree of Glory in it*, and many other great Priviledges, to be injoy'd here, before they came to Heaven; and this Promise the *Pope* makes, not singly by himself, but in, and with the consent of the *greatest General Council Rome* ever had. *Innocent* the Third is the Pope, and the (*t*) fourth *Lateran* is the Council I mean; in which (*u*) there were, above Twelve hundred Fathers. By the Authority of this (*x*) Council, an Army was to be raised for the (*y*) *Destruction of Hereticks* (the poor *Waldenses*) and they were to have the same (*z*) Priviledges which were granted to those who fought against the *Turks* to recover the *Holy Land*. What those Priviledges were Pope *Innocent* (in his (*a*) Bull) tells us.

(*t*) Conc. Lateranmagnum sub Innocentio 3. Ann. 1213.
(*u*) Ita Abbas Urlperg. in Chronoco ad dictum Ann. 1215. Binius in Hist. Concil. Later. 4. præfixa.
(*x*) Can. 3. *De Hereticis.*
(*y*) *Ad Hæreticorum Exterminium. Accedentibus ad terræ Sanctæ subsidium conceditur.* Ibid. dicto Can. 3. 12. data Lateran. 19. Cal. Jan. 1215.
(*z*) *Illa Indulgentia & Privilegio muniti sunt, quod* (*a*) Const. Innocent. 3.

1. They were to be freed from (b) *all Taxes, Impositions, and all Burdens whatsoever.*

2. They were to be *received into the* (c) *Protection of St. Peter and the Pope*; there is nothing of *God's Protection* mention'd. The Pope (*who sits in the Temple of God, (d) shewing himself that he is God*) thought (and would have them think so too) that he was sufficient to protect them.

3. If they had borrowed any Money upon Use, and had solemnly sworn to pay it; yet the Pope *Commands* that they *shall be freed both from their* (e) *Oath, and paying any Use.*

4. If they went to kill and extirminate Hereticks *in Person*,

(b) *A Collectis, Tallis, aliisque gravaminibus sunt Immunes.* Bullæ dictæ, § 10.
(c) *Quorum Personas & Bona sui Beati Petri & Nostra Protectione suscipimus.* Ibidem.
(d) 2 Thess. 2. 4.
(e) *Si ad præstandas usuras Juramento teneantur astricti, creditores ut remittant Juramentum & usuras, compelli præcipimus.* Ibid. § 12.

and

and at their *own Expences*, then *A Full* (f) *and Plenary Pardon of All their Sins here*, and *A Greater Degree of Glory hereafter*, is (by the Pope and that great General Council) *promised them*.

By the Premisses I think it evident, that if any of Queen *Elizabeths* Subjects (after her Damnation and Excommunication by the Pope) had by raising Arms against her publickly, or by Poyson or Pistol privately taken away her life, it had neither been *Rebellion*, *Treason*, nor *Murder*, but an innocent Action; And that not one of those which *Aristotle* calls τὰ μέσα, *Naturæ Mediæ*, and Indifferent, which are morally neither good nor bad; but (in the Judgment of the Church of *Rome*, and upon those her approved Principles) it had been an Action *Morally Good*, nay, (which is far more) *Meritorious*: For which they *should have Remission of All their Sins here*, and not *only Heaven*, but (in it) *A higher Degree of Glory* hereafter: And if it happened, that any of them miscarried in this their *meritorius* Act of killing Heretical Kings, and were (according to their desert) hang'd for Treason, then (with the Pope and his Party) they pass for *Martyrs*, and as such, shall be honour'd, and highly commended to Posterity. I wrong them not, *Ribadeneira* the Jesuite (to omit many others) in a (g) Book *Licenced by the* (h) *Vice-Provincial of Toledo*, approved by the Bishop of (i) *Antverp*, and (k) *other Grave and Learned Men* (as they are there call'd) I say, in this Book he has a (l) *Century of Martyrs* of his Society; and amongst them, reckons (m) *Campian*, (n) *Walpoole*, (o) *Southwell*, (p) *Garnett*, (q) *Oldcorne*, &c. and calls them *Martyrs*; who were *Legally Convict* here, and *Justly Executed* as *Impious Traitors*. God Almighty preserve our Gracious King from the Traiterous and Pernicious Conspiracies of those men, who (by a strange delusion) believe such Principles, and call Impious Traitors Holy Martyrs.

(f) *Plenam peccatorum Veniam Indulgemus, & Salutis Æternæ pollicemur Augmentum*. Ibidem §. 17. In Bullario Rom. Romæ 1638. Tom.1. p.78.Col.7. vide Matth. Paris ad Ann. 1213. in Johanne. pag.241.

(g) Catalogus Scriptorum Religionis Societatis Jesu; Auctore Pet. Ribadeneira, Ejusdem Societ. Theol. Antverp.1613.

(h) Ferdinandus Lucero in Censura Libro præfixa, Madriti,17.Sep.1607.

(i) Lavin. Torrentius in Oda ad Societat. Libr. præfixa.

(k) *Gravium doctorumque hominum Judicio probatus*. Ferd. Lucero in dicta Censura.

(l) Dicti Libri, p.357.358. &c.

(m) Ibid. p. 366.   (n) Ibid. p.371.   (o) Ibid. p. 372.   (p) In supplemento ad dictam Centuriam. pag.375.   (q) Ibidem.

The Premisses consider'd, there can be little reason to doubt, but the Popish Party (as ever since the Reformation they constantly have, so they) always will indeavour by secret Plots and Conspiracies, by Poyson, Pistols, or (when they have Ability) by open War, to ruin and utterly extirpate and destroy all the Protestants of this Nation (King and Subjects) who are by the Pope Declared and Excommunicated Hereticks, seeing there are such exceeding great Rewards (afore-mention'd) assured to them, for doing it; not only by private and fallible persons, but by the Constitutions of their Popes, and the Canons of their greatest and approved General Councils; their Supream Judge and Infallible Guide, which all Papists (by the Principles of their Religion) are bound to *obey, and all according to such Canons and Constitutions.* And were they indeed (what they pretend to) Infallible, it were great folly and madness not to do so. For he is certainly a Fool, who (having a Journey to go, on which the Eternal misery or felicity of his Soul depends) will not follow an Infallible Guide. And (which is further very considerable) *All their* (r) *Dignitaries in all Cathedral and Collegiate Churches, All who have Cure of Souls, All who are provided for, and preferr'd to any* (s) *Monastery, or Religious House whatsoever, be they of whatsoever Order of Regulars.* And not only these; but (t) *All Doctors, Masters, Regents, and Professors of any Art or Faculty, whether they be of the Laity or Clergy, or Regulars of any Order whatsoever, in any University, Publick School, or any where else, in Cities, Universities,*

(r) *Omnes, quas Cathedralibus & Superioribus Ecclesiis præfici, vel quibus de illarum dignitatibus, Canonicatibus & aliis quibuscunque Beneficiis Ecclesiasticis, curam Animarum habentibus, providere contingat, publicam Orthodoxæ fidei professionem fateri, seque in Rom. Ecclesiæ obedientia permansuros, Spondere & Jurare teneantur.* Vide Bullam Pij 4. super forma Juramenti Professionis fidei, in Concilio Trident. Sess. 24. De Reformat. Cap. 12. pag. 450. Edit. Antverp. 1633. (s) *Etiam per quoscunque quibus de Monasteriis, Conventibus, Domibus, & aliis quibuscunque locis, Regularium quorumcunque Ordinum, etiam Militiarum, quocunque nomine providebitur, idem servari.* Idem. pag. 451. Extat etiam in Bullario Romano. Edit. Romæ 1638. Tom. 2. pag. 97. Dat. Ibid. Novem. 1564. Pontificatus sui Ann. 5. (t) *Nullus Doctor, Magister, Regens, vel alius cujuscunque Artis & Facultatis Professor, sive Clericus, sive Laicus, ac Secularis, vel cajusvis Ordinis Regularis, sit, in quibusvis Universitatibus aut Gymnasiis publicis, aut Alibi Lectoris Cathedram obtinere, aut obtentam retinere, seu alias Theologiam, Canonicam vel Civilem censuram, Medicinam, Philosophiam, Grammaticam vel alias Artes Liberales; publice vel privatim profiteri, nisi Juramento prius præstito,* &c. Bulla Pij 4. in Bullarij Rom. Tom. 2 p. 96 & cap. In Sacro Sancta. 2. De Magist. & Doctoribus in 7.

Towns.

Towns, Churches or Monasteries; whether they profess *Divinity, Canon or Civil Law, Physick, Philosophy, Grammar*, or any other *Liberal Art, publickly or privately*, and all who take any *Degrees* in any *University*; *All those* (that is, almost all the Learned men in the Papacy) by the (u) *Disposition and Appointment of the Pope and Council of* Trent, are to (x) *promise, vow, and swear to obey the Pope as* Peter*'s Successor and* Christ*'s Vicar, and to receive, and without* **All Doubting** *to Profess all Things deliver'd, defin'd,* **and declared in the Sacred Canons, and General Councils,** *especially in the Council of* Trent; *and all this they swear to do most constantly so long as they live, and to take care* (to the utmost of their Ability) *that all under them, or committed to their Charge, shall do so too.* And the Pope there further tells us, (y) *That God Almighty did by the Holy Ghost Inspire the Trent Fathers to require, That this Oath should be taken.* Seeing then there are so many thousands in the Church of *Rome*, who do and must take this cursed Oath, to Obey the Pope, and *receive*, and without doubting believe all their Rebellious Canons before-mention'd, and (to the utmost of their Power) to perswade and induce all who are under their Cure and Charge (that is, all the Laity in the whole *Roman Church*, for all of them are under the Charge and Cure of some of those who take their Oath) to *receive* and believe them too. Hence it manifestly follows, 1. That the Church of *Rome* approves those impious and rebellious Doctrines to which so many thousands swear, by the Command of the Pope and *Trent* Council. 2. That all their Ecclesiasticks (Secular and Regular) who have any Cure of Souls and Charge over others, are bound, not only by their Papal Constitutions and Decrees of their General Councils; but by a Personal Promise, **Vow,** and Oath, (*in facinus Jurasse putes*) to believe and profess, **and** (as there is opportunity) to practise according to these Principles. 3. And hence it appears, That Queen *Elizabeth* was (and all Protestant Kings and Princes are, and in the like case, will be) in most eminent Danger of Assassination by her Popish Subjects, especially after Pope *Pius* the Fifth had damn'd and deposed her,

(*u*) Juxta dispositionem Conc. Trid. in Constit. 89. Pii 4. Bullar. Rom. Tom. 2. pag. 97.

(x) *Romano Pontifici, Petri Apostolorum Principis Successori, & Christi Vicario veram Obedientiam Spondeo, ac Juro. Cætera item Omnia à Sacris Canonibus & Œcumenicis Conciliis, Præcipuè à Trident. Synodo tradita, definita ac declarata, Indubitanter recipio & profiteor, & ad ultimum vitæ spiritum constantissimè retinere ac profiteri, & à meis subditis, illisq; quorum Cura ad me spectat, teneri, quantum in me est, Curaturum. Ego N. Spondeo, Voveo, Juro, &c.* p. 98. §. 2. dictæ Bullæ.

(y) *Deus Omnipotens Patribus (Tridentinis) Divinitus Inspirare Dignatus est.* Ibidem, in dictæ Bullæ Initio.

her, absolved all her Subjects from their Oaths of Allegiance, and Commanded them (on pain of Excommunication) never to obey her, or any of her Laws or Commands; it being also declared, by their Supream Infallible Power, That the killing the Queen, by open War publickly, or privately by Poyson or Pistol, had neither been Rebellion, Treason, nor Murder, but an Act morally good and meritorious; by which they should merit, not only Heaven, but a higher Degree of Glory in it, and be, as Glorious Martyrs (if they died in that Cause) commended to Posterity; Nay; when their Ecclesiasticks (both Secular and Regular) who had any Cure of Souls, or Authority and Charge over others, had promised, vow'd, and solemnly sworn, That they would obey the Pope as Christ's Vicar, &c. I say, those who had such great Promises to allure them, and their Promise, Oath and Vow to oblige them to it, would certainly indeavour (as indeed they did, as will appear anon) the ruin and destruction of that good Queen. Neither is this all. For,

6. Lastly; the Pope and his Party have further Inducements, more efficacious and powerful to perswade their Instruments to Assassinate Princes and Extirpate Hereticks, *especially* (z) *Protestants*, the *greatest* Enemies of their Antichristian Tyranny and Papal Usurpations. For although to pious men, (who really desire, and use the just meanes to obtain it) the promise of Eternal Joys in Heaven, is the

(y) They are more affraid of Protestants, then of all others they call Hereticks, and there is good reason for it. For truth (which the Protestants constantly maintain, is more destructive of their Popish Errors, then any one Error can be of another. *Extrema (Errores & Vitia) facile coexistunt ; Media (virtutes & veritates) Extrema destruunt.* This appears 1. Because they will not permit their Italian Papists to live in any Protestant County. *Prohibentur nunc Itali Catholici habitare, seu commorari extra Italiam Occasione Mercimonij absque Licentiâ Inquisitorum, si in illis partibus non viget Libertas Religionis Catholicæ.* Vide Const. 42. Clem. 8. in Bullario Rom. Tom. 3. p. 42. 2. They permit no Hereticks (Protestants you may be sure especially) to inhabit in *Italy*, or the adjacent Isles, on pretense of Merchandize, &c. *Gregorius* 15. *sub gravissimis pœnis vetuit, Hereticos quoscunque etiam sub pratextu Commercij habere domum apertam propriam vel conductam in Italiâ, vel adjacentibus insulis.* Gregorius 15. in Constitut. 38. In dicto Bullario. Tom. 3. pag. 314. Edit. Romæ, 1638. Vide Corp. Jur. Canon. Lugduni. 1661. & ibi Annotationes in Calce, Tom. 2. pag. 55. 3. Because 'tis notoriously known, that they permit Jews, (who deny Jesus Christ, and the whole Gospel) to live and have Houses, even in *Rome* it self, and yet they will not permit Protestants. It is a less Crime (it seems) at *Rome*, to deny Jesus Christ, then to deny (what all Protestants do) that the Pope is his Vicar, and Monarchical Head of the whole Christian Church. greatest

greatest Motive and Incouragement imaginable; yet to such Impious and Prodigious Villains (who will undertake to kill Kings and murder Innocents) Heaven signifies no more, then the Diamond did to *Æsop's* Cock in the Fable, who preferr'd a Grain of barly before it. And therefore, for such, (and none but such will serve them in the Execution of such Execrable Villanies) they have present and more prevailing Incouragements; I mean Money and great Sums of Gold, or some vast Temporal Advantages to be injoy'd here; which prevails more with such Persons, then the Promise of Heaven hereafter: I shall (out of many) give two or three Instances. As,

1. In the year 1596. (*a*) *Roderigo Lopez* (a Jew and Physician) *Stephen Ferriera Gama*, and *Emanuel Loisie* (two *Portugals*) by the Roman Arts and Impiety, were hired, and undertook to Poyson Queen *Elizabeth*. *Lopez* had a rich Jewel sent him, and was (by Contract) to have (*b*) Fifty thousand Duckets; which evidently appeared (at their Trial) by their own Confessions. And though Letters intercepted, and the Good Providence of God (by whom King's Reign) their Villany was detected, and they (as Traitors) justly Executed; yet their Popish Desires and Indeavours were not to less mischievous and impious, because the Good Providence of God graciously prevented the Execution of their Designs.

2. This by the Mercy of God not taking Effect, (for there is no Power or Policy can prevail against Divine Providence) a little after in the (*e*) same year, *Edmund York* and *Richard Williams*, were (by the same Roman Arts and Impiety) hired to *Kill the Queen*. *York* (at his Trial) confess'd That *Holt* the Jesuit, *Hugh Owen*, *Jacomo de Francisco*, and others, had offer'd him an Assignment of (*d*) Forty thousand Duckets, if he would *Kill the Queen* himself, or assist *Richard Williams* in *Killing Her*. This *York* confess'd at his Trial; and that *Holt* the Jesuit (in whose Hand the Assignment of Forty thousand Duckets was deposited) kissing the Holy Host, swore that the Money

(*a*) Cambdens Eliz. l. 4 ad An. 1594. p. 430. 431. Edit. Lond. 1635.

(*b*) Fifty thousand Duckets promised by the Popish Party, for Poysoning Q. *Elizabeth*.

(*c*) Cambd. Eliz. l. 4. ad Ann. 1594. 1596. p. 440. vide Plura in Statuto de Ann. 3. Jac. c. 2.

(*d*) Forty thousand Duckets promised for killing Q. *Elizabeth*.

Money should be paid so soon as the Queen was kill'd; and bound *York* and *Williams* by an Oath, and the Sacrament of the Eucharist, *To Dispatch it*.

In short, many others (besides these named) conspired the Assassination and Death of the Queen. For Instance; (to omit others) 1. Dr. (*e*) *Story, Ann.* 1572. 2. (*f*) *Somervil, Ann.* 1583. 3. Dr. (*g*) *Parry, Ann.* 1585. by the Approbation and Incouragement of the Pope and Cardinal *Como.* 4. *John* (*h*) *Savage, Ann.* 1586. 5. *Ant.* (*i*) *Babington*; and five or six more with him are incouraged and perswaded to Murder the Queen, in the same year, 1586. 6. (*k*) *Moody, Ann.* 1587. 7. *Patrich* (*l*) *Cullen, Ann.* 1594. 8. *Edward* (*m*) *Squire, Ann.* 1598. 9. (*n*) *Winter* and *Tesmond* the Jesuite, *Ann.* 1602. *&c.* We see there were many (too many) desperate Villains, who valued not their own, so that they might take away the Queens life; and yet too few (Divine Providence preventing their Impious Designs) to Effect and Compass that (more then Pagan) *Popish Conspiracy*, which at (so vast an Expence of Money) the Pope and his Party designed and earnestly desired, and indeavour'd to Execute.

3. When all this would not do; and the Pope and his Party plainly saw, that they could not cut off the Queen by Pistol, Poyson, or private Assassinations, *horrendum & majus machinantur scelus:* they design by Fire and Sword, by open War, utterly to destroy that good Queen, and all her Heretical (that is, Loyal) Subjects. And to this end, (besides Plenary Indulgence and Pardon of all sins here, and the Kingdom of Heaven hereafter) *Pius* the Fifth promises, and immediately gives two whole Kingdoms (*England* and *Ireland*) to *Philip* the Second, King of *Spain*; as is notoriously known, and (*o*) confess'd by their own Popish Writers His Successors, *Gregory* the Thirteenth, and *Sixtus* the Fifth, renue and confirm the Excommunication of *Elizabeth*, and the Donation of her Kingdoms; and accordingly (not with Gods,

---

(*e*) Cambd. Eliz. l. 2. p. 144. 145.
(*f*) Ibid. l. 3. pag. 257.
(*g*) Ibid. l. 3. pag. 272.
(*h*) Ibid. l. 3. pag. 302.
(*i*) Ibid. p. 303.
(*k*) Ibid. p. 336.
(*l*) Ibid. l. 4. pag. 431.
(*m*) Ibid. l. 4. pag. 498.
(*n*) Ibid. l. 4. pag. 578.

(*o*) *Pius 5. in Depositione Eliz. Jus Britanniæ, Hiberniæque ad Philip.* 2. *Hispaniæ Regem transtulit; vi cujus donationis, demandatus postea Sidonius sult. Anno 1558. Classe Hispanica Instructus, ut Regna Britanniæ Possideret.* F. R. Caron, Remonstrant. Hibernorum, part. c. 3. §. 4. p. 7.

against Queen Elizabeth. 193

Gods, but) with the Popes (p) *Approbation* and Blessing, in that memorable year 1588. the (vainly supposed) Invincible Armado was sent to destroy the damn'd Hereticks (the Queen and her Loyal Subjects) and take Possession of her Kingdoms, which the Pope had given him. The Pretences the Pope had to give those Kingdoms, (for they were but miserable Pretences, void of all Reason and Justice) were Two. 1. King *John's* Donation and (q) Resignation of his Crown to Pope *Innocent* the Third, about the year 1213. when the King and the whole Nation groaned under many Miseries and Papal Oppressions. Which Act of King *John* was Invalid and absolutely Null; he having no just Power to give away his Kingdom. And even then declared to be Null; not only by the English Barons and Nation, but by the King of (r) *France* and his Nobility, as *Matthew Paris* tells us. 2. Nor is it only *Matthew Paris* who says that the Kings of *England* and *Ireland* are (since King *John's* time) Tributaries to the Pope, (as they pretend) but their Historians, Canonists, and the Popes themselves. So (s) *Matthew Westminster*, *Henry* (t) *Knighton*, Cardinal *Tuscus*, &c. The Cardinal tells us, *That the Pope is the Supream* (u) *Judge of All. That he can Depose the* (x) *Emperor, Kings, Dukes, and All who Acknowledge no Superior; and that the Kings of* England, *and* Sicilie *are* (y) *Tributaries to the Church of* Rome. *And he who denies this Papal* (z) *Power, is no Christian.* And for *Ireland,* Pope *John* the Two and twentieth, in a Bull to our King *Edward* the Second, tells him, That his Predecessor, *Adrian* the Fourth, Gave the Kingdom of *Ireland* to *Henry* the Second, King of *England*, upon certain Conditions, which Conditions our King had not kept. And this ridiculous Bull we have in *Matthew Paris, ad Ann.* 1156. *pag.* 95. where he tells us, *That all the Islands in the World, which are Christian, belong to Pe-*

(p) *Sixtus* 5. was Pope, and it was in the fourth year of his Popedom. Vide Cambd. Eliz. l. 3. ad Ann. 1588. p. 350, 351.
(q) Matth. Paris ad dictum Ann. 1213. pag 426.
(r) *Rex Francorum respondet, Regnum Angliæ Patrimonium Petri nunquam fuit; Nec est, Nec erit. Nullus Rex potest dare Regnum suum, sine assensu Baronum suorum. Qui Regnum tenentur defendere. Tunc Magnates Omnes uno Ore clamabant, quod isto Articulo starent usque ad mortem, non Rex vel Princeps per Solam voluntatem suam possit Regnum dare, vel tributarium facere, unde Nobiles regni essent servi.* Matth. Paris in Johanne ad An. 1213.
(s) Matth. Westm. ad Ann. 1213. pag. 271. Johannes Rex est Papæ Tributarius seu feudatarius.
(t) Hen. Knighton de Event. Angl. l. 2. c. 15. p. 2402.
(u) Card. Tuschus Pract. Conclus. Juris

Tom. 6. Conclus. 41. (x) *Papa potest deponere Imperatorem, Reges, Duces, & Omnes qui de facto Superiorem non recognoscunt.* Ibid. §. 49. (y) *Rex Angliæ & Siciliæ sunt Tributarij Ecclesiæ Romanæ.* Ibid. §. 34. (z) *Qui negat potestatem Papæ, Negat se Christianum.* Ibid. § 37.

E e ter,

ter, *and so to the Pope.* See Archbishop *Usher* of the Religion profess'd by the Ancient *Irish,* pag. 51. 92. 93. 94. &c. And upon these (and such like ridiculous) Pretenses, the Pope required *Edward* the Third to do him (*a*) *Homage* for the Kingdoms of *England* and *Ireland,* and the Arrears of One thousand Marks *per Annum.* All the Popes pretenses were in a full Popish Parliament declared vain and evidently null; as appears by my Lord (*b*) *Cooke,* and the Record before-mention'd. Besides, 'tis certain that *John* was an Usurper, and had only Possession of the Crown, but no just Right and Title to it. For *Elinor,* Daughter to *Jeffery* his elder Brother, was living, and was the true Heir of the Crown; so that King *John*'s Resignation of the Crown to the Pope, was absolutely null; it being impossible he should give a Just Title to another, who had none himself. His second Pretence was, that the Queen being an Excommunicate and Deposed Heretick, (as he was pleased to miscall her) her Kingdom was forfeited to him, by the Canon of their great *Lateran Council.* Wherein 'tis (*c*) declared, That such obstinate Persons (as they call the Queen) when they stood Excommunicate, and would not give Satisfaction, the Pope was to absolve their *Subjects from their Oaths of Allegiance,* and give their *Lands and Kingdoms to Catholicks:* who by that Canon, were bound to Extirminate or Extirpate (*d*) all Hereticks. Upon the aforesaid Sandy Foundations, the Popes successively since King *John*'s time, build their Right to the Crown of *England*; and believe, (or at least say, and would have others believe) that the Imperial or Royal Power of *England* and *Ireland* is in them; and our Kings only *Beneficiarij & Feudatarij* (as the Civil Law calls them) Feudataries to the Pope, of whom (as their Supream Lord) they hold their Kingdoms. Whence it was, that Pope *Innocent* the Third, in his Letter to *Philip* King of *France,* calls the King of *England* his (*e*) *Vassal.* And his Successor, Pope *Innocent* the Fourth (with a Prodigious Antichristian Pride and Impiety) calls our King

(*Henry*

(*a*) Vid. Const. 4. Johan. Papæ 22. in Bullar. Rom. Tom. 1. p. 172. Edit. Rom. 1638.
(*b*) My Lord *Cooke* Inst. Part. 4. c. 1. p. 13.

(*c*) *Significetur Pontifici, ut ipse Vasallos à fidelitate absolvat, & Terram Expunat Catholicis occupandam.* Concil. Lateran. 4. Can. 3. De Hæreticis. And it now goes for Law. Cap. 13. Extra. de Hæreticis.
(*d*) *Qui terram illam Extirminatis Hereticis absque ulla contradictione possideant, & in fidei puritate conservent.* Ibidem.
(*e*) *Papa Philippo Francorum Regi Literas mittit, in quibus rogat ut Regem Angliæ non inquietaret; sed ut Romanæ Ecclesiæ Vassallum protegeret.* Matth. Paris Hist. an Ann. 1216. p. 280. In Johanne.

against Queen Elizabeth. 195

(*Henry* the Third was then King) *His Vassal*, and (which is more) his *Slave*. What (says he) (*f*) *Is not the King of England our Vassal?* Nay, that *I say more, our Slave?* These are his words, and expressions, of such prodigious Pride, as is absolutely inconsistent with that great and exemplary *Humility*, which our blessed (*g*) Saviour practis'd in his own Person, and *Commanded all* (even (*h*) *Peter and his Apostles*) *to imitate*: But yet congruous enough, and consistent with *the Hypocrisie* of him, who would be call'd *Servus Servorum Dei*, the Servant of all God's Servants; and yet as *the Man of Sin* (mention'd by the (*i*) Apostle) *Exalts himself above all that is called God*, and (with Pope *Innocent* the Fourth, in the place now cited) calls Kings his *Slaves* and *Vassals*.

(*h*) Matth. 20. 45, 46, 47. & Matth. 23. 11. 12. Luc. 22. 24, 25, 26.   (*i*) 2 Thess. 2. 4.

'Tis true, we believe and know, that the Pope indeed had no Power to perform those aforesaid Promises; and so in making them was (to all intelligent, sober, and pious Persons) not only impious, but ridiculous; yet to those of his Popish Party, who (having strong delusion to believe a Lye) were perswaded he had power to make good his Promises; that he was Christ's Vicar, Supream Head and Monarch of the Church; that he had the Power of the Keys, and so could shut and open, keep out and let into Heaven whom he pleased, that he could by his Power Depose (*k*) Kings, and was *Infallible* and (*l*) *never Err'd* (for these Erroneous and Impious Positions are (*m*) approved and received at *Rome*) I say, such Promises, made by such a person, were very great. And (to such deluded persons, who were perswaded of the truth and reality of them) prevailing Incouragements, to make them despe-

(*f*) *Papa non secipiens præ ira & indignatione* (it was *Grosthead's* Letter had angred him) *torvo aspectu, & superbo animo, ait: Nonne Rex Anglorum noster est Vasallus, & ut plus dicam Mancipium?* Matth. Paris Hist. in Hen. 3. ad Ann. Dom. 1253. p. 872. in Edit. G. Watsij. London. 1640.

(*g*) Matth. 20. 28. Luc. 22. 27.

(*k*) *Greg.* 7. deposeth *Hen.* 4. Emperor, by the Power of the Keys. *Potestas Ligandi & Solvendi in Cœlo & Terrâ, mihi à Deo data. Hac ide fiducia fretus, Henrico totius Regni Teutonici & Italiæ gubernacula Interdico, & Omnes Christianos, à vinculo Sacramenti, quod sibi fecere, absolvo.* Baronius Annal. Tom. 11. ad Ann. 1076. §. 25. 26.

(*l*) *Ecclesia Rom. Nunquam Erravit, nec in perpetuum* (Scripturâ testante) *Errabit. Inter dictatus Papæ.* Ibid. apud Bar. §. 33. p. 479. Edit. Antv. 1608.   (*m*) *Dictatus seu Sententiæ Breviores Gregorij Papæ, Quæ Hactenus in Ecclesia Catholica usu receptæ, ut ex his reprimeretur audacia schismaticorum Episcoporum & Principum.* Baron. Ibid. §. 31. p. 479. And Pope *Leo* 10. in their General *Lateran* Council, 1513. and in his Bull in Bullario Rom. Romæ 1638. Tom. 1. p. 451 says the same thing, that the Church and Pope of *Rome* have never err'd. Ibid. in Constit. Leo 10. 40. §. 3. & 6.

E e 2   rately

rately indeavour to Affaffinate and Murder Queen *Elizabeth*. Forty or Fifty thousand Duckets promised, was great and inticing Wages for doing such a Work, and actually prevail'd with many to indeavour it. But when (what the Pope promised *Philip* King of *Spain*) two whole Kingdoms here, and the Kingdom of Heaven hereafter are promised for destroying the Hereticks (the Queen and her Loyal Subjects) this was such an offer, as could not be refused by any who desired (as most do) Wealth or Honour here; or (as all should do) the Joys of Heaven hereafter. These were the Impious Policies, and Bloody Practices of *Rome*, to destroy Queen *Elizabeth* and her Protestant Subjects: and as their fear of the Protestant Religion, (destructive of their Superstition and Idolatry) continued, so their hate of it, and their desire and indeavours to destroy all the Professors of it. For the Queen being dead, in the beginning of K. *James* his Reign (upon the afore-mention'd, or the like motives) they undertook the Gunpowder (n) Conspiracy, (such a horrid and hellish Villany, as no Turkish or Pagan Story can parallel) wherein they indeavour'd, and (if the Powerful Providence of Heaven had not hinder'd it) had Assassinated, not the King only, but the whole Kingdom, in its Representative. And further, (to omit the bloody and barbarous Assassinations of (o) *Henry* the Third of *France*, by *Jaques Clement*, and of *Henry* the Fourth, by *Raviliac*, (p) incouraged to those Villanies by Jesuitical and Popish Principles and Promises; for *Ravaliac* confess'd, *That it was the Book of* Mariana *the Jesuite, and the Traiterous Positions maintain'd in it, which induced him to that Prodigious Villany, the Murder of the King*; for which Cause that Book (Damn'd by the Sentence of the Parliament and *Sorbon*) was publickly burnt in *Paris*. I say, to let these, and such Instances pass it is too well known and believ'd, that in the late (q) horrid and hellish Conspiracy (conti-

(n) Vide Stat. 3. Jac. Capp. 1. & 2. *A Conspiracy undertaken by Malignant and evilish Jesuits and Priests.* Ibid. c. 1. *A Design so barbarous and cruel, as the like was never before heard of.* Ibidem. *The most wicked barbarous, execrable, and abominable Treason that ever enter'd into the heart of the most wicked man.* Ibid. cap. 2.

(o) Vid. Thuani Hist. Tom. 4. lib. 95. ad Ann. 1598.

(p) Vide Anticoton. by *Peter Du Moulin*. In that Pyramid erected in *Paris* upon the Murder of *Henry* the Fourth, the Jesuites are noted as men, *Maleficæ Superstitionis, Quorum Instinctu, piacularis Adolescens* (Raviliac) *Dirum facinus* (the Murder of the King) *Instituerat*. (q) Ann. 1678. & 1679.

nued

nued and carried on, principally by the Jesuits) to take away the Life of our Gracious King (whom God preserve) one of the Assassins had Fifteen thousand pounds pay'd or promised, and another, Thirty thousand Masses to be said for him, if he miscarried, to Incourage them to that Monstrous Popish Villany. Now their Impiety in this their Ingagement, was equal; both undertaking the Commission of the same Sin, the Murder of their King: But their folly seem'd unequal. For Fifteen thousand pounds might possibly (in this World) have been some benefit to him who contracted for it: But the 30000. Masses, were altogether Insignificant, and could be no way beneficial or profitable to him to whom they were promised, either in this, or the World to come. The poor Miscreant was cozen'd by his Party, with the noise and number of their Masses. For they knew, and (had he not been a Fool as well as Knave and Villain) so might he too; that those Masses could never do him any good. For even by their own approved and received Principles, killing of Hereticks (especially an Excommunicated Prince) was such a meritorious Work, as (without any Masses) deserved a Plenary Indulgence and Pardon of all his Sins, and an higher place in Heaven; and therefore he could *not go to* (r) *Purgatory* (had there been any such Place) nor could the Devil or the Pope punish him there, for such Sins as were absolutely pardon'd, and all the Punishment due to them remitted; I say, they could not justly do it: or admit the Devil (had he power and permission) might be willing to punish an innocent Soul, which had no Sin to punish: yet sure his Holiness (who as Christs Vicar has the Keyes of Purgatory as well as Heaven) would not do, or at least not own (for otherwise he does, and has done as Impious things) the doing of that, which is so evidently injust. So that (if their own principles be true) those Thirty thousand Masses could no way be profitable to that miserable deluded Person, in Purgatory, whither he was never to come; and I suppose, they will not say, that their Masses here, are profitable to the glorifi'd Saints and Martyrs in Heaven.

(r) *Cum pœnæ pro culpis debitæ delentur & remittuntur, tum crimina velentur & remittuntur. Quo sensu Ecclesia per Indulgentias concedit peccatorum Omnium plenissimam veniam, id est, Pœnarum Omnium, quas peccando contraximus.——Quia non est plene remissa culpa, quamdiu peccator Reus est Solvendæ Pœnæ.* Melch. Canu: Locorum Theol. l. 12. c. 13. §. Ex quo Ambrosij pag. 694. Edit. Colon. Agrip. 1605.

12. And

Observations on the Pope's Bull

Observ. 12.

12. And here, (for a more clear and distinct Explication of their Jesuitical and Popish Assassination) it will neither be Impertinent nor Improper to observe further, That although since the time of *Hildebrand* or (ſ) *Gregory* the Seaventh, the Antichristian Pride or Tyranny of the Pope and his Party, has been exceeding great, and pernicious to the Western Part of the World; they both approving and practising the Excommunications and Depositions of Kings and Emperors, Absolutions of their Subjects from all Oaths of Allegiance, with Injunctions (against the Law of Nature and Scripture) never to Obey them : yet I do not find that the Popes or their Party approv'd or practis'd the Assassinations of Princes before *Ignatious Loyola*, and the unhappy Approbation and Confirmation of his Society, *Anno*. 1540. Nay I find it Condemned, as Impious, Inhuman, and Barbarous; not only by their Learned men, (even their Canonists) but by their Popes and Councils. That this may appear, I desire it may be consider'd,

(ſ) It was the saying of this *Gregory*; *Intelligant omnes, Imperia, Regna, Principatu, & quicquid habere mortales possunt, auferre & dare nos posse.* Plat. in vita Greg. 7. Edit. 1485. And *Baronius* tells us, that this, and such dictates of that Pope —— *In Ecclesia Catholica Hactenus usu recepti sunt.* Annal. Tom. 11. ad Ann. 1076. § 31.

1. That Pope *Innocent* IV. about the year 1245. or 1246. makes a (*t*) Constitution in the General Council at *Lions*, (and with the (*u*) *approbation* of that Council) wherein he calls Assassinations (*x*) *horrid Inhumanity*, and *Detestable Cruelty*, and an indeavour to *Body and Soul:* and then adds, *That if any Prince or Prelate, any Person Ecclesiastical or Civil, shall procure any Assassin to kill any Christian, (though the Effect do not follow) or receive, conceal, or any way favour such Assassin, then such person is* (*Ipso facto*) *Excommunicate, Deposed, and Deprived of all his Honour, Dignity and Revenue.* This was the Judgment of Pope *Innocent* IV. about 35. years since; and although for Antichristian Pride and Tyranny (as in other things, so) in his Impious Excommunication and Deposition of the Emperor *Frederick*, he was as bad as his Predecessors;

(*t*) Constitutio illa extat, in Corpore Juris Can. de Homicidio, cap. pro humani. 1. In. 6.

(*u*) *Sacri approbatione Concilij Statuimus.* Ibid.

(*x*) *Quâ Hortenda Impietate Detestandaque Saevitiâ Mortem sitiunt alienam, ut Ipsos faciant per Assassinos occidi, non solum corporum, sed mortem procurent Animarum* —— *Statuimus,*
ut quicunque Princeps vel Pralatus quempiam Christianorum per pradictos Assassinos interfici fecerit, vel mandaverit (quanquam mors non sequatur) Excommunicatus & Depositus à Dignitate, Honore, & Officio, Ipso facto, sit bonis etiam Mundanis Omnibus à toto Christiano populo perpetuo diffidatus. Ibid. & Conc. Tom. 11. Part. 1. p. 672. Edit. per Labbe Parif. 1671.

yet

against Queen Elizabeth.

yet neither they nor he, were (as yet) arrived at the height of Impiety to approve Mahometan and Turkish Assassinations of Kings and Emperors.

2. About Eight and forty years after the making of this Constitution by *Innocent* the Fourth, *Boniface* the Eighth (as Impious and Tyrannical as his Predecessors) was made Pope, and approved this Constitution of *Innocent* against Assassinations, and referr'd it into the Body of their (y) Canon Law; where it still (z) remains in all Editions of that Law, even to this Day: and that (to give (a) Authority to it) with the Approbation and Confirmation of succeeding Popes; particularly of *Pius* the Fourth, *Pius* the Fifth, and *Gregory* the Thirteenth.

(y) Cap. *pro humani.* 1. De Homicidio, In. 6. Decretalium.

(z) Vid. Edit. Juris Canonici, Parif. 1612. & 1618. Lugduni, 1661. &c.

(a) *ut hujus utilissimi & gravissimi Codicis non vacillaret Authoritas, placuit Pio 4. dein Pio 5. & Greg. 13. ut illi Corrigendo Summa opera daretur, &c.* Ita admonitio ad Lect. præfixa Corpori Juris Can. Parif. 1612. & Lugd. 1661.

3. And hence it is, that eminent Writers of the Church of *Rome* (except the Jesuites and their party) do, even to this Day, generally Condemn all such Assassinations, as impious, and to the Publick pernicious. This evidently appears (to say nothing of the Gloss) by Cardinal (b) *Turrecremata*, Cardinal (c) *Cajetan*, Cardinal (d) *Tuschus*, Henry (e) *Spondanus* (Bishop of *Pamiez* in *France*,) *Didacus* (f) *Covarruvias* (Bishop of *Segobia* in *Spain*, &c.) And here it is further observable, 1. That Pope *Innocent* the Fourth, in the aforesaid Decretal Constitution, speaks only of those Ancient, and properly so call'd *Mahometan-Assassins*; and though he censures their Assassinations as impious, yet he appoints not their Punishment. I know that the Author of the Gloss upon that Constitution (*John Andreas Bononiensis*, was the man) tells us; (g) *That the Punishments express'd there, are denounc'd against the Assassins, as well as those who procured or hired them to Assassinate any Christians.* But Ann. 1231. §. 3. 4. 5. &c. (f) Operum, Tom. 1. p 528. De Delict. & Contr. §9. (g) *Papa volens obviare hujusmodi malis, profert plures pœnas in istos Assassinos, & illos qui eis mandabant.* Glossa ad dictum Cap. 1. De Homicidio, In. 6.

(b) Summa de Ecclesia, l. 2 5.35. & 36. as he is cited (for I have not the Book by me) in the Margent of the Canon Law; ad Cap. 1. de Homicidio. In. 6.

(c) In Summula. verbo Assassinus.

(d) Concluf. Pract. Juris, Lit. 6. verbo Assassinus. Concluf. 531.

(e) Continuat. Annal. Baronij. ad

the

(h) Non contra ipsos Assassinos, utpote Infideles sed contra Mandantes, per ipsos aliquem occidi, Innocentius 4. Excommunicationem promulgavit. Cajetan. in Summula. verbo Assassinus.

(i) Papa cum prius esset Purus Homo, nunc Vices Veri Dei gerit. Johan. Andreas, in Glossa ad Procœmium. 6. Decret. verbo Bonifacius.

(k) Et hi non comprehenduntur sub censura dicta, quamvis digni sunt & Morte Temporali & Æternâ. Cajetan Ibid.

(l) Qui cum quolibet Christiano aut Infideli, pecunia data vel promissa pactionem inierit, de homine Christiano occidendo, in ipso Mandandatario, si ad actum proximum processerit, ut per eum minime steterit; quin scelus peregerit, notant puniendum fore pœna Ordinariâ; id est, Morte. D. Covarruvias, Part. 2. Relect. Clem. *Si furiosus, de Homicidio, de delictis & Conat.* num. 9. Operum. Tom. 1. p. 258. Col. 1.

the man is miserably mistaken; for 'tis Evident, and (*h*) Confess'd *That the Punishments contain'd in the Constitution, are denounced only against those Christians who hire and imploy those Impious Assassins.* Excommunication (and the Consequents of it) is the Punishment mention'd in that Constitution; which neither did, nor possibly could concern those Mahometan Assassins. For although the said Author of the Gloss, else where tells us, *That the Pope is* (*i*) *more then a pure man; and Gods Vice Roy*; yet certainly, he cannot do Impossibilties, and Excommunicate Mahometans and Infidels; unless he can turn those out of the Christian Church, who never were, nor would be in it; and deprive them of that Communion, which they never had. But although Pope *Innocent the Fourth* (in the afore-mention'd Constitution) speaks only of the Infidel and Mahometan Assassins, and of those Christians who procure or hire them to Murder Princes, and has nothing of any other, who are not of that Mahometan Society; though they undertake and act the same Villanies; yet those Great and Learned Canonists and Writers of the Popish Church (before-named) upon proportion and parity of Reason, justly Condemn all Christians who shall undertake and effect, or indeavour such Assassinations. Of these Christian Assassins, Cardinal *Cajetan* says ——— (*k*) *That though they be not comprehended under the censures of that Constitution, yet they Deserve both a Temporal and Eternal Death.* And to the same purpose *Covarruvias* tells us, (and he says it is the Common Opinion) (*l*) *That whosoever he be* (*Christian or Mahometan*) *who for Mony given or promised, undertakes the Assassination of any Christian; in this Case, both the Mandans and Mandatarius, both he that hires, and he who is hired to do such Villany, are highly guilty, and under the Censures, and the Severity of them: though he who is hired, do not actually effect the Assassination, if he really indeavour it.* Nor is it only these I have named, who Damn this Impious, Mahometan and Turkish Doctrine of Assassinating Kings and Princes. I believe, and (from good

good Authority) know, that many thousands more in the Communion of the Church of *Rome* do equally abhorr and detest it, especially in *France*, where their Divines and Parliaments (famous for Learning and their General Defence of the Liberties of the *Gallican Church*, against the Usurpations and Tyranny of *Rome*) in the year 1594. publickly Condemn'd this Mahometan and Jesuitical Doctrine, and declared it to be (what indeed it is) (m) *Heretical, Prodigious, and* **Diabolical**.

4. But all this notwithstanding, the Jesuites (and others of their Party and Principles) did, and do approve and practise that Diabolical Doctrine; and when they concieve Princes to be Enemies to their Interest, or the Catholick Cause, (as they call it) indeavour (by Lying Calumnies) to disaffect the people, and to raise Rebellions against those Princes; that so they may cut them off, by publick War and Seditions; and when this succeeds not, by private Assassinations. This is (by sad Experience) notoriously known to our Western World; as my appear by the Premisses, and further Testimonies of their own *Roman Catholick Historians* (in this Case) of Indubitable Truth and Veracity. *Thuanus* tell us, (n) *That in those Bloody Wars in* France, *in the Reign of* Henry *the Third; it was some of the Religious and Regulars, especially the Jesuites, who by an Industrious, and* (I add) *Impious Diligence, did first Alienate the People from their Obedience to their Prince, and then sollicited them to Rebellion.* I know that those words (*Ac Jesuitarum Patrum Imprimis*) are not to be found in those Editions of *Thuanus* we

(m) Hen. Carter. Davila in his Hist. of the Civil Wars of France, ad Ann. 1594. in Cake istius Anni.

(n) *Accidente ad hoc Sacri ordinis favore & quorandam Religiosorum non signi Opera, & Jesuitarum Patrum Imprimis, qui fascinatum per scrupulosas in Arcanis Confessionibus quæstiones, plebem sensim à Principis obsequio alienatam, Ad Defectionem Sollicitabant.* Thuanus Hist. Tom. 3.

lib. 75. p. 561. A. B. Edit. 1620. & Tom. 4. l. 86. p. 170. ad Ann. 1587. And the same excellent person (*Thuanus*) gives us this account of the Society of the Jesuites.

Nata Magistratum convellere, nata Ministris
Subtrahere obsequium, præsulibusque suum.
Et viles Regnantum animas, ipsosque Necandos
Horrenda Regis proditione docet;
Servandamque fidem Negat, argutisque cavillis
Detorquet magni jussa severa Dei.

Hi sunt Amplis. Præsidis Thuani versus de Jesuitarum Sectâ, in Elegia sua eleganti in Parricidas, sub finem Sacræ Poeseos.

F f   have

Observations on the Pope's Bull

have, being left out by the Arts and Frauds of those who corrupt all Authors who have any thing against their Errors or Impieties; but we are assured that those words were in the (o) *Original Copy of Thuanus his History*. But when this would not do, and they saw the King could not be cut off by a Rebellious War, and publickly; they perswade and incourage *Jaques Clement* (a Desperate Villain) to Assassinate his Prince; who *August* the first, 1589. did the Execrable Act, and Murder'd his *King*. *Thuanus* tells us, (p) *That Friar* Clement *was incouraged to commit that Prodigious Parricide by the furious Sermons and Declamations of their New Divines,* (q) *Especially of the Jesuites, who publickly taught them, That it was lawful, nay* (r) *Meritorious to kill a Tyrant, and if he outlived the Fact, he should be a Cardinal at* (s) Rome; *and if he died, a* (t) *Saint in Heaven. And accordingly when he was dead (by a Death he Deserved) his Party caused his* (u) *Picture to be cut in Brass, adorned their Churches and Chambers with it, counted him a Saint and Martyr, and (as such) made their addresses and Prayers to him.* Horrid Superstition and Popish blindness, not to put a vast difference between a Martyr of *Jesus Christ*, and an *Impious Traytor and Murtherer of his King*. After this, in the year 1594. *Johan Chastell* undertakes and indevours the Assassination of *Henry* the Fourth of *France*, struck him in the Mouth, but (the good Providence of Heaven protecting that Prince) did not effect his Impious Design. Now if you ask, How any who pretends to be a Christian, could have a Conscience so seared, or a Soul possess'd with so Prodigious an Insensibility, as not to tremble at the very thought of Committing such a horrid and inhuman Villany? (x) *Davila* will tell you, *That he was Disciple of the Jesuites*; *That he himself freely confessed, that he was bred*

(o) Vide Thuanum Restitutum Amstolodami. Ann. 1663 p.490.

(p) Thuanus Hist. Tom.4.l.95. p.454. A. *Facundis Concionatorum Declamationibus, & Novitiorum, Theologorum, ac praecipuè Jesuitarum disputationibus, qui Tyrannum Impune occidere Licere affirmabant, Incitatus Clemens, &c.*

(q) Vide Thuanum Restitutum. p. 84.

(r) *Non solum inoffensa conscientiâ facere posse, sed multam apud Deum Merituram.* Thuanus dicto Tom.4 & p. 454.

(s) Hen. Cart. Davila, in his Hist. of the Civil Wars in *France*, Lib. 10. ad Ann 1589.

(t) *Si in actu ipso moriatur, procul-dubio inter Beatorum choros animam ejus Evolaturam.* Thuan. dicto Tom. 5.& p.454 & Davila l.10.ad Ann.1589.

(u) Historical Collections of the most Memorable Accidents, and Tragical Massacres in *France*, under Hen. 2. Francis 2. Charles 9. Hen. 3. and Hen. 4. ad Ann. 1589. in the beginning of Hen. 4. & Thuan. Tom. 4 ad dictum Ann p. 458. (x) Hen. Carter. Davila, in his History of the Civil Wars of *France*, lib.14.ad Ann. 1594. sub finem istius Anni. See to the same purpose the Author of the Civil Wars of France under Hen. 2.Franc.2. Charl.9. Hen.3. and Hen. 4. In Henry the Fourth, ad Ann.1594 a little before the end of that year.

up in the Schools of the Jesuites, and had often heard it discours'd and disputed, That it was not Only Lawful, but Meritorious to Kill Henry of Bourbon, a Relapsed Heretick, and Persecutor of the Holy Church; That Father Gueret a Jesuite, was his Confessor, &c. so that being possess'd with their Impious Principles and Perswasions, he undertook that prodigious and damnable Parricide. In short, it was notoriously known to all France, that the Jesuites both approved and designed the Execrable Assassination of their King. Whence it was, (as Davila goes on) that the Parliament of Paris pass'd this Sentence —— That Father Guignard and Gueret (Jesuites) should be Condemned to the Gallows; that the rest of the Jesuites (profess'd or not profess'd) should be banished out of France, as Enemies to the Crown and publick Tranquility, their Goods and Revenues seiz'd and distributed to pious Uses, &c. And it had been well for France had they stood banished still, and never return'd. For about Sixteen years after, what Johan. Chastell impiously indeavour'd, that bloody Villian *Raviliac*, May the Fourteenth, 1610. effected; and with Monstrous Impiety, and a Cursed hand Murder'd his King *Henry* the Fourth; And it was the Jesuites, and their Traiterous Principles, which moved and incouraged him to Commit that Monstrous Unchristian and Antichristian Parricide. For (after the Fact was done) *Raviliac* freely and publickly confessed, *That it was the Jesuite* Mariana's *Book which moved and incouraged him to that Impious Design*. I know that the Jesuites did then indeavour to (b) *free themselves* from the Odium of that Impious Fact; as if they had neither approved nor incouraged that Monstrous and Mahometan Assassination. *Sed quid verba audiam, cum facta videam?* This (c) was only a ridiculous indeavour, *Æthiopem Lavare*, to wash a Blackamore, and do Impossibilities. It is evident, *That their approved Doctrine and Principles in* Mariana, (*and many others*) *was the Motive which induced* Raviliac *to Murder his Prince*. Which Doctrine has never been Condemned by any Publick Act of their Society, nor by the Inquisitors in any *Index Expurgatorius*; now for them

(b) See Father *Cotton*, the Jesuites Declaration, with the Bishop of *Paris* his Preface prefixed to it, to this purpose.

(c) See *Anti-Cotton* by *Peter Du Moulin*.

them to approve those Traitorus Principles, and deny the Consequents of them, is most irrationally to approve and grant the Premisses, and yet deny the Conclusion.

5. But this (though bad enough) is not all, For it is not only the Jesuites and their Accomplices, but the Pope too, (their Supream Judge, whom they (d) believe to be Infallible, both in Matters of Faith and Fact) who approved their Seditious and Traiterous Principles of Rebellion and Assassination of Princes. *Thuanus* speaking of the Jesuites Practices to stir up the People to Rebellion in the time of *Henry* the Third of *France*, he adds —— (e) *That these things were well known to the Pope, who sent Breves and Bulls secretly to the Heads of those Rebels, whereby they were incouraged to Rebel.* Afterwards, when that Prodigious Villain *Jaques Clement* had Murder'd the said King, (f) *Sixtus* the Fifth then Pope, did not only *approve the Fact, but* (in a premeditated Oration, publickly spake in the Consistory (blasphemously compares it (in respect of its greatness and amiableness) to our blessed Saviours Incarnation and Resurrection: and then highly Commends the Murderer (for his Virtue, Courage, and zealous Love of God) above Eleazer and *Judith, &c. And* (to omit the rest) *pronounceth the Murder'd King Eternally Damn'd as having Committed the* (g) *Sin against the Holy Ghost.* This the Historian (though a Papist) modestly and justly Censures, as a Fact (h) *Extreamly Insolent* and *Unworthy the Moderation of a Pastor*, (especially the supream Pastor of the Church Christs Vicar, and St. *Peter's* Successor, as they call him). And then he tells us of *Anti-Sixtus*, (or the Answer to Pope *Sixtus* his Oration) and says, 1. *That it had been more for the* (i) *Credit of the Pope and the Holy Apostolick Sea, that his Oration had been suppress'd, then* (as it was by those of the League) *Published.* 2. *That Anti-*

(d) *Christus Petro & Successoribus Ecclesiæ regimen commisit, & eandemquam habebat ipse, Infallibilitatem concessit, quoties è Cathedra loquerentur. Datur, Ergo, in Rom Ecclesiâ, Controversarum Fidei Judex Infallibilis, etiam extra Concilium Generale, tum in Quæstionibus Juris, tum Facti.* Hæc erat Thesis in Coll. Claromontano à Jesuitis proposita & expositâ Decem. 12. Ann. 1661.

(e) *Quæ omnia Conscio Pontifice gerebantur, crebro commeantibus ad tum Emissariis, qui brevia & occulta Diplomata ad partium Duces adferebant, & indies magis plebem ad seditionem incendebant.* Vid. Thuanum Restitutum, p. 45.

(f) *Sixtus Papa 5. Oratione præmeditata. 3. Idus Sept. in Consistorio habita, factum Clementis Operi assumptæ à Domino Carnis, & Resurrectionis, propter magnitudinem, & rei administrationem comparat. Tum virtutem hominis, animi robur, & ferventem Erga Deum Amorem, supra Eleazarum & Juditham, Multis verbis, Extollit, &c.* Thuanus Hist. Tom. 4, l. 95. ad Ann. 1589. p. 458 Edit. 1620. (g) *Peccato in Spiritum Sanctum admisso, quale erat Regis peccatum.* Ibid. p. 458. E. (h) Thuanus ibid. *Summè Insolens,* & Pastoris moderatione indignum. (i) *Supprimi potius quam publicari, famæ Sixti Sanctæ Sedis Interfuit.* Ibid.

Sixtus

Sixtus (*or the Answer to it*) *though it was something sharp and bitter,* (k) *yet the Popes Oration abundantly deserved it, in which were Many Things Absurd and Impious.* This was the Judgment of that Faithful and Excellent Historian, (though a Papist) concerning the Erroneous and Impious Principles of the Pope and Jesuites.

6. Nor is this all; For although, only privately to approve and incourage Rebellion and Assassination of Kings and Princes, be an Execrable Villany, to be abhorr'd by all men (especially Christians) as being repugnant to that clear Light of Nature and Scripture, to common Reason and Religion; yet in publick Writings to vindicate and justifie such Actions, to perswade the World, *that they are not only morally good, but meritorious*: This argues a higher degree of Impiety and Impudence. We know (by sad Experience) that may Pagans and Christans, have blasphem'd their Gods, committed Adulteries, Murders, Perjuries, &c. yet we do not find, that any Christans, (tho Jesuites and their Accomplices excepted) or any sober Pagan (who acknowled'gd a God) did ever justifie Blasphemy, Adultery, Murder, or Perjury; but when they were Apprehended, Convict and brought to Execution, they would confess the Crime, pray for Pardon, and desire others to pray for them. But the Jesuites (and those possess'd with their Principles) though they be Convict, & Legally Condemn'd for rebellion and assassination of Princes, yet they neither do, nor can repent; believing such Actions not to be any Vices, but Vertues, and themselves (if they suffer for them) not Traytors or Murderers, but Holy Martyrs. That this is their approved and received Doctrine, which they publickly defend, and industriously (in their publick Writings) indeavour to justifie, is evident to the Western World, and may appear by the Premisses. Yet being a thing of such great concern, (omitting *Mariana Emanuel Sa, Sanctarellus,* and others before mentioned) I shall only add Two or Three Eminent Testimonies, in further confirmation of it. First then, *Fran.* (l) *Suarez,* publick and prime Professor of

(k) *Responso acerbior, sed tali Oratione prorsus Digna, in qua Multa Absurda & Impia notantur.* Ibidem.

(l) Franc. Suarez. in Defens Fidei Cathol. adversus Angl. Sectæ Errores cum Respons. ad Apolog. Jacobi Regis, &c. Colon. Agrip. 1614. l. 6. c. 4. pag. 814. &c.

of Divinity in the University of *Conimbra* in *Portugal* handling that Point, how and in what Cases a Tyrant may, (by any private Person) be Murder'd: And having told us that a Tyrant was either, 1. *Tyrannus*(m) *Titulo*; one who, (without any just Title) usurp'd the Government, to the ruine of Common-weal. 2. *Tyrannus* (n) *Administratione*; one who, having a just Title, ruled Tyrannically. And he there tells us, *That all Christian* (o) *Kings are such Tyrants, who induce their Subjects to Heresie, Apostasie, or Schism.* So that all Protestant Princes (we may be sure) are such Tyrants, though he there name only King *James* of happy Memory. Having Premised this, he gives the state of the Question: Thus,

1. He does (in the General) gives us two Cases, wherein it is Lawful for a Subject to kill his King. 1. *In defence of his* (p) *own Life.* If a King invade *Sempronius* to kill him, *he may, in defence of his own life, take away the Kings.* 2. *In defence of the* (q) *Commonwealth.* This in the General. But then

(m) *Tyrannus titulo, qui vi, & injustè Regnum occupat, qui Revera Rex non est, sed locum illius occupat.* Ibid.§.1.

(n) *Qui licet justo Titulo Regnam possideat, quoad usum tamen & gubernationem, Tyrannicè regnat.* Ibid.

(o) *Inter Christianos, Maximè ist numerandus in hoc Ordine Princeps, qui Subditos suos in Hæresin, aut aliud Apostasiæ genus, aut Schisma inducit.* Ib. §.2.p.811.Col.1.

(p) *Si defensio sit propriæ vitæ, quam Rex violentèr auferre aggrediatur, tunc quidem Ordinarie licebit Subdito, seipsum defendere, etiamsi Mors Principis sequatur, quia jus tuendæ vitæ est Maximum,* &c. Ibid.p.815.b. (q) *Si Rex Actu aggrediatur Civitatem, ut Cives perdat,* &c. *tunc certe licebit Principi resistere, Etiam Occidere Illum, si aliter sibi defensio,* &c. Ibid.§.6. C. *Tunc enim Civitas habet justum bellum defensivum, contra Injustum Invasorem, etiamsi proprius Rex sit.* Ibid.D.

2. For a *Tyrant in Title*, he absolutely declares it, as a thing (r) commonly received amongst them; *That such a Tyrant may be lawfully kill'd, by Any Private Person, who is a Member of that Commonwealth, if there be no other Means to free it from such a Tyranny:* And least it should not be observ'd 'tis set in the (ʃ) Margent, *That such a Tyrant may lawfully be kill'd.* So that the Case is (with him) out of all doubt, *That any private man may kill a Tyrant in Title*; and the Pope is Judge who is such a Tyrant. Whence it evidently follows, *That no Princes can have any Security* (as to the *Preservation* of their *Kingdoms* or *Lives*) longer then they please the *Pope*. For if he declare any of them Tyrants, (as many times, with Execrable

(r) *Communitèr asseritur Tyrannum quo ad Titulum, Interfici posse, à Quacunque privata Persona, quæ sit Membrum Reipubl. qua Tyrannidem patitur,* &c. Ibid.§.7.F.

(ʃ) *Tyrannus in Titulo Licitè Occiditur.* Ibid. §.7. Margine.

Pride

Pride and Impiety, he has done) Excommunicate and Depose them; then by this Jesuitical and Papal Doctrine, any Private Person, (any of their Subjects especially) may Assassinate and Murder them.

3. For those Princes who have a *just Title* to their Dominions, and are (as they call them) *Tyrants not in Title*, but in their Injustice and Impious Government: He tells us, 1. That (t) all *Protestant Princes being Hereticks are such Tyrants*, 2. That *being Hereticks, they are by their* (u) *Heresie*, Ipso facto, *and presently deprived* (aliquo modo) *in some manner, of all Right to their Dominions.* 3. That *the Pope* (as their (x) *Superior, to whom even Supream Princes are Subjects*) *may totally and absolutely depose and deprive them of all their Dominions and right to Govern.* 4. *When the Pope has pass'd such Sentence, and deprived them of their Dominions; if afterwards they meddle with the Government, they become every* (y) *way Tyrants* (both Titulo & Administratione) *And then,* 5. *After such* (z) *Sentence pass'd by the Pope, such Kings or Smpream Princes may be dealt with, as Altogether, and Every Way Tyrants, and Consequently may be kill'd by Any Private Person.*

(t) *Inter Christianos Maximè in hoc Ordine (Tyrannorum ex Administratione Tyrannica) numerandus est Princeps, qui Subditos in Hæresin aut aliud Apostasiæ Genus, aut publicum Schisma inducit.* Ibid. c. 4. §. 1.

(u) *Rex Hæreticus Statim per Hæresin ipso Facto privatur, Aliquo Modo, proprietate & Dominio Regni sui.* Ibid. c. 4. §. 14. p. 819.

(x) *In summo Pontifice est hæc potestas tanquam in Superiori habente Jurisdictionem ad corripiendum Reges, etiam Supremos, tanquam sibi Subditos, &c.* Ibidem. (y) *Si Rex post depositionem Legitimam, in sua pertinacia perseverans, Regnum per vim retineat, incipit esse Tyrannus in Titulo, quia non est Legitimus Rex, nec justo Titulo Regnum possidet.* Ibidem. (z) *Ergo Extunc poterit Rex tanquam Omnino Tyrannus Tractari; & Consequentèr A Quocunque Privato Poterit Interfici.* Ibidem. p. 819. B.

4. And though these be Prodigious Errors, Unchristian, and indeed Antichristian Impieties; such as neither ours, nor any Language can fully express; yet this is not all: The Jesuite further declares, *That though* (a) *Pagans anciently had, and still have Power, to Depose their Tyrannical Kings; yet in Christian Commonwealths, they have such dependence upon the* (b) *Pope, that without his Knowledg* p. 820. A. (b) *Regna Christiana quoad hoc (scilicet depositionem Regum suorum) habent dependentiam & subordinationem ad Pontificem Romanum; qui potest Regno præcipere, ut se Inconsulto, Regem non deponat, nisi prius Causa & Ratione Ab Ipso Cognita propter pericula, & Animarum dispendia, quæ in his tumultibus popularibus interveniunt.* Ibid. A.

(a) *Respublica (prout inter Gentiles, & nunc inter Ethnicos) habet potestatem, se defendendi à Rege Tyranno, & illum deponendi si necessarium fuerit, &c.* Ibid. §. 17.

and

and *Authority*, they *should not depose their King: For he may Command and Prohibit the People to do it.* And he gives Instances, when People have consulted the Popes, and by their Counsel and Consent Deposed their Kings. So (he says) (c) *Chilperick was Deposed in France, and Sancius Secundus in Portugal.* And (to make up their Errors and Impieties full) he further tells us, ———— (d) *That all Christian Kingdoms and Commonwealths do so far depend upon the Pope, that he may not only Counsel the People, and Consent to their Deposition and Assassination of their Tyrannical Princes*; *But he may Command and Compel them to do it, when he shall think it fit, for avoiding Schisms and Heresies*: That is indeed, *for the rooting out and ruine* of the true Protestant Religion, and establishing their *Roman Superstition and Idolatry.* And to conclude, he further declares, *That* (in such Cases *the Popes Command* (to Murder a Deposed King) *is so far from being any Crime, that it is* (e) *Superlatively Just.* I might here cite Cardinal (f) *Telet, Guliel.* (g) *Rossæus*, and a hundred such others, who approve, and in their Publick Writings (Approved and Licenced, according to the Decree of their (h) *Trent* Council, by the *Authority of their Church*) justifie this Impious and Antichristian Doctrine of Deposing and Assassinating Heretical Kings: but this I conceive a needless work, For, 1. *Suarez* himself declares it to be the received Doctrine of their Church, and cites many of their Eminent Writers to prove it ; which, any may see, who is not satisfied with those before cited. 2. The Licencers of *Suarez* and his Book are (for Dignity in their Church and for Learning) so great, and (for Number) so many, and the Commendations they give *Suarez* and his Work so high, that there neither is, nor can be any just Reason to doubt, but this Doctrine was approved at *Rome*, **and** by the Ruling part of that Church (the Pope and his Party, believed and incouraged, as a Doctrine asserting the Popes Extravagant, and (as they call it) *Supernatural* (i) *Power*, and so their Common Interest. Let the Reader consult the Censures prefix'd to *Suarez* his Book, and

he

(c) Ibid. p. 820. C
(d) *Pendet Regnum Christianum à Pontifice in hoc, ut posset Pont. non solum consulere, aut consentire, ut Regem sibi perniciosum deponat, sed etiam præcipere, & cogere ut id faciat, præsertim cum ad vitandas Hæreses & Schismata necessarium esse Judicaverit.* Suarez. ibid. p. 820. B. C.

(e) *Quia tale præceptum in illo Casu Justissimum est.* Idem Ibidem.

(f) Instruct. Sacerd. l. 5. c. 6. §. 17. p. 738.

(g) G. Rossæus de Justa Reipub. Christiana in Impios, &c. Authoritate, Cap. 3.

(h) Conc. Trid. Sess. 4. in Decreto de Editione & usu Sacrorum librorum.

(i) *Firmis & inconcussis Argumentis potestatem summi Pontificis supernaturalem tuetur.* Ita in Censura Illust. D. D. Alphon. A Mello, Epis. Lamecensis, Suaresij Libro præfixa.

he will find all these following to Approve and Licence it. First, Three great Bishops, all of them Counsellors to his Catholick Majesty. 2. Two Provincials of the Society; one of the Jesuites in *Portugal*, the other of those in *Germany*. 3. *Academia, Complutensis,* the University of *Alde Henares* approves it too. 4. Lastly, the (*k*) *Supream Senate* (Court or Congregation) of the Inquisitors, do also approve and licence it, and this they do by (*l*) Commission from *Peter de Castello, Vice Roy of Portugal, and in Matters of Faith Supream Inquisitor.* The Premisses impartially consider'd, I think we may truly say, That it is not only *Suarez*, or some particular or private Persons, but the Church of *Rome*, and her Ruling part, which approves this Impious and Trayterous Doctrine: Which may further appear (besides their Approbations and Licences) from the great Commendations they give *Suarez* and his Book and Doctrine. And here

(*k*) *Facultas Supremi Senatus S. Inquisitionis.*

(*l*) *Ex Commissione Illustrissimi Episcopi, D. Petri de Castillo, Lusitaniæ Proregis, & Supremi in rebus Fidei Inquisitoris.* In Censura Alphonsi à Castello, Episc. Conimbricensis, à Consiliis Catholicæ Majestati.

1. For *Suarez*; They say, (*m*) *That he was a Contemner of Humane things, and a most Valiant Defender only of Piety and Catholick Religion:* And (*for his Excellent Wisdom*) *the Common Master, and another Augustine of that Age.* —— *That for this great zeal for the Catholick Faith, he was a most Famous Author, and a most Eminent Divine. That he was a* (n) *most Grave, and most Religious Writer, whose Works the World,* (the Popish World) *does Honour, Admire, and Love, &c.*

(*m*) *Humanarum rerum Religiosus contemptor, & unius Pietatis & Religionis fortissimus Defensor, & propter Eximiam Sapientiam, Communis hujus ætatis Magister, & Alter Augustinus.*

(*n*) *Religiosissimus juxta ac Gravissimus Auctor, cujus Ingenij monumenta, Orbis Suspicit, Miratur, Amat.*

2. And for this Book, and the Doctrine contained in it, They say, *That all* (o) *things in his Book, are Religiously Consonant to Sacred Scripture, to Apostolical Traditions, General Councils, and Papal Decrees*; (this last we admit, and they profess it to be true). And hence, if they may be believed, who expresly affirm it themselves, it evidently follows, That this Traiterous Doctrine is approved by the Pope, and is Consonant to his Decrees. And those

(o) *In quâ non solum S. Scripturæ Authoritati omniæ Religiosè consonant, Apostolicis traditionibus Piè correspondent, Oecumenicis Conciliis, summorum Pontificum Decretis eruditè consentiunt.*

G g

those publick Censors of *Suarez* his Boook severally add; *That they find* (p) *Nothing* (and therefore not the Assassinations of Kings) *in it, against the Orthodox Faith,* (the Roman Faith they mean) *but many things which do defend the Faith.* The University of *Alcala de* (q) *Henares* (to omit the rest) more fully testifies ———— *That they read Suarez his Book with all possible Diligence, and found Nothing in it repugnant to the Catholick Faith; nor was there Any Thing in it which ought not to be Approved and Commended.* And then add, (that we may be sure they spoke cordially and deliberately) *That there was Nothing in that whole Work, which All of them did not approve; so that they were all of the same Mind and Judgment.* Nay, we are further told, *That he had Composed that Work, by* (r) *More then Human Helps*; and therefore they Judge it (s) *Most Worthy to be Published, for the Publick, and Common Benefit of the whole Christian World, and a Signal Victory of their Faith over Heresies.* Such are the Commendations of *Suarez* his Book and Doctrine; so that we may be sure that it is Approved and Received at *Rome*.

(p) *Quâ in defensione nihil planè ostendi, quod Fidem offendat, quâ verò defendant, inveni multa.* So it is in the Censure of *Ferdinand Martinez* Counsellor to his Catholick Majesty.

(q) *Librum Suarisii quantâ potuimus diligentiâ, evolvimus, in quo Opere nihil veritati Catholicæ fidei Alienum, nihil devium, nihil dissonum deprehenditur: Nihil quod probari laudarique non debeat. Denique nihil à nostrô omnium Sensu discordans, cum hac in re, sit omnium nostrum eadem vox, idem Animus, Eademque Sententia.* (r.) *Plusquam Humano studio.* In *Censura Alphon. A Castello, Episc. Conimbricensis*. (s) *Dignissimum ut in Lucem eat, ad Fidei nostræ Victoriam de Hæresibus Insignem, & totius Orbis Christiani Publicam & Communem utilitatem.* In *Censura Illustris. D.D. Alphons. A Mello, Episc. Lamec. A Consiliis Cathol. Majesta. L.*

And here let me further add, that when King *James* had published his Apology for the *Oath of Allegiance*, and Sir *Henry Savil* Translated it into Latin; the Latin Copy was (by the Popish Party) immediately sent to *Rome*, and (by the Pope) (t) *Condemned* there, as Impious and Heretical: From *Rome* it was sent to *Suarez*, who (by the Popes Command) was to Confute and Answer it. He undertook and finished the Answer, sent it to *Rome*, where it was highly approved, and afterwards printed and published with all those Approbations and Commendations before-mentioned. But these Positions need no further proof, that they are own'd and publickly approved by the Pope and his Party

(t) By Pope *Paul* 5. who in his Damnatory Breve, says, ——*Juramentum illud, salva fide Catholica, & salute Animarum, præstari non potest; cum multa contineat, quæ fidei saluti apertè adversantur.* Vide *Remonstrant. Hibernorum, per R. Caron. p. 9.*

ty. I shall only add; When King (*u*) *James* had charged *Bellarmine* and the Church of *Rome*, with this Rebellious and Impious Doctrine, of Deposing Kings, Absolving Subjects from all Oaths of Allegiance and Fidelity, &c. (*x*) *Gretser* is his Answer, has these memorable words— (*y*) *We do not deny,* (says he) *but freely profess, that the Pope upon just cause,* (and he is Judge of that) *may Excommunicate and Depose Princes, and Absolve their Subjects from their Oath of Allegiance.* And then he adds —— (z.) *That the Subjects are bound in Conscience to Obey the Popes Sentence; not only in the Cases mentioned, But in* (a) *All other of the like Nature.* And this impious and traiterous Doctrine of *Gretser*, is not only approved by (*b*) *the Provincial of the Jesuites* in *Germany*, and the Rector and Vice-Chancellor of the University of *Ingolstade*, but his whole Book (and so those mentioned, and many more such Rebellious and Impious Positions) *Was Approved at* Rome, *by the Suffrage of Most Learned Divines.* This the said Provincial of the Jesuites, and the (*c*) Rector of the University of *Ingolstade* expresly testifie, in their publick and printed Approbations of *Gretser's* Book. The Premisses, and Traiterous Popish Principles consider'd, (which are received and believed at *Rome*) though men may (*d*) wonder at the Beast, (the Pope and his Party) and that any, (who would not only be thought Christians, but the only Catholicks in the World) should maintain, and publickly justifie such Principles: yet we need not wonder, that such persons should practise and act according to such Principles, and continually indeavour (especially after the Anathema of *Pius* the Fifth) by Rebellions at home, and Invasions from abroad, to rob Queen *Elizabeth* of her Crown and Kingdoms, and of her Life too, by Roman and Mahometan Assassinations. I say, we need not wonder at this. For let the aforesaid Doctrines (which they approve and constantly contend for) be granted, (*That the Pope is Su-*

(*u*) In Apolog. pro Juramento fidelitatis.

(*x*) In Commentario Exegetico contra Jac. Regem Ingolstadij, Ann. 1610.

(*y*) *Non dissitemur, sed libere profitemur, quod rata, supposita legitima causa possit Principes Excommunicare, Deponere, Subditos à Juramento Fidelitatis Exsolvere,* &c. Gretser Ibid. p. 255.

(*z*) *Subditi in Conscientia tenentur stare Sententiæ Pontificis.* Ibidem.

(*a*) *Et si qui sint alij casus hujus generis.* Ibid.

(*b*) Ibid. p. 1½. Apolog. Jac. Gretseri, Romæ, à Deputatis ad id Theologis lectam & approbatam ego quoque Theod. Busæus Approbo, &c.

(*c*) *Hunc Librum Jac. Gretseri, Doctissimorum Theologorum Suffragiis Romæ approbatum, ego itidem approbo, ut quamprimum, Antipharmaci loco, (parsistex Britannia Venenis, opponatur,* opto ego, *Petrus Steuartius, Academiæ Ingolstadiensis Pro-Cancellarius, & hoc tempore Rector.* Ibid. p.12.   (*d*) Rev. 13. 3.

pream *Judge* and *Monarch* of the *World*, directè or indirectè) that all *Kings* and *Emperors* are his *Subjects*, that he has power to *Depose* and *Deprive* them of their *Kingdoms*, that when he has *Judicially* deprived them, any private *Person* may *Murder* them; that he has power to absolve their *Subjects* from all *Obligations* and *Oaths of Allegiance*, and to *Command* them, upon pain of an *Anathema*, never to obey any of their *Princes Laws or Commands*; that the People may *Depose* their *King*, with *His Consent* and *Counsel*; and that he may *Command* and *Compel* them to do it; and this so (d) oft as he shall think it *Good* for the *Spiritual Health* of the *Kingdom*. (Prodigious Error and Impiety! as if Rebellion, Assassinations and Murdering their Kings, conduc'd to the Salvation of the Subjects.) I say, these Erroneous and Impious Doctrines granted, and (as they are at *Rome*) believ'd it is certain, that (so far as they have opportunity and ability) they will (as they ever have done) prosecute their Interest, and practise according to those Principles; and all Christian Kings will be in perpetual danger to loose their Crowns, their Kingdoms, and their Lives too; unless they can please the Pope and become his dutiful Servants, and indeed Slave to his Anti-Christean Tyranny. I say no Christian King, *Tros Tyriusve*, Papist or Protestant can be out of eminent Danger, where such Doctrine is by such Docters maintain'd we have sad and and certain Instances of this Truth: For, 1. *Henry* the Third and Fourth of *France* were neither *Calvinists* nor *Lutherans*, but declared Sons of the *Roman Synagogue*; yet because they did not Comply with the Popish Interest,

(d) *Potest Pontifex non solum consulere, aut consentire, ut Regnum Regem suum sibi perniciosum Deponat; sed etiam præcipere, & cogere, ut id faciat; quando saluti Spirituali Regni, & præsertim ad vitandas Hæreses necessarium esse Papa Judicaverit.* Suarez dicto.l 6 cap.4. p.820.B.C. This place is before cited, but that the Reader may not be troubled to look back for it, I have again put it here. Where in the Margent, (which I before omitted) Suarez cites others, (to shew he was not singular in this Opinion) Azorius, Tom.3.l.2.c.7.Quæst.30. A Castro, lib. 2. De justa Hæreticorum Punitione; cap. 14. vid. Hist. Conciliorum General. per Ed. Richerium Doctorem Sorbonicum, lib 1. cap. 13.§.3.p.398.Colon. 1680. where he acknowledges that *Bellarmine, Suarez, Becanus*, and the Jesuites maintain this Doctrine of Deposing and killing Kings —— *Jesuitæ non modo docent, Papam habere potestatem Regum Abdicandorum rerum etiam à capite Paniendorum in Officio Sacræ Inquisitionis, ut vocant, &c.* And the same *Sorbon* Doctor, Ibid. cap 8 §.13.pag.191. tells us, that 'tis the Jesuites Doctrine; *Licere Pontifici Reges sibi immorigeros, haud aliter abdicare, quam Pastor Canes, quos minus habet ad manus, Occidet.* And that it is their Practise, to accuse those Princes who do not please them, to the People, of Tyranny, Schism or Heresie, *Hacque via illos tanquam arietes, aut Canes furiosos, Parricidis mactandos Exponere.*

in that degree and measure, the Pope and his Party expected, they fatally fell by the Traiterous and Prodigious Villany of Bloody Assassins, *Ridente & gaudente Roma*; The Pope and his Jesuitical Party, (with an Extasie of Joy) Approving and Commending the Treason, and (in their Writings and Pictures) Canonizing the Traitors.

2. For Protestants, and (as they call them) Heretical Princes, their danger (proportionable to *Romes* hatred of them) is greater. They may (by the Power and Gracious Providence of God) want ability, but they neither do, nor (unless they renounce their Erroneous and Impious Principles) ever will want a desire and indeavour to ruine those they call Hereticks, either by open Hostility and Rebellions, or by Poyson, Pistols, and private Assassinations. Their many known Plots and Conspiracies against Queen *Elizabeth* King *James*, *Charles* the Martyr, and his Gracious Majesty now Reigning, (whom God preserve) are undeniable Demonstrations of this Truth. The Ark of God and Dagon, Light and Darkness, Truth and Error the Bible and Popish Bullary, Protestancy and Popery cannot Possibly Consist, and be in Peace. Nothing is (or can be) so destructive of Darkness and Error, as Truth and Light; And 'tis evidently known to this Western World, That the Evangelical Light and Truth, which the Protestants have happily and clearly discovered, to the long deluded Church of God, have awakened thousands, to a detestation of that Superstition and Idolatry, under which they formerly lay, to the dishonour of God, and ruine of their Souls, and to a shaking and great diminution of the Papal Monarchy and Tyranny; so many Kingdoms forsaking *Rome*, and shaking off the Heavy and Intolerable Yoake of Sin and Popish Servitude. *Et hinc illæ Lacrymæ*; Hence it is, that the Pope, and his inraged Party, when they cannot, by any probable pretence of Reason confute, what they call Heresie, (the Protestant Religion) they indeavour to Confound and (by Fire and Sword) Consume the Hereticks.——— *Æterna bella pace sublata gerunt, Jurant odium,*

(e) This is evident (to omit others) by the Bull of Pope *Paul* the Third, wherein K. *Hen.* 8. is Excommunicated and Deposed. For in that Bull having declared that King an Heretick and deposed him; he commands all Christian Princes (Kings or Emperor) to take Arms against King *Henry* and his Adherents —————— *Insuper, tam Principes, prædictos (quacunque etiam Imperiali aut Regali dignitate fulgentes. §. 15.) quam quoscunque alios, etiam ad stipendia quorumcunque Christi fidelium militantes & alias quascunque personas, tam per Mare quam per Terras, Armigeros habentes, eis Mandantes, ut contra Henricum Regem, eique adhærentes, dum in erroribus adversus Sedem prædictum permanserint, Armis Insurgant, eosque & eorum singulos persequantur, &c.* And then (such is his liberality) he gives those Souldiers all the Goods of those Anathematiz'd Hereticks, wherever they can find them —————— *Eorumque Bona, Mobilia, & Immobilia, Mercantias, Navigia, Credita, Res, & Animalia, etiam extra territorium Henrici Regis, ubi libet Consistentia, Capiant, &c.* Vide Pauli Papæ 3. Constit. 7. datum Romæ, Decemb. 17. Ann. Dom. 1538. Pontificatus sui, Ann. 5. In Bullario Romano, Romæ 1938. Tom. 1. p 516. Col. 2. §. 16.

odium, nec prius hostes esse desinunt quam esse desinunt. They excite and incourage (*e*) *Princes of their Profession*, to persecute and destroy all protestants in their Dominions; and their barbarous and bloody Poet has told us, how they desire it to be done;

Utere Jure Tuo Cæsar, *Sectámque* Lutheri
Ense, Rora, Ponto, Funibus, Igne neca.

Use thy Power *Cæsar*, let *Lutherans* be slain,
By Fire, Rack, Halter, Sword, or drown'd ith' Maine.

DAM-

EXCOMMUNICATIO
Henrici VIII.
REGIS
ANGLIÆ
EJUSQUE
FAUTORUM,
Cum aliarum
ADJECTIONE POENARUM.
Paulus Episcopus, Servus Servorum Dei.
Ad futuram Rei Memoriam.

Ædita.A.D.1538
& 1538.

EJUS qui immobilis permanens, sua Providentia, Ordine mirabili dat cuncta moveri, disponente Clementiâ, vices, licet immeriti gentes in Terris, & in Sede Justitiæ Constituti, juxta quoque Prophetæ Hieremiæ vaticinium dicentis: *Ecce Te Constitui super Gentes, & Regna, ut evellas, & destruas, ædifices, plantes,* præcipuum super Omnes Reges Universæ Terræ, cunctósque

Exordium.

cunctósque populos obtinentes Principatum, ac illum qui pius, & misericors est, & vindictam ei, qui illam prævenit paratam temperat, nec quos Impœnitentes videt severa ultione Castigat, quin prius Comminetur, in assiduè autem peccantes, & in peccatis perseverantes, cum Excessus Misericordiæ fines præteriunt, ut saltem metu pœnæ ad Cor reverti cogantur, Justitiæ vires Exercet, imitantes, & Incumbenti Nobis Apostolicæ solicitudinis studio perurgemur, ut cunctarum Personarum nostræ Curæ Cœlitus Commissarum salubri Statui solertius Intendamus, ac Erroribus, & Scandalis, quæ hostis Antiqui versutia imminere conspicimus, propensius obviemus, Excessúsque, & Enormia, ac scandalosa Crimina congrua severitate Coerceamus, & juxta Apostolum inobedientiam ovium promptius ulciscendo, illorum perpetratores debitâ Correctione si Compescamus, quod eos Dei iram provocasse pœniteat, & ex hoc aliis Exemplum Cautelæ salutaris accedat.

Henricus postquam à Leone decimo Titulo Defensoris Fidei donatus fuit, ex Causa hic expressa, à Catholica fide deviavit, & multa enormia commisit.

Sect. 1. Sane cum Superioribus Diebus nobis relatum fuisset, quod Angliæ Rex, licet Tempore pontificatûs Fel. recor. Leonis Papæ decimi Prædecessoris nostri diversorum Hæreticorum Errores sæpe ab Apostolica Sede, & Sacris Conciliis præteritis Temporibus damnatos, & novissimè Nostra Ætate per Perditionis Alumnum Martinum Lutherum suscitatos, & innovatos, zelo Catholicæ Fidei, & Erga dictam Sedem, devotionis fervore inductus, non minus doctè, quam piè per quendam Librum per eum desuper Compositum & eidem Leoni Prædecessori, ut eum Examinaret, approbaret, oblatum Confutasset, ob quod, ab eodem Leone Predecessore, Ultra dicti Libri cum magna Ipsius Henrici Regis Laude & Commendatione, approbationem, Titulum Defensoris Fidei reportaverit, à recta Fide & Apostolico tramite devians, ac propriæ salutis, famæ & honoris immemor, postquam Carissima in Christo Filia nostra Catherina Angliæ Regina, Illustri sua Progenie Conjuge, cum qua publice in facie Ecclesiæ Matrimonium Contraxerat, & per plures Annos Continuaverat, ac ex qua, dicto constante Matrimonio prolem pluries susceperat, nulla Legitima Subsistente Causa, & contra Ecclesiæ Prohibitionem dimissa, cum quadam Anna Bolena, Muliere Anglica, dicta Catherina adhuc vivente, de facto Matrimonium Contraxerat, ad deteriora prosiliens, quasdam Leges,

seu

seu Generales Constitutiones edere, non erubuit, per quas, subditos suos ad quosdam Hæreticos, & Scismaticos Articulos tenendos; Inter quos & hoc erat, quod Romanus Pontifex Caput Ecclesiæ, & Christi Vicarius non erat, & quod ipse in Anglicâ Ecclesiâ Supremum Caput Existebat, *sub Gravibus etiam mortis pœnis* cogebat. Et his *non Contentus, Diabolo Sacrilegij* Crimen *suadente* quamplures *Prælatos etiam Episcopos, aliásque Personas* Ecclesi-sticas, *etiam Regulares, necnon Seculares sibi ut* Hæretico, & Schismatico *adhærere, ac Articulos prædictos sanctorum Patrum decretis, & sanctorum Conciliorum Statutis, immo etiam Ipsi Evangelicæ veritati contrarios, tanquam tales alios damnatos approbare, & sequi nolentes, & intrepidè recusantes capi, & carceribus mancipari. Hisque similiter non Contentus, mala malis accumulando, bonæ mem.* Jo. H. S. *vitalis Presbyter Cardinalis* Roffen. *quem ob Fidei Constantiam, & vitæ sanctimoniam, ad Cardinalatus Dignitatem promoveramus, cum dictis Hæresibus & Erroribus consentire nollet, horrendâ immanitie & detestandâ sævitiâ publicè Miserabili supplicio tradi, & decollari mandaverat, & fecerat Excommunicationis, & Anathematis, aliásque gravissimas sententias,* censuras, *& pœnas in Literis, ac Constitutionibus recolendæ mem.* Bonifacij Octavi, Honorij Tertij, Roman. *Pontificum Prædecessorum Nostrorum desuper Editis Contentas, & alias in tales a jure latas damnabilitèr incurrendo ac Regno* Angliæ, *& Dominiis, quæ tenebat, necnon* Regalis fastigiis Celsitudine, *ac præfati Tituli prærogativâ, & honore se Indignum reddendo.*

Sect. 2. *Nos licet ex eo, quod prout non Ignorabamus,* Idem Henricus *Rex in Certis Censuris Ecclesiasticis quibus a Piæ Memoriæ* Clemente *Papa Septimi etiam Prædecessore nostro, postquam humanissimis literis, & paternis Exhortationibus, multisque Nunciis, & mediis, Primo & Postremo,* etiam Judicialiter, *ut præfatam Annam à se dimitteret, & ad Prædictæ* Catherinæ *suæ veræ Conjugis Consortium rediret frustra monitus fuerat, innodatus Extiterat,* Pharaonis *duritiam imitando, per Longum Tempus in Clavium* Contemptum *Insorduerat, & Insordescebat, quod ad Cor rediret vix sperare posse videremus ob Paternam tamen Charitatem, qua in minoribus Constituti donec in Obedientiâ, & Reverentiâ Sedis prædictæ permansit, eum prosecuti* fue-ra-

Clemen. 7. (ejus Constit.hic non habes) tandem illum Excommunicavit, quin in Censuris insordescendo deterior evasit.

fueramus, utque clarius videre Possemus, an Clamor qui ad nos delatus fuerat (quam certè etiam Ipsius Henrici *Respectum falsum esse disiderabamus) verus esset, statuimus ab ulteriori contra Ipsum* Henricum *Regem processu ad Tempus abstinendo, hujus Rei veritatem diligentius Indagare.*

Ideo Pont. Iste contra Regem, Complices, & Fautores decrevit, procedere, ut hic.

Sect. 3. *Cum autem debitis diligentiis desuper factis clamorem ad Nos, ut præfertur, delatum, verum esse, simúlque, quod dolentèr referimus, dictum* Henricum Regem *ita in Profundum malorum descendisse, ut de Ejus Resipiscentiâ nulla penitùs videatur spes haberi posse, reperimus. Nos attendentes veteri Lege Crimen Adulterij notatum, lapidari Mandatum, ac Auctores Schismatis hiatu terræ absorptos, eorúmque sequaces Cœlesti Igne Consumptos,* Elimámque Magnum *viis Domini Resistentem per Apostolum Æterna severitate damnatum fuisse, volemésque ne in districto Examine Ipsius* Henrici *Regis & Subditorum suorum, quos secum in Perditione trahere videmus, Animarum Ratio à Nobis Exposcatur, quantum Nobis ex alto conceditur providere contra* Henricum Regem, *Ejúsque Complices, Fautores, Adhærentes & sequaces; & in Præmissis quomodolibet culpabiles contra quos, ex eo quod Excessus, & delicta prædicta adeo manifesta sunt notiora, ut nulla possint tergiversatione celari absque ulteriori morâ ad Executionem procedere Possemus, benignius agendo, decrevimus infrascripto modo procedere.*

Regem itaque hortatur, ut ab hujusmodi erroribus desistat.

Sect. 4. *Habita itáque super his cum venerabilibus Fratribus Nostris S. R. E. Cardinalibus deliberatione maturâ, & de Illorum Consilio, & Assensu præfatum* Henricum Regem, *Ejúsque Complices, Fautores, Adhærentes, Consultores & Sequaces, ac quoscunque alios in Præmissis, seu eorum aliquo quoquomodo Culpabiles, tam Laicos, quam Clericos, etiam Regulares, cujuscúnque Dignitatis, Status, Gradus Ordinis, Conditionis, Præeminentiæ, & Excellentiæ existant: (quorum Nomina, & Cognomina perinde ac si Præsentibus Intersererentur, pro sufficienter expressis haberi volumus) per viscera Misericordiæ Dei Nostri hortamur, & requirimus in Domino, quatenus* Henricus Rex *à prædictis Erroribus prorsus abstineat, & Constitutiones, seu Leges prædictas, sicut de facto eas fecit, revocet, Casset, & annullet, &*
                                                                                                        Coactione-

Henrici 8. Regis Angliæ, &c.

Coactione Subditorum suorum ad eas Servandas, necnon Carceratione, Captura, & Punitione illorum, qui ipsis Constitutionibus, seu Legibus Adhærere, aut eas servare noluerint, & ab aliis Erroribus prædictis penitus, & Omnino abstineat, & si quos Præmissorum occasione Captivos habeat, relaxet.

Sect. 5. *Complices vero, Fautores, Adhærentes, & Sequaces dicti* Henrici *Regis in præmissis, & circa ea Ipsi* Henrico *Regi super his de cetero non adsistant, nec adhæreant, vel faveant, nec ei Consilium, Auxilium, vel Favorem, desuper præstent.*

Complices vero & Fautores monet ut abstineant Regi d. super favere, vel adhærere.

Sect. 6. *Alias si* Henricus Rex, *ac Fautores, Adhærentes, Consultores, & Sequaces hortationibus, & requisitionibus hujusmodi modi non audiverint cum Effectu,* Henricum Regem, *Fautores, Adhærentes, Consultores & Sequaces, ac alios Culpabiles prædictos, Authoritate Apostolica, ac ex certa nostra Scientia, & de Apostolicæ Potestatis Plenitudine tenore Præsentium in virtute Sanctæ Obedientiæ, ac sub Majoris Excommunicationis Latæ Sententia, à quo etiam prætextu cujuscunque Privilegij, vel facultatis, etiam in forma Confessionalis, cum quibuscunque efficacissimis Clausulis à Nobis, & Sede prædicta quomodolibet Concessis, etiam iteratis vicibus innovatis, ab alio quam à Romano Pontifice, præterquam in mortis Articulo Constituti, ita tamen, quod si aliquem absolvi contingat, qui postmodum Convaluerit, nisi post Convalescentiam, Monitioni, & Mandatis Nostris huiusmodi paruerit cum Effectu, in eandem Excommunicationis Sententiam reincidat) absolvi non possint.*

Inobedientésque Majoris Excommunicationis sententia innodat.

Sect. 7. *Necnon Rebellionis, & quod* Henricum Regem, *etiam Perditionis Regni, & Dominiorum Prædictorum, & tam quoad eum, quam quoad alios Monitos supradictos, supra & infra scriptis pœnis, quas si dictis Monitione & Mandatis, ut præsertur, non paruerint, eos, & eorum singulos, Ipso facto respectivè incurrere volumus, per Præsentes Monemus; eisque, & eorum cuilibet districtè præcipiendo Mandamus, quatenus* Henricus Rex *per se, vel Procuratorem Legitimum, & sufficienti Mandato suffultum, Infra Nonaginta, Complices vero, Fautores, Adhærentes, Consultores & Sequaces, ac alij in Præmissis quomodolibet*

Hh 2 *Culpabiles*

Rebellionis quóque, & Amissionis Regni pœnam Imponit. Regémque & Complices monet, ut infra, certum Terminum Compareat alioquin in pœnas hic expressas incidisse declarat.

Culpabiles supradicti, Seculares & Ecclesiastici, etiam Regulares, Personaliter, Infra Sexaginta dies Compareant Coram Nobis, ad se super Præmissis legitimè Excusandum, & Defendendum, alias videndum, & Audiendum Contra eos, & eorum singulos etiam Nominatim quos sic Monemus, quatenus expediat, ad Omnes, & singulos Actus, etiam Sententiam Definitivam, Declaratoriam, Condemnatoriam, & Privatoriam, ac Mandatum Excusativum procedi. Quod si Henricus Rex, *& alij Moniti prædicti Intra dictos terminos eis, ut præfertur, respectivè præfixos, non Comparuerint, ad Prædictam Excommunicationis Sententiam per tres dies, post Lapsum dictorum Terminorum Animo, quod absit, sustinuerint Indurato, Censuras Ipsas aggravamus, & successivè reaggravamus,* Henricúmque Regem *Privationis Regni, Dominicorum prædictorum, & tam eum, quam alios Monitos Prædictos, et eorum singulos, Omnes et singulas alias pœnas prædictas Incurrisse, ab omnibúsque Christi Fidelibus, cum eorum bonis perpetuo diffidatos esse. Et si Interim ab humanis decedat, Ecclesiastica debere carere Sepulturâ. Auctoritate et Potestatis Plenitudine prædictis devernimus, et Declaramus, eósque Anathematis, Maledictionis, et Damnationis Æternæ mucrone percutimus.*

Et quascunq; **Civitates Ecclesias & alia Loca, ad quæ Ipsi declinaverint, Interdicto, Ecclesiastico supponit.**

Sect. 8. *Necnon quæ præfatus Rex* Henricus *quomodolibet, & ex quavis Causa tenet, habet, aut possidet quam diu* Henricus Rex, *et alij Moniti prædicti, & eorum singuli in aliis per dictum* Henricum Regem *non tentis, habitis, aut possessis permanserint, & Triduo post eorum inde recessum, & alia quæcunque, ad quæ* Henricum Regem, *& alios monitos prædictos post Lapsum dictorum Terminorum declinare contigerit, Dominia, Civitates, Terras, Castra, Villas, Oppida, Metropolitanásque, & alias Cathedrales, cetérásque Inferiores Ecclesias, necnon Monasteria, Prioratus, Domos, Conventos, & Loca Religiosa, vel Pia Cujuscunque, etiam S.* Benedicti, Cluniacen. Cistercien. Præmonstraten. *ac Prædicatorum, Minorum, Eremitarum. S.* Augistini, Carmelitarum, *& aliorum Ordinum, ac Congregationum, & Militarium quarumcunque in Ipsis Dominiis, Civitatibus, Terris, Castris, Villis, Oppidis, & Locis Existentiâ,*

Ec-

Henrici 8. Regis Angliæ, &c.

Ecclesiastico supponimus Interdicto; ita ut illo durante in iIlis etiam præt...u cujuscunque Apostolici Indulti Ecclesiis, Monasteriis, Prioratibus, Domibus, Conventibus, Locis, Ordinibus, aut Personis, etiam quacunque Dignitate Fulgentibus Concessi, præterquam in Casibus à jure permissis, ac etiam in illis alias quam Clausis Januis, & Excommunicatis & Interdictis Exclusis, nequeant Missæ, aut alia Divina Officia Celebrari.

Sect. 9. Et Henrici Regis, Complicúmque, Fautorum, Adhærentium, Consultorum, Sequacium, et Culpabilium, prædictorum Filij, Pænarum ut hic in hoc Casu par est participes sint, Omnes et singulos ejusdem Henrici Regis ac dictæ Annæ, ac singulorum aliorum prædictorum Filios natos, et nascituros, aliosque descendentes, usque in eum gradum, ad quem Jura pœnas in Casibus hujusmodi extendent (Nemine excepto, nulláque minoris ætatis, aut Sexus, vel Ignorantiæ, vel alterius cujusvis Causæ habita ratione) Dignitatibus et Honoribus in quibus quomodolibet Constituti Existunt, seu quibus gaudent, utuntur, potiuntur, aut muniti sunt, necnon Privilegiis, Concessionibus, Gratiis, Indulgentiis, Immunitatibus, Remissionibus Libertatibus, et Indultis, ac Dominiis Civitatibus, Castris, Terris, Villis, Oppidis, et Locis, etiam Commendatis, vel in Gubernium Concessis, et quæ in feudum, emphyteusim, vel alias à Romanis, vel aliis Ecclesiis, Monasteriis, et Locis Ecclesiasticis, ac Secularibus, Principibus, Dominiis Potentatibus, etiam Regibus et Imperatoribus, aut aliis Privatis, vel publicis Personis quomodolibet habent, tenent, aut Possident, Ceterísque Omnibus bonis, Mobilibus et immobilibus, Juribus et Actionibus, eis quomodolibet Competentibus privatos, dicta bona feudalia, vel emphyteutica, et alia quæcunque, ab aliis quomodolibet obtenta, ad directos Dominos, ita ut de illis libere disponere possint, Respectivè devoluta, et eos qui Ecclesiastici fuerint, etiamsi Religiosi existant, Ecclesiis etiam Cathedralibus, et Metropolitanis, necnon Monasteriis & Prioribus, Præposituris, Præpositatibus, Dignitatibus, Personatibus, Officiis, Canonicatibus, & Præbendis, aliisque Beneficiis Ecclesiasticis per eos quomodolibet obtentis, privatos, & ad alia, ac alia in posterum obtinenda Inhabiles esse, simpliciter decernimus, & declaramus.

Filiósque eorum de dignitatibus, gratiis & privilegiis ac dominiis & bonis omnibus privatos, & ad alia de cetero obtinenda inhabiles esse declarat.

ramus; eósque sic respectivè Privatos, ad alia et alia quæcunque similia ac dignitates, honores, administrationes, et officia, jura, ac feuda in Posterum obtinenda, Auctoritate et Scientia, ac Plenitudine similibus Inhabilitamus.

Subditósque à juramento fidelitatis & subjectione liberat. Et eisdem mandat ut ab obedientia omnino recedant.

Sect. 10. *Ipsiúsque* Henrici Regis, *ac Regni omniúmque aliorum Dominiorum, Civitatum, Terrarum, Castrorum, Villarum, Fortaliciorum, Arcium, Oppidorum, & Locorum suorum, etiam de facto obtentorum, Magistratus, Judices, Castellanos, Custodes & Officiales quoscunque, necnon Communitates, Universitates, Collegia, Feudatarios, Vassallos, Subditos, Cives Incolas, & Inhabitatores etiam Forenses, dicto Regi de facto Obedientes, tam Seculares, quam si qui ratione alicujus temporalitatis Ipsum* Henricum Regem *in Superiorem recognoscant, etiam Ecclesiasticos, à Præfato Rege, seu Ejus Complicibus, Fautoribus, Adhærentibus, & Consultoribus, & Sequacibus supradictis deputatis, à juramento fidelitatis, jure vassilitico, & omni erga Regem, & alios prædictos subjectione absolvimus, ac penitús liberamus, eis Nihilominús sub Excommunicationis pœna Mandantes, & ab ejusdem* Henrici Regis, *suorúmque Officialium, Judicum, & Magistratuum quorumcunque. Obedientiâ penitús, & omnino recedant, nec illos in Superiores recognoscant, nèque illorum Mandatis obtemperent.*

Henrico & Complicibus alias pœnas hic Expressas Imponit.

Sect. 11. *Et ut alij eorum Exemplo perterriti, discant ab hujusmodi Excessibus abstinere, eisdem Auctoritate, Scientiâ & Plenitudine, volumus, & decernimus, quod* Henricus Rex, *& Complices, Fautores, Adhærentes, Consultores, Sequaces, & alij in præmissis Culpabiles, Postquam alias pœnas prædictas, ut præfertur respectivè incurverint, necnon Præfati descendentes, exunc Infames existant, & ad Testimonium non admittantur, Testamenta, & Codicillos, aut alias dispositiones, etiam Inter vivos concedere, & facere non possint, & ad alicujus Successionem ex Testamento, vel ab Intestato, necnon ad Jurisdictionem, seu Judicandi potestatem, & ad Notariatus Officium, Omnésque Actus Legitimos quoscunque (ita ut eorum Processus, sive Instrumenta atque alij Actus quicunque, nullius sint Roboris, vel momenti) Inhabiles existant; & Nulli Ipsis, sed ipsi aliis super*
quocunque

quocunque debito, & Negotio, tam Civili quam Criminali, de jure respondere teneantur.

Sect. 12. *Et Niholominus Omnes, & singulos Christi fideles, sub Excommunicationis, & aliis Infrascriptis pœnis, monemus, ut moniti, Excommunicatos, aggravatos, interdictos, privatos, maledictos, & damnatos prædictos evitent, & quantum in eis est, ab aliis evitari faciant, nec cum eisdem, seu Præfati Regis Civitatum, Dominiorum, Terrarum, Castrorum, Comitatuum Villarum, Fortaliciorum, Oppidorum, & Locorum prædictorum Civibus, Incolis, vel Habitatoribus, aut Subditis, & Vassallis, Emendo, Vendendo, Permutando, aut quamcunque Marcaturam, seu Negotij Exercendo, Commercium, seu aliquam Conversationem, seu Communionem habeant, aut vinum, granum, sal, seu alia victualia, arma, pannos, merces, vel quasvis alias Mercantias, vel Res per Mare in eorum Navibus, Triremibus, aut aliis Navigiis, sive per Terram cum Mulis, vel aliis Animalibus deferre, aut Conducere, seu deferri, aut Conduci facere, vel delata per illos recipere, publicè vel occultè, aut talia facientibus auxilium, consilium, vel favorem, publicè, vel occultè, vel indirectè quovis quæsito colore, per se, vel alium, seu alios quoquomodo præstare præsumant, quod si fecerint, ultra Excommunicationis prædictæ, etiam Nullitatis Contractuum, quos inirent, necnon Perditionis Mercium, Victualium, & bonorum omnium delatorum, quæ Capientium fiant, pœnas similiter eo Ipso Incurrant.*

Christi fidelibus sub pœnis hic expressis præcipit, ut Infidelium Commercium evitent.

Sect. 13. *Ceterum quia Convenire non videtur, ut cum his qui Ecclesiam Contemnunt, dum præsertim ex eorum pertinaciâ spes Corrigibilitatis non habetur, hi qui Divinis Obsequiis vacant Conversentur, quod etiam illos tutè facere non posse dubitandum est, Omnium & singularum Metropolitan: & aliarum Cathedralium, Ceterarùmque Inferiorum Ecclesiarum, & Monasteriorum, Domorum, & Locorum Religiosorum & Piorum quorumcunque, etiam* S. Augustini, S. Benedicti, *Cluniacen. Cistercien. Præmonstraten. ac Prædicatorum, Minorum, Carmelitarum, aliorùmque quorumcunque Ordinum, Militiarum, etiam Hospitalis* Hierosolymitani, *Prælatibus, Abbatibus, Prioribus, Præceptoribus,*

Prælatis quoque & cæteris Personis Ecclesiasticis mandat sub pœnis hic contentis quatenus de Regno Angliæ discedant, ut hic.

bus Præpositis, Ministris, Custodibus, Guardianis, Conventibus, Monachis, & Canonicis, necnon Parochialium Ecclesiarum Rectoribus, aliisque quibuscunque Personis Ecclesiasticis in Regno & Dominiis prædictis Commorantibus, sub Excommunicationis, ac Privationis administrationum, & Regiminum Monasteriorum, Dignitatum, Personatuum, Administrationum, ac Officiorum, Cannonicatuúmque, & Præbendarum, Parochialium Ecclesiarum, & aliorum Beneficiorum Ecclesiasticorum quorumcunque quomodolibet qualificatorum, per eos quomodolibet obtentorum pœnis Mandamus, quatenus Infra quinque dies post Omnes & singulos Terminos prædictos Elapsos, de ipsis Regno, & dominiis, dimissis tamen aliquibus Presbyteris in Ecclesiis, quarum Curam habuerint pro administrando Baptismate parvulis, & in Pœnitentia decedentibus, ac aliis Sacramentis Ecclesiasticis, Quæ Tempore Interdicti Ministrari permittuntur, exeant, & discedant, néque ad Regnum, & Dominia prædicta revertantur, donec Moniti, & Excommunicati, aggravati, reaggravati, privati, maledicti, & damnati prædicti Monitionibus, & Mandatis nostris hujusmodi obtemperaverint, & meruerint à Censuris hujusmodi absolutionis Beneficium obtinere, seu Interdictum in Regno, & dominiis prædictis fuerit sublatum.

Ducésq;& alios monet sub pœnis supradictis, ut Henricum & ejus Complices de Regno expellere & expelli procurent.

Sect. 14. Prætereà si Præmissis non obstantibus Henricus Rex, Complices, Fautores, Adhærentes, Consultores, & Sequaces prædicti in eorum pertinacia perseveraverint, nec Conscienciæ stimulus eos ad Cor Reduxerit, in eorum forte Potentia, & armis Confidentes Omnes & singulos Duces, Marchiones, Comites, & alios quoscunque, tam Sæculares, quam Ecclesiasticos, etiam forenses, de facto dicto, Henrico Regi Obedientes, sub ejusdem Excommunicationis, ac Perditionis bonorum suorum (quæ, ut Infra dictus similiter Capientium fiant) pœnis, requirimus, & monemus, quatenus Omni mora, & Excusatione Postposita, eos & eorum singulos, ac Ipsorum Milites, & Stipendarios, tam Equestres, quam Pedestres, aliósque quoscunque qui eis cum armis faverint, de Regno & Dominiis prædictis, etiam vi armorum, si Opus fuerit, expellant, ac quod Henricus Rex, & ejus Complices, Fautores, Adhærentes, Consultores, & Sequaces Mandatis nostris non obtemperantes prædicti de Civitatibus, Terris, Castris,

Castris, Villis, Oppidis, Fortalitiis, aut aliis Locis Regni, & Dominij Prædictorum, se non Intromittant, procurent, Eis sub Omnibus & singulis pænis prædictis Inhibentes, ne in favorem Henrici *ejúsque Complicum, Fautorum Adhærentium, Consultorum & Sequacium, aliorúmque Monitorum Prædictorum Mandatis Nostris non obtemperantium, arma Cujuslibet Generis offensiva, & defensiva Machinas quoque bellicas, seu tormenta (artellarias nuncupata) sumant, aut teneant, seu illis utantur, aut armatos aliquos, præter Consuetam familiam parent, aut ab* Henrico *Rege Complicibus, Fautoribus, Adhærentibus, Consultoribus, & Sequacibus, vel aliis in Regis Ipsius favorem paratos, quomodolibet, quavis occasione vel Causa, per se, vel alium, seu alios publicè vel occultè, directè vel indirectè teneant, vel receptent, aut dicto* Henrico *Regi, seu Illius Complicibus, Fautoribus, Adhærentibus, Consultoribus, & Sequacibus Prædictis, Consilium, Auxilium, vel quomodolibet ex quavis Causa, vel quovis quæsito Colore sive Ingenio, publicè vel occultè, directè vel indirectè, tacitè vel expressè, per se vel alium seu alios Præmissis, vel aliquo Præmissorum præstent, seu præstari faciant quoquomodo.*

Sect. 15. *Præterea ad dictum* Henricum *Regem facilius ad sanitatem, & præfata Sedis Obedientiam reducendum, Omnes & singulos, Christianos Principes, quacúnque etiam Imperiali & Regali Dignitate fulgentes, per viscera Misericordiæ Dei Nostri (Cujus Causa agitur) hortamur & in Domino Requirimus, eis Nihilominus, qui Imperatore & Rege Inferiores fuerint, quos propter Excellentiam Dignitatis à Censuris Excipimus, sub Excommunicationis pœna Mandantes ne* Henrico *Regi Ejúsque Complicibus, Fautoribus, Adhærentibus, Consultoribus, & Sequacibus, vel eorem alicui per se vel alium seu alios, publicè vel occultè, directè vel indirectè, tacitè vel expressè etiam sub prætextu Confœderationum aut Obligationum quarumcunque, etiam Juramento, aut quavis alia firmitate roboratarum, & sæpius geminatarum, à quibus quidem Obligationibus, & Juramentis Omnibus, nos eos, & eorum singulos eisdem Auctoritate & Scientia, ac plenitudine per præsentes absolvimus, Ipsásque Confœderationes*

Principum Christianorum Confœderationes, & Obligationes Contractas cum Henrico nullas & invalidas declarat.

fœderationes & Obligationes tam factas, quam in Posterum faciendas, quas tamen (in quantum Henricus Rex & Complices, Fautores, Adhærentes, Consultores, & Sequaces prædicti circa præmissa, vel eorum aliquod se directè vel indirectè Juvare possent sub eadem pœna fieri prohibemus, nullius Roboris vel Momenti, nulláfque, irritas, Cassas, inanes ac pro Infectis habendas fore decernimus & declaramus, consilium, auxilium, vel favorem, quomodolibet, præstent; quinimo si qui illis, aut eorum alicui ad præsens quomodolibet assistant, ab Ipsis omnino, & Effectu recedant. Quod si non fecerint postquam Præsentes publicatæ & Executioni demandatæ fuerint, et dicti Termini lapsi fuerint, Omnes & singulas Civitates, Terras, Oppida, Castra, Villas, & alia Loca eis Subjecta, simili Ecclesiastico Interdicto supponimus, volentes Ipsum Interdictum donec Ipsi Principes à Consilio, Auxilio & Favore Henrico Regi & Complicibus, Fautoribus, Adhærentibus, Consultoribus, & Sequacibus prædictis præstando, destiterint, perdurare.

Principibus & aliis mandat, ut contra Henricum & Complices Arma Capiant.

Sect. 16. Insuper tam Principes prædictos, quam quoscunque alios, etiam ad Stipendia quorumcunque Christi fidelium Militantes, & alias quascunque personas, tam per Mare, quam per Terras, Armigeros habentes, similiter hortamur, & requirimus, & nihilominus eis in virtute Sanctæ Obedientiæ Mandantes, quatenus contra Henricum Regem, Complices, Fautores, Adhærentes, Consultores, & Sequaces prædictos, dum in Erroribus prædictis, ac adversus Sedem prædictam rebellione permanserint, Armis Insurgant, eosque & eorum singulos, persequantur, ac ad Unitatem Ecclesiæ, & Obedientiam dictæ Sedis redire cogant, & compellant, & tam eos, quam Ipsorum Subditos, & Vassallos, ac Civitatum, Terrarum, Castrorum, Oppidorum, Villarum, & Locorum suorum Incolas, & habitatores, aliásque Omnes singulas Personas supradictis Mandatis nostris, ut præfertur, non obtemperantes, & qui præfatum Henricum Regem Postquam Censuras & Pœnas prædictas incurrerit, in Dominum quomodolibet etiam de facto recognoverint, vel ei quovis modo obtemperare præsumpserint, aut qui eum, ac Complices, Fautores, Adhærentes, Consultores, Sequaces, ac

alios

alios non obtemperantes prædictos, ex Regno & Dominiis prædictis, ut præfertur, expellere noluerint, ubicúnque eos invenerint, eorúmque bona, mobilia & immobilia mercantias, pecunias, navigia, credita, res, & Animalia, etiam extra territorium, dicti Henrici Regis *ubilibet Consistentia, Capiant.*

Sect. 17. *Nos enim bona, Mercantias, Pecunias, Navigia, Res, & Animalia prædicta sic capta, In proprios eorum usus convertendi, eisdem Auctoritate, Scientia, & Potestatis Plenitudine, Plenariam Licentiam, Facultatem & Auctoritatem concedimus, illa omnia ad eosdem Capientes plenariè pertinere, & spectare, & Personas ex Regno, & Dominiis prædictis Originem trahentes, seu in illis Domicilium habentes, aut quomodolibet habitantes, Mandatis nostris prædictis non obtemperantes, ubicúnque eos Capi Contigerit, Capientium servos fieri decernentes, Præsentésque Literas, quoad hoc, ad omnes alios cujuscúnque Dignitatis, Gradus, Status, Ordinis, vel Conditionis fuerint qui Ipsi* Henrico Regi, *vel ejus Complicibus, Fautoribus, Adhærentibus, Consultoribus, & Sequacibus, aut aliis Monitionibus, & Mandatis nostris hujusmodi, quoad Commercium non obtemperantibus, vel eorum alicui victualia, arma, vel pecunias subministrare, aut cum eis Commercium habere, seu Auxilium, Consilium, vel Favorem per se vel alium, seu alios publicè vel occultè, directè vel indirectè, quovis modo contra tenorem Præsentium præstare præsumpserint extendentes.*

Infideles & inobedientes capientium servos, & corundem bona occupantium fieri decernit.

Sect. 18. *Et ut præmissa facilius iis quos concernunt innotescant, universis & singulis Patriarchis, Archiepiscopis, Episcopis, & Patriarchalium Metropolitan. & aliarum Cathedralium, & Collegiatarum Ecclesiarum Prælatis, Capitulis, aliísque Personis Ecclesiasticis Sæcularibus ac quorumvis Ordinum Regularibus, necnon Omnibus, & singulis etiam Mendicantium Ordinum Professoribus Exemptis, & non Exemptis, ubilibet, Constitutis, per easdem Præsentes, sub Excommunicationis & Privationis Ecclesiarum, Monasteriorum, ac aliorum Beneficiorum Ecclesiasticorum, Graduum quoque & Officiorum, necnon Privilegiorum,*

Prælatis & aliis Mandat sub pœnis de quibus hic, ut in eorum Ecclesiis Henricum & Complices qui supradictas pœnas, & Censuras Incurrerint, Excommunicatos publicè enuncient, & evitari faciant.

Damnatio & Excommunicatio.

vilegiorum, & Indultorum quorumcunque etiam à Sede prædicta quomodolibet Emanatorum pœnis ipso facto Incurrendis, præcipimus, & mandamus, quatenus Ipsis ac eorum singuli, si, & Postquam vigore Præsentium desuper requisiti fuerint, Infra tres dies Immediaté sequentes præfatum Henrici Regem, Omnesque alios & singulos, qui supradictas Censuras, & pœnas Incurrerint in eorum Ecclesiis, Dominicis, & aliis Festivis diebus, dum Major Inibi populi Multitudo, ad divina Convenerit, cum Crucis vexillo, pulsatis Campanis, & accensis, ac demum Extinctis, & in Terram projectis, & Conculcatis Candelis, & aliis in similibus servari solitis Cæremoniis servatis, Excommunicatos publicè nuncient, & ab aliis nunciari, ac ab Omnibus Arctius evitari faciant, & mandent, necnon sub supradictis Censuris & Pœnis, Præsentes Literas, vel earum transumptum, sub forma Infrascripta Confectum, Infra Terminum trium Dierum, Postquam, ut præfertur requisiti fuerint, in Ecclesiis, Monasteriis, Conventibus, et aliis eorum Locis, publicari, et affigi faciant.

Publicationem Istius Const. Impedientib. easdem pœnas Imponit.

Sect. 19. *Volentes, Omnes, et singulos cujuscunque Status, Gradus, Conditionis, Præeminentiæ, Dignitatis, aut Excellentiæ fuerint, qui quominus Præsentes Literæ, vel earum transumpta, Copiæ seu Exemplaria, in suis Civitatibus, Terris, Castris, Oppidis, Villis, et Locis Legi, et affigi, ac publicari possint, per se, vel alium, seu alios, publicè vel occultè, directè vel indirectè impediverint, easdem Censuras, et Pœnas Ipso facto Incurrere. Et cum fraus et dolus nemini debeant Patrocinari, ne quisquam ex his, qui alicui Regimini, et Administrationi deputati sunt Infra Tempus sui Regiminis, seu Administrationis, Prædictas Sententias, Censuras, et Pœnas sustineat, quasi post dictum Tempus Sententiis Censuris et Pœnis prædictis amplius Ligatus non existat, quemunque qui dum in Regimine, et Administratione existens, monitioni, et mandato nostris quoad pramissa, vel aliquid eorum obtemperare noluerit, etiam deposito Regimine, et Administratione hujusmodi, nisi paruerit, eisdem Censuris, et Pœnis subjicere decernimus.*

Sect.

Sect. 20. *Et ne* Henricus, *Ejusque Complices, et Fautores, Adhærentes, Consultores, et Sequaces, aliique quos præmissa Concernunt, Ignorantiam eorundem Præsentium Literarum, et in eis Contentorum prætendere valeant, Literas ipsas* (*in quibus Omnes et singulos, tam juris, quam facti, etiam solemnitatum, et Processuum, Citationúmque Omissarum defectus, etiamsi Tales sint, de quibus Specialis, et expressa mentio facienda esset, propter Notorietatem facti, Auctoritate, Scientia, et Potestatis plenitudine similibus, supplemus*) *in Basilicæ Principis Apostolorum, et Cancellariæ Apostolicæ de urbe, et in partibus in Collegiata Beatæ* Mariæ Brugen. Tornacen. *et Parochialis de* Dunkercæ, *Oppidorum Moriensis Diœcesis, Ecclesiarum valvis Affigi, et Publicari Mandamus, decernentes quod earundem Literarum Publicatio sic facta,* Henricum Regem, *Ejúsque Complices, Fautores, Adhærentes, Consultores et Sequaces Omnésque alios, et singulos, quos Literæ Ipsæ quomodolibet Concernunt, perinde eos arctent, ac si Literæ Ipsæ eis Personalitèr Lectæ et Intimatæ fuissent, cum non sit verisimile, quod ea, quæ tam patentèr fiunt, debeant apud eos incognita remanere.*

Publicari Mandat hanc Const. in locis hic expressis. Sed hæc forma immutata est, ut hic in fine.

Sect. 21. *Ceterum quia difficile foret Præsentes Literas ad singula quæque Loca, ad quæ necessarium esset deferri, volumus, et dictâ Auctoritate decernimus, quod earum transumptis manu publici Notarij Confectis, vel in Almâ Urbe Impressis, ac Sigillo alicujus Personæ in Dignitate Ecclesiastica Constitutæ munitis, ubique eadem fides adbibeatur quæ Originalibus adhiberetur si essent exhibitæ vel ostensæ.*

Transumptis credi jubet.

Sect. 22. *Nulli ergo Omnino hominum liceat hanc paginam Nostræ Monitionis, Aggravationis, Reaggravationis, Declarationis, Percussionis, Suppositionis, Inhabilitationis Absolutionis, Liberationis, Requisitionis, Inhibitionis, Hortationis, Exceptionis, Prohibitionis, Concessionis, Extensionis, suppletionis Mandatorum, Voluntatis, et Decretorum Infringere, vel ei ausu Temerario*

230   Damnatio & Excommunicatio

merario contraire. Si quis autem hoc attentare Præsumpserit, Indignationem Omnipotentis Dei, ac Beatorum Petri, et Pauli Apostolorum ejus se noverit Incursurum.

D.P.An.1. Die 30. Aug.

Dat. Romæ apud S. Marcum, Anno Incarnationis Dom. 1435. 3. Kal. Septemb. Pont. Nostri Anno Primo.

A

A SHORT ACCOUNT OF THE CONTENTS OF THIS BOOK.

I.

THE *Bull of Pope* Pius *the Fifth* (*containing the Damnation and Excommunication of Queen* Elizabeth) *in Latin and English.* P. 1.

II. *The*

The Contents.

II.

The first Observation, That Pius V. *was neither the first nor last Pope, who Excommuicated and damn'd Kings and Emperors. For,* 1. *before him Pope* Constantine, Gregory *the Second,* Gregory *the Third,* Gregory *the Seventh,* Gregory *the Ninth,* Innocent *the Fourth,* Paul *the Third* &c. *did the same thing: And,* 2. Gregory *the thirteenth, and* Sixtus *the Fifth, after him.* p.7.

III.

The second Observation, concerning the Ἐπιγραφὴ *or Title prefix'd to* Pius *the Fifth his Bull; that it is* Damnatio & Excommunicatio Elizabethæ. *Where it is proved,* 1. *That not only* Pius *the Fifth, but other Popes (not short of him in time or impiety) use the same hard word* (Damnation) *in the Titles prefix'd to their damnatory Bulls, wherein they Excommunicate Kings and Emperors.* 2. *The uncharitable Error, and Invalidity of their reasons they do, or can pretend for doing so.* p.13.

IV.

The third Observation, wherein, 1. *The notion and significations of the word* Damnation *are explain'd.* 2. *That by the word* Damnation *in their* Anathema'*s and Damnatory Bulls, not only some temporal loss or punishment (as to their Bodies or Estates) but eternal* Damnation *of Body and Soul, is meant, by the Pope and his Party; together with the invalidity of their reasons and pretences to justifie them in this particular.* p.18.

V.

The fourth Observation, wherein we have, 1. *The grounds on which* Pius *the Fifth, and other Popes, build their Power to Excommunicate and Depose Kings; and that in the Supremacy and Plenitude of Power, which (they pretend) our blessed Saviour gave to* Peter, *and in him to all his Successors. So that*

Peter

The Contents.

Peter (*and so every Successor of his*) was constituted a Prince over all Nations and Kingdoms, to pull up, and throw down, to dissipate and destroy, to plant and build, &c. 2. That such Power was (*by our blessed Saviour*) given to Peter and his Successors, they indeavour to prove out of Scripture, (*and in their Bulls, cite the places*) Gen 1. 16. and Jer. 1. 10. 3. *The ridiculous inconsequence and impertinence of such Papal reasoning, which shews them rather to be Fools, then Infallible.*
p. 26.

VI

The fifth Observation, against the Pope's pretended Supremacy. 1. *That Peter's Supremacy* (*much less the Popes*) *cannot be proved from* Matth. 10. 2. *where he is called* πρῶτος, primus (*or as in the Latin Fathers*) Princeps Apostolorum. 2. *Nor from that place,* Matth. 16. 18. 19. 3. *That St.* Paul *in Scripture, hath a far better pretence to the Supremacy and the Bishoprick of* Rome, *then St.* Peter; *and yet neither he, nor any for him, ever pretended to any Papal Supremacy.* 4. *How our blessed Saviour and the Apostles* (yet Peter *no more then the rest*) *are in Scripture, said to be* Foundations *of the Church.* 5. *That the Power of the Keys was given to every Apostle, as well and as much as to* Peter. Nay, 6. *To every Bishop and Priest, as is expresly affirm'd in the* Authentick Offices *of the* Roman Church, *and in their* Trent Council and Catechism. 7. *That every Apostle was* Christ's Vicar *as well as* Peter; *that the Jesuites profess,* (*and in their Institutions do publish it*) *that their Superiors are* Christ's Vicars. 8. *That* Pasce Oves, Joh. 21. 15. 16. 17. (*though usually*) *is most impertinently urged to prove* Peter's *Supremacy.* 9. *That the 28. Canon of the Council of* Chalcedon (*which utterly overthrows the Popes Supremacy*) *is basely corrupted by* Gratian *and the Canonists and* (*that it might not appear*) *left out of their* old *Editions of the* Councils. p. 30. 31

The Contents.

VII.

The sixth Observation, In which a further examination and confutation of the Popish pretended grounds for the Popes Supremacy. That they neither do, nor can prove that Peter *ever had any such Monarchical Supremacy over the Apostles and all Christians, with the reasons why they cannot.* 2. *If it were granted (which is evidently untrue) that he had such a Power, yet it neither does, nor can appear (by Scripture, or any just Medium) that it was hereditary, and to pass to his Successor, but might be personal, and (as his Apostleship did) dye with him.* 3. *And if it were granted (which neither is nor ever can be proved) that that Power was hereditary, and to be transferr'd to his Successor, yet they neither have, nor can have any just grounds to prove, that the Bishop of* Rome *is that Successor, and not the Bishop of* Antioch, *where (they say)* St. Peter *first sate.* 4. *That 'tis certain from Scripture, that* Peter *neither was nor could be (as they pretend)* 25. *yeares Bishop of* Rome. 5. *Nor can it (by Scripture) appear that ever he was at* Rome, *nor can* Rome *be meant by* Babylon, 1 Pet. 5. 13. 6. *Nor can it appear by any just Testimonies of antiquity, that ever he was at* Rome. Papias *is the ground and Author on whom they rely for that Fable; and he an ignorant Person, and Arch-Heretick.* 7. *That to get credit to* Papias, *they have impiously corrupted* Eusebius. 8. *If it were granted, that he was at* Rome, *yet they have no ground or probability for it, that he was Bishop there; seeing there are far greater probabilities grounded on Scripture, that* Paul *was Bishop there, than* Peter *(or any for him) can pretend to; and yet they do not say, nor (without contradiction to their own Priciples) can say, that he was Bishop there.* 9. *That those other honorary Titles or Epithites, which their Authors every where use as proper to the Pope, and marks of his Supremacy, or (at least) superiority over all Bishops (such as* Apostolicus, Pontifex Summus, Papa, Sedes Apostolica, Vicarius Christi, Cathedra Apostolica, Successor Petri *&c.) are impertinently* made use *of, without any proof or probability.*

The Contents.

VIII.

The seventh Observation, concerning the Censures, Punishments and Curses contain'd in this Bull; and the Antichristian impiety of them. 1. *He miscalls the* **Queen**, an Heretick, a favourer of Hereticks, a Slave of Impiety, and then Anathematizes her, and cuts her off from the Unity of Christ's Body. 2. He deposes and deprives her of her pretended Right to the Crown, and of all manner of Dignity Dominion and Priviledge. 3. He absolves her Subjects, and all others, who are bound to her by any Oath, from all their Oaths, and all debt of Fidelity and Obedience, and that for ever. 4. *He severely prohibits them all, to obey any of her Laws or Commands.* 5. *If any of them do otherwise, he excommunicates and Curses them, whether they be Papists or Protestants.*
p. 115. 116. &c.

IX.

The eighth Observation, That the Pope *is the great Antichrist, the Man of Sin, and* Son *of Perdition, spoken of* 2. Thess. 3. 4. *That the Opinons of* H. Grotius, (*that* Caius Caligua) *and of Dr.* Hammond, (*that* Simon Magus *was Antichrist*) *are inconsistent and contradictory to each other, and to themselves. That they are (both of them) repugnant to Scripture, the Judgment of the primitive Fathers, of Protestants and Papists, and the sense of Christendom for about 1600. years after our blessed Saviour, &c.* 120. 121. ad. 157.

X.

The ninth Observation, What *the Popes Power is,* (*and whence they pretend to have it*) *which inables them with Authority to sit Judges, and, pass damnatory Sentences against Supream Princes, for Heresie.* 2. *What that Heresie is, and who the Hereticks, who by the Pope are so severely damn'd.* 3. *What those punishments are, which they pretend they may, and* (*when and where*
they

The Contents.

they can) *actually do inflict on such Hereticks.* 4. *Of the Waldenses, that* (*by the testimony of their Enemies*) 1. *They had continued ever since the Apostles time.* 2. *That there was scarce any Christian Country in which they were not.* 3. *That they lived justly before men, and believ'd all things well of God, and all the Articles of the Creed: but their fault was, They said* Rome *was* Babylon *and the* Pope *Anrichrist, &c.* 157. 158.

XI.

Observation the Tenth, That Queen Elizabeth *stood Excommunicate, before the Damnatory Bull of* Pius *the Fifth, and by whom, &c.* 169.

XII.

Observation the Eleventh, Of the damnable and pernicious Doctrines and Conclusions, which evidently follow, upon their approv'd and practised Principles, of Deposing and Anathematizing Kings and Supream Princes. That 'tis neither Treason, Murder, or any Sin, for Subjects to Assassinate their King, if he be Excommunicate by the Pope. Nay, that it is a meritorious act, for which they promise them vast rewards here, and an higher degree of glory in Heaven hereafter, &c. p. 174. 175. &c.

XIII.

The Damnation and Excommunication of Henry *the Eighth by Pope* Paul *the Third,* Decemb. 17. Anno 1538.

FINIS.

www.ingramcontent.com/pod-product-compliance
Lightning Source LLC
Chambersburg PA
CBHW021349230426
43666CB00006B/454